research methods in education

F. E. PEACOCK PUBLISHERS, INC.
ITASCA, ILLINOIS 60143

william wiersma

University of Toledo

research methods in education

an introduction ▪ second edition

To Joan and Susan and Lisa

Preface

This book is primarily designed for an introductory course in research methods for students in education. The main purpose of such a course is to provide instruction in basic research techniques so that the student can begin the pursuit of independent research associated with the graduate program. In order to meet this purpose it is important that the student attain some technical and methodological competence through which he can pursue his research ideas. This text, along with conscientious study, should enable the student to rise above the stage of ideas and pursue his research in a meaningful and correct manner.

Like the first edition published in 1969 by J. B. Lippincott Company, this book was fundamentally prepared as a text for an introductory course. It can, however, serve a wider audience. Students should find it helpful as a supplement for any course that emphasizes research studies. Practicing educators, whether teachers, administrators, supervisors, or specialists, will find the content of the text helpful in pursuing their own research and in acquiring an understanding of research reports. Since considerable emphasis is placed upon the underlying reasoning of methodology, the book can be used as a supplement by graduate students, either independently or in connection with more advanced courses. Of course, it also can be used independently as a reference. Since education draws on several disciplines for its research methods, students in other areas, especially the behavioral sciences, should find the text beneficial.

The orientation of the text is toward the design of research studies and the quantitative procedures of dealing with research data. The procedures discussed have wide application and are illustrated with examples. The ideas presented are general enough so that they apply to many specific research problems. Although formulas occasionally appear, especially in the chapters on hypothesis testing, this is not a statistics text. Computation, when it appears, is included only for the purpose of illustration and to enhance understanding. A minimum mathematical background is necessary; a course in elementary high school algebra should suffice. Nevertheless, the student of educational research needs to be cognizant of the existence of statistical procedures, the reasoning underlying them, and their significance. This text provides such a background, but it does not attempt to develop computational proficiency in the use of the procedures studied.

The organization of the material is somewhat changed from that of the first edition. The content is divided into three parts. The first five chapters deal with general concepts, research design, principles, and types of research. Two chapters on measurement and a chapter devoted to sampling comprise the balance of Part One. Although many specific procedures are discussed, it is the more general principles that are covered in this part.

Part Two, comprised of Chapters 9, 10, and 11, discusses specific procedures for testing hypotheses by parametric, nonparametric, and correlational techniques. These chapters emphasize the reasoning of inferential statistics.

Part Three is concerned with the research literature. Chapter 12 deals with searching the literature and reading research reports with understanding and a critical eye. The final chapter discusses the preparation of research proposals and research reports.

Teaching aids have been designed to be of help in the classroom or in self-teaching situations. These include exercises at the end of each chapter; where applicable, solutions to these exercises are provided in Appendix 1. All necessary tables of underlying distributions are given in Appendix 2. Lists of key concepts discussed in each chapter are provided for Parts One and Two. Also included, at the back of the book, are a glossary of research terms and a selected bibliography.

The content of the text basically follows a sequential form of development. The general scope of educational research methods and design is considered first, and the more specific methods are reserved for Part Two. However, all users of the book need not consider the entire text in sequence. For example, a reader with mastery of elementary statistics could omit Part Two. One who is limited in time could make a meaningful study of the early chapters, say 1 through 5 or all of Part One, to develop some mastery of general research methods and design. Some users of the text may want to consider Part Three before the chapters on hypothesis testing which comprises Part Two. A reader interested primarily in locating research reports, for example, would find Chapter 12 helpful, while one anticipating the writing of a research proposal would find the information he needs in Chapter 13. Thus there are numerous options for considering the content of the book, depending on the user's needs, time, and background.

Although this is an introductory text, it is not simplistic and was not meant to be. Research procedures are too precise and complex to be superficially dismissed as "easy." Educational research is a demanding activity, requiring interest, concentrated study, and attention to details. On the other hand, the text is not intended as a treatment of advanced, specialized topics. Excellent textbooks on these topics are available, and occasional references to such texts are made throughout this book. The reader who masters the ideas of this text, however, should be well on his way to competency in the methods of educational research.

WILLIAM WIERSMA

Table of Contents

PART ONE

GENERAL PRINCIPLES OF EDUCATIONAL RESEARCH

chapter 1

Educational research: Characteristics and definition

The word "research" as commonly used in contemporary society has wide and varied meanings, as evidenced in popular newspapers, books, and journals. What does all the concern with research, especially educational research, have to do with individual educators or students of education? Intuitively, we associate a positive value judgment with research, and the word generally carries an aura of respect. But we are not clear about who does research and under what type of conditions it is done. Is doing research something like playing golf, involving a repertoire of skills to be mastered? How does the student get involved in whatever it is that comprises research?

OVERVIEW

Research is carried on in a host of situations by a variety of individuals. Scholars of various levels of sophistication in the disciplines and professions engage in it. They meditate in secluded rooms, work in laboratories with equipment of various degrees of elaborateness, search in the ruins of ancient civilizations or investigate modern cities, to mention just a few of the possible research settings. Large industrial concerns pour vast sums of money into research activities to which advances in all fields have been attributed.

The beginning graduate student hardly identifies with any of these situations. He does not have the experience or knowledge of the sophisticated scholar. His financial resources are usually very limited, so he cannot entertain the approach of industry. Yet to pursue his degree successfully, he is required to produce some original research. He may realize that research is necessary and hears the term repeatedly, but this does not provide him with much knowledge or direction as to how to go about it.

The situation of the average elementary or high school teacher, guidance counselor, or administrator is not much better than that of the beginning graduate student when it comes to matters of research. In fact, a considerable proportion of the graduate student population is often made up of school personnel pursuing a graduate program on a part-time basis. The professional educator may not be called upon to produce an original piece of research, but to ignore research entirely is to do both himself and the profession an injustice. A great deal of change, innovation, and experimentation is occurring in education today, some prompted and supported by federal programs, but much of it initiated from within the profession itself. It is essential for the professional educator to know and understand the research related to his area before he can participate in a meaningful way in educational innovation and change. Much of the educational research is reported in such a way that a knowledge of methodology is invaluable. In fact, such knowledge may be essential for a meaningful implementation of research results.

The physical and behavioral sciences have long placed a premium upon research. Statements to the effect that the behavioral sciences are becoming more "scientific" and developing better research procedures are frequently made. The graduate schools of the nation's universities attach a marked premium to the ability to carry out "original" research. Consequently, for the graduate student and the practitioner alike, knowledge of research methods is essential.

Educational research is a complex and demanding endeavor. Many research activities utilize various research methods, ranging from relatively simple, single operations to complex combinations of procedures, both qualitative and quantitative. An entire research project, from the initial identification of the research problem to the completed report can call for an extensive effort requiring considerable study and numerous activities involving a variety of interrelated procedures.

While educational research is a demanding task, it is not an impossible one. There are often frustrations, and errors are made along the way, but with organized and concentrated study the aspiring educational researcher should be able to master necessary research methods. Basically, the only way to acquire competence in research is by doing. Before research can be put into practice, however, some skills must be acquired. The matter of knowing what to do in specific situations is important. How is a research problem started? What procedures apply in the pursuit of the solution to a specific problem? How are the data to be collected and interpreted? How can a satisfactory and lucid report be produced? Viewed in the context of a specific research project, all these questions call for certain skills.

Many universities and colleges have courses designed to help the student master research skills, and related books also serve as aids to understanding the research process and learning the skills. Courses and books vary greatly in their levels of sophistication: some are abstract and theoretical, while others place a great deal of emphasis on application. The approach of this text is more of the latter persuasion, although some of the underlying ideas may seem to be abstract when initially presented. This abstraction is in the interest of enhancing understanding of basic concepts of research.

While this text presents basic concepts, the potential researcher must project them into his own research situation. A misconception sometimes develops with the idea of the "typical research project." There is no typical project; each has its unique problems and conditions. Further, research is a personal matter, and every researcher develops his own style of solving his research problem. There may be considerable similarity among various types of projects, but doing a research project is not like baking a cake from a recipe.

The researcher should always aim for a respectable, competent product. However, since it is extremely unlikely that there has ever been a perfect study, he should not become discouraged if his result is less than perfect. Nor will any finished project be totally immune from criticism. There are many potential pitfalls, and errors are likely to occur. Criticism of research should be offered and accepted in a strictly constructive sense, for the purpose of improving a particular project or future projects. Any researcher, regardless of his degree of sophistication, should seek the criticism of his professors or peers and be willing to accept their suggestions.

THE NATURE OF RESEARCH

A work of research may be discussed as if "research" were a noun; at other times it is considered as expressing action and therefore viewed as a verb. Research can take on various broad or restricted meanings.

In order to develop a more succinct concept of research, and educational research in particular, we will consider two statements from contemporary authors. George Mouly describes the nature of research as "the process of arriving at dependable solutions to problems through the planned and systematic collection, analysis, and interpretation of data." Specifically, he states that "we can define educational research as the systematic and scholarly application of the scientific method interpreted in its broadest sense to the solution of educational problems."[1]

Note the idea of a systematic approach applied through the scientific method. This idea is important to our study, and we will develop the meaning of the term "systematic" below. Note also that educational research involves the solution of educational problems, including both practical and theoretical problems.

A definition of scientific research is presented by Fred N. Kerlinger as "systematic, controlled, empirical and critical investigation of hypothetical propositions about the presumed relations among natural phenomena."[2] The idea of a systematic approach, along with the idea of control, characterizes scientific research as ordered and disciplined so that the researcher can have confidence in the outcome of his endeavors. By empirical is meant that in scientific research the conjectures of the researcher are put to an objective test. The outcomes are subjected to the critical scrutiny of the researcher himself and others.

When these relatively broad concepts of research are considered in the context of educational research, the emphasis is on a systematic approach, in essence a scientific approach, to the study of problems and phenomena related to education. We can consider scientific as an adjective summarizing those characteristics that essentially make the method of inquiry more systematic. The characteristics that a research study or activity possesses if it is to be considered systematic can be described in a general sense.

In systematic research, a general system is followed whose elements are (1) identification of the problem, (2) data collection, (3) data analysis, and (4) drawing conclusions. First, in order for a research study to be systematic, the nature of the problem to be studied must be understood. The related area of knowledge is identified and, in essence, a framework is established in which to conduct the research. Closely related to establishing the framework or foundation for the research is identification of any necessary assumptions related to the research problems.

---

1. G. J. Mouly, *The Science of Educational Research,* 2d ed. (New York: Van Nostrand Reinhold Co., 1970), pp. 12–13.
2. F. N. Kerlinger, *Foundations of Behavioral Research,* 2d ed. (New York: Holt, Rinehart & Winston, 1973), p. 11.

The collection of data relevant to the problem is the second step in systematic research. But data cannot be collected in any available haphazard or *ad hoc* manner. The process of data collection requires proper organization and control so that the data will enable valid decisions to be made about the research problem at hand. Third, the data must be analyzed in a manner appropriate to the problem. Finally, after the analysis, a process of drawing conclusions or making generalizations takes place. These conclusions are based upon the data and the analysis within the framework of the research study.

The scientific method

The scientific method is a general set of procedures or steps through which the systematic approach is developed. In some ways, certainly at points in the procedures, the scientific method and a systematic approach are synonymous, even redundant. In going from the more general ideas of systematic research to the scientific method, however, we can focus more directly on the specificity of the research process.

The scientific method is usually broken down into a series of steps beginning with the encounter of some problem to the final step of drawing conclusions and integrating them into the existing body of knowledge. The terminology for the various steps of the scientific method varies somewhat from writer to writer, as do the numbers of steps. The scientific method is a general formulation of steps and should not be viewed as a single correct method (e.g., experimentation, historical) for attacking all problems.

The initial step of the scientific method, that of observing some phenomenon, represents an insight into some experience. This may manifest itself as a problem or obstacle or some unexplained situation. The need to resolve the problem or situation is felt, and the individual prepares to do something about the need or difficulty.

The second step is to identify the problem more precisely. This step involves the formulation of tentative hypotheses, based on the observed phenomenon. The factors involved with the problem are more closely identified, and their relationships are clarified. Observations related to the problem are made.

The third step of the scientific method is to develop and apply a design for the solution of the problem. Theories or hypotheses may be used as tentative explanations of the facts being observed. Hypotheses are tested and either retained, modified, or discarded.

The next step usually identified is a continuation of the third step— the continued testing and refinement of theories and hypotheses. Results from initial tests are subjected to further analyses and tests.

The final step is that of drawing conclusions based on data and tests and integrating these conclusions with the existing body of knowledge. In connection with the observed facts and the procedures conducted in the research, the individual arrives at what is to him the most reliable solution to the problem or most accurate explanation of the situation.

The method by which the steps of the scientific method are presented (that is, the one, two, . . . fashion) may give the impression that the steps will necessarily follow a definite order and time sequence. This may, in fact, be true, but the use of the scientific method is not rigid, and the researcher rarely follows the pattern in such an orderly fashion. Individual steps are not isolated. The researcher may be involved with two or more steps simultaneously, he may take them out of order, or he may fluctuate back and forth among the steps. They are not an end in themselves but a means to an end—the systematic solution of a research problem.

The use of the scientific method rests upon certain fundamental assumptions. Deobold Van Dalen has identified these as (1) the nature of reality, (2) the uniformity of nature, and (3) assumptions concerning the psychological process. Accompanying these assumptions are several postulates, that is, basic principles assumed to be true without proof.[3]

The assumption of the nature of reality is that we assume we are living in a real world; that is, there exists an objective reality, independent of whether or not it has been discovered. The real world is not dependent upon discovery or creation by the individual human mind; there is more to its existence than a basis in the minds of men. To be sure, scientists do not necessarily agree on the nature of reality, but nevertheless it exists.

The assumption of the uniformity of nature is that what has been found to be true will continue to be true and that similarity of circumstances will produce consistently similar results. In essence, the assumption is that nature is orderly. The postulates related to this assumption are those of (1) natural kinds, (2) constancy, and (3) determinism.

The postulate of natural kinds is the principle that natural phenomena can be classified according to common characteristics. Thus we can, for example, classify objects according to physical characteristics such as shape or color, and we can classify student behavior or performance. Countless taxonomies and classification schemes are in continuous use in education; the grading system employed in most schools is a classification system of student performance. By using classification schemes the researcher attempts to increase and organize his knowledge.

The postulate of constancy assumes that in nature there is a certain degree of consistency. Certainly all phenomena are not universally con-

3. D. B. Van Dalen, *Understanding Educational Research,* 3rd ed. (New York: McGraw-Hill Book Co., 1973), pp. 18–26.

sistent, but related to specific phenomena relatively constant conditions exist, and these can be discovered. We are aware of the many physical changes that take place, and we can predict such changes with relative certainty. A rate of change, in fact, may be one of the factors that is quite stable or constant. The performances of students under certain conditions are expected to be the same as they have been in the past, given the same conditions.

The postulate of determinism assumes that within the orderliness of nature, the occurrence of a phenomenon is preceded by certain antecedent events or conditions. Events are not random or accidental occurrences. If a student has a severely hostile attitude toward school, we assume that this is the result of antecedent factors or events.

The assumption dealing with the psychological process is basically that the researcher can acquire knowledge through the processes of perceiving, remembering, and reasoning. The three postulates, one related to each of these psychological processes, are very similar, namely the postulates of reliability of perceiving, remembering, and reasoning. In each case we do not assume absolute reliability; we are aware that errors can and do occur in connection with each of these processes. Despite the possibility of error, the researcher assumes that these psychological processes can aid him in acquiring knowledge and securing solutions to his problems.

In our discussion of research the emphasis has been primarily on the systematic approach as exemplified by the scientific method. From this discussion, it can be assumed that if educational research is to be considered a legitimate part of the research endeavor, it must involve a scientific approach. The general goals of educational research coincide with those of all scientific research: explanation, prediction, understanding, and control. In order to enhance the understanding of what we mean by educational research, we often classify specific educational research endeavors on the basis of the goals to be attained. There are any number of classification schemes for educational research based on the goals of the research; to a large extent these are arbitrary schemes, based on what appears to be most useful at the time. Two such classification schemes identify research as basic or applied and as problem solving, theory developing, or theory testing.

Basic and applied research

The terms "basic" and "applied" research have been used for some time. Unfortunately, some misconceptions have developed with their use. One such misconception is that basic research is complex, whereas applied research is simple in its methodology. A related misconception is the idea that applied research is carried on by an unsophisticated practitioner, and basic research is performed by an abstract but impractical thinker. Another misconception is that applied research is often sloppy and haphazard but of great practical value, while basic research is precise and exacting but of little or no value in a real situation.

Basic and applied research are not differentiated by complexity or value but by their goal orientation, that is, the goals they pursue. The aim of applied research is to solve an immediate, practical problem. It is oriented to a specific problem. Basic research has a more general orientation—addition to the existing body of knowledge in the discipline. Basic research does not necessarily provide results of immediate, practical use, although such a possibility is not ruled out. If this result does occur, however, it is supplemental and not the result of the primary goal. It should also be noted that applied research, in its solution of a specific problem, may contribute to the general knowledge of the field. Both basic and applied research are important; they should not be differentiated by a hierarchy of value judgments.

An example of basic research would be conducting an experiment concerning learning in a laboratory setting. The purpose of such an experiment would be to contribute to the knowledge about how learning takes place. The experiment might be focused on one or a very limited number of factors associated with learning, such as the difference between presenting the learning materials in a figural or verbal manner.

An example of applied research might result when a biology department proposes that a team-teaching approach would be more challenging and effectual than individual teachers. The members of the department would then set about conducting a research study to help them decide between the feasibility and effectiveness of the two approaches in their specific situation.

Another term which has come into recent use in education is *developmental research*. This type of research for the most part is applied research; its orientation is to the solution of practical problems. If developmental research is directed to the development of educational products, it is referred to as *product research*. The advent of the federally funded research and development (R & D) centers undoubtedly did much to foster developmental research. (It should not be inferred, however, that R & D centers conduct only developmental and applied research.) The development of Individually Guided Education (IGE)[4] at the Wisconsin Research and Development Center for Cog-

---

4. There are numerous publications devoted to various factors of IGE developmental research, many of them published by the Wisconsin Research and Development Center for Cognitive Learning. See, for example, H. J. Klausmeier

nitive Learning is an example of a large-scale developmental research effort. Numerous individual studies related to IGE and its implementation have been conducted. Certainly all developmental research is not of the magnitude of the IGE development, but often the term is associated with continuing, relatively large-scale efforts.

The distinction between basic and applied research may not be an extremely useful one, primarily because of the considerable overlap between the two. We introduce the terms at this point to describe the distinction between them and to clear up any misconceptions you may have concerning this terminology.

Problem-solving, theory-developing, and theory-testing research

Another method of classifying research which may be more definitive than simply basic or applied is a three-category system: problem solving, theory developing, and theory testing.[5] This method of classifying research is also based on the goal orientation of the research, and often there is an overlap between these three major goals. Most educational research projects, however, can be viewed in terms of a major goal orientation. There is no hierarchy of value judgments, either *a priori* or empirically based, that labels one type of goal orientation superior to the others. Educational research involves all three types, and the types not only overlap to some degree, but they often support one another.

Problem-solving research is directed toward an applied goal, usually the solution of a specific problem. It is not performed for the purpose of developing or testing theories, although the actual problem may be more or less related to some theoretical constructs. Research associated with the instructional programs of specific schools is often of this type. For example, suppose the teachers in a school are concerned about whether to use additional group work involving overhead projection or an individual programmed text as a supplement to the regular textbook and classroom instruction for teaching elementary science. The teachers are concerned about the relative effectiveness of the two methods in their particular situation. They want to make a decision that they can apply. They have little concern, if any, for theory development and testing.

Theory-developing research is oriented toward clarifying a tentative guess, and it is therefore exploratory in nature. The research is conducted in order to formulate a theory or to refine it further. Very basic

et al., IGE and the Multiunit Elementary School (Madison: University of Wisconsin, 1971).

5. W. A. Scott and Michael Wertheimer, *Introduction to Psychological Research* (New York: John Wiley & Sons, 1962), pp. 4–8.

aspects of the theory may be under consideration, for example not only the type of effect a certain stimulus may have but whether it has any effect at all. Suppose an educational psychologist has an idea that the frequency of encountering instructional materials (e.g., word lists, mathematics problem solutions) has an effect upon the retention of the concepts involved in the materials. Note that he conjectures some effect, not that increased use would either decrease or increase retention. The theory to be developed relative to this idea may be part of a larger theory of learning. The educational psychologist is developing theory at this point, he is not formally testing any part of the theory.

The greatest amount of overlap is between theory-developing and theory-testing research. Theory-testing research in essence requires some formulation of the theory, usually through hypotheses which can be either supported or refuted. The support (or lack thereof) of initial hypotheses may lead to additional theory developing which would include revision if necessary. In theory-testing research, the researcher may be making a decision among several alternative hypotheses.

Suppose that the educational psychologist in the above example had formulated the hypothesis that increased use enhances retention. Along with this idea there might be formulated several conditions relating to factors such as complexity of the materials and level at which continued use would no longer affect retention. It is likely some relationships among factors would be hypothesized as well. Theory-testing research would enable the researcher to test his theory with its major and related hypotheses. Presumably his research would either confirm or refute his theory.

THE ROLE OF THEORY

While we have discussed theory-developing and theory-testing research, little has been said about the meaning of a theory and the role that theory has in educational research. Kerlinger has defined theory as "a set of interrelated constructs (concepts), definitions, and propositions that presents a systematic view of phenomena by specifying relations among variables, with the purpose of explaining and predicting the phenomena."[6] May Brodbeck[7] includes many of the same ideas in her discussion of theory, adding that a theory is a deductively connected set of laws and that all statements in a theory, both explained and

---

6. Kerlinger, *Foundations of Behavioral Research,* p. 9.
7. May Brodbeck, "Logic and the Scientific Method in Research on Teaching," in N. L. Gage, (ed.), *Handbook of Research on Teaching* (Chicago: Rand McNally & Co., 1963), p. 68.

explaining, are generalizations. The laws doing the explaining are the axioms and those explained are the theorems.

A *theory,* then, is a generalization or series of generalizations by which we attempt to explain some phenomenon in a systematic manner. Theories can range from a single, simple generalization to a complex formulation of laws. The definition of theory also allows for flexibility in the stage of development or formulation. Most theories in education require a process of refinement through revision and extension.

We have mentioned the goal orientation of theory-developing and theory-testing research, but what of the role and purpose of theory in research? Basically, theory helps to provide a framework for research by serving as the point of departure for the pursuit of a research problem. The theory identifies the crucial factors. It provides a guide for systematizing and interrelating the various facets of the research. However, it not only provides the systematic view of the factors under study but may very well identify gaps, weak points, and inconsistencies which then alert the researcher to the need for additional research. Also, the development of the theory may light the way for continued research of the phenomena under study. Thus, it serves as a tool of science in the research context.

In educational research, theory serves a synthesizing function, combining ideas and individual bits of empirical information into a set of constructs which provides for deeper understanding, broader meaning, and wider applicability. In a sense, a theory attaches meaning to facts and places them in proper perspective. Through this process the theory aids in defining the research problem; that is, it helps identify the proper questions to be asked in the context of the specific research project.

As indicated in Kerlinger's definition, a theory also serves the purposes of explaining and predicting. It provides an explanation of observed phenomena, and it can also predict as yet unobserved or undiscovered factors by indicating their presence if the theory is consistent. The researcher is then "tipped off" in terms of what to look for.

Another function of theory is to provide the researcher with one or more generalizations that he can test and either refute or retain. These generalizations can then be used in practical applications and further research. This development of generalizations is based on the assumption that generalizations do exist in education or any area under study and that individual observations are special cases of such generalizations.

In a very real sense, research and theory go hand in hand. Integral parts of any specific research project are the various conditions under which the research is conducted and the data collected. The conditions and data must be incorporated into a meaningful whole; standing alone, they are not likely to mean much. As the facts of the research study, the data derive significance from the theory or theories into which they fit. Conversely, the theories become acceptable to the extent that they enhance the meaning of the data. Through this process more adequate theories and unobstructed facts are secured. Theory stimulates research, and, conversely, research stimulates theory development and theory testing.

The purposes and functions of theory are certainly not independent of the goals of scientific research. The criterion by which we judge a theory is not its truth or falsity, but rather its usefulness. Theories sometimes decrease in usefulness in the light of new knowledge, and they are combined, replaced, and refined as more knowledge is made available.

A "good" theory is developed in such a way that the generalizations can be tested. The theory must be compatible with the observations made relative to it and with the already existing knowledge. It must adequately explain the events or phenomena under study. The greater the generalizability of the theory, the more useful it will be, because of its wider applicability.

Another characteristic of a good theory is reflected in the *law of parsimony,* which holds that theories should be stated in the simplest form but one that adequately explains the phenomena. This does not mean that all theories should be simple statements, but that they should be stated succinctly and precisely, avoiding ambiguities and unnecessary complexity. Important factors must not be overlooked, and the comprehensiveness of the theory must be adequate for its purpose.

THE IMPORTANCE OF DEFINITION

Another matter of considerable importance in educational research concerns precise definition. Because words mean different things to different people, potential problems of ambiguity, confusing semantics, and misinterpretation are very real.

Educational research problems, hypotheses, and related theories are stated in words and sentences. These words and sentences convey meanings and concepts, but, as semanticists point out, the definition of words is not in the words but in ourselves.[8] We put meaning into words by the use we make of them. It does not take extensive reading or con-

8. S. I. Hayakawa, *Language in Thought and Action* (New York: Harcourt, Brace & World, 1949), p. 292.

versation to realize that educational research means different things to different people. Yet when we are dealing with specific research projects, precise definition is necessary to ensure that the words and sentences mean to our audience what we intended them to mean.

We usually ascribe to the researcher the right of definition within the context of existing use and knowledge. What this means is that the researcher can assign his intended meaning to the words he uses. The right of definition also carries the responsibility of adequately communicating this meaning to the audience. Every area of study contains a great many defined terms, but the definitions of all objects, concepts, and so on are not equally easy or difficult. It may be relatively simple to transmit what is meant by the color yellow to a group of individuals who can be shown examples of physical objects that have as one of their characteristics the color yellow. It is considerably more difficult to transmit the meaning of anxiety, a characteristic that an organism might take on under certain conditions and that is manifested more by behavior than by physical characteristics.

Some things in nature are essentially defined through repeated use and common experience. Many objects encountered in direct experience need no definition because the mere association of the object with the name transmits a precise meaning. Other objects and concepts need qualifying terms. A physical object can be defined by naming its observable characteristics. If a science student is asked to define a rattlesnake, for example, he can list observable characteristics such as rattles and their position on the tail and color patterns of the skin until he has provided adequate information for recognition of an instance of a rattlesnake.

Of course, all objects that require definition do not possess observable physical characteristics that can be identified and listed. In defining an abstract concept such as cognition we can say, to begin with, that cognition is a process that involves knowing or perceiving. This knowing or perceiving could be evidenced by immediate discovery, awareness, rediscovery, or recognition of information. We also could provide synonyms for cognition, such as knowledge or perception. In attempting to secure a definition, we replace certain words with other words. In essence, we are using conceptual expressions in place of the word or words being defined. In our definition of cognition, we must decide what immediate discovery, awareness, and so on mean. Where does the word-replacement process stop? It stops when there is no longer any ambiguity about the referents of the original term being defined. Essentially, a chain of definition is set up. The more abstract the concept being defined, the longer is the chain of definition before it terminates. This approach to definition is sometimes called a *constitutive definition*.

Brodbeck has summarized the conditions for an adequate definition as follows:

An adequate definition permits us always to tell when a sentence containing the defined term is true and when it is false. An adequately defined concept is also called "reliable." If a concept is reliable, then different people or the same person at different times always agree about whether or not there is an instance of the concept.[9]

The operational definition

The educational researcher often deals with objects that do not readily manifest themselves. If we are interested in the weights of the pupils in a first-grade class, we can measure these using a common weight scale. But if we want to measure and quantify ability to learn or reading comprehension, we must have some tool to do it with. Perhaps we could set up the chain of definition for ability to learn and meet the criterion of an adequate definition. But in order to achieve empirical measurement we need something more in the definition; we must include the processes or operations that are going to be used to measure or quantify the phenomena under study. Such a definition is called an *operational definition*.[10] In the example dealing with ability to learn we might "measure" this as the pupil's score on an IQ inventory, specifically the score attained on the LM form of the *Stanford-Binet Intelligence Scale*.

The operational definition is stipulative in that it specifies the operations to be used for the measurement. By adequately describing the operations to be used, the researcher enhances understanding of the term being defined.

SELECTION OF A RESEARCH TOPIC

Our discussion of the research process thus far has dealt primarily with how good answers, that is, solutions to research problems, are secured. But educational research initially involves asking good questions as well. The selection of an appropriate research topic is in part a matter of asking such questions. Without a workable research topic, the most carefully designed procedures for securing answers will be to no avail.

There is no standardized set of procedures that can be prescribed for

9. Brodbeck, "Logic and the Scientific Method," p. 48.
10. For a detailed discussion of operational definition, see R. H. Ennis, "Operational Definitions," *American Educational Research Journal* 1 (May 1964): 183–201.

selecting a research topic. However, certain factors can be considered which will aid in the selection.

The research topic should be of interest not only to the individual researcher but to at least some recognized segment of the educational community. Its place in the context of education should be assured. The matter of originality should also be considered, especially if the research topic is being selected for a thesis, but a completely original research idea is rare. It is more likely that the research will be a takeoff or extension of some already completed project. The extent of duplication or replication that is desirable in such studies depends upon the specific area and conditions of the research.

Another factor is the significance of the research topic for education, from either a practical or a theoretical viewpoint. Trivial problems can be procedurally researched, for example, the proportions of elementary students wearing canvas and leather shoes and the relationship of this choice of footwear to achievement. But such a problem has no theoretical framework and no significance, regardless of what the resulting proportions happen to be. The research problem should add to the existing knowledge or contribute to education in a meaningful way.

Not all problems in education are researchable. Some topics are philosophical in nature and can be discussed but not researched. An example is a question such as: "Should the history requirement in the senior high school be one or two courses?" Chances are that if the requirement is two courses the students will learn more history. But the question remains whether it is *important* that they have two courses. Answers to such questions are for the most part based on value judgments. If no additional conditions are stipulated, the questions are not researchable.

Some problems may be researchable but doing the research is not feasible. The necessary data for the study may be excessive or too difficult to obtain. Ethical considerations may be involved; for example, the testing required to obtain the necessary data may be an invasion of the individual's privacy. There are also problems that could be researched if the necessary funds were available. Other necessary resources, such as laboratory facilities or computer time, may also not be available. There are any number of these kinds of conditions which can make research on a specific problem unfeasible.

Research topics are not selected in a vacuum of information or experience. The aspiring researcher should familiarize himself with the area in which he plans to work. He should know the relevant theories, and his research question should be framed in the context of such theories. A premium is put on original and creative thinking, but the possibility of such thinking is very remote if the individual has no knowledge on which to base it.

A study of related research and familiarization with practical or theoretical problems in the area will aid the researcher in formulating appropriate questions which will help him focus on the research topic he has chosen. Suppose an individual is interested in doing research related to learning, and specifically to transfer. He could consider the identical-elements theory of transfer, which assumes that elements present in the original learning are also present in the new learning, to be the basis for considering transfer. But he would have to decide what actually comprises identical elements. Suppose it were desirable to test the theory relative to a unique learning task and the visual stimuli involved in that task. Would an identical element of color be adequate for transfer? Would shapes or sizes by themselves be adequate? Are some combinations of the possible elements conducive to transfer? What implications would the results have for a practical learning situation? How could the results be used for testing the theory in a practical learning situation? What would these visual stimuli mean in terms of confirming or refuting the theory?

These are examples of questions related to the theory and the specific area of research. In any research study it is not adequate to simply accumulate empirical results. Such questions, along with the theory and the statement of the research problem, provide meaning to the results to be derived from the study.

STATEMENT OF THE RESEARCH PROBLEM

The statement of the research problem should be well defined and specific. If the problem selected is stated in vague or overly broad terms, considerable difficulty will result in applying the research procedures, since it will be unclear as to what is actually under investigation. The tendency may be for the beginning researcher to state his problem too broadly at the outset. This is not undesirable if the problem is later systematically restricted through a review of the literature and in the initial stages of organizing the research effort. It is better to work in this direction than to start with a problem that is too narrow and then attach pieces to it in order to expand the problem.

There is extensive discussion of factors related to the identification of a research problem in Chapter 3. At this point, we want only to illustrate the procedure with some unsatisfactory and satisfactory statements. A problem such as "the elementary curriculum" is far too broad. A more satisfactory statement would be: "the effects of elementary curriculum practices upon the reading achievement of fourth-grade students of City A." Following are several examples of original statements and their subsequent restatement into more manageable statements of the problems.

Original: Creativity of elementary school students.
Restatement: A study of the relationship between divergent thinking scores and selected factors of fifth-, sixth-, and seventh-grade students.

Original: Achievement and teaching techniques.
Restatement: The effect of three teaching techniques upon science achievement of junior high school students.

Original: The elementary primary school.
Restatement: A study of the effects of the ungraded primary school organization upon the personality scores of the students.

Original: The role of the guidance counselor in the high school.
Restatement: A survey of the practices of the guidance counselors in the high schools of City B.

A good statement of the problem should provide the researcher with considerable direction in pursuing the project. The statement should identify certain key factors in the research project. For example, in the first statement above the word "relationship" implies certain procedures. The grade level limits and defines the population under study. The term "divergent thinking scores" is certainly more specific than the word "creativity" used in the original statement. Divergent thinking requires an operational definition, likely as the score on a specific divergent thinking test.

It should be noted that in the restatements of the above problems, considerable definition of terms would be necessary. The selected factors in the first example would require identification and definition. The three teaching techniques of the second example would require definition for the specific situation. Such definitions should accompany the statement of the problem, but they are usually not included in the statement because they would make it excessively long, cumbersome, and awkward. Assuming that adequate definition accompanies the statement of the problem, there should be no ambiguity about what is to be investigated.

Some researchers prefer to state the research problem in question form, which may aid in focusing it. Using question form can be an especially effective technique when subproblems are included within the larger research problem. For example, in considering the statement of the research problem above dealing with guidance counselors, the following research questions could be raised:

1. What proportion of the guidance counselors' working day is taken up with nonguidance activities?

2. What are the major strengths of the guidance counselors' practices, as perceived by the students?
3. What are the major weaknesses of the guidance counselors' practices, as perceived by the students?
4. What practices are perceived by the guidance counselors as being most effective?

Stating research problems in question form does not eliminate the need for definition. If we are to obtain student perceptions, for example, some type of measuring instrument for such perceptions must be defined and developed. Whether or not research problems are stated in question form is to a large extent dependent upon the preference of the researcher. If question form appears to be helpful, by all means it should be used. Actually, the form for stating the problem is relatively unimportant. What is important is that the statement be precise and definitive enough so that there is no confusion as to what is under study.

THE ROLE OF HYPOTHESES

By itself, the statement of the research problem usually provides only general direction for research procedures. More specific direction is afforded by hypotheses associated with the problem. Hypothesis can effectively tie the statement of the problem to related theory and knowledge.

In the context of a research project, a hypothesis may be considered a conjecture or a tentative statement of the situation. It approximates a hunch or guess of what the existing situation is truly like. In this general sense, a hypothesis takes on some of the characteristics of a theory, which is usually considered as a larger set of generalizations about a certain phenomenon. Thus a theory might include several hypotheses. Logically, the approach is to proceed so that a decision can be made about whether or not the hypotheses are tenable. This is called *testing the hypothesis*. The test of a hypothesis does not prove or disprove it; it merely sustains or refutes the hypothesis.

The purpose of stating hypotheses, like the purpose of theories that may be involved, is to provide a framework for the research endeavor. Either directly or indirectly, the hypotheses formulate the statement of the problem. They may also imply research procedures to be used and necessary data to be compiled. The conclusions of the research problem may also be stated in the context of the initial hypotheses.

A research project need not proceed from a statement of hypotheses, however. Such hypotheses are not ends in themselves but rather aids to the research process. Objections have been raised against stating hypotheses. One is that hypotheses bias the researcher in favor of certain conclusions and hence threaten his objectivity. Closely allied is the objection that in his pursuit of the stated hypothesis the researcher may overlook other possibly worthwhile hypotheses. The statement of hypotheses in some situations also may appear premature. A research situation might develop about which there is very little background information. Perhaps considerable theory development is necessary. The researcher may decide to defer any hypotheses or theories until he has some empirical evidence upon which to base them.

Nonetheless, the overall consensus is in favor of stating hypotheses *whenever they are feasible.* It should be emphasized, however, that hypotheses are not stated in a vacuum. They should be formed not on the basis of sporadic or irrelevant bits of information or data but on the basis of the available body of organized information and the related theory, if such a theory exists. Certainly hypotheses should relate to and reflect the research problem.

Forms of hypothesis statement

Different forms may be used for stating hypotheses. We will not develop elaborate categorizing systems for them, but this text does place considerable emphasis upon hypothesis testing using inferential techniques. Therefore we will introduce here two forms, one which implies a direction of results and the other a nondirectional form.

Suppose we have a research situation in which we are experimenting with a new technique of teaching third-grade spelling. We hypothesize that the spelling achievement of third-grade pupils being taught with the new technique exceeds that of students being taught with traditional methods. This is a directional hypothesis in that a direction of results is implied, namely that the pupils taught by the new technique will register the greater achievement. Other examples of directional statements of hypotheses are:

1. The mathematics achievement of high-ability students exceeds that of average-ability students.
2. The reading level of first-grade girls is higher than that of first-grade boys.
3. There is a positive relationship between academic aptitude scores and scores on a social adjustment inventory.
4. As a teacher's salary scale increases, he has a more favorable opinion of school administrative personnel.

A second form of stating hypotheses is the nondirectional form. The statement in such a form hypothesizes no difference or no relationship. The nondirectional form is also referred to as the *"null" form* or *null hypothesis,* especially when it is used in a statistical context. The null hypothesis is often used when statistical procedures are employed to test the hypothesis.[11] Null hypotheses corresponding to those stated above would be as follows:

1. The mathematics achievement of high-ability students equals that of average-ability students, or there is no difference between the mathematics achievement of average- and high-ability students.
2. The reading level of first-grade girls is the same as that of first-grade boys.
3. There is no relationship between academic aptitude scores and scores on a social adjustment inventory.
4. A teacher's salary scale is independent of his opinion of school administrative personnel.

The researcher should not hesitate to be specific in the statements of hypotheses. A weakness of many hypotheses is that they are too broad to pinpoint the specific problem under study. Consider the following hypothesis: "Bright students have good attitudes toward school." The terms "bright" and "good" represent some types of broad, undefined generalities. Some type of vague relationship between brightness and good attitude is implied, but little direction for research procedure is provided. To convert the statement into an acceptable hypothesis, it might be changed to read:

Students aged nine through eleven who score in the upper 25 percent of their class on the (standardized) IQ test have a higher mean score on the "X-Y-Z Attitude toward School Inventory" than students scoring in the lower 75 percent of the class on the IQ test.

Another version could state:

A positive relationship exists between the scores on the (specific) IQ test and the (specific) attitude inventory, for students aged nine through eleven.

In null form, it might state:

There is no relationship between the scores on the (specific) IQ test and the (specific) attitude inventory, for students aged nine through eleven.

The elaborateness or complexity of the hypothesis depends on what is necessary to state it adequately. The language in the hypothesis should be concise and understandable. It is generally not good policy to run several hypotheses together, since this tends to make for both cumbersome wording and confusion. In order to be useful, hypotheses run

---

11. It should be noted that if the null hypothesis is used in a statistical context, specific statistics such as means would be identified. This point will be discussed in the chapters of Part II. The purpose here is to illustrate generally the directional and nondirectional forms of hypothesis statement.

together would likely require separation once the research study is underway.

A research problem may have several hypotheses associated with it, and they may be more specific than those stated above. When statistical procedures are anticipated, the hypotheses often refer to the specific statistics that will be involved. In the context of statistical tests of hypotheses, the definition of a hypothesis becomes more restrictive, as will be discussed after the necessary terminology has been introduced. The terminology is introduced in the next chapter and it is extensively used in Part II.

RESEARCH METHODOLOGY

The methods of research provide the tools by which the research problem is attacked. Methodology consists of the systematic procedures by which the researcher travels from the initial identification of the problem to its final conclusions. The role of the methodology is to carry on the research job in a scientific, applicable, and valid manner. A host of procedures and techniques, both simple and complex, come under the heading of methods of research.

Generally, no one would attempt to tighten a bolt with a hammer or drive a nail with a screwdriver. By the same token, the research methods utilized must fit the requirements of the specific research problem. Such tools as hypotheses, data-gathering techniques, analyses, and interpretations must be the appropriate ones for each research study. This common-sense requirement may not on the surface seem to merit discussion, but the use of improper methods, unfortunately, does occur in educational research.

The tools in themselves will not get the job done, just as all the available hammers and nails placed side by side will not get the nails driven. Research procedures are of little value unless they are used, and used properly. The proper use of research methods must be learned.

Our analogy between nail-driving and educational research methods begins to break down in relation to understanding the results. It is enough to realize that a nail has been driven without understanding how to drive the nail. Understanding the results and conclusions of a research study is more demanding. The reason why many teachers and educators say that they have difficulty understanding the research in an area is because they do not understand the methodology behind the research. For the same reason graduate students encounter unnecessary difficulties when they identify research problems and immediately want to inspect relevant data and press to conclusions without proper regard for the research methodology to be used along the way. Mastery of the methodology invariably enhances understanding of the research.

Research methodology involves such general activities as data collection, measurement, review of the literature, identifying problems, formulating hypotheses, procedures for testing hypotheses, analyses, interpreting analyses, and drawing conclusions, not necessarily in that order. For a specific research study the procedures within each of the general activities should be identified. In pursuing a study, the researcher will bring many procedures to bear. Some of these may involve the specific measurement necessary to acquire the desired data. Others may involve the manipulation of the data in order to make decisions about the hypotheses. Another procedure is a review of the literature in order to pull together the existing information about the problem under investigation. And so it goes, until by use of the procedures the various facets of the research study are pieced together and brought to a conclusion.

Research activities

In summarizing the general activities involved in conducting a research study, we may appear to be emphasizing the sequential nature of the research process. To a certain extent this is fine, but we do not want to leave the impression that the research process is rigid or completely structured. Activities overlap to some degree, and at times two or more activities can be in process simultaneously. There may also be some fluctuation in the sequence of activities; for example, preliminary analysis may begin while data collection is still in process. It is helpful, however, to impose some order on the various research activities.

Figure 1.1 presents a sequential pattern of activities in flowchart form which should provide an overview of the various research activities. The top line of boxes represents the general activities. Within each of these, more specific activities could be listed. For example, the review of related literature would be an activity aiding in the identification of the research problem. The lower boxes and the corresponding arrows reflect the relationships between the activities and existing knowledge, related theory, and expanded, revised, and new theory. Related theory is considered to be a part, but not necessarily all, of the body of knowledge relative to the research problem. Expanded, revised, and new theory, if forthcoming from the research project, then becomes part of the existing body of knowledge, as does new information not considered to be theory. Obviously, all general activities draw on existing knowledge, but for the purposes of this figure we consider the major impact of the body of knowledge as relative to the research problem.

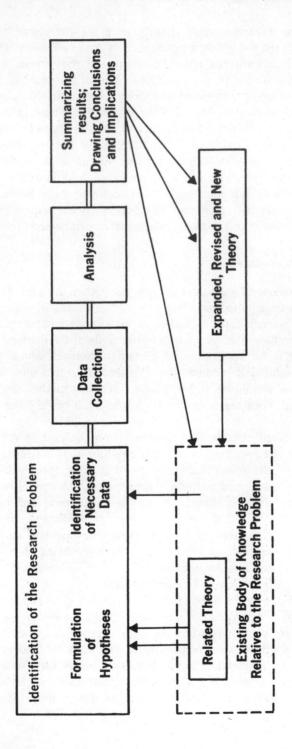

FIGURE 1.1. Sequential pattern of general activities in conducting a research study, and the relationship of such activities to existing knowledge

The naïve researcher may attempt to begin the research study by breaking into the pattern at a point such as data collection. This results in working backward (or possibly seesawing). Sometimes hypotheses are formulated on the basis of available data or the analysis of existing data. An attempt is then made to extract a research problem from the hypotheses so generated. Breaking the sequential pattern in this manner tends to result in confusion and inefficiency. As has been indicated, there often are both fluctuation in the pattern and a possible reordering of activities. However, the nature of these variations depends upon the specific project and where in the sequence such variations occur. Generally, breaking in at a point such as data collection is to be discouraged. The more nearly the researcher can adhere to the sequential pattern, the more efficiently and precisely the activities can be conducted.

Statistical procedures

The development of statistical techniques within the past four or five decades has contributed greatly to the advancement of educational research as a science. The invention of high-speed computers has made possible the analysis of great quantities of data. Computers have also made possible the application of certain techniques which previously had been prohibitive because they required excessive time and effort. But statistical techniques and computers are only methodological tools, to be applied when they can do the job at hand better than any other method.

There is often considerable reluctance on the part of students and educators to become associated with anything that concerns statistics. Formulas and the manipulation of numbers can appear difficult and foreboding. This type of attitude is unfortunate, since avoiding statistics renders many research studies impossible to complete and many completed studies difficult, if not impossible, to understand. Some of the actual computation involved in analysis may be extensive and complex. Nevertheless, the basic ideas and underlying reasoning should be mastered. This is essential for meaningful reading of research articles, as well as for participation in research studies.

One additional point about the use of statistical procedures: Statistical treatment of data does not necessarily make the research good. Such procedures are good only when they are appropriate, when they relate to the research hypotheses or questions, and when the necessary conditions for their application exist. Wherever statistical procedures are presented in this text, you should focus attention on the underlying reasoning. Formulas are introduced only for illustration; it is not necessary for you to memorize any of them. Computation is minimal and is required only for a limited number of the suggested study exercises.

CONCLUDING REMARKS: SUMMARY OF EDUCATIONAL RESEARCH CONCEPTS

The various specific definitions of educational research that can be generated all indicate that it is broad in scope, including many activities and diverse areas of study. We have noted that educational research can be considered in the context of the scientific method. But we might also caution against viewing educational research as being rigid and invariably following a lockstep set of procedures. In fact, some writers would reject the notion of a single, simple scientific method or formula as the procedure for conducting educational research.[12] Certainly scientific knowledge is arrived at through a variety of procedures and by a host of individuals who manifest personal behaviors. Therefore, when considering something like the scientific method as a general model for conducting research, you should keep in mind that it embodies great flexibility.

In this chapter we have discussed topics such as theory, definition, hypotheses, and so forth in an attempt to describe the components of educational research and thus arrive at a general understanding of what is meant by the term "educational research." The characteristics of "scientific" and "systematic" were discussed. Various research activities were identified, described, and interrelated (see Figure 1.1).

One who reads the research literature but does not himself conduct research might get the impression (to some extent a false one) that educational research is very orderly and organized. The research report is usually arranged in logical sections, beginning with a statement of the research problem and concluding with a discussion of results and their implications. What the reader may not realize is that the actual research might not have been so well organized or conducted in so orderly a fashion. Problems can and do arise in conducting educational research which may call for adjustments to be made, procedures to be redone, and the like. What we attempt to do is show you how to structure and conduct the research effort, according to the conditions of the specific study, in order to minimize problems and difficulties and still meet the goals of the research. However, you should not expect a single "recipe" for conducting educational research; no such thing exists.

Educational research involves many different kinds of activities. Some

---

12. See, for example, R. M. W. Travers, *An Introduction to Educational Research,* 3rd ed. (New York: Macmillan Co., 1969), p. 2.

of these activities are simple and others are complex; in fact, an entire continuum from simple to complex is encompassed. The research is done in many different areas: curriculum, learning, educational administration, to mention just a few. It takes place at many different levels, from the individual to the massive projects conducted in R & D centers, universities, and other large agencies. Therefore, the description of educational research must be broad and include many components. Even broad concepts, when projected into reality, are made up of specifics, however, and it is the specifics of research methods (activities, procedures, underlying reasoning, and so on) that are of major consideration in this text.

The function of educational research

At the conclusion of this first chapter it is well to consider the role of educational research in a general sense. The question might be raised by an already overloaded teacher: Why bother with educational research at all? What type of a role or function does educational research have in the overall enterprise of education and in its specific facets? One measure of its importance is its widespread use. The federal government and various foundations have allotted considerable funds for the pursuit of educational research, and numerous universities have for years been more or less involved in it. Such involvement is often on the basis of individual professors, but with federal funding there has been a trend toward more extensive projects involving several individuals and in some cases more than one university. School systems are becoming increasingly willing to utilize the results of research. In some instances, schools conduct research themselves, especially as it relates to educational development. (It should probably be assumed that the purpose of such expenditures in money and effort is not simply to keep educational researchers off the rolls of the unemployed.)

We might say that the overall function of educational research is to improve educational procedures through the refinement and extension of knowledge. The refinement of existing knowledge or the acquisition of new knowledge is essentially an intermediate step toward the improvement of the educational process. This step is extremely important and may occupy a considerable proportion of the time allotted to the research endeavor. The refinement of existing knowledge should not be taken lightly, since in many situations the initial ideas and procedures of a research study may be relatively crude and remain adequate for only a short time.

Within the broad framework of educational improvement, the specific roles of educational research are viewed differently by the people associated with various aspects of education. Consider two examples. The researcher concerned with a learning experiment may be attempting to reinforce or refute his theory of how learning takes place. The function of research here is to aid in making a decision concerning the refinement or extension of knowledge in this particular area. The classroom teacher, on the other hand, grappling with the problem of coming up with a more effective technique for teaching slow learners how to read, looks to research for tangible evidence on how to solve this immediate problem. For research to meet its function it should satisfy both requirements. That is, it should aid the theorist in making a decision about his theory, and it should provide the teacher with information that will lead to the solution of the nontheoretical classroom problem. The long-range goal of both theorist and teacher is to improve the educational process, the teacher in a much more immediate situation and the theorist on the assumption that knowing more about learning will increase the effectiveness of the learning process.

The demands of contemporary culture upon the educational systems of today are many and intense, as the various areas of education are exposed to objective examination. The problems associated with the development, operation, and improvement of educational systems must be met with extensive and systematic applications of knowledge. Educational research provides the impetus, background, and vehicle by which systematic examination, development, and improvement can take place.

The teacher, the administrator, the specialist of any kind in the schools, the college professor, the researcher—all of these are taking part. All concerned should be consumers of research findings. Almost everyone should at some stage or another also be an active participant in research studies. The practitioner, such as a teacher, will use research primarily to shed light on some immediate problem. It is likely that he will become a better educator because of his research involvement. Teachers, administrators, and the like should engage in on-the-job research as a normal part of their professional activity and growth. To be sure, there will be different types of research and different amounts of involvement. Educational research should have the image of a helpful mechanism which can be used by all educators, in one way or another, for the improvement of the educational process.

SUGGESTED STUDY EXERCISES

1.1. Suppose a researcher were interested in doing research on the effects of individualizing instruction upon scholastic performance of elementary school students. What terms would require operational definition? Provide examples of operational definitions for these terms.

1.2. Develop an argument against the assertion: "Theory is useless in educational research."

1.3. Suppose someone decides to do research on team teaching in the elementary school. This, of course, is not an adequate statement of a research problem. Choose an aspect related to this more general topic, identify a research problem, and formulate a statement of the problem.

1.4. Consider the question, "What should be the objectives of mathematics instruction in the senior high school?" Can this question be formulated into a research problem? If your answer is yes, develop a satisfactory statement of the research problem. If your answer is no, provide an argument for why this is not a researchable question.

1.5. What is the essential characteristic of the statement of a hypothesis in null form?

1.6. Restate each of the following hypotheses in null form:
   a. As students receive increased positive reinforcement, their error rate will decrease.
   b. Senior high school age students display more efficient performance on a concept-attainment task than junior high school age students.
   c. The achievement of fifth-grade students on a divergent thinking test is greater than that of third-grade students.

1.7. Consider the following inadequate statements of a research problem. Restate each, being specific enough so that it becomes a satisfactory statement of a research problem.
   a. Attitudes and scholastic achievement.
   b. Behavior modification with children who are discipline problems.
   c. The use of behavioral objectives in teaching science.
   d. Accountability and teacher attitudes toward school administration.

1.8. For each of your restatements of the previous exercise, formulate two hypotheses that might be associated with the research problem. State one of each of the pairs of hypotheses in null form.

1.9. Publications such as the *Journal of Educational Psychology* and the *American Educational Research Journal* often contain articles dealing with research studies. Select three or four articles from such publications and identify the statement of the problem for each. Decide whether or not the research problem is clear to the reader. Consider the adequacy of the definition of terms used in each research study.

chapter 2

Basic concepts of summarizing data

The identification of a research problem and the formulation of viable hypotheses are generally recognized as the beginning points of a research study. The researcher cannot proceed far, however, before realizing that he requires data in order to pursue the research, make decisions about his hypotheses, and make generalizations from the study. He soon arrives at the point where information must be secured about the phenomena under study.

DATA AND OBSERVATIONS

Data consist of specifically identified bits of information. In a research study, data are collected under the conditions specified by the study.

Suppose, for example, a researcher is interested in the effects of two different teaching methods upon the science achievement of fifth-grade students. He must secure information (data) about the science achievement of two groups of students, one group taught by each of the methods. After the methods have been used, the students most likely would be measured by using some type of science achievement "test." The scores on this test would be the observations or data, and the fifth-grade students would be the units or individuals being observed.

For a second example, consider a research study conducted in a learning laboratory in which high school seniors are required to perform individually a learning task consisting of solving a problem. The researcher records the time required by each senior to arrive at a correct solution; this is an observation, or score. These scores comprise the data of the study. The individual seniors are the units being observed. If each senior solved one problem, the researcher would secure as many observations as there are seniors participating in the learning task. In this example, the seniors might be referred to as the *subjects* (*S*s) of the research study. This use of the term "subject" to refer to the individual participants of the research study is common when conducting experiments.

Observations are not necessarily always taken on individuals. We could, for example, take an observation on a class, such as the amount of time spent in discussion. Assuming that classes are of a standard length, the data would consist of the numbers of minutes spent in discussion, one observation for each class. In contrast to the previous two examples, here classes rather than individuals would receive scores.

In each of the above examples, it is unlikely that the researcher would draw conclusions on the basis of a single observation or score. Rather he would obtain a considerable number of scores, and the set of scores would comprise the data for the study.

CONSTANTS, VARIABLES, AND MEASUREMENT SCALES

Before we can conveniently discuss procedures for conducting research or consider the underlying reasoning of research procedures, it is necessary to establish the appropriate terminology. Much of this chapter is devoted to defining terms and describing their commonly used meanings. It also suggests how these terms are related and how the concepts they represent fit together.

A *constant* is a characteristic or condition that is the same for all the observed units or *S*s of a study. A *variable*, on the other hand, is a characteristic which takes on different values for different *S*s. In the science achievement example discussed above, the grade level (i.e., fifth grade) is a constant. Science achievement is a variable, since it is unlikely that all Ss would obtain the same score on the science test. Suppose the researchers were doing a more comprehensive achievement study; it might be possible to observe the same group on reading achievement and spelling achievement as well. These achievement scores would also be variables. The achievement scores are variables not because there are two or more measures of achievement but because for any one type of achievement the fifth-grade students do not all attain the same score. The data would consist of the observations or scores on the one or more variables included.

A distinction is made between independent and dependent variables. In some research studies an *independent variable* is simply a classifying variable; it classifies the Ss of the study. In the science achievement example, teaching method would be an independent variable. A fifth grader in the study would be taught by one of the two methods, and the two methods would comprise the two classifications or "levels" of this variable. Two is the minimum number of levels for a variable.

A *dependent variable* is the consequent of the independent variable (or is at least presumed to be). It is the variable we are attempting to explain in the light of the independent variable. Referring again to the science achievement example, the score on the science test is the dependent variable. The terminology of dependent and independent variable comes from mathematics. In a general sense we say that the values of the dependent variable are dependent upon the independent variables. However, a word of caution is in order: Simply assigning names does not establish a cause-and-effect relationship between variables. Pursuing such relationships and effects is often the purpose of conducting the research.

To further illustrate the use of variable and constant, consider the following example. Suppose a study is conducted to determine the effect of three different teaching methods upon achievement in elementary algebra. Each of three ninth-grade algebra sections in the same school, taught by the same teacher, is taught using one of the methods. Both boys and girls are included in the study.

The recognized constants in the study are grade level, school, and teacher. (This assumes the teacher can hold constant teaching effectiveness, except for the method.) The independent variables in the study are teaching method and sex of the student. Teaching method has three levels which we can arbitrarily designate as methods A, B, and C, and the sex of the student has, of course, two levels. Achievement in algebra, as objectively measured at the end of the instructional period, is the dependent variable. (You should not interpret this example as a complete research design but only as an illustration of the terms "variable" and "constant.")

Types of measurement scales

In attempting to define the meaning of the term "measurement," it soon becomes apparent that not all measurement is the same. If we had a zoo full of animals we could decide whether each animal happens to be similar to another animal. We can tell that zebras are different from bears, and so on; the measurement here says only that the animals are different. Now suppose we consider measuring attitudes. If one S says that he is highly favorable toward something and another S says that he is neutral, we not only say that they are different but we can also order the Ss on degree of favorableness on the attitude being measured. Thus, in addition to having difference, we also have order.

Now, consider the measurement of something like IQ. If three S's have scores of 105, 110, and 115, respectively, we say that the difference between S_1 and S_2 is five points, as is the difference between S_2 and S_3. This gives not only difference and order but also a unit of equal differences established in the measurement. Finally, consider the weight of different quantities of apples. If we have two bags of apples, a 50-pound bag and a 100-pound bag, we say that the 100-pound bag weighs twice as much as the 50-pound bag. We can say twice because having no apples is the zero point in quantity of apples. Thus we not only have difference, order, and a unit, but also a comparison in terms of the ratio of one observation to another. We can say that a 100-pound bag of apples weighs twice as much as one of 50 pounds, but we cannot say that a S with an IQ of 140 has twice whatever IQ measures as does a S with an IQ of 70. In order to establish a ratio, the scale must have a true zero point.

The four different types of measurement scales identified above comprise a hierarchy in terms of the number of necessary conditions needed to attain the scale. These measurement scales can be defined and summarized as follows:

1. *Nominal.* Categorizes without order; simply indicates that two or more categories are different. *Example:* color of eyes.
2. *Ordinal.* Categorizes with order; indicates that the categories are different and can be rank ordered. *Example:* the letter grading system.
3. *Equal unit.* Has all of the characteristics of an ordinal scale, plus the establishment of numerically equal distances on the scale. *Example:* performance on an IQ test. (This type of scale is also called an equal-interval or interval scale.)

4. *Ratio.* Contains an absolute or true zero point, in addition to equal units. *Example:* height.

This classification of types of scales may be considered a hierarchy, with the ratio scale being the highest level.

Variables whose measurement scales are ordinal or higher may be divided into those that are numerically scaled and those that are not. For example, observations for variables such as weight in pounds are on a numerical scale. However, if we used more general categories such as light weight, medium weight, and heavy weight, then the variable weight would still be ordered, but it would no longer be numerically scaled. A variable measured as poor, fair, good, or excellent is another example of one ordered but not numerically scaled.

Numerically scaled variables are considered as discrete or continuous in their measurement. A variable is said to be *discrete* if it can assume only certain or "discrete" values in the range of measurement. If we repeatedly flipped 20 coins simultaneously, the number of heads to appear would be a discrete variable, because only whole numbers of heads could occur. A *continuous* variable, in contrast, can take on any values in the range of measurement. The height of individuals, for example, is considered continuous because the possible scores include fractions of an inch as well as whole numbers of inches. If an accurate measuring stick were available, a person could be measured to a thousandth or ten-thousandth of an inch. Even with this precision, it would still be possible for the variable to assume only a finite number of values. The precision of measurement is never absolute, and the researcher must round off at some point. For our purposes the practical distinction between discrete and continuous variables is not a difference in reality of a finite or infinite number of possible values. The important distinction lies in the theoretical continuity of the variable.

DISTRIBUTIONS

We have noted that the data of a study consist of the observations on one or more variables. The set of observations or the data on a single variable is called a *distribution*. Suppose we have a set of scores on an achievement measure and we simply record the scores in some order, say the order in which the answer sheets were turned in. Such a set of scores is usually not easily interpreted. By inspection we could determine the extreme scores, but by and large we would find that some reordering of the scores was necessary. One common way of reordering is to arrange the scores from the smallest to the largest and tabulate the frequency of occurrence for each score. Such a reordering is called a *frequency distribution*.

As an example, consider the set of scores in Table 2.1, which could

TABLE 2.1.   Set of hypothetical scores on an arithmetic test

82	79	72	85	99
72	72	80	83	61
89	93	76	84	66
72	92	87	82	66
89	94	69	90	80
98	86	82	81	77
84	86	83	75	81
75	67	74	93	97
75	98	78	66	74
91	95	78	60	95

represent the achievement scores on an arithmetic test. There are 50 scores, and we assume that measurement was on at least an interval scale. We can tabulate the frequency of each score as follows: The extreme scores are 99 and 60. A tabulation of the frequencies of the scores between the values 99 and 60, inclusive, gives the frequency distribution which appears in Table 2.2. Note that including all possible integer val-

TABLE 2.2.   Frequency distribution of arithmetic test scores

Score	f	Score	f	Score	f	Score	f
60	1	70	0	80	2	90	1
61	1	71	0	81	2	91	1
62	0	72	4	82	3	92	1
63	0	73	0	83	2	93	2
64	0	74	2	84	2	94	1
65	0	75	3	85	1	95	2
66	3	76	1	86	2	96	0
67	1	77	1	87	1	97	1
68	0	78	2	88	0	98	2
69	1	79	1	89	2	99	1

ues between 99 and 60 requires 40 values, even though some of these values have frequencies of zero. In the distribution of Table 2.2, the observed scores are tabulated and ordered, the only change from the original set of scores. Sometimes the original set of scores is referred to as the *raw scores,* Table 2.2 would then be called a frequency distribution of raw scores.

The distribution presented in Table 2.2 is in tabular form. We can also present the distribution in graphic form by indicating the frequency on the vertical axis and the values of the possible scores on the horizontal axis. Such a representation is called a *histogram*. The histogram for the arithmetic test scores example is quite flat and spread out, due to relatively small frequencies and a wide range of scores. Figure 2.1 presents the histogram.

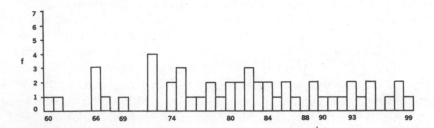

FIGURE 2.1.   Histogram for the frequency distribution of the raw scores on an arithmetic test

Describing a distribution of scores

While developing a frequency distribution or constructing a histogram does pull together the observed scores, these procedures are hardly adequate for describing the scores and identifying all the information they obtain. We could hardly report all research studies by merely reproducing the frequency distributions of the scores and constructing the related histograms. What we need are measures by which we can efficiently describe a distribution. Such measures are sometimes called *descriptive statistics,* one of the many tools we have for understanding research data.

Basically, there are three requirements for describing a distribution of scores. One is that we must know something about where the distribution is located on the scale of measurement. Secondly, we must have information about how the distribution is "spread out," how it is dispersed. The third requirement for describing a distribution is identification of its shape.

We can compute statistics that indicate the location of a distribution; such statistics are called *measures of central tendency.* Correspondingly, we can compute statistics that indicate the dispersion of the distribution; these are called *measures of variability.* In determining the shape of a distribution we could plot the scores and produce a histogram, but more commonly we infer a shape from knowing something about the variable under study. More will be said about this in a later section which considers the shapes of specific distributions.

Measures of central tendency

Measures of central tendency are what we commonly refer to as *averages*. In this sense they give an indication of what a "typical" observation in the distribution is like. The measures of central tendency are *locators* of the distribution; that is, they locate the distribution on the scale of measurement. They are points in the distribution which derive their name from a tendency to be centrally located in the distribution.

The mean, median, and mode are the most commonly used measures of central tendency. *Mean,* used in this context, refers to the arithmetic mean. To determine the mean we simply add the scores in a distribution and divide by the number of scores in the distribution. The *median*, by definition, is the point on the scale of measurement below which one-half of the scores of the distribution lie. The *mode,* which is the least frequently used of the three measures of central tendency, is simply the score with the greatest frequency. There are other measures of central tendency, but their infrequent use in educational research does not warrant their consideration in this text.

To illustrate the idea of a locator, suppose we have two distributions of weights: one for adult men and the other for adult women. Suppose that the mean weight of the distribution for men is 170 pounds and for the women's distribution it is 132 pounds. Both distributions have the same measurement scale, that of pounds, and both can be located on the measurement scale by their means. If we set the distributions on the measurement scale the distribution for the men would be located to the right, that is, further up the scale, than the distribution for the women.

The following example by which the mean for a distribution is determined must introduce some statistical computation. Its primary purpose is to introduce and define some elementary notation which will facilitate the presentation of ideas and enhance understanding.

Suppose we have the following distribution of ten scores: 9, 7, 8, 6, 7, 5, 4, 7, 7, 6. We could arrange them in order from lowest to highest, which would give 4, 5, 6, 6, 7, 7, 7, 7, 8, 9. An inspection of the data quickly reveals that the mode is 7. The sum of the ten scores is 66. In terms of notation this sum could be noted by

$$\sum_{i=1}^{10} X_i = 66.$$

The symbol Σ is a summation sign; it is simply an indication to add the numbers represented by the letter symbol which follows. The letter symbol X_i stands for a particular number in our distribution. The i is a subscript which is used as a substitute for the values 1 to 10 inclusive, since we have ten scores in our distribution. The $i = 1$ immediately below the summation sign tells us to begin adding with the first X (i.e., first score in our distribution), and the 10 above the summation sign tells us to stop with the tenth X. The mean of the distribution is defined as the sum of the scores divided by the number of scores. Thus, our mean would be 66 divided by 10, or 6.6.

The median of the example above would occur between the fifth and sixth scores, as they are listed in order. Since both the fifth and sixth scores are 7, the median, at least the rough median, is 7. With more extensive distributions (greater numbers of scores), computation of the median can become complicated. For the purposes of this discussion it is enough that you know the definition of the median as the point below which one-half, or 50 percent, of the observations lie.

Measures of variability

The ideas of shape and central tendency or location were introduced in describing a distribution, but this description is not comprehensive enough. The variability or dispersion of a distribution also should be considered. *Variability* refers to the spread or scatter of the distribution scores, thus the measures of variability give an indication of the spread in a distribution. In contrast to measures of central tendency, which are points, measures of variability are intervals. That is, they occupy or are designated by a number of units on the measurement scale.

There are several measures of variability which can be used in describing a distribution. Probably the crudest of these is the *range,* defined as one plus the difference between the two extreme scores. When determining the range we want to include both extreme scores in the interval; hence the one plus. It is very easy to calculate, since it can usually be determined by a quick inspection of the scores. However, the range has serious limitations. Since it considers only the two extreme scores, it does not reveal the pattern of variation between the scores. Two distributions could have identical ranges but different dispersion throughout the distributions.

The measures of variability most commonly used are the variance and the standard deviation. Before these measures can be defined, we must consider the meaning of a deviation in this context. *Deviation* means the difference between an observed score and the mean of the distribution. In the example of computing a mean for the distribution given in the preceding section, an observed score of 8 would have a deviation of

+1.4 from the mean of 6.6. There are as many deviations as there are scores in the distribution, although some of the deviations might be zero. If an observed score corresponds exactly with the mean, the deviation is zero.

To illustrate, we can use the summation notation and notation for the scores introduced earlier. We will let n be the number of scores in the distribution and $\bar{X}$ (read X bar) represent the mean of the distribution. Then the variance of a distribution[1] is given by:

$$\text{Variance} = \frac{\sum (X_i - \bar{X})^2}{n}.$$

That is, the deviation of each score from the mean is squared, the squares of these deviations are then summed, and this sum is divided by the number of observations in the distributions. The *standard deviation* is defined as the positive square root of the variance. The variance and standard deviation are undoubtedly the most important measures of variability in terms of theoretical and practical usefulness.

Our discussion of measures of central tendency and measures of variability as elements in providing a description of the distribution of observations may have made it intuitively clear that both types of measures are necessary, as well as knowing something about the shape. When distributions are described as being alike, for example, it is important to specify in what way they are similar. Figures 2.2 and 2.3 illustrate distributions alike in one respect, yet very different in the other.

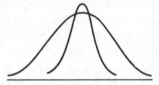

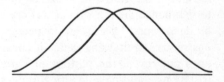

FIGURE 2.2. Distributions with like central tendency but different variability

FIGURE 2.3. Distributions with like variability but different central tendency

---

1. The denominator of the variance formula is given here as n, since we are not considering sampling and inferential statistics at this point, only the matter of describing a distribution. A discussion of the use of $n - 1$ as the denominator of the variance formula appears later.

Shapes of distributions

Distributions may take on an unlimited number of shapes. The shape of the histogram in Figure 2.1 above has no specific name, but there are distributions whose shapes have been named. A distribution which (at least theoretically) occurs frequently in educational research is the "normal" distribution. The *normal distribution* is not a single distribution with a specific mean and standard deviation. Rather it is a smooth, symmetrical distribution which follows the general shape of the distributions in Figure 2.4 (sometimes called bell shaped). There is con-

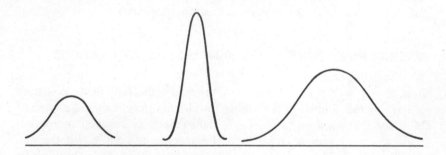

FIGURE 2.4.   Examples of normal distributions

siderable evidence that many educational variables, such as achievement in academic areas, are normally distributed.

When considering the shape of a distribution of scores comprising the data of some research study, the important consideration is not identifying the exact shape of the distribution. We seldom actually construct histograms, for example. The important questions about the distribution's shape are: Theoretically, what shape should the data from this variable take? Can we assume a specific distribution will be the shape if we have all possible scores for the group under study? What kind of assumed distribution is required for the intended procedures to be applied to the data? These are the kinds of relevant questions to be raised about the shape of the distribution of observed scores. In contrast to working with measures of central tendency and variability, for which we compute the specific values, we are usually less concerned with the actual shape of the distribution of observed scores and more concerned with its assumed or theoretical shape. This point will be illustrated later when the reasoning of inferential statistics is discussed.

The importance of adequate descriptions of the distributions under study should not be overlooked or dismissed lightly. Sometimes providing descriptions is looked down upon as too simple a task, and for many research studies descriptions are not adequate for the purposes of the study. Nevertheless, providing descriptions is often an essential preliminary task, and it can certainly be a valuable contribution to the research study. The possibility of a descriptive study of this nature is often overlooked, especially in areas where the information about the distributions is incomplete or inconclusive.

The measures discussed in connection with describing a distribution and the procedures for determining them are referred to as descriptive statistics. In this sense, descriptive statistics are the measures by which we pull together the facts in order to describe the distribution under study. As we shall see shortly, this is not the only meaning that the term "statistics" has in the context of educational research.

MAKING INFERENCES FROM SAMPLES TO POPULATIONS

Few, if any, educational researchers are interested only in the collection of data or feel limited to describing the distribution of the data at hand. Most researchers want to generalize their results and make inferences to some group or groups larger than the specific one for which the data were obtained. However, in developing generalizations or making inferences, acceptable procedures must be used. It is not enough to simply "eyeball" the data and then make ad hoc inferential leaps to conclusions, many of which would likely be unwarranted. In summarizing and interpreting data, the researcher seeks to obtain all the information he can from the data.

In many situations the interest is in studying a specific group with the expectation that it will be possible to generalize to some larger group. For example, a research director for a large city school system might set up five third grades and expose them to some experimental treatment, with the purpose of generalizing to all third-grade students of the system. In a more ambitious vein the goal might be to generalize to third-grade students in all school systems. In any event, an attempt is made to infer something about a relatively large group by the investigation of a segment of that group. The smaller group under investigation is a sample of the larger group which is called a *population*. A *sample* is, then, a subgroup or subset of the population, and is the group that is measured. The distribution of observations that is acquired is the *dis-*

tribution of the sample. A descriptive measure of the sample distribution is a *statistic*. For example, if the mean of the sample is determined, this mean is a statistic.

A descriptive measure of a population is called a *parameter*. Typically, the entire population is not measured; rather, inferences are made and conclusions are drawn about parameters from the statistics of the sample. Had the mean been determined for a set of population observations, this would be called a parameter. The distinction between a statistic and a parameter is very important in the logic of making inferences from samples to populations. Further emphasis will be placed on this distinction in the chapters in Part II on hypothesis testing.

Associated with the terminology of parameters and statistics are notations which tend to reduce confusion and enhance consistency of meaning. The notation used for parameters is indicated by Greek letters, and the notation for statistics employs letters of the English alphabet. As examples, consider means and variances. The population mean is indicated by μ (mu), and $\bar{X}$ is the sample mean. (The symbol $\bar{X}$ has been introduced earlier in connection with descriptive measures of a distribution.) The variances of the population and sample are given by σ^2 and s^2, respectively. The standard deviations are the correspondingly positive square roots.

The basic idea in making an inference from statistics to parameters is to observe the sample distribution and then employ accepted and scientific techniques to make the inference to the population. We compute statistics from the sample data, and on the basis of these statistics we generalize to the parameters (population measures). The theory and methodology underlying this procedure are known as *inferential statistics*. In order to construct the reasoning for inferential statistics, we must employ some basic concepts of probability and distributions (for the most part theoretical) related to the probability. In this way, we arrive at an established and conceptually sound procedure for making inferences from research data, now summarized by statistics, from the sample to some larger population.

THE CONCEPT OF UNDERLYING DISTRIBUTIONS

In order to construct the chain of reasoning from statistics to parameters, we can begin by considering some basic ideas about probability. Everyone at some time or other encounters probability notions. We talk about odds on the outcomes of various sports events. Sweepstakes are entered but intuitively we feel (and rightly so) that the probability of winning is very small. Certain combinations of winners at the race track pay many times the initial investment because their occurrence is a rare event. The same is true for the appearance of certain combinations on a slot machine.

The probability of an event occurring is often referred to as small, large, or with some other descriptive word implying magnitude. For the sake of consistency, computational ease, and mathematical tradition, the probability of an event can take on values from zero to plus one, inclusive. A probability of zero indicates no possible chance of occurrence, and a plus one probability indicates certainty of occurrence. *Probability* can be considered as a ratio: it is the ratio of the number of possible favorable ways an event can occur to the number of all possible ways of occurrence, both favorable and unfavorable.

Consider the toss of an unbiased coin. Suppose we define the appearance of a head as favorable. There is only one head on a coin and hence only one way for a head to appear. However, there are two sides to the coin; thus, the probability of a head appearing is $1/2$. This is sometimes referred to as a 50–50 chance.

The tossing of a pair of dice poses some interesting probability problems. We know that there are six faces on each die. In a single throw of both dice there are 36 possible different ways the dice may appear. This can be quickly established by considering that each face of one die may appear with the six faces of the other. Suppose that the appearance of a sum of 7 on the two faces is considered a favorable event. How many ways can a sum of 7 appear? Combinations of 6 and 1, 2 and 5, and 3 and 4 are three favorable events. But the above combinations could also appear on the opposite dice. Thus, combinations of 1 and 6, 5 and 2, and 4 and 3 are also favorable. This gives a total of six possible favorable events. The probability of a sum of 7 appearing in a single throw of a pair of unbiased dice is $6/36$ or $1/6$.

Most of the probability associated with sampling and statistics is not so simple an enumeration as in this example. We must consider the underlying distribution of the number of ways an event can occur. Given this distribution, we can designate the area under the underlying distribution curve to be 1. This corresponds to the total number of all possible ways of occurrence, and hence the probability 1. If we designate certain events to be favorable, we can determine the proportion of the area occupied by the numbers of these events. This, then, is the probability of the favorable event.

Consider again the example of the throw of two dice. We can illustrate the concept of underlying distribution by considering all possible ways the two dice can roll as the underlying distribution. The possible sums that can appear in a single roll of two dice are 2 (double 1) to 12 (double 6), inclusive, or 11 possible values. But we know that there are 36 different combinations of faces. There is only one way that a double 1 can appear, namely, a 1 on each die, for a sum of 2. A sum of 3 can appear in two ways, a sum of 4 in three ways, and so on through the 11 possible values. Finally we arrive at a sum of 12, which can appear in only one way or combination of faces, that of a 6 on each die.

The distribution of possible sums should contain 36 equal areas, each representing one combination of faces. The areas are equal because, assuming unbiased dice, each combination has equal probability of occurrence. If we put each of the corresponding areas with the sum that it represents, this gives us the distribution of all possible outcomes of a single throw of two dice. The distribution appears in Figure 2.5, with the sums designated on the horizontal scale.

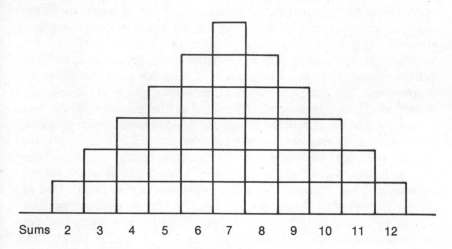

Sums 2   3   4   5   6   7   8   9   10   11   12

FIGURE 2.5.   Distribution of possible outcomes of a single roll of two dice

The distribution of Figure 2.5 can be considered the underlying sampling distribution of the outcomes of a single roll of two dice. The area of the distribution is designated as 1.0, since if we throw the dice some outcome of the 11 possible will appear. Thus, each area represents 1/36, and the probability of the combination which it represents is 1/36. It can be seen by inspection that the probability of a 7 appearing is 6/36, or 1/6. What would be the probability of getting a 5 or less? It would be the proportion of the area occupied by the sums 5, 4, 3, and 2. This area is 10/36, or 5/18. We could take the area between any two points that divide specific sums. Consider the probability of getting a sum greater than 5 but less than 11. This probability is 23/36. In this case, the favorable event is rolling a sum greater than 5 but less than 11. The area occupied by the favorable event is 23/36.

The dice-throwing example provides an illustration of an underlying distribution in that there is a distribution of possible outcomes of a single throw of two dice. The outcome in our example was defined as the sum on the two dice. Since we know the underlying distribution, we can determine the probability of any of the possible outcomes. As a specific sum is an outcome in the dice-throwing example, so a statistic such as a mean may also be considered an outcome. A specific sum appears from the throw of the dice, and a statistic appears from the sample of observations. Thus, statistics may be considered events in the probability sense.

Just as the probability of the appearance of a specified sum on two dice can be determined if we know the underlying distribution of these sums (Figure 2.5), so the probability of a specified mean (or other statistic) appearing can be determined if we know its underlying distribution. This requires a distribution of the possible values of the statistic. To know a distribution is to know its shape, location, and dispersion. These underlying distributions of statistics are called *sampling distributions*. They are theoretical distributions which are commonly arrived at through mathematical proofs. For the purposes of this text we are not concerned with the proofs and development of these distributions but with the ideas underlying their use.

The theoretical underlying distributions are based on certain conditions. Recall that we are working with a sample from which we get statistics and are attempting to make inferences to parameters. One of the conditions is that the sample be a random sample. A simple *random sample,* by definition, is one drawn in such a manner that every member of the population has an equal probability of inclusion.[2] A simple random sample also requires the selection to be made in such a way that the inclusion of any member in the sample in no way affects the probability of the selection of any other population member. With a small population, a random sample is not difficult to obtain; a table of random numbers can be used to draw the sample. When sampling from large populations, however, the sampling procedure can become quite complex. Approaches to sampling other than simple random sampling are discussed in Chapter 8.

---

2. If we sample from a finite population without replacement, a slight adjustment in the definition is necessary. A sample is then considered to be a simple random sample if drawn in such a way that every possible sample of a given size has an equal probability of being selected.

The underlying distribution of the mean

The sampling distribution or underlying distribution of the mean is the distribution of the values of the means of all possible random samples of a given size, say n, drawn from the population. From each possible sample one and only one value is contributed to this distribution of means. As a distribution, this distribution of means has its own shape, mean, and variability. Since the mean is a statistic, we now have a distribution of a statistic. This is analogous to the distribution of outcomes in the dice-throwing example, except that it involves means that come from samples rather than sums observed on two dice.

We want to know about the location (central tendency), shape, and dispersion (variability) of our distribution of means. Eventually we want to make our inferences from the statistic to the parameter, in this case from the sample mean to the population mean.

To locate the distribution of means, we consider its mean in terms of the location of the population mean. It can be mathematically shown that the mean of this distribution of means of all samples of a given size, n, randomly drawn from the population, is equal to the mean of the population. You should not interpret this as indicating that if we select a sample and determine its mean, this one sample mean will exactly equal the population mean, however. This one sample mean is only one of the scores in the distribution of sample means.

Next, we consider the shape of the distribution of means. We have already mentioned the general shape of the normal curve. If the population of observations is normally distributed, the distribution of means will also be approximated by a normal distribution. If sample size is large—30 or greater—the distribution of the means will approximate a normal distribution, regardless of the shape of the population distribution.

Now that we have the shape and location of the distribution of means, we can consider its dispersion or variability. The specific measure of dispersion that we will consider is the variance (which was defined earlier), letting σ^2 represent the variance of the population. The variance of the distribution of means is generally less in magnitude than σ^2; in fact, it can be mathematically shown that this variance is equal to the population variance divided by the sample size, that is σ^2/n. (Remember that throughout this discussion of the distribution of the means, the sample size remains constant. The variability of the underlying distribution of means, as indicated above, depends on the sample size. As sample size is increased, variability decreases.) The positive square root of this variance $(\sigma/\sqrt{n})$ is the standard deviation of the distribution of means. This standard deviation is called the *standard error of the mean.* The term "standard error" is often used in connection with the distribution of a statistic. The standard error of a statistic is simply the standard deviation of the distribution of the statistic.

At this point we have the shape, location, and dispersion or variance of our distribution of means. All of this can be summarized by one of the most important theorems of statistics, namely the *central limit theorem,* which can be stated as follows:

> Given any population with mean μ and finite variance σ^2, as the sample size increases without limit the distribution of the sample means approaches a normal distribution with mean μ and variance σ^2/n.

The question might arise as to how large the sample size must be in order for the distribution of means to be normally distributed. The answer depends upon the extent to which the specific population under study deviates from normality. However, as indicated earlier, if sample size is 30 or greater, the distribution of means will approximate a normal distribution even if the population distribution is not normal in shape.

Consider a very small distribution of six scores and the underlying distribution of the mean of samples of size 2. We must consider all possible combinations of the observations in pairs and compute the mean of each pair. There are 15 such possible pairs or samples of size 2, so there will be 15 means in the underlying distribution of the mean. (We are sampling without replacement and the order of the numbers in the sample is irrelevant, since we are only interested in the combination.) The original observations are 10, 9, 8, 8, 7, and 6, that is, these six values make up the original distribution. The 15 samples of size 2 and their means appear in Table 2.3. Note that there are two 8's in the original distribution. Hence, there are two samples of, say, 9, 8, but they include different 8's.

The 15 sample means make up the underlying distribution of the mean. It should be noted that if we changed the sample size, the distribution would change. If, for example, we had selected samples of size 3, there would have been 20 possible samples.

Let us inspect more closely the distribution of means in relation to the original population distribution. The distribution of means contains more scores.[3] However, the scores are not spread out as much, since they go from 6.5 to 9.5. We will not compute the standard deviation, but we

---

3. Generally the distribution of means contains more values than the original population distribution. The exceptions are: if sample size is the same as population size when there is only one sample, and if sample size is 1 or one less than the population size, the number of means is the same as the number of observations in the population distribution.

TABLE 2.3.   Sample observations and
sample means of all samples of size 2
from a distribution of six observations

Sample	Sample mean
10,9	9.5
10,8	9
10,8	9
10,7	8.5
10,6	8
9,8	8.5
9,8	8.5
9,7	8
9,6	7.5
8,8	8
8,7	7.5
8,6	7
8,7	7.5
8,6	7
7,6	6.5

will consider the means. The mean of the original distribution is 48/6, or 8. To find the mean of the distribution of means we add the 15 values and divide by 15. This gives 120/15, or again, 8. This provides an example of the fact that the mean of the distribution of means is equal to the mean of the original distribution. The underlying distribution of the mean is pictured in Figure 2.6.

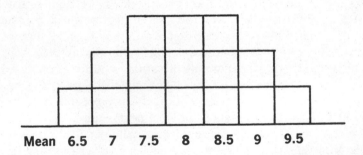

Mean   6.5   7   7.5   8   8.5   9   9.5

FIGURE 2.6.   Distribution of the means of all samples of size 2 drawn from six observations

Figure 2.6 can be used to illustrate a probability question about a sample mean. Suppose we draw a random sample of size 2 from the original six observations. What is the probability that we would draw a sample with a mean of 8? We go to the underlying distribution of the mean (Figure 2.6) and see that three of the 15 equal areas are occupied by 8. In the probability sense we consider the area under the entire distribution as 1. Therefore the probability of drawing a sample with a mean of 8 is 3/15, or 1/5. In like manner, the probability of drawing a sample with a mean of 7.5 to 9 inclusive is 11/15.

Tables of underlying distributions

The above example illustrates a specific underlying distribution. We developed the underlying distribution of a specific statistic, the mean, of all possible samples of a given size, namely size 2. The original distribution contained only six observations. In practice, we would rarely develop an underlying distribution in such a manner. As has been mentioned, the underlying distributions are theoretical distributions developed through mathematical proofs. The mean of a sample is one statistic, and we have developed the underlying distribution of this statistic. You may intuitively realize that there is a multitude of statistics and consequently a multitude of underlying distributions. Fortunately, the underlying distributions of many statistics behave in a similar manner; that is, they have common shapes. Thus, when trying to determine the underlying distribution of a statistic, if we know its shape, location, and dispersion (or variance), we know its distribution. The shape is determined by the type of statistic. This has already been done for us by the mathematicians. The location and dispersion can be estimated from the sample observations.

The use of inferential statistics, that is, inferring from statistics to parameters, invariably involves the use of tables which contain the values of common underlying distributions. Just as Figure 2.6 represents the underlying distribution of our example, so do the tables in Appendix 2 represent underlying distributions of various statistics. Figure 2.6 was specifically constructed for the example, and therefore it can be used directly to determine the probabilities of the appearance of specific values of the statistic. The tables in the appendix are designed for more general use, and they call for applying additional techniques to the sample observations. The use of these tables involves selecting the correct one (knowing the shape of our underlying distribution) and converting our observations to coincide with the same scale as that of the table. These procedures are discussed and illustrated in following sections. The idea introduced here is that underlying distributions are provided, and therefore it is not necessary to develop the distribution for each specific situation.

A very important and common underlying distribution is the normal distribution. In the following section the use of the normal distribution is illustrated in considerable detail, to provide an example of the use of the appendix tables in connection with the concept of underlying distribution, in this case Table A. The principle is exactly the same for the use of the other tables, which will be illustrated at appropriate points in Chapters 9, 10, and 11, on hypothesis testing.

The preceding discussion of underlying distributions can be summarized briefly. An underlying distribution is simply a theoretical distribution. Usually it is the theoretical distribution of a statistic. If we consider the area contained by the underlying distribution as 1.00, in a probability sense, this corresponds to the total number of all possible occurrences of the statistic. If we know the specific underlying distribution, that is, its shape, measures of central tendency, and variability, we can compute the probabilities associated with the appearance of specific values of the statistics.

THE NORMAL DISTRIBUTION

The normal distribution was introduced earlier in this chapter in connection with shapes of distributions (Figure 2.4 above shows some normal distribution shapes). Normal distributions may be flat or peaked, spread out or close together, but they all have in common a general bell shape. The normal distribution is symmetrical around a vertical line which divides the area of the distribution into two equal parts. We could not conceivably construct tables for all the possible specific normal distributions that could occur, so we must have a procedure by which we can convert an observed distribution to coincide with the distribution in the table. (Appendix 2, Table A). This procedure is commonly called converting to standard scores.

A specific normal distribution, whether a distribution of observations on Ss, a distribution of means, or some other statistic that is normally distributed, depends on its mean for location and on its standard deviation for dispersion. It would be impossible to construct tables which would cover all possible combinations of these two descriptors of the distribution. Recall, too, that for the probability concept we define the total area under the curve of an underlying distribution as 1.

The technique used to arrive at a common base is to convert an existing normal distribution of observations to the standard normal distribution. (This may also be called the standard normal curve.) The standard normal distribution, by definition, has a mean of zero and a standard deviation of 1, and the area under the curve is designated as 1. As a normal curve it is symmetrical. Approximately 68 percent of the area is contained within one standard deviation on each side of the mean. Within two standard deviations of the mean, about 95.5 percent of the area is contained, and within three standard deviations of the mean, approximately 99.7 percent of the area is included. Theoretically, the standard normal distribution extends from $-\infty$ to $+\infty$ on the scale of measurement.

The conversion of observed distribution scores to the corresponding values in the standard normal distribution is accomplished by the following formula:

$$z_i = \frac{X_i - \bar{X}}{\sigma},$$

where z_i is the score in the standard distribution or the standard score of the ith S, $\bar{X}$ is the observed mean, X_i is the observed score of the ith S, and σ is the standard deviation of the observed distribution. All this formula indicates is: Subtract the mean from an observed score and divide this difference by the standard deviation. This gives the corresponding score in the standard normal distribution. By inspection it can intuitively be seen that this conversion relocates the distribution around zero, and the scores (z_i's) are now given in terms of standard deviation units. Since the mean is zero and since in a symmetric distribution one-half of the scores are below the mean, one-half (or approximately one-half, depending on rounding errors) of the standard scores will be negative. The algebraic sign of the standard score should be carefully retained.

Thus far we have a distribution with an area of 1 (sometimes called a unit curve) and a procedure for converting any normal distribution of observations to this curve. To illustrate the use of the standard normal table (Table A Appendix 2), suppose we have a normal distribution whose mean and standard deviations are 65 and 8, respectively. Consider the question: What proportion of the scores are greater than 77? The standard score corresponding to 77 is $z_{77} = 1.50$. We find the z value of 1.50 in the table and note that the corresponding area is .433. However, the table is constructed to give the area from the mean to the z value. Since the curve is symmetric, the area from the mean to $z = 1.50$ (our z_{77}) is .433. Hence, the area above (to the right) of $z = 1.50$ is $.500 - .433$, or .067. This is illustrated graphically in Figure 2.7.

This example may be considered in terms of probability. Suppose we had the above distribution of scores and we were to randomly select one score. What is the probability that this score would be greater than 77? The probability of this event is .067, or about 7 chances out of 100. For another way of looking at this, suppose the number of observations in the population distribution is 100 or greater and we draw a sample of

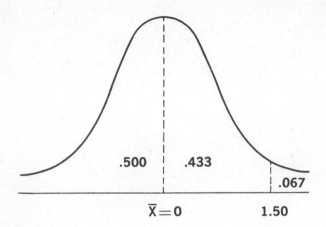

$$\bar{X}=0 \qquad\qquad 1.50$$

FIGURE 2.7.   Area in a standard normal distribution relative to a standard score of 1.50

100. How many scores would be expected to exceed 77? Clearly the answer is 6.7, or approximately 7. Note that this is what we would expect before the sample is drawn. In any one specific sample the result may deviate considerably from this expected result.

Another illustration involves areas on both sides of the mean. Suppose, in the previous distribution example, we want to determine the proportion of scores between the values of 55 and 71. We convert to the appropriate standard scores and find $z_{55} = -1.25$ and $z_{71} = +.75$. The corresponding areas (from the table) are .394 and .273, respectively. The areas lie between the mean and the standard scores, and since the standard scores lie on opposite sides of the mean, we add the areas and obtain the result .667. Thus we would expect 66.7 percent of the scores to be included between 55 and 71. (The curve is symmetrical, so negative z values are not given in the table.) The solution in terms of area is pictured in Figure 2.8. If the standard scores had both been on the same side of the mean, a subtraction operation would have been necessary to determine the proportion of scores (or area) between the two standard scores.

We have established that the standard deviation of a distribution of means of random samples of size n is given by $\sigma/\sqrt{n}$. If the samples had been drawn from a normal population with a known mean and standard deviation, we could determine the probability of obtaining a

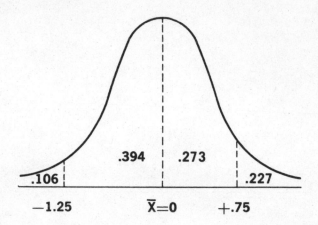

FIGURE 2.8.   Area in a standard normal distribution relative to standard scores of −1.25 and +.75

sample mean between two specified values. The underlying probability distribution is the normal curve. Another way to state this is: The normal distribution is the underlying distribution for the mean.

Consider an example involving a mean. Suppose that the two parameters, population mean (μ) and standard deviation, are known to be 50 and 12, respectively. The size (n) of the random sample to be drawn is 64. What is the probability that this sample mean will exceed 53? We know that the distribution of means is normally distributed and that this theoretical distribution has a mean of μ and a standard deviation of $\sigma/\sqrt{n}$. To locate 53 in this distribution we consider the expression $\dfrac{\bar{X} - \mu}{\sigma/\sqrt{n}}$, which will convert the 53 to its corresponding value in the standard normal. (This corresponding value we will designate by z_{53}.) Note that we let $\bar{X}$ be a score in our distribution of means, subtract the mean of the distribution of means from it, and divide by the standard deviation of the distribution of means. Substituting and solving for the z_{53} value, we get 2.00. In checking the table we find the probability of a mean of 53 or greater appearing is .023. This probability is found by finding the standard score of 2.00 and its corresponding value in the area column of .477. However, the .477 represents the area between the mean and the score of 2.00. Therefore, 1 − .477 or .023 is the remaining area in that tail and the probability of obtaining a mean of 53 or greater.

The value of the expression $\sigma/\sqrt{n}$ is clearly dependent upon sample size. If σ is held constant, the variability of the mean decreases as sample size increases. We see that the maximum value for variability is when $n = 1$, in which case the variance of the mean would be the same as the variance of the original distribution of observations. This is immediately apparent because for sample size of 1 the means coincide with the original observations.

As sample size is increased (with σ held constant), the means of repeated samples would tend to cluster closer together. We say that the increase of sample size makes the mean more stable. This can be illustrated by the example above. We know that $\mu = 50$, so in sampling we would expect to get a sample mean close to 50. The sample size of 64 may be considered a substantial sample. In this case the appearance of a mean of 53 or greater is a relatively rare event. Suppose sample size had been 16. The corresponding value of the expression $\dfrac{\bar{X} - \mu}{\sigma/\sqrt{n}}$ would be 1, i.e., $z_{53} = 1$. Under these conditions the probability of a mean of 53 or greater appearing is about .16. Note that everything was held constant except sample size.

Parameters, being measures of the population, are rarely known, and therefore it is necessary to estimate them from sample measures, or statistics. Estimates of parameters from statistics may be biased or unbiased. A statistic is said to be *unbiased* if the mean of its underlying distribution is the parameter being estimated. The sample mean is an unbiased estimate of the population mean, since the mean of the distribution of all sample means, selected from a sample of a given size, is the population mean. An estimate is said to be *biased* if the mean of its underlying distribution does not equal the parameter being estimated.

An example of a biased estimate is the estimate of the population variance, σ^2, using the formula

$$\frac{\sum_{i=1}^{n}(X_i - \bar{X})^2}{n},$$

in which n is the sample size. In order to obtain an unbiased estimate of σ^2, we make a slight adjustment in the formula by changing the numerator to $n - 1$. Usually the following notation is used:

$$s^2 = \frac{\sum_{i=1}^{n}(X_i - \bar{X})^2}{n - 1},$$

is an unbiased estimate of σ^2. Then if we are estimating the standard deviation of the distribution of the mean (the standard error of the mean), we would compute the esimate with the formula $s/\sqrt{n}$. The s is being used instead of the σ because this is a sample measure which estimates a parameter.

INFERENCE FROM STATISTICS TO PARAMETERS: A REVIEW

The basic ideas of inference from statistics to parameters which have been discussed thus far play an extremely important role in educational research. These basic ideas, of which the concept of underlying distribution is a part, comprise the foundation for testing hypotheses using statistical techniques.

The chain of reasoning from statistics to parameters is a part of what we call inferential statistics, as we have noted. The inference is from the statistics to the parameters. The chain of reasoning (illustrated in

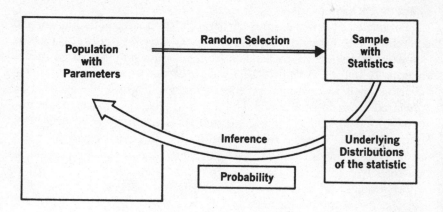

(a) We have a population and we want to make decisions about measures of the population, namely parameters.

(b) We select a random sample and compute measures of the sample which are statistics.

(c) The statistics reflect the corresponding parameters and sampling fluctuation.

(d) We observe the statistics, which are the facts that we have, and infer back to the parameters in the light of the underlying distributions and probability.

FIGURE 2.9.   Chain of reasoning for inferential statistics

Figure 2.9) is linked as follows: We have a population and we want to know something about the descriptive measures of this population, namely, the parameters. It is undesirable or impossible to measure the entire population, so a random sample is drawn. The descriptive measures of the sample are statistics, and the statistics can be determined. Since the sample is a random sample, we know that the statistics reflect the parameters within fluctuations due to sampling. It is at this point that the underlying distributions of the statistics come in. If we know the underlying distribution we know how the statistic behaves. The appropriate underlying distribution for a specific statistic has been determined for us by mathematical theory and has been tabulated in table form. Underlying distributions are commonly theoretical distributions.

It would be impractical, and in many cases impossible, to draw all possible samples of a specific size and tabulate the distribution of, say, the mean of all these samples. From the information of the statistic and its underlying distribution, we can reason back to the parameter. The parameters are never known for certain unless the entire population is measured, and then there is no inference. We look at the statistics and their underlying distributions and from them we reason to tenable conclusions about the parameters.

MEASURES OF RELATIONSHIP

Thus far we have been primarily concerned with describing the scores on a single variable, that is, a single set of data. Frequently, however, the educational researcher is interested in considering two variables simultaneously to determine how they relate to one another.

This extent of relationship is approached through the distributions of scores that represent the two variables. The two distributions are commonly made up of paired scores from a single group of Ss. In any event, the distributions make up sets of ordered pairs of scores. We are interested in how the scores in the distributions correlate or covary. To *covary* means to vary together—high scores with high, low with low, high with medium, whatever the case may be. The relationship between the two distributions (and hence the variables represented by the distributions) is based on how the pairs of scores vary together. We are concerned about changes (variation) in one variable compared with changes in the other variable. The degree of relationship or association between two variables is referred to as *correlation*. Thus, in correlational studies we are not concerned with a single distribution but with two distributions of observations.

The measure of correlation is called the *correlation coefficient* or the *coefficient of correlation.* The correlation coefficient is an index of the extent of relationship between two variables. It can take on values from −1.00 through zero to +1.00, inclusive. The end points of the interval indicate a perfect correlation between the two variables. As an example of a perfect correlation, suppose an individual is earning $500 per month and we correlate the number of months worked with the total amount of money earned. At the end of one month the total amount of money earned would be $500; at the end of two months, $1,000; after three months, $1,500; and so on. Note the relationship between these two variables. Each increase of one month corresponds to an increase of exactly $500. A difference of two months yields an increase of $1,000. The correspondence between one month and $500 is uniform throughout; the unit change on one variable corresponds to a designated uniform change in the other. We have a perfect +1.00 correlation between these two variables. The algebraic sign on a correlation coefficient simply indicates the direction of the relationship, that is, if high scores on one variable go with high scores on the second variable, we have a positive correlation. Conversely, if high scores on one variable go with low scores on the other variable, we have a negative correlation. A correlation coefficient of zero indicates no relationship.

Suppose we have a single group of Ss measured on two variables and we are interested in the relationship between the variables. Each S has two scores, one on each variable. To illustrate the concept of correlation, consider the plot of the scores in a two-dimensional space or plane. Such a space is sometimes referred to as the Cartesian plane. Any point in this plane can be located by two values, one for the horizontal axis and one for the vertical axis. In order to plot the scores we assign the scale of one variable on the horizontal axis and the scale of the other on the vertical axis. Thus each S's pair of scores may be plotted in the usual manner, by being represented as a point in the plane. Such a plot is called a *scattergram*. There will be as many points in the scattergram as Ss measured on both variables.

Figures 2.10 and 2.11 illustrate two possible scattergrams. The two variables are designated by X and Y. The horizontal scale increases to the right and the vertical scale increases upward. By locating any specific S (point), we can determine his score on the Y variable by going to the left to the Y scale, and his score on the X variable by going down to the X scale.

An inspection of the scattergram gives some idea of the relationship between the variables, although it does not provide a quantified measure of the strength of the relationship. The correlation coefficient provides such a measure, or numerical index. Since it is an index, even though

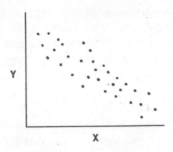

FIGURE 2.10.   Scattergram indicating a positive correlation coefficient

FIGURE 2.11.   Scattergram indicating a negative correlation coefficient

the greater the absolute value of the coefficient the stronger the relationship, it is not measured on an equal-unit scale. Nor can the correlation
coefficient be interpreted as some kind of direct percentage.

Figure 2.10 illustrates a positive relationship between variables and
hence a positive correlation coefficient. The high values of variable X
are associated with high values of variable Y. The opposite situation
is true for a negative correlation, i.e., high values of variable X go with
low values of variable Y and vice versa, as shown in Figure 2.11. In
order to have a perfect correlation ($+1.00$ or -1.00), the points of
the scattergram must fall on a straight line. (If the example presented
earlier of months worked and total money earned were plotted, all points
would fall on a straight line.) The direction of the line indicates the
algebraic sign. It is extremely rare in educational research to discover
two variables that have a perfect correlation.

For example, two variables which seem to be positively correlated are
intelligence and achievement in science; that is, students who score high
on IQ tests tend to be the highest scorers on science tests. Of course, for
any one correlation coefficient the scores of only one IQ test and one
science test would be correlated. An example of a negative correlation
coefficient might be the relationship between intelligence scores and time
to perform a learning task. That is, the more intelligent Ss should tend
to perform the task in less time if correlation exists. Two variables which
probably have zero correlation are amount of loose change in pocket
and intelligence.

The correlation coefficient does not necessarily indicate a cause-and-effect situation between the two variables. This is to say that it does not necessarily follow that one variable is causing the scores on the other variable to be whatever they are. For example, there usually exists a positive correlation between the salaries paid teachers and the percentage of graduating seniors going on to college in a particular school or system; that is, schools with higher teachers' salaries tend to have greater percentages of graduating seniors going on to college. However, it would be difficult to argue that paying higher teachers' salaries is causing greater percentages of seniors to go on to college or, vice versa, that sending seniors to college increases teachers' salaries. A third factor or a combination of external but common factors may be influencing the scores on both variables. Multiple causation is not uncommon when dealing with educational variables.

The "scatter" or dispersion of the points in the scattergram gives an

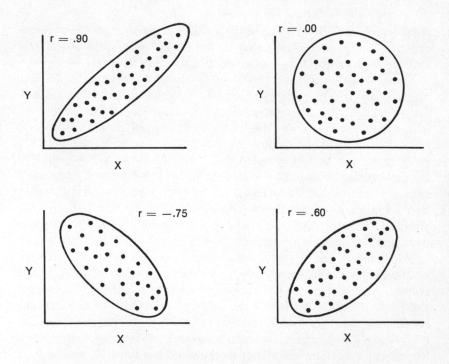

FIGURE 2.12. Examples of scattergrams and corresponding correlation coefficients

indication of the extent of relationship. As the positions of points tend to deviate from a straight line, the correlation tends to decrease. If a relationship exists but is not +1.00 or −1.00, the points generally fall in an elliptical ring. As the ring becomes narrower, that is, approaches a straight line, the relationship becomes stronger and the absolute value of the correlation coefficient increases. The direction of the ring indicates whether the relationship is positive or negative, lower left to upper right being positive and upper left to lower right, being negative. When the points of the scattergram fall within a circle we have a correlation of zero. Figure 2.12 presents some examples of scattergrams with the corresponding magnitude of the correlation coefficient given by r.

Different types of correlation coefficients can be computed, depending upon the conditions of the situation, such as the type of measurement scales used. Different types of correlation coefficients are discussed in Chapter 11. The correlation coefficient can be used in a descriptive manner, as a descriptor of the relationship between two variables, or it can be used in inferential statistics. That is, we can test hypotheses about the correlation coefficient. The concept of relationship or association is important, since there are many educational research studies that are concerned with determining the extent of relationship between two variables.

THE MEANING OF STATISTICS

The term "statistics" has multiple meanings in educational research. Probably its simplest meaning is "bits of information." If we say that 1,231 students are enrolled in a specific school, this can be referred to as a statistic. The salary schedule and the number of teachers at each salary level for a specific school system are sometimes called salary statistics.

Statistics has a much broader meaning than simply bits of information, however. It also refers to the theory, procedures, and methodology by which we summarize and analyze data. It has been suggested that statistics is like a foreign language to many people. Actually the understanding and use of statistics is not so much identifying new terminology and symbols for already known concepts as it is a new way of reasoning and drawing conclusions. In this way statistics and the reasoning involved can be a highly useful tool for the researcher working with data. Where the layman often views statistics as an accumulation of facts and figures, the researcher views it as the method used to describe data and make sense out of them.

A common classification scheme is to divide statistics into descriptive and inferential statistics, which have been introduced earlier in this chapter. When working with descriptive statistics we are essentially describing a distribution, or possibly the relationship between distributions. Inferential statistics are used when we have an observed sample and, on the basis of the sample, we make inferences to the population from which the sample was drawn. The theory and procedures which enable us to make the inferences are statistics in a broad sense. However, in a specific situation the statistics are the sample facts. In this sense they are the sample means, standard deviations, and the like. Although the word "statistics" does have multiple meanings, the specific meaning can usually be recognized by the context of its usage.

The major emphasis on inferential statistics in this text will be in the chapters on hypothesis testing found in Part II. Statistical concepts were introduced at this point because both descriptive and inferential statistics provide useful methods for obtaining information from research data. It is important in designing educational research studies that the researcher have some idea as to what kinds of procedures will be useful in enabling him to understand his data. The researcher must have some knowledge about the kinds of factors that may be influencing his data, and he must be knowledgeable about the characteristics of his data.

SUGGESTED STUDY EXERCISES

2.1. Classify each of the following variables in terms of the type of measurement scale (nominal, ordinal, equal unit, or ratio):
   a. Type of residential dwelling: duplex, single family residence, multiple apartments.
   b. Amount of calcium deposits in the organs of rats that have been subjected to different experimental treatments (assume the organs are removed).
   c. Performance on the essay section of an American history test.
   d. Ratings assigned to the performance of student teachers.
   e. Strength of junior high boys on a physical task as measured in pounds of force by an electronic device.
2.2. A study is conducted to determine the effects of three sets of instructional materials upon fourth-grade reading achievement. Three random samples of fourth-grade boys are selected within the same school. These three groups are then taught by three different teachers, each using one set of instructional materials. At the end of ten weeks of instruction the students are tested on reading achievement. Identify the constant(s), independent variable(s) and dependent variable(s) of this study.
2.3. The following 80 scores represent the distribution of scores on a variable. The scores are listed from low to high. Tabulate the frequency distribution for these scores and plot the histogram for the frequency distribution.

20	29	32	34	36	38	41	45
23	29	32	34	36	39	42	45
24	29	32	35	37	39	42	46
24	30	32	35	37	39	42	46
25	30	33	35	37	40	43	47
27	30	33	35	37	40	43	47
27	30	33	35	37	40	44	48
27	30	33	35	38	41	44	49
28	31	33	36	38	41	44	51
28	31	34	36	38	41	45	52

2.4. Discuss the difference between measures of central tendency and measures of variability. Why are both types of measures necessary in describing a distribution? Present some examples of educational variables that are alike in measures of central tendency but different in variability; alike in dispersion but different in location.

2.5. What is the probability of getting a sum less than 5 or greater than 8 in a single roll of two dice? Getting either a sum of 6 or an 8? Use the distribution of Figure 2.5 of this chapter.

2.6. Suppose we have a distribution which has a mean of 50 and a standard deviation of 5. We know that the distribution is normally distributed. What is the probability of randomly selecting a score from this distribution of 57 or greater? A score between 55 and 65? Less than 40 or greater than 60? Between 40 and 55?

2.7. A researcher wants to know the end-of-the-year reading level of approximately 1,000 first-grade students of a city school system. The entire population cannot be tested. Discuss how sampling and inferring from statistics to parameters would be used. Identify the statistic and parameter involved in this situation. Reconstruct the chain of reasoning used to arrive at some conclusion about the reading level of the entire first-grade population.

2.8. Distinguish between a statistic and a parameter in the context of inferential statistics. Discuss the role of the underlying distribution. Specifically, of what is it the underlying distribution?

2.9. Discuss what is meant by a correlation coefficient. What are the possible values the coefficient can take? Interpret the meaning of a correlation coefficient of +1.00, of −1.00.

2.10. Would you expect the correlation coefficients for the following combinations of two variables to be positive or negative, and low, moderate, or high in absolute value?
   a. Reading performance of fifth graders and distance a baseball is thrown.
   b. Performance on a mathematics exam and score on an attitude toward school inventory.
   c. I.Q. score and performance on a geometry exam.
   d. Divergent-thinking test score and time required to solve problems in logic.
   e. Reflex time score and number of errors on a simulated driving task.

2.11. Suppose a researcher has measured a group of 150 teacher education students on three measures of scholastic achievement and a measure of performance on a professional knowledge exam. Thus, he has four "dependent" variables. Under what conditions (purposes of his study) would he

a. Compute only descriptive statistics for the four dependent variables.

b. Use inferential statistics.

c. Compute correlation coefficients between pairs of the dependent variables?

chapter 3

Research design: Planning and problems

KEY CONCEPTS

Research project
Experimental research
Nonexperimental research: historical, *ex post facto*, and survey
Format for organizing a research design
Review of the literature
Identification of constants and variables
Formulation of hypotheses
Identification of necessary data
Selection of measuring instrument
Pilot study
Reliability checks
Sample selection
Collation of data
Biased and unbiased data
Confounded variables
Statistical precision
Experimental control: randomization, holding factors constant,
      building in independent variables, statistical adjustments
Stating and testing hypotheses
Interaction of variables
Missing or unusable data
Adequacy of measurement

The broad term "research design" includes all the numerous aspects of planning, structuring, and proceeding in a research endeavor. Designing a research project,[1] basically means developing a plan, usually sequential, that is specific enough to bring the project to a successful conclusion. The development of any research design must simultaneously consider numerous factors.

The design of the research for a given project deals with the specifics of that project. Nevertheless, it is possible to identify some general characteristics and procedures which tend to enhance good research design, regardless of the specific project. This chapter deals with these

---

1. The word "project" used in this discussion has a very broad meaning. It can mean any research endeavor, of short or long duration and of any level of complexity.

more general concepts, especially as they concern organization and planning. It also gives some help in avoiding the potential pitfalls of poor research design.

CLASSIFYING EDUCATIONAL RESEARCH BY METHODOLOGY

There is no inherent classification system for educational research and the various methods that apply to it. Authors vary in the categories and classifications they have applied to methodological approaches in educational research, but most have included experimental, historical, and survey research somewhere in their classifying schemes.[2] Others also include such methodological approaches as clinical research and case studies. For the purposes of this text, the methodological approaches are dichotomized into two large categories, experimental and nonexperimental research. These are discussed separately in Chapters 4 and 5. Nonexperimental research is further categorized into historical, *ex post facto,* and survey research.

An experiment in educational research is a situation in which one or more factors are systematically varied according to some preconceived plan in order to determine the effects of this variation. The researcher must have control over at least one factor to the extent that he can systematically vary it. Suppose, in a laboratory situation, that a researcher wanted to test three different types of instructions used in training Ss to perform a concept-attainment task. The dependent variable would be some measure of efficiency in performing the task, say time required to attain the concept. The factor being systematically varied would be the type of instruction. The researcher would be attempting to determine what effect, if any, the type of instruction had upon the dependent variable.

In nonexperimental research, the researcher does not systematically manipulate the independent variables. Historical research deals with determining and interpreting past events. Survey research, a second type, is conducted to determine the status quo, that is, the status of the phenomena under study. For example, if we wanted to determine the status of the achievement level in science and mathematics of a defined group of middle school students, we would conduct survey research.

A third type of nonexperimental research, *ex post facto,* may not appear much different from survey research. The emphasis, however, is

---

2. The definitions of these methodological approaches are not necessarily identical from author to author. Some definitions are more restrictive than others, and, of course, the wording will vary somewhat. In any discussion the definitions given should be carefully considered.

more on the relationships between variables than on the status quo of the variables. Fred N. Kerlinger defines *ex post facto* research as: "systematic, empirical inquiry in which the scientist does not have direct control of independent variables because their manifestations have already occurred or because they are inherently not manipulable. Inferences about relations among variables are made, without direct intervention, from concomitant variation of independent and dependent variables."[3]

In *ex post facto* research, the researcher studies the independent variables as he finds them and attempts to relate them to the dependent variables. Suppose that in the middle school example above the researcher were investigating how factors (independent variables) such as the type of community or the socioeconomic level of the students related to achievement in mathematics and science. The research would be *ex post facto*.

The methodological approach necessarily influences the research design. For example, in an experiment the researcher must design or at least define the manipulation of the independent variable or variables. In *ex post facto* research such manipulation would not be present. However, it should not be inferred that certain procedures, such as statistical analysis, are unique to specific methodological approaches. Computing means, for example, is not confined to experimental or any other type of research, and inferential statistics is not limited in application to any specific methodological approach. The type of statistical analysis to be used depends upon the specific hypotheses of the research project.

THE NEED FOR ORGANIZATION

The case for organization in a research project can hardly be overstated. The basic reason for planning and organizing is to facilitate the research. While research endeavors which initially seemed lacking in organization have been completed, and with apparent success, the odds are high against that outcome.

Any research project is made up of specifics. For example, specific hypotheses referring to the variables, conditions, factors, or Ss of the project are required. We may speak in terms of generalities in regard to a research project, but to complete the project the generalities must be applied or translated into the specifics. These specifics will vary with the nature and complexity of the research study, but it is attention to the details of the specifics that brings a research project to a successful

---

3. F. N. Kerlinger, *Foundations of Behavioral Research,* 2d ed. (New York: Holt, Rinehart & Winston, 1973), p. 379.

conclusion. Organization will avoid haphazard activities as the specifics are put together to produce the final product.

Any researcher may feel overwhelmed as he begins a research project. The first impulse may be to acquire something tangible, possibly to collect some data. To follow such an impulse would very likely be an unfortunate beginning, however. Any research effort is susceptible to error; the sophisticated researcher will take precautions against making mistakes. Adequate organization provides such a precaution, although it will not necessarily eliminate all errors. Possible errors are mentioned at various points in this chapter, and one of the final sections gives special attention to potential problems in research design. The mistiming of data collection mentioned above is such an error.

A FORMAT FOR ORGANIZATION

This chapter presents a general format for organizing a research project. We recognize, however, that there should be considerable flexibility in procedures from project to project. In fact, there may be considerable flexibility within a single project. In proposing a general format, we do not preclude the possibility of variation from the standard design.

The organization of a research project is divided into four general parts with several subtopics under each part, as indicated in the outline below. These parts and their subtopics can be related to the sequential pattern of general activities discussed in Chapter 1 and illustrated in Figure 1.1. The subtopics are flexible, and for certain projects their order may be concurrent or even possibly reversed; for example, the delimiting of the problem might involve simultaneous review of the literature. There also might be some overlap between parts; for example, in a study that is quite exploratory in nature, some data collection might actually precede the final identification of the necessary data. Also, for certain studies, one or more of the subtopics may not apply; for example, test revision is unnecessary if a standardized test is used for a population or sample for which the test was intended. Nevertheless, the four major parts would generally follow the order indicated in the outline.

An outline of the organization of procedures for a research project is as follows:

I. Identification of the Problem
   1. Review of the literature
   2. Delimiting and stating the problem
   3. Identification of constants and independent and dependent variables

    4. Formulation of hypotheses
    5. Identification of necessary data
II. Data Collection
    1. Development or selection of the measuring instrument(s)
    2. Training for data collection procedures
    3. Pilot study or trial run with the measuring instruments
    4. Reliability checks and any necessary revision
    5. Sample selection for the actual project
    6. Application of experimental treatments
    7. Data collection for the actual project
    8. Assembling the data
III. Analysis
    1. Superimposing the analysis design on the data
    2. Completion of the actual analysis procedures
    3. Assembling the results
IV. Conclusion of the Research
    1. Interpretation of the results
    2. Synthesis
    3. Preparation for writing

The climax of a research endeavor is usually the writing of a report or thesis or some other means of written communication. This is an important step, since research findings are of little value unless they are communicated to other people. Chapter 13 gives suggestions for writing about research.

IDENTIFICATION OF THE PROBLEM

The clear and concise identification of the problem is not an easy matter. Some research studies are pursued in such a way that it is difficult to determine what the researcher is trying to investigate. In fact, the literature contains reports in which the problem is never clearly identified, such as a report of a study which seems to have no problem but proceeds with only technical direction. Other studies tend to leave the problem too general, so that it is difficult to identify the specifics by which to proceed. Either situation is unsatisfactory.

Thus an essential preliminary step is to satisfactorily identify the research problem. (See Chapter 1 for introductory comments about the statement of the problem.) Initial ideas must be pulled together and initial statements need to be revised. The identification of the problem should develop from a background of information. Once the specific topic of interest has been selected (supposedly the researcher knows what general topic he wants to research), a review of related literature will aid in the satisfactory identification of the problem.

Review of related literature

The review of related literature serves multiple purposes. One has already been mentioned, that of helping to identify the problem. Upon the selection of a topic for research, the researcher must determine what has already been done concerning this topic. The review of literature should supply information that will more minutely and accurately describe the problem and help to bring it into better focus.

Research is not done in a vacuum; it should fit in the educational context of its specific area and indirectly in the overall educational setting. If a direct case is not made for the value of the research, its importance should certainly be implied by relating it to what has been done in the area. The review of literature thus provides a setting for the research.

The review should also be an enlightening experience for the prospective researcher. Although it may not make him a scholar in the area, he can assimilate considerable information and ideas. Design and methodological procedures may be suggested which can be the initial step in worthwhile modifications in the proposed research. The existing literature may indicate accepted, orthodox methods, and the researcher may be forewarned of unanticipated difficulties. Specific information about the distributions of the variables under study may be valuable in deciding on sample size.

Although we usually associate the review of literature with the identification of the problem and the research setting, it can contribute valuable information to any part of the research project. In the time sequence, however, the review comes early, and it is initially associated with the identification of the problem.

Delimiting and stating the problem

The establishment of the limits of the problem is also facilitated by the review of the literature, although the extensiveness of the study will often be determined by the resources for the research project. This is the step of delimiting the problem, or stating it in as precise terms as possible. The researcher should be careful that his definitions and terminology are consistent with the accepted usage in the literature. If terms are used which have multiple or ambiguous meanings, they should be precisely defined within the context of the research project.

The problem may be identified in the form of a statement, a question, or a series of either. A problem statement such as "The secondary curriculum" is far too broad to be considered an adequate identification of a problem. A better choice of a research topic might be: "The effects of two types of curriculum materials upon achievement in geometry at the tenth-grade level." Even this statement might need additional de-limiting; for example, the researcher may be proposing to consider only students enrolled in a college preparatory course. A statement of a problem that is too broad will lead to confusion and lack of direction in pursuing the project.

The choice of form for stating the problem as a question or a direct statement is arbitrary. The question form may have an advantage in that it is more direct and brings the problem into clearer focus. When it is stated in question form, the goal of the research is to provide an ade-quate answer to the question.

The statement of the problem alone does not adequately identify the problem; additional information is required. For example, the problem concerning geometry achievement has no stated hypotheses, although they may be implied. Before an attempt is made at stating hypotheses, however, there must be a means of expressing them—namely the varia-bles and constants (or conditions) of the study.

Identification of constants and variables

The dependent variable implied in the statement of the problem for the geometry example is geometry achievement. However, geometry achieve-ment needs more precise definition. Are the students to be tested only on factual knowledge, or on some combination or all of the elements that make up the discipline—logical reasoning, constructions, proof develop-ment, factual knowledge? If all of these areas comprise achievement, are they to be combined or measured separately? These are examples of questions that must be considered in identifying the dependent variable or variables.

The independent variable implied in the geometry example is type of material. The two levels of this variable would require complete defini-tion. Other independent variables might also be identified; for example, the students might be classified according to high and average ability.

We might prefer to hold ability level constant and consider only high-ability students. The tenth-grade level also is a constant, and other constants, such as the instructional time devoted to each type of ma-terial, must also be identified.

At this point we are concerned primarily with the identification of constants and variables. Later in the chapter, when discussing the char-acteristics of good research design, additional concepts will be introduced as to why we may want to include certain factors as variables or constants.

Formulation of hypotheses

The intuitive formulation of hypotheses can be intermixed with the identification of the variables. Certainly there would be some idea of what to hypothesize about before the variables are specifically spelled out. However, the precise formulation of the hypotheses requires the use of the independent variables or factors under study. The hypotheses as stated also imply the statistics if sampling is used and the statistical procedures to be used for testing the hypotheses. The matter of design, which ensures that anticipated procedures will adequately test the hypotheses, is important at this point. An error not uncommon in educational research is to state quite complex hypotheses and then realize that there is no provision for a statistical test of them. The precise statement of hypotheses should sharpen the focus on the specifics of the research design.

The hypotheses may be stated in different forms. One form is to indicate the direction of expected results, based on previous experience or on some *a priori* reasoning. Another form is the null hypothesis, in which the statistical procedures commonly test the hypothesis directly. Research such as historical research might not include a statistical test of a hypothesis, in which case the term "null hypothesis" is usually not associated with the research.

Identification of necessary data

The identification of the variables and the formulation of hypotheses lead to the identification of the data necessary for the project. The independent variables may require personal data on the S. This would be true in *ex post facto* research, where the levels of independent variables are not assigned to Ss but consist of existing characteristics of the Ss or existing classifications in the natural situation. For example, it might be necessary to determine the socioeconomic levels of the Ss.

A good deal of the necessary data is identified by the dependent variables. The identification may need some refinement at this point, possibly the development of an operational definition of the dependent variable. Also, the type of measurement scale chosen must be adequate. For example, if the researcher plans to compute means, the necessary measurement scale would be at least an interval scale. Whatever statistics the researcher is planning to compute must be available from the data.

DATA COLLECTION

The second major part of the research project, that of data collection, follows directly from the identification of the necessary data. Once the researcher knows what data he needs, he must work out the procedures for collecting those data. The first matter to be determined is what to measure the dependent variables with in order to secure the necessary data.

Selection of measuring instrument

The researcher may have available existing measuring instruments such as tests or scales, published or otherwise, that will secure the necessary data for him. If this is the case, the initial step in data collection is considerably simplified. Otherwise, a good deal of effort must be put into the development of the instruments. The items must be carefully constructed and the content of the items must reflect the objectives of the research. This is true whether a test battery, an interview, or a questionnaire is being developed. The items may differ considerably between measuring instruments, but their construction is a major task.

The selection of measuring instruments is not always a case of what is or is not available. The researcher may have existing instruments which can serve only as a starting point or base and need considerable revision for the purposes of the particular research project. Consider a situation in which a researcher is measuring the performance of two groups of teacher education students in two different countries on scholastic and professional achievement tests (assume both are English-speaking countries). There are quite a number of achievement tests available, in the United States at least. An achievement test in an area such as mathematics could be used in both countries without revision. However, a test on professional education knowledge would be unsatisfactory for use in both countries in its original form, as it is published in the United States. The test items are used as the basis for the measurement, but in this case they would need considerable revision to make their meaning consistent in both countries. If the meaning of an item could not remain consistent, it would have to be eliminated or replaced. The final instruments for both countries would have to be constructed so that they measure the same thing and the scoring is consistent.

The measuring instruments need not be tests, attitude inventories, questionnaires, interviews, or the like, but some sort of equipment. A researcher in physical education, for example, may require quantitative measurements of hand grip or muscle strength. An experiment in the learning laboratory may require arrangement of blocks or selections on pictorial boards. Learning psychologists working with animals often use a maze or some kind of lever device to induce the animal to learn a procedure by offering a reward. Thus the step of developing or selecting the measurement instruments can be viewed very broadly in the general context of educational research. In any one research project, however, the development and selection of the instrument is very specific and is dictated by the data necessary for the project.

Training for procedures

Training for data collection procedures covers a wide variety of possibilities, depending again upon the specific research project. Very little training may be necessary if the administration of a test is straightforward and simple. A brief review of the administration procedures with the testers may be all that is required. On the other hand, complex experiments or extensive interviews may require a great deal of effort to master and standardize the procedures.

The pilot study

Sometimes the conditions of the research project require that a pilot study be conducted before the major research is done. A pilot study is a small-scale model or trial run of the major study, done for the purpose of obtaining additional information by which the major study can be improved. Often when a pilot study is used it is for the purpose of refining the measurement instrument or the data collection procedures. However, if the pilot study is specifically concerned with the effectiveness of the measuring instrument itself, the data collection procedures should be carefully developed before the pilot study is attempted. Otherwise inconsistencies or other defects may be due to the data collection procedures rather than the instrument.

Not all research projects require a trial run of the measuring instruments, but for some, it is essentially impossible to refine the procedures without one. If such a test is required, it is for the purpose of revising items, eliminating ambiguities, and the like. It may not be possible to eliminate all adjustments in the data collection procedures during the trial run, however.

Reliability checks

Reliability is a concept associated with measurement; a more detailed discussion of reliability of measurement is given in Chapters 6 and 7.

For our purposes at this point, it is sufficient to define *reliability* as the consistency or accuracy of the measurement. If a pilot study is used, its results should lead directly into revisions of the measuring instrument and reliability checks where these are considered necessary. If extensive revisions are made it may be necessary to have a second trial run with the revised instrument.

Reliability checks are a necessity when self-developed tests are used or if standardized tests are used for any populations except those designated in the test manual. The lack of a pilot study does not eliminate the possibility of a reliability check. Reliability coefficients[4] can be computed on the data collected for the analysis, and they should be computed whenever applicable and considered necessary. This computation would follow the actual data collection of the project, of course.

Sample selection for the trial run

The choice of Ss for the trial run should correspond with the population from which the anticipated sample will be selected. In some cases, instruments are pretested on any Ss that are readily available; the value of such a procedure is questionable. The desirable situation is to use a representative sample of the population. Sometimes a special subpopulation is sampled or included in its entirety for the trial run. The effectiveness of this procedure depends upon whether the use of the instrument with such subpopulations adequately reflects its use with the proposed population or sample. This is a trial run in a very limited sense. It is essentially part of instrument development and would likely have little or no value in establishing reliability.

The researcher should not attempt to generalize the use of an instrument across diverse populations. For example, he cannot give a mathematics test constructed for junior high arithmetic to fifth graders and expect the procedures, reliability coefficients, and so on to apply. Neither should an instrument constructed for fifth graders be administered to eighth graders for the trial run, although errors of using inappropriate Ss for a trial run are usually not so glaring as this example. Such errors can lead to difficulties in securing valid data for the research study.

Selecting Ss for the research study

Before data collection can begin it must be established from whom or what the data will be collected. If an entire population is to be measured,

---

4. The conceptual meaning of a reliability coefficient and suggested procedures for determining such coefficients are discussed in Chapter 6.

the researcher must be certain that all members are included. An experiment may require all the members of a subpopulation, such as all the third graders enrolled in a certain school, but the members will have to be randomly assigned to the experimental groups. The same situation would apply to an experiment in a learning laboratory, for example. The Ss would be randomly selected from the population and assigned to the experimental treatments.

We introduced the idea of selecting random samples in the preceding chapter, and Chapter 8 describes different procedures for the process. This is often a task of considerable magnitude, especially in some survey research projects. The researcher should have his sampling procedures carefully developed, so that this step can proceed efficiently and the sampling procedures do not break down.

Application of experimental treatments

The time between sample selection and the data collection for the project varies with the type of study. In the case of an experiment, the application of the experimental treatments takes place during this interval. In a learning laboratory experiment, the Ss may participate shortly after being assigned, and the data consist of measures of their performance during the experimental session. On the other hand, a considerable period may elapse while the Ss are exposed to the experimental treatments, with the data consisting of measures taken at the close of the experimental treatment. An experiment involving the use of different types of materials over an instructional period of several weeks would be an example. In the case of a survey in which no experimental treatments are applied, the interval between sample selection and data collection is usually quite short.

Collecting the data

The data collection may take place at different times for either the same or different Ss. Longitudinal studies requiring several measures on the same Ss over an extended time period would be an example. Any studies involving pre- and posttesting would require some time interval between tests of the same S. Different Ss would be measured at different times in the case of cross-cultural studies if, for example, they were measured at the end of the school year, since school years conclude at different times in different countries.

The total time required for the data collection also varies considerably from project to project. All Ss may be measured simultaneously within a very short interval, or the time span may be considerable as Ss are measured individually or in small groups in interviews or on individual learning tasks. The researcher should be careful to allow enough time for the data collection, since insufficient time can introduce bias and possibly result in invalidating the data.

The data collection should proceed according to the specified plan as developed by the researcher or indicated in the manual accompanying the instrument, if a published instrument is used. Attention to detail must be exercised, not only the detail of administering the instrument but associated details as well. The data collector must be certain that he has the appropriate tests for the Ss he is planning to test, as well as special pencils, answer sheets, or stop watches that may be required. The matter of being at the right place at the appointed time is important. Careless data collection will undoubtedly lead to difficulties immediately following this step in the research endeavor.

Assembling the data

Once the data are acquired, the researcher prepares for the analysis. However, the data in original form are usually not ready for the process of analysis. If tests, questionnaires, interviews, and the like have been used, the responses of Ss will have to be transmitted from the answer sheet to a data card or data sheet. If data are put on IBM cards,[5] the data must be assembled in such a manner that the keypunch operator can transmit the information to the cards efficiently and with a minimum of error.

The data may require some coding when transferred to IBM cards. The levels of the independent variables are usually coded by numbers in the identification columns of the card. At least one column (but seldom more) is needed for each independent variable. If pre- and post-testing have been done, the pre- and posttest scores of each S must be put into proper order, or *collated*. Often the Ss are assigned numbers for identification. All of this type of information must be assembled before cards can be punched.

The researcher may not anticipate using a computer for the analysis, however. A desk calculator may be sufficient if the necessary computations are not extensive. Qualitative data may not require any compu-

---

5. For those unfamiliar with an IBM card, a description is given in Chapter 7. If the data are to be analyzed using a computer, IBM cards provide one way of putting data into the computer. However, data must be appropriately assembled, identified, and transferred to the cards. IBM cards are prepared by punching holes in columns; the machine for doing this is called a keypunch.

tations at all. With quantitative data such as test scores, some grouping and assembling are necessary prior to analysis. The scores of each dependent variable must at least be grouped together. Responses on questionnaires, especially responses to open-end questions, require categorization, and quantitative responses require tabulation. Data of the type collected in a historical study require sorting, categorization, and evaluation. Thus any type of research project that involves quantitative data calls for some assembling of the data after it has been collected.

The problem of missing data is often associated with studies involving large samples, but it can occur in situations with few Ss and small amounts of data. The seriousness of missing data depends upon the research study. If a correlation study involves a large number of Ss, the absence of a single observation is of little concern. On the other hand, one or more missing observations in an experimental design requiring equal numbers of observations for all groups will introduce serious analysis and interpretation difficulties. More comments are made on the problem of missing data in the section on potential problems in research design.

Accuracy checks should be made on the data recording and coding. A possible source of error is in copying when making entries onto a data sheet; the recorder may copy the entry incorrectly or place it in the wrong box on the data sheet. If IBM cards are punched they should be verified, a process which allows errors committed in putting the data on the cards to be identified and corrected.

ANALYSIS

The third major step in organizing and actually conducting a research project is the analysis of the data. If careful preparation has been made in the identification of the problem and the data collection has been adequate, the analysis should proceed with little difficulty. The formulation of the hypotheses and the type of data collected will dictate to a large extent the specific analysis procedures. Suppose, for example, that an experiment is conducted involving two different experimental treatments as the two levels of the independent variables. The dependent variable is some type of performance score and the null hypotheses is: The means of the populations receiving Treatment A and Treatment B are equal. This clearly implies a statistical test for determining the difference between two means. It would be necessary that means and variance estimates be computed from the dependent variable data, as at least part of the analysis.

The analysis design and the data

The analysis is not an end in itself but a means to an end; it is the tool by which the results are generated from the data. The analysis can only be altered within the bounds of the hypotheses. Usually adjustments consist of only minor alterations in such things as the number of Ss in a group. Unexpected *mortality* (dropout of Ss), for example, may necessitate such an adjustment, but the basic analysis would not be changed. Other analyses that were not initially anticipated may be carried out because of interesting results appearing in the data. These are peripheral to the major problem and should not be viewed as a replacement for the major or primary analysis.

A serious error can be made by departing markedly from the analysis as originally designed. The researcher may unwittingly and in varying degrees depart from his problem and hypotheses. Sometimes, because of unfortunate data collection, major adjustments in the analysis seem unavoidable, but this is a very tenuous procedure. Actually, the research procedures have begun to break down prior to this step, in the matter of data collection. The researcher will have to decide whether or not he can salvage enough of the data to proceed with the original problem; if not, it may be necessary to redo the data collection.

Analysis procedures

When the analysis design is satisfactorily superimposed upon the data, the researcher is ready to proceed with the actual analysis. If the data are in good shape and the analysis procedures well defined and applicable, this step should proceed efficiently. Yet on many research projects this is the step where difficulties and frustrations are encountered, largely due to inadequate data and inappropriate analysis procedures. Lack of sufficient resources also occasionally poses a problem; an example is the absence of a computer when one is required. Although such a problem manifests itself at this point, it is a result of poor planning earlier in the research project. If difficulties of this type occur, a careful reassessment of the research project must be made to determine what can be retained in the light of available data and resources. Sometimes it is possible to use an alternate but more feasible analysis technique.

Technical difficulties can usually be overcome. A more serious resource deficiency would be one in which the results of the data collected are not appropriate or meaningful in terms of the proposed study. Again, by careful planning, this could have been avoided. Such a situation is more likely to occur in a project where several people are working on a single problem and there is lack of communication and coordination between members. The outcome of this difficulty becomes more apparent when interpreting the results.

Assembling the results

Upon the completion of the analysis, some assembling of the results is necessary, regardless of the type of research project. If the analysis is done by a computer, some translation and reorganization of the computer output are necessary. An analysis done on a desk calculator requires reorganization, and the actual computations are usually deleted. A historical researcher will need to pull together various facets of his results, although the assembling of results may be more of an ongoing process and not quite as definitive a step as in a project requiring statistical analysis.

The assembly of results should not be confused with the assembly of data. Suppose a researcher does a survey study and assembles the responses in categories or pulls them together in some other manner. This is assembling data. Then he analyzes these categories. The statistics or tabulations, whatever he generates from the categories, are results, and pulling these together is assembling the results.

Descriptive statistics and results of statistical tests are commonly reported in tables. The researcher will have to decide upon the organization for these tables. If he has means and standard deviations for several dependent variables, for example, he must consider whether it is more meaningful to group by statistics, such as putting means only or means and standard deviations in a table, or by variables, that is, placing all the statistics relative to a variable or group of variables in the same table.

The organization of a table is a flexible matter and several forms are acceptable. (This is discussed further in Chapter 13.) Whatever form is chosen, the organization of the tables should facilitate the interpretation of results, and all items should be clearly defined. Confusion may result not only from poorly defined headings but also from an excessive amount of information in a single table. Tables that have many different types of entries and are spread over more than one page are often difficult to read. The use of tables is often necessary, but the technique should facilitate the reporting of results and not serve as a source of confusion.

CONCLUSION OF THE RESEARCH

The emphasis of this chapter is upon planning and organizing the research, not writing the research report. To be sure, these two activities cannot be completely separated, since in doing the research many things are written which may appear in the research report, although it is likely they will be revised for the final version. The fourth (and final) major aspect of the organization of a research project as outlined above deals with the activities prior to writing the report. These should not be confused with the "conclusions" section of the written research project (or the conclusion of this chapter, for that matter).

Interpretations of results

The interpretation of the results is often confused with the results themselves. In a certain sense, the results are the facts and the interpretations are what the researcher makes of the facts. Alternative interpretations should be presented and entertained if there is no basis for discrediting them. If hypotheses have been tested, the researcher should interpret the meaning of the results (reject or fail to reject the hypotheses) in the context of the specific project. The interpretations should be based on the results which, of course, are based on the data.

The use of appropriate research methods up to this point is necessary, but this is not the only condition for valid interpretations. While the methods are largely of a technical nature, the interpretations involve more than technical procedures. For one thing, the researcher should be well informed about the problem under study so he can make valid interpretations of the results of the research effort.

Synthesis

A synthesis or pulling together of the various parts of a research project is a necessary part of the research effort. Actually this process should be going on during the entire project so that no one part (or researcher) gets too far afield, and also to avoid duplication and "excess baggage." Examples of excess baggage would be retaining unnecessary procedures or collecting data which initially seemed necessary but were replaced or deleted.

The synthesis also guards against inadvertently overlooking important segments of the research. The researcher should have an overall grasp of the entire project as it approaches completion. This is not to say that this grasp should be lacking at earlier stages, but it should now be in terms of what has been done. The synthesis will help to tie things together and reveal the connections between the various parts of the research.

The three subsections of the conclusion of the research as presented in the outline cannot really be separated. The synthesis may be done prior to or simultaneous with the interpretation of the results. For example, certain conditions or irregularities of data collection which may be revealed by the synthesis can have a direct bearing on the interpretation of the results. The interpretation of results, almost without exception, does require some synthesis, so that these two steps should be considered as taking place simultaneously.

Preparation for writing

The finished, tangible product of a research project is usually the written report. In a general sense, all of the research activities are done as a preparation for writing. As the research is completed, the activities and results more directly reflect this preparation. The researcher is beginning to consider how he will present the results and discuss the interpretations. The preparation for writing thus is not an isolated activity but is occurring simultaneously with other activities of the project. The researcher should conduct the study in such a manner that he can account adequately and accurately for all he does. Haphazard and isolated procedures make the writing very difficult and inefficient. More will be said in Chapter 13 about ways to enhance the writing activity.

The format for organizing the activities of a research project presented here can do much to enhance the research design. Indeed, in a broad sense it is an integral part of the design. To complete our discussion of research design, we will consider some characteristics of good design and suggest some potential problems.

CHARACTERISTICS OF GOOD RESEARCH DESIGN

What makes for a good research design as contrasted with one that is poorly conceived? In a general sense we could answer that question with such statements as the design should be appropriate for the hypotheses, or the design should be feasible within the limits of available resources. We can be more specific, however.

Freedom from bias

One characteristic of a good research design is that it will provide data that are free from bias. This means that the data and the statistics computed from them do not vary in any systematic way, but only as would be expected on the basis of random fluctuation. Any differences that appear, therefore, can be attributed to the independent variables under study. If some type of bias exists in the data and differences, say between group means, appear that cannot be attributed to random fluctuation, we cannot make a decision as to whether this difference is due to the bias or to the effect of the independent variable.

Bias can enter into the data in a number of ways, such as a biased assignment of Ss to experimental treatments, the levels of the independent variable. An example would be if the dependent variable were a measure of performance on a science test and the higher ability Ss were assigned to one level of the independent variable, while the lower ability Ss were assigned to another.

Bias in the data *may* be eliminated by random assignment of Ss or random sampling, but the bias also can be introduced independent of the random procedure. In the example above, random assignment of the Ss to the levels of the independent variables would have eliminated the bias of putting the higher ability Ss in one level. (The possibility of a "wild assignment" does exist, but its probability would be very small.) It would still be possible to introduce bias if, for example, the two levels of the independent variable were two methods of teaching science, say M_1 and M_2, and after the random assignment of Ss a superior science teacher is assigned M_1 and a less able teacher is assigned M_2. In this case possible bias has been introduced after the random assignment of the Ss.

Freedom from confounding

Closely related to the matter of bias in the data is the possibility of confounding the variables. Two (or more) independent and/or extraneous variables are confounded when their effects cannot be separated. A good research design eliminates confounding of variables or keeps it to a minimum so the results can be interpreted separately. In the example where two methods of science teaching are used, teacher and method have been confounded. The teacher is an extraneous but relevant variable that may affect the dependent variable, performance on the science test. The effects of method and teacher cannot be separated because each teacher teaches with only a single method, M_1 or M_2, not both.

Statistical precision

Another characteristic of a good research design is that it will provide appropriate statistics, and with enough precision to test adequately those hypotheses that require statistical tests. In a statistical sense, precision means the inverse of variance.[6] In order to test adequately at least some statistical hypotheses, it is necessary to obtain an estimate of random variance from the analysis. The more precise this estimate, the more likely it is that the statistical test of the hypothesis will reach statistical significance. Extraneous factors inflating the estimate of random variance will tend to make the statistical tests insensitive to the real differences that exist.

Ways to enhance control

Bias in the data, confounding of variables, and lack of statistical precision can be avoided, basically, by securing a high degree of control through the research design. The term "control" is most commonly used with experiments; by experimental control, the researcher can manipulate one or more independent variables. In this sense, control refers to the experimenter's ability to manipulate, in a reliable manner, the Ss and the conditions of the experiment, perhaps by limiting them. In a broader context, we can define control as restraints on the research conditions that will provide greater focus for the research and ensure the interpretability of the results. Thus another characteristic of good research design is securing adequate control.

There are basically four ways by which control can be enhanced. These are:

1. Randomization.
2. Holding conditions or factors constant.
3. Building conditions or factors into the design as independent variables.
4. Statistical adjustments.

The first three are procedures that bear directly on the research design. The fourth includes computational analyses performed on the data in an attempt to obtain control. These four suggested procedures can be illustrated in the context of a single example.

Suppose a research study is to be conducted in which three methods for teaching high school chemistry, M_1, M_2, and M_3, are to be used as the levels of the independent variable. The dependent variable is performance on a chemistry achievement test, to be administered after one

6. After you have completed a study of the three chapters on hypothesis testing, especially Chapter 9, the concept of precision and reducing the variance of statistics will be more meaningful. For the discussion here you can simply accept the assertion that for many research situations it is desirable to reduce the variance in a set of data or to identify additional factors that may explain a portion of the variance.

semester of instruction. Assume that the same teacher will be used, the students (Ss) are all juniors, and they are enrolled in the same school. A group of 90 Ss is available to participate in the project, and it comprises a representative sample of some larger population. One purpose of the research is, of course, to determine whether the three methods have differing effects upon the dependent variable. The 90 dependent variable scores will not be identical, that is, their distribution will have variance. This may be due to a variety of causes. The methods may have different effects. Some Ss will undoubtedly be more able than others, regardless of the instructional method. Possibly the time of day that instruction takes place will have some effect. There is undoubtedly some inherent variation in the way Ss respond to a chemistry test. Any number of factors might be operating to cause variance in the dependent variable scores.

Let us focus on the ability level of the S's. Using randomization as a control, we would assign at random 30 S's to each of the three methods. Thus ability level would be randomly distributed among the three methods, and we would expect the effect of ability level to be the same in each of the three groups of 30 Ss, one group for each method. Although this procedure distributes the effect of ability level evenly, it does not allow for the separation of the variance due to ability level.

If we were going to reduce ability level to a constant we would do the research with only one defined ability level of S, say those scoring between 98 and 108 on a standardized IQ test. If ability level does affect performance on the dependent variable, it would now tend to be more homogeneous than if we had a large range of ability level. This would tend to reduce the variance of the chemistry test scores. But it might be difficult to do the study with this restriction, since several of the original Ss would likely be eliminated. Also, the results would now generalize to a restricted group. This research project already has several constants built into the design, such as teacher and length of instruction.

The ability level could also be structured as an independent variable. One approach which is arbitrary but does find some use in educational research is to categorize performance on an ability measure into three levels: high, average, and low. For the purposes of this study we could take the 30 highest ability-measure scores and arbitrarily classify them as high, the middle 30 as average, and the lowest 30 as low. (The ability-measures scores, of course, would have to be available prior to beginning the actual chemistry instruction with M_1, M_2, and M_3.) Then we would randomly assign to each of the three methods ten Ss of high ability, ten of average ability, and ten of low ability. Ability level would now be balanced across the three methods. Not only would it be balanced, but the effect of the ability level could be separated from the methods effect, since we are analyzing the variance of the dependent variable scores.

The design with ability level and method as the independent variables is diagrammed in Figure 3.1. The fact that each independent variable has

		Ability level			
		High	Average	Low	Totals
	M^1	10	10	10	30
Method	M^2	10	10	10	30
	M^3	10	10	10	30
	Totals	30	30	30	90

FIGURE 3.1.   Diagram of 90 Ss studied in three methods, with the Ss classified into three ability levels

three levels is coincidental. Different independent variables can, and usually do, have different numbers of levels. Note that in this design the researcher is not manipulating ability level in the sense that he is randomly assigning an S to an ability level. Rather, the effect of ability level is being controlled by balancing it across the levels of method.

The final method of control to be considered is by statistical methods. Suppose we had an ability score for each of the 90 Ss and there exists a positive relationship between the ability score and the dependent variable score; that is, high-ability Ss tend to score high on the chemistry test and low-ability Ss tend to score low. If we could somehow adjust the dependent variable scores to account for this ability-level effect, we would be controlling the effect of ability level. The adjusted scores on the dependent variable would also tend to be less variable, since the adjustment in this case, with a positive relationship between ability level and chemistry test performance, would tend to make the scores more homogeneous. There are statistical procedures for making these types of adjustments, assuming the necessary technical conditions can be met.[7]

Note that in the example, for all the procedures except randomization, it would have been necessary to have available ability-measure scores for the Ss. With the exception of statistical adjustments, these ability-measure scores would be required prior to conducting the research, since they would be used for placing Ss in the design. In many practical situations it is difficult to obtain such antecedent measures, however.

The four procedures for enhancing control can be used singly or in combination in the research design. One procedure might be used for

---

7. Readers with some statistical background may be interested in reading the section in Chapter 9 dealing with analysis of covariance at this point.

one extraneous variable and another for a second. The method used in the example of instructional methods and chemistry achievement would likely be an experiment, since the independent variable methods are directly manipulated by the researcher. However, the concepts of control can also be extended to nonexperimental research.

Carefully designing a research project does much to enhance the research, but there exists no foolproof guard against problems that can arise. To a large extent these problems are due to poor research design rather than to unforeseen technical difficulties.

POTENTIAL PROBLEMS IN RESEARCH DESIGN

We could, of course, say that problems arise when the characteristics of good research discussed above are not met, for example problems in obtaining biased data or not having adequate control in the design. However, there are more specific difficulties which, if not avoided, tend to make for poor research design. To some extent, we can also view these problems as arising from errors on the part of the researcher.

Inadequately stating and testing hypotheses

One potential source of difficulty is inadequately stating the hypotheses of the research project. If hypotheses are ambiguous and not clearly stated, it may be difficult to focus the research. Operational definitions may be missing for key (or other) words in the hypothesis. The researcher should not hesitate to use technical terms in stating hypotheses, since such terms often tend to be less ambiguous or general in meaning than common terms. This does not mean that hypotheses should be complicated; on the contrary, they should be stated as simply as possible. The use of technical language does not necessarily complicate hypotheses, but it does tend to make them more precise. A problem can also arise if hypotheses are not limited in scope or if two or more hypotheses are run together.

Another problem which occurs in research studies is that the hypotheses are not testable. All problems or topics are not researchable, and, hypotheses can be developed which are either unmanageable or lacking in definition, so that they cannot be researched. Consider the hypothesis, "Boy Scout training makes youths better citizens." We might infer that this is true in some vague sense, but without better definition this hypothesis is not testable.

Untestable hypotheses can be a problem in another way; the design, data, and/or the analysis for the study may not provide for testing the hypothesis. To examine an example of the potential problem of an untestable hypothesis, a new term, "interaction," is introduced. In the context of research design, *interaction* can be defined as the effect of one independent variable upon another. Interaction can also be described as the failure of the effect of one independent variable to remain constant over the levels of another. Suppose a researcher were studying the effects of a stimulant and the age of the S upon performing a psychomotor task. Two doses of the stimulant, D_1 and D_2, are used as the two levels of the independent variable, and two age groups, A_1 and A_2, are the two levels of the age independent variable. Thus there are four groups in the study, Ss of age A_1 receiving dosage D_1; those of A_1 receiving D_2; those of A_2 receiving D_1; and those of age A_2 receiving D_2. The means of each of the four groups can be computed, and statistical tests exist that can be used to test interaction hypotheses.[8]

If an interaction exists, the means will position themselves to indicate such an interaction. There are any number of possible ways they can do this, but let us consider the example in Figure 3.2. One independent

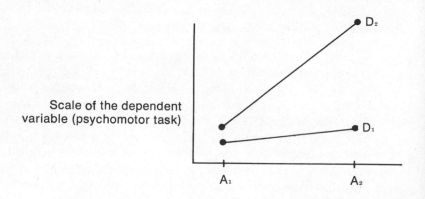

FIGURE 3.2.   Possible plot of means indicating an interaction between two independent variables

variable is arbitrarily positioned on the horizontal axis, and the other is represented by the lines connecting the means of specific levels. The vertical axis represents the scale of the dependent variable. The spacing on the horizontal axis is arbitrary.

---

8. Statistical tests for interaction in the analysis of variance are discussed in Chapter 9. Additional examples are also introduced in that chapter.

In considering the interaction illustrated in Figure 3.2 we note that the effect of drug level is not the same as we go from A_1 to A_2. To be sure, D_2 always exhibits a greater mean than D_1, but the increase from A_1 to A_2 is much greater for D_2 than for D_1. Thus, because the effect of the drug levels is not the same as we go from A_1 to A_2, we say the two independent variables are interacting. There are any number of possible interaction plots for means. The lines could intersect or cross over, for example. The example illustrated has only four means, two independent variables with two levels each, which is the simplest situation. If independent variables had more than two levels, we would have more points (means) to connect.

If there were no interaction in the above example, the D_1 and D_2 lines would be parallel, or approximately so. We can also say that when, in a situation such as the one above the two variables do not interact they are independent, that is, they do not affect each other. More will be said about interaction in Chapter 9.

If the hypotheses are not testable, it is a consequence of faulty research design. In the interaction example above, suppose the researcher had hypothesized that an interaction existed between the age of the S and stimulant dosage. The hypothesis might be, "Stimulant dosage has different effects upon the S's performance on a psychomotor task, depending upon the age of the S." If both age groups had not received both stimulant doses there would be no possibility for interaction to take place. Possibly, too, necessary assumptions could not be met for the statistical test. The researcher must carefully check the hypotheses and the design to avoid the problem of untestable hypotheses.

Missing or unusable data

Missing data can be another problem, especially in projects where the researcher has less than maximum control over the Ss, as in research studies in natural educational situations in which some Ss may be absent when data are collected. There is no completely satisfactory procedure for dealing with the problem of missing data, although procedures do exist which enable the research project to continue. One way is to delete an S whose data are missing. This procedure may be applied if very little data are missing, there appears to be no bias introduced by missing data, and deleting data will not invalidate the research design. However, before the data of many Ss are left uncollected, some checking must be done on the possible introduction of bias. For example, in a study involving achievement it would not be satisfactory to delete the low-ability students because they had managed to be absent the day of the achievement testing. In such a situation it is best not to announce the testing beforehand and to provide for immediate make-up testing.

A second procedure for dealing with missing data is to substitute a value for the missing observation. The question, of course, is what value to substitute. One procedure is to substitute the mean value of the group, on the assumption that for a single value the mean is the best estimate. If some other information is available for the S, it may be possible to substitute some predicted value. For example, if we knew a S's IQ score, it might be possible to predict his achievement score. This would require information about the relationship between IQ and the achievement score and the assumption that the relationship holds for the group under study. The use of substitute scores can be quite tenuous, and if this procedure is followed a rationale for the substitution must be developed.

A research project can also involve some unusable data. A response may be completely out of context so that it is obvious that the S misunderstood the question. Scores may be unreasonably high or low due to an error in the data collection. If an observation falls outside of the range of possible values it is clearly unusable. The rules for discarding unusable data should be developed and then applied during the data-assembling process. It is not proper to analyze the data and then discard data so that the results will more closely resemble expectations. If considerable data are unusable, a check on the Ss should be made to determine whether a certain group of Ss consistently produces unusable data. If this is true, it is likely that a bias has been introduced. The problem of missing or unusable data is often due not to a faulty design but to unanticipated S behavior.

Bias in sampling

The research project will encounter a problem if the sampling of the design introduces a bias. We have discussed the definition and rationale for random sampling, but not all educational research projects use random samples. The important question is whether the sample is representative of the population under study. When volunteer Ss are used, they are rarely representative of any general population except possibly a population of volunteers, since their motivation level undoubtedly differs from nonvolunteers. If Ss begin dropping out of the study (bringing the problem of missing data when the analysis takes place), the sample may become biased. The sampling for a research project should be designed and conducted with great care, because the interpretation and generalization of the results depend extensively on the representativeness of the sample.

Inadequate measurement

The success of a research project in meeting its objectives is dependent upon the adequacy of the measurement techniques used. Possible problems can be introduced into the research due to inappropriate or faulty measurement. The actual measurement instruments may be defective, or they may be inappropriate for the Ss of the study. Data collection or scoring procedures can become inconsistent and thus introduce a bias into the data. If the data collection involves observer judgment, there may be inconsistencies between two or more observers, or a single observer may not be consistent from observation to observation. The measurement for a research project must be carefully defined and structured to avoid problems of this type. Concepts and procedures of measurement are discussed in Chapters 6 and 7.

We have introduced some possible sources of problems connected with research design in quite broad areas such as the formulation of hypotheses, sampling, and measurement. You should not view this as a compendium of possible problems, however, since a complete list would be impossible to compile. Any number of technical and logistical problems can arise in pursuing a research project. Avoiding such problems is basically a matter of good organization or planning and good research design. Problems can arise in any research project, but with good planning and design they can be minimized or overcome so that the project can proceed to a successful conclusion.

CONCLUDING REMARKS

The emphasis of this chapter has been upon organizing and designing a research project. A format for organization was presented early in the chapter. In the first part of the outline, identification of the problem, five subparts were identified. The research design is ultimately dependent on three of these: identification of constants and dependent and independent variables, formulation of hypotheses, and identification of necessary data.

The process of conducting a research project is made up of separate but interrelated activities or parts. Some activities can be more easily isolated than others, and while many follow a logical sequence, others may vary in order of occurrence or may overlap. The overall scope of the research project must be accurately identified. Getting the research completed, however, is a matter of doing it piece by piece. Various generalizations can be considered and applied, but for a single research project it is attention to the details of the specifics that gets the job done.

Detailed planning, following the guidelines suggested in this chapter, is an important aspect of doing a research project. Resources and effort must be devoted to it. Attending to all of these matters will not guarantee an adequate research study, but it will help to enhance efficiency, avoid errors, and improve research efforts.

SUGGESTED STUDY EXERCISES

3.1. Discuss possible reasons for the review of the literature early in a research project. What are some items of specific information that may be supplied by the review? Prepare a list of specifics. Would there be any reason for doing additional literature review toward the close of a research project? If so, why?

3.2. A researcher plans to do a study for which the dependent variable is "history achievement" at the secondary level. Discuss how you would arrive at a more precise definition of history achievement. Consider the various facets of history achievement and develop what you consider a satisfactory definition.

3.3. A guidance counselor is doing research on the effects of parental educational level upon the performance of their children in academic subject areas as seniors in high school. What type of methodological research approach is the guidance counselor most likely using? Identify possible constants in this study. What are some possible extraneous variables that might make it difficult to interpret results?

3.4. An educational administration professor is planning to survey the superintendents in a large area, using a questionnaire of seven pages. Why would a trial run or pilot study with the questionnaire be a good, possibly essential procedure? Suggest some appropriate subgroups for the trial run.

3.5. Suppose an experiment in instructional methods were designed in which the levels of the independent variable consisted of five different instructional methods. The methods were used in five different elementary schools with students of age ten, but only one method was used in each school. Discuss how bias would enter into the data with this type of research design. Describe how the independent variable could have been manipulated to provide data free from bias. Suggest additional variables that would merit controlling in the experiment.

3.6. An educational psychologist is interested in designing an experiment in which three different types of motivational techniques will make up the levels of the independent variable. The dependent variable will be performance on a cognitive task, which has been shown to be positively related to an ability-level measure. The Ss will be college freshmen enrolled in an introductory psychology course. Sixty Ss will be randomly selected to participate. Discuss possible variables that might be controlled in this experiment and suggest procedures for enhancing such control.

3.7. Define what is meant by confounding of variables and describe a research project in which confounding could occur. What is the difference between two variables being confounded and two variables exhibiting interaction?

3.8. From a research journal, select an article which is the report of a research project. Read the article carefully and attempt to identify the specific parts of the format for organization discussed in this chapter that apply to the report you are reading. This may take some reading between the lines, since the parts may not be explicitly defined in the report.

chapter 4

Designs for
experimental research

KEY CONCEPTS

Experiment
Experimental design
Experimental control
Control group
Contamination of data
Statistical precision
Confounding of variables
Random selection
Parsimony
Experimental validity: internal and external
Posttest-only control group design
Differential mortality
Pretest-posttest control group design
Solomon four-group design
Factorial designs
Fractional factorial
Counterbalanced designs
Latin square design
Multiple-treatment interference
Quasi-experimental designs
Time designs
Nonequivalent control group design
Selection of subjects
Regression effect
Differential maturation

The word "experiment" has a vaguely familiar, broad meaning in contemporary usage. Many procedures, both in research and outside the
area, are referred to as experiments. The use of the concept of experiment in educational research was introduced in the preceding chapter,
where it was noted that it has a somewhat restricted meaning as a research situation in which one or more factors are systematically varied
according to some preconceived plan in order to determine the effects
of this variation.

The preconceived plan which is superimposed upon and essentially
lends structure to the research is the experimental design. Another descriptive definition of experimental design indicates what is included in

the preconceived plan: "those ideas, issues, principles, and techniques peculiar to those investigations in which the control of natural processes is actually attempted and directly observed."[1] Note that the design is preconceived, that is, it is conceived before actually doing the research. The research is not conducted first and then a design sought to give meaning to the results.

The reference to control in the definition implies the manipulation of the factors which comprise the independent variables of the experiment. The extent to which other variables or factors are controlled depends upon the scientific situation in which the experiment is conducted. Experiments in education are certainly not limited to research in a laboratory setting; they can also be conducted in natural or field settings such as a classroom. In this sense, experimental design applies to a wide variety of settings.

CRITERIA FOR A WELL-DESIGNED EXPERIMENT

Many of the criteria for good research design discussed in the preceding chapter also apply to good experimental design. Criteria such as obtaining data that are free from bias are, of course, equally important in designing experiments. Therefore, some of the comments in this section may be repetitive, but they bear emphasis in relation to experimental design.

Experimental control

The matter of experimental control, in this case restraints on the experimental conditions, is very important in experimental design. The control in an experiment must be sufficient to meet the objectives and test the hypotheses of the experiment. In an experiment, the researcher is concerned that he be able to observe a direct cause and effect (or lack thereof) between the independent variables and the dependent variable of the experiment. In order to meet this end, many experiments have numerous restraints imposed by any one or a combination of the four procedures for enhancing control that were discussed in Chapter 3. However, where randomization might be used heavily in an *ex post facto* study, in an experiment control is often achieved by reducing extraneous variables to constants or building them in as additional independent variables. In some cases, experiments are designed so that only the experimental variables are operating. This extent of control makes the

---

1. W. S. Ray, *An Introduction to Experimental Design* (New York: Macmillan Co., 1960), p. 1.

interpretation of experimental effects more straightforward, but it may also have some undesirable outcomes.

Lack of artificiality

Another desirable characteristic of a well-designed experiment that is related to extensive experimental control is that it be lacking in artificiality, at least to the extent that generalizations can be made to the groups or populations intended. When an experiment, especially in education, tends to have extensive, almost complete control, an artificial situation may be created in the experiment's structure, so that the results are no longer applicable in a wider sense. It may be that so many variables are reduced to constants that if the experimental variable were applied in a nonlaboratory or nonexperimental setting, its effect would change. Possibly, too, the experimental variable would interact with variables in a natural setting, which would give different effects of the variable than were obtained in the experiment.

Another way that artificiality can be introduced is in the nature of the experimental material. Suppose an experiment is designed to study some aspect of learning, but in order to avoid the possibility that Ss will vary in their familiarity with the meaningful materials to be learned, they work with nonsense symbols in the experiment. The question would then arise whether the results of this experiment would be applicable with Ss working with meaningful materials. The use of nonsense symbols was introduced in order to control the extraneous variable of the Ss' familiarity with meaningful materials. However, it is possible that the introduction of nonsense symbols makes for an artificial situation, the results of which have no generalizability except to nonsense materials. One criticism of some research studies reported in psychological journals (among others) is that the experiment reported was to a large extent artificial, and its application is extremely limited. In any experiment, the matter of avoiding artificiality must be considered, and enough realism must be maintained so that the results can be adequately interpreted for the purposes of the experiment.

Use of control groups

An experimental design should provide for adequate comparison. Sometimes this may require the inclusion of a control group, which is essentially a group of Ss who do not receive an experimental treatment. This does not necessarily mean that nothing happens to the Ss in a control group. For example, in instructional experiments, a group of students taught by traditional methods is sometimes referred to as a control group.

The fact that changes occur in the Ss of an experimental group does not conclusively establish the existence of an experimental effect. In order to determine whether or not an experimental effect exists, a comparison group which has not had the experimental treatment may be necessary. The change in the experimental group between the initiation of the experiment and the time of data collection may have occurred because of the passing of time, regardless of the experimental treatment. In other words, the experimental group might have shown a similar change without the experimental treatment. Such a situation requires that the control group be built into the design so that a valid comparison can be made to determine whether or not there is an experimental effect. It is not satisfactory to begin searching for a comparison group after the experiment has been conducted.

Consider an example of an experiment designed to determine the effects of different size doses of a drug upon the performance of rats running a maze. For adequate comparison, it might be important to include a group of rats which are not given any of the drug. Suppose there were three doses of major interest, 10 cc., 20 cc., and 30 cc. Performance may increase as dosage increases, but possibly the 10 cc. dose has no more effect than none at all, and the drug may have no effect until the dosage exceeds 10 cc. Without a control group it would be impossible to determine the complete pattern of the drug effect. Essentially the zero dosage the control group would receive becomes another level of the independent variable "drug dose," which is, in this case, the experimental variable. The rats to be used in the experiment should, of course, be randomly assigned to the four groups, three receiving doses of the drug and the control group.

For educational experiments that involve new teaching methods, new materials, or some condition of the instructional setting as the experimental variable, it is often necessary to include a control group which receives usual or traditional treatment. Without such a control group it is impossible to determine whether any of the levels of the experimental variable produce an improvement over what already exists. Certainly not all educational experiments require control groups, but in many instances such a group is necessary for adequate comparison.

Uncontaminated data

The well-designed experiment guards against the contamination of the data. Contamination may enter into the data if the Ss of the experimental groups and control group are allowed considerable interaction which has an effect upon the dependent variable. For example, in an achievement study involving different techniques with several groups of seventh graders, if the students of the various groups study together after school it would undoubtedly affect the achievement scores. This might also be considered a lack of control over a relevant factor, obviously a very difficult factor to control. In some experiments it is considered undesirable if the experimental group is aware of its experimental status. This awareness alone may affect the performance of the group.

Statistical precision

As in any good research design, a criterion for a well-designed experiment is that the precision be adequate to test the hypotheses. One way to increase the precision of an experiment is to decrease the variability of the Ss on factors that increase the variability of the dependent variable scores. For example, if an experiment is being conducted in which the age of the S is related to the dependent variable score, if the range of age for Ss is restricted, the variance of the dependent variable scores decreases. Age or grade level of elementary school children is often related to performance on standardized achievement tests covering several grade levels. Limiting the age of the students tends to make the tests scores more homogeneous.

Since the variability of many statistics depends inversely upon the number of observations, another way of increasing precision is to increase the number of Ss in an experiment. It is not good experimental practice, however, to take a "more the merrier" approach. We would not continue increasing the number of Ss just for the sake of having large numbers of Ss, since this would be wasteful of time and resources. Usually the researcher has information from previous experience or a review of the literature that gives some indication about the minimum number of Ss necessary for adequate statistical precision.

Occasionally experiments are conducted in education for which the use of large numbers of Ss is not feasible. If the experimental procedure is very time-consuming or if it is expensive to run Ss through the experiment, possibly because of costly expendable equipment, it may be possible to include only a small number of Ss. An example might be an experiment in health education in which the Ss participate in extensive physical exercise programs, each requiring the individual attention of the experimenter. In such situations it is necessary to control variation through the experimental design. The experiment might be limited to more homogeneous Ss, or other variables causing variance in the dependent variable might be controlled through extending and improving the experimental design. Other variables might be built into the design as independent variables, for example.

No confounding of relevant variables

A possible experimental error is allowing relevant factors to be confounded with the independent variables. Recall, from Chapter 3, that when two variables are confounded it is impossible to separate their effects. A well-designed experiment guards against confounding of relevant variables.

Consider an experiment of limited scope in which only one teacher is using a specific teaching technique. There are as many teachers as experimental treatments, but each teacher is involved in only one. "Teacher" is therefore confounded with the experimental treatment, which is teaching technique. To be sure, the teachers may be equated on several factors, but it is difficult to equate teachers on teaching effectiveness. In many situations, too, it is not feasible to have all teachers teach with all techniques. A better design would involve several teachers for each technique. If we compare two teachers they may be quite different, but if we compare two groups of teachers, the two groups may in fact be quite similar. The inclusion of several teachers for each technique would extend the scope of the experiment. Preferably, the teachers would be randomly assigned to the techniques.

Note that confounding variables is not the same as allowing variables to inflate the variance. In the case of confounding, the effect of an extraneous variable cannot be separated from the effect of an experimental treatment. When the variance is inflated, an uncontrolled source of variation is included in the variance, thus decreasing precision. A good experimental design guards against both of these errors.

Random selection

The condition of randomness is essential to a well-designed experiment. We discussed in the preceding chapter how random assignment can be used to control for bias or systematic variation entering the data. At the beginning of the experiment, the groups will be equivalent within the limits of random fluctuation. For the purpose of inferential statistics, random selection is a requirement if we plan to generalize to some larger population.

Parsimony

In listing the criteria for a well-designed experiment we can also include parsimony, which means that with all other characteristics equal, the simpler design is preferred to the more complex one. Complexity is not encouraged for its own sake. The simpler experimental design is usually easier to implement and possibly easier to interpret. A complex design may be wasteful of time and resources.

Experiments are susceptible to technical and procedural errors, as is any type of educational research. The development of an appropriate experimental design and its adequate implementation require considerable careful planning, but they provide the best safeguard against errors. Experimental design requires simultaneous attention to a variety of details. A well-designed experiment that is properly conducted will result in adequate experimental validity.

EXPERIMENTAL VALIDITY

The term "experimental validity" is used in this discussion as it has been defined by Donald Campbell and Julian Stanley.[2] Validity is considered to be of two types: internal and external.

Internal validity is the basic minimum necessary to make the results of the experiment interpretable. Internal validity questions whether the experimental treatment really makes a difference in the dependent variable. An adequate answer to this question requires adequate internal validity. Before it can be answered the researcher must be confident that extraneous variables have not produced an effect that is being mistaken as an effect of the experimental treatment.

External validity of an experiment deals with the generalizability of the results of the experiment. To what populations, variables, situations, and so forth do the results generalize? Adequate external validity is required for securing answers to this question that are in keeping with the objectives of the experiment.

The goal is to use experimental designs that are high in both types of validity. However, in some cases securing one type tends to jeopardize the other. As more rigorous controls are applied in the experiment, less carry-over can be anticipated between what occurred in the experiment and what would occur in a natural educational setting. For example, in research on instructional techniques, the control of the experiment may be so extensive that essentially an artificial situation is created and

---

2. D. T. Campbell, and J. C. Stanley, "Experimental and Quasi-Experimental Designs for Research on Teaching," in N. L. Gage, (ed.), *Handbook of Research on Teaching* (Chicago: Rand McNally & Co., 1963), pp. 171–246.

only the experimental variables are operating. This would greatly enhance internal validity, but the generalization might be so limited that the results could not be applied to a real classroom situation. This is not to say that it is never desirable to achieve maximum control; the objectives of the experiment dictate the extent of the validity requirements. Obviously an experiment whose results are uninterpretable is useless even if wide generalizability would have been possible. On the other hand, it is unsatisfactory to do an experiment and then discover that the results cannot be generalized as anticipated in the objectives of the experiment.

Internal validity involves securing adequate control over extraneous variables, selection procedures, measurement procedures, and the like. The experimental design should be so developed that the researcher can adequately check on the factors that might threaten the internal validity. To be sure, all possible factors are not operating in all experiments, but the researcher should have some knowledge about his variables and the possible difficulties that may arise in connection with internal validity. Then he can design his experiment accordingly so that his results can be interpreted adequately.

External validity certainly concerns the populations to which the researcher expects to generalize his results, but it is not limited to these. It also may include generalizing his findings to other related independent variables or modifications of the experimental variable. There may be factors such as size of class, type of school, etc., across which the researcher hopes to generalize. For example, suppose an experiment is being conducted in a suburban school with fourth-grade pupils. Would the results apply to an inner-city school? To eighth graders? Most likely not, but again this depends on the variables and the details of the experiment. The researcher may also desire to generalize to different measurement variations. For example, would the results of an experiment including pretesting be applicable to a classroom situation with no pretesting? External validity is concerned with these types of questions.

Experimental designs in educational research are rarely, if ever, perfect. Through experimental design we attempt to embrace adequate validity, both internal and external. Since enhancing one type of validity may tend to jeopardize the other, we often must attempt an adequate compromise. The compromise is essentially that of attaining sufficient control to make the results interpretable while maintaining enough realism so that the results will generalize adequately to the intended situations. As we consider the various experimental designs, comments will be made about their experimental validity.

POSTTEST-ONLY CONTROL GROUP DESIGN

The designs discussed in this chapter are those commonly found in the educational research literature. Two terms often used in connection with experimental design are "pretest" and "posttest." *Pretest* refers to a measure or test given to the Ss prior to the experimental treatment. *Posttest* is a measure taken after the experimental treatment. Not all designs involve pretesting, but posttesting is necessary to determine the effects of the experimental treatment.

Experimental designs commonly involve two or more groups: one for each of the experimental treatments and possibly a control group. The posttest-only control group design in its simplest form involves just two groups: the group that receives the experimental treatment and the control group. The Ss are randomly assigned to the two groups, prior to the experiment. The experimental group receives the experimental treatment. Upon the conclusion of the experimental period the two groups are measured on the dependent variable under study. Preferably, this measurement is taken immediately after the conclusion of the experiment, especially if the dependent variable is likely to change with the passing of time.

The posttest-only control group design is an efficient design to administer. It does not require pretesting, which for many situations is not desirable or applicable. Pretesting and posttesting require that each individual S be identified so that their pre- and posttest scores can be matched. The posttest-only design requires the Ss to be identified only in terms of their group and possibly other independent variables, if such variables are in the design.

The posttest-only control group design is high in internal validity. The random assignment of Ss rules out selection bias. Any effects of extraneous factors are, of course, functions of the experimental control; but with the random assignment such effects should be equally spread over the groups at the beginning of the experiment. Such effects may not be eliminated, but if they do not interact with the experimental treatment, they do not threaten the internal validity.

However, the posttest-only control group design does have some possible weaknesses that could threaten internal validity. If there is considerable subject mortality during the experiment, the design is weak for checking on differential mortality between the groups. *Differential mortality* means that the dropouts in one group have different characteristics than those of the other group and that these characteristics may be relevant to the experimental and dependent variables. Without additional information it is essentially impossible to rule out a possible effect of differential mortality, if there is a considerable dropout of Ss. If there is a suspicion that it will be difficult to keep the initial groups intact it might be well to consider another design. Another possible threat to internal validity is if some relevant but nonexperimental factors enter during the experiment and operate in one and not the other group. (The entrance of such factors would be due to a lack of control.) These factors may have a direct effect upon the dependent variable, or they may interact with the experimental or control treatment to affect the dependent variable. Such factors are relevant only as they affect the dependent variable, in one way or another.

The external validity of the posttest-only control group design is high, provided that the generalizations can be made from the experimental to the nonexperimental setting. The random assignment of Ss is assumed to have eliminated the possibility of selection biases interfering with generalization.

The posttest-only control group design may be extended to include more than two groups. Two or more experimental treatments may be used, increasing the number of groups to three or more. The Ss would be randomly assigned to the groups from the population. The effects of the various experimental treatments could be investigated by comparing means or some statistics of the treatment groups and the control group.

The posttest-only control group design can be diagramed[3] in a straightforward manner, as follows:

$$
\begin{array}{cccc}
G_1 & R & X_1 & O_1 \\
G_2 & R & X_2 & O_2 \\
\cdot & \cdot & \cdot & \cdot \\
\cdot & \cdot & \cdot & \cdot \\
\cdot & \cdot & \cdot & \cdot \\
G_k & R & X_k & O_k \\
G_{k+1} & R & - & O_{k+1}
\end{array}
$$

In this diagraming scheme G indicates group and R indicates that the members of the group are randomly assigned or selected. An X indicates an experimental treatment, and the subscripts on the Xs indicate different possible experimental treatments or levels of the independent variable. In the general case there are k possible experimental treatments. The O's indicate an observation or testing, in this case post-testing; the vertical line of O's indicates that they are taken at the same point in time. The posttest score is the dependent variable. The final group is the control group, and the dash indicates no experimental treatment for this group.

---

3. The diagraming format used here is very similar to that used by Campbell and Stanley in "Experimental and Quasi-Experimental Designs," pp. 171–246.

In its simplest form this design would have two groups, in which case $k = 1$. There would only be one experimental treatment and, of course, the control group. In a situation in which it is not necessary to have a control group, it would be necessary to have at least two experimental treatments. The design would then no longer be called a control group design but a posttest-only randomized groups design. The posttest-only control group design is a type of randomized groups design.

PRETEST-POSTTEST CONTROL GROUP DESIGN

The addition of a pretest given prior to the experimental period essentially extends the posttest-only control group design to the pretest-posttest control group design. The Ss are randomly assigned to the two or more groups and tested just prior to the experiment on a supposedly relevant antecedent variable, possibly a second form of the test which measures the dependent variable.

What is gained by pretesting? It may be that the pretest score can be used for a statistical control in the analysis, and thus statistical precision will be enhanced. It has an advantage over the posttest-only design if subject mortality is a problem. The dropouts can be checked on the pretest, and thus the researcher has an indication as to whether or not there is a differential mortality between the groups. Generally, the pretest-posttest control group design is strong in internal validity.

The external validity of the pretest-posttest control group design has a possible threat from the existence of an interaction between the pretesting and the experimental treatment. The pretesting itself may have some sort of an effect upon the Ss so that the results do not generalize to the nonpretested population. The problem of pretesting effects must be considered in the context of the specific experiment. For some dependent variables, it may have a substantial effect, and for others no effect at all. For example, an attitude inventory administered prior to the experimental period might arouse certain feelings and yield different end results than if there had been no pretest. In an achievement study which has different teaching techniques as the experimental and control treatments and which covers a substantial instructional period such as one or two semesters, pretesting is unlikely to be a threat to validity.

The random assignment of Ss is assumed to remove selection bias as a threat to external validity. The question of generalizing to the nonexperimental setting may be raised, however. External validity cannot be pinned down through objective computations. It has a logical context that is relative to the specific experiment. The researcher should have some knowledge about what is operating in his experiment relative to external validity.

The pretest-posttest control group design may be extended to additional groups. In all cases, the Ss of all groups are randomly assigned. The pretests for all groups are given at the same time, and so are the posttests.

The pretest-posttest control group design can be diagramed in general form as follows:

$$
\begin{array}{cccccc}
G_1 & R & O_1 & & X_1 & O_2 \\
G_2 & R & O_3 & & X_2 & O_4 \\
\cdot & \cdot & \cdot & & \cdot & \cdot \\
\cdot & \cdot & \cdot & & \cdot & \cdot \\
\cdot & \cdot & \cdot & & \cdot & \cdot \\
G_k & R & O_{2k-1} & & X_k & O_{2k} \\
G_{k+1} & R & O_{2k+1} & & - & O_{2(k+1)} \\
\end{array}
$$

The notation of the diagram is defined the same as in diagraming the pretest-only control group design. The indication of the subscripts is, of course, arbitrary. In this diagram any O (observation) with an odd-numbered subscript is a pretest score, and an O with an even subscript is a posttest score. If there were no need for a control group, the design could be called a pretest-posttest randomized groups design. Again, the minimum number of groups, whether or not a control group is used, is two.

SOLOMON FOUR-GROUP DESIGN

The extension of the pretest-posttest control group design to the Solomon four-group design[4] is sort of a "have your cake and eat it too" situation when it comes to pretesting and the possible effects of pretesting. This design in its four-group form includes two control and two experimental groups. Only one of each of the two types of groups is pretested, and all four groups are posttested at the conclusion of the experimental period. The assignment of Ss to all groups is random.

The diagram for the Solomon four-group design is given by:

$$
\begin{array}{ccccc}
G_1 & R & O_1 & X & O_2 \\
G_2 & R & O_3 & - & O_4 \\
G_3 & R & - & X & O_5 \\
G_4 & R & - & - & O_6 \\
\end{array}
$$

---

4. R. L. Solomon, "An Extension of Control Group Design," *Psychological Bulletin* 46 (1949): 137–50.

Note that, since it is a four-group design, only four groups are included and only one experimental treatment is used, the effects of which are determined by comparison of the posttest scores of the experimental and control groups. Since there is only one experimental treatment, no subscript appears on the X. Groups 1 and 3 are experimental groups and Groups 2 and 4 control groups, indicated by the absence of X.

By including in this design the groups that are not pretested, the researcher is able to determine both the main effects of pretesting and the interaction of pretesting with the experimental variable. Thus, of the three designs discussed so far, the Solomon four-group would seem to be the highest in validity. The comments made for the pretest-posttest control group design relative to generalizing to the nonexperimental setting hold for this design. It may be extended to include additional experimental treatments, but two groups—one pretested and one not— are required for each treatment.

Comparisons to determine the existence of an experimental effect can be done independently for the pretested and nonpretested groups (compare O_2 and O_4; O_5 and O_6). A statistical control using pretest scores could be built in only for the posttest scores of the first two groups. It would be possible to consider pretesting and the lack thereof as the two levels of an independent variable when analyzing posttest scores.

Various additional comparisons can be made on the data of a Solomon four-group design. The pretest data may be compared with the posttest scores of the nonpretested control group (O_1, O_3 with O_6). If the assignment of Ss has been genuinely random, this comparison is a measure of the effect of the passing of time in the usual (control) situation. The comparison would be between statistics computed for the groups, not between scores of individual Ss. In this comparison the Ss pretested are not the same as those supplying the posttest data.

By various comparisons in combinations of two, the effect of the experimental treatment can be checked in four different ways. First, comparison of the pre- and posttest scores within the experimental group (O_1 with O_2) gives an indication of the actual gain due to the experimental treatment. Second, comparison of the posttest scores of the two pretested groups, one experimental and one control (O_2 with O_4), is an indication of the effect (or lack of effect) of the experimental treatment when the Ss are pretested. Third, a similar comparison in the remaining two groups (O_5 with O_6) checks the same thing for nonpretested Ss. A comparison of the pretest scores of the control group and the posttest scores of the nonpretested experimental group (O_3 with O_5) is the fourth comparison involving the effect of the experimental treatment. This comparison provides an indication of the gain due to the experimental treatment when Ss are not pretested. In all these comparisons there is considerable crossing over of groups, that is, comparison of pretest scores from one group with posttest scores of another. The random assignment of the Ss enables us to assume that the groups were initially equivalent, thus making these cross-group comparisons possible.

FACTORIAL DESIGNS

A design which is becoming increasingly more common in the educational research literature actually comprises a family of designs called the factorial designs. The basic construction of a factorial design is that all levels of each independent variable are taken in combination with the levels of the other independent variables. (Technically this is referred to as complete factorial.) The design requires a minimum of two independent variables with at least two levels of each variable. This minimum design is called a two by two (2×2) factorial. Theoretically there could be any number of independent variables, with any number of levels of each. The number of digits indicates the number of independent variables. The numerical values of the digits indicate the number of levels for the specific independent variables. These numbers need not be the same for the independent variables. A $2 \times 3 \times 5$ factorial has three independent variables, with two, three, and five levels, respectively. An example which fits this factorial is two teaching methods, three ability levels, and five grades.

The number of different groups involved in a factorial design increases very rapidly with the increase of the number of independent variables and number of levels. The 2×2 factorial has four groups. To add just one independent variable with two levels would increase this to a $2 \times 2 \times 2$ (commonly denoted by 2^3) factorial with eight cells. If one level is added to each of the independent variables of a 2×2 factorial, the number of groups is increased to nine. Since the levels must be taken in all combinations, the number of groups is the product of the digits which specify the factorial design.

The $2 \times 3 \times 5$ factorial design shown in Figure 4.1 contains 30 groups. Suppose we designate the independent variables by A, B, and C, respectively. The different levels of the independent variables may be designated by the subscripts 1, 2, etc., to the required number.

The control group may be built into the factorial design by considering "no experimental treatment" as one of the levels of the independent variable called experimental treatment. In an experiment involving only an experimental treatment and no experimental treatment in combination with other independent variables, one half of the Ss would be in control groups. It should be noted that a control group is not a require-

		Variable A					
		1			2		
		Variable B			Variable B		
		1	2	3	1	2	3
	1	$A_1B_1C_1$	$A_1B_2C_1$	$A_1B_3C_1$	$A_2B_1C_1$	$A_2B_2C_1$	$A_2B_3C_1$
Variable	2	$A_1B_1C_2$	$A_1B_2C_2$	$A_1B_3C_2$	$A_2B_1C_2$	$A_2B_2C_2$	$A_2B_3C_2$
C	3	$A_1B_1C_3$	$A_1B_2C_3$	$A_1B_3C_3$	$A_2B_1C_3$	$A_2B_2C_3$	$A_2B_3C_3$
	4	$A_1B_1C_4$	$A_1B_2C_4$	$A_1B_3C_4$	$A_2B_1C_4$	$A_2B_2C_4$	$A_2B_3C_4$
	5	$A_1B_1C_5$	$A_1B_2C_5$	$A_1B_3C_5$	$A_2B_1C_5$	$A_2B_2C_5$	$A_2B_3C_5$

FIGURE 4.1.   Diagram of a $2 \times 3 \times 5$ factorial design. The 30 cells (groups) could all be designated by the letters with subscripts, as they are in the body of the figure. Note that no cell designation is exactly like any other. Any two cell designations differ in at least one subscript.

ment of the factorial design; its inclusion depends upon the objectives of the experiment. It is assumed that Ss are assigned at random to the levels of the experimental variable.

The factorial design is considered high in internal validity. The design may be used whether or not the Ss have been pretested, but it is used more often for experiments in which no pretests are administered. Under these conditions the validity comments are essentially the same for the factorial design as for the posttest-only control group design.

The real advantages of a factorial design over alternative designs are not necessarily great gains in validity, however, but two other factors: the economy of a single design rather than separate designs for each of the factors or variables, and the fact that the factorial design provides for investigating the interactions between the variables. For many research studies a knowledge of interaction is of major importance, and investigating the existence of interaction is a primary objective of the study.

The factorial design also allows for the manipulation or control of more than one independent variable. For this reason it is often used as a design for enhancing control by including relevant factors as independent variables. Theoretically, the factorial design may be extended to include any finite number of variables and levels. However, complex designs should be considered with caution, one reason being that such a design may not be economically feasible in terms of the available Ss. Also, the interpretation of complex interactions involving more than two independent variables may, for all practical purposes, be impossible.

The use of a complete factorial may for some reason be impossible or undesirable. If several independent variables are included in the same design, each with numerous levels, the number of cells and, correspondingly, the number of Ss necessary rapidly increase. In such a situation a *fractional factorial* may be an appropriate design. A fractional factorial design is one in which only selected combinations of variable levels are used. The valid use of a fractional factorial requires the assumption that certain complex interactions are of little interest and do not contribute a significant effect. This assumption is necessary for the technique of deliberate confounding. Recall from Chapter 3 that confounding involves an effect being attributable to more than one variable (or interaction) in such a manner that the single effects of the variables confounded cannot be separated. The fractional factorial confounds complex interactions with the effects of independent variables on the assumption that the higher order interactions do not contribute to an effect. Extensive discussion of both complete and fractional factorial designs appears in the more advanced experimental design texts.[5]

COUNTERBALANCED DESIGNS

The counterbalanced designs make up a family of designs in which experimental control is enhanced by entering all Ss into all levels of the experimental treatment variable. They also go by other names such as cross-over, switch-over, or rotation designs. (It should be noted that this is not a unique usage of the term "rotation" in experimental design.) These designs may be referred to as multiple-observation or repeated measures designs if any one S is observed more than once.

Campbell and Stanley[6] discuss these designs under the heading of quasi-experimental designs. As will be noted in the section below, their applications are directed to naturally assembled groups rather than groups to which the Ss have been randomly assigned. In this discussion of counterbalanced designs, however, we will assume the random assignment of Ss.

The device by which the design is structured is a *Latin square,* an $n \times n$ array in which the n letters or numbers appear once and once only in each row and column. The size of the square may vary from a 2×2 as a minimum to, at least theoretically, any finite number. The number of different possible squares increases greatly with an increase in n. For example, there are 12 different ways of arranging the letters of a 3×3 square and 161,280 ways for a 5×5 square. The size of the Latin square used in a specific experiment depends upon the number of experimental treatments to be assigned by the square.

---

5. See, for example, D. R. Cox, *Planning of Experiments* (New York: John Wiley & Sons, 1958).

6. Campbell and Stanley, "Experimental and Quasi-Experimental Designs," pp. 220–22.

Suppose a researcher has randomly selected three groups of Ss: a group each of eighth graders, tenth graders, and twelfth graders. Each S is to singly solve three different problems, say P_1, P_2, and P_3, in some sequence. These might be unique problems administered under standardized conditions in a learning laboratory. The dependent variable could be one of several measures such as time required for solution or number of errors. (More than one dependent variable might be measured, but the design would apply in the same manner for each dependent variable.) The different positions in the sequence of problems make up different ordinal positions which are actually the first, second, and third times in the solution sequence.

The above experiment would require a 3×3 Latin square. Suppose the researcher has six Ss in each of the three grade levels. In the diagram of the experimental design in Figure 4.2, the 18 Ss are numbered consecutively, with the first six subscripts assigned to the eighth grade, the second group of six to the tenth grade, and the final group of six to the twelfth grade. T_1, T_2, and T_3 represent the three times in the solution sequence.

The specific Latin square used in this design is:

$$
\begin{array}{ccc}
1 & 2 & 3 \\
3 & 1 & 2 \\
2 & 3 & 1
\end{array}
$$

Note that the numbers of the Latin square make up the subscripts on the problems as assigned to the first three Ss. After this, the Latin square repeats for each group of three Ss. The Latin square has only complete replications and is repeated the same number of times for each grade level. Thus, all sequences of problems, as designated by the rows of the Latin square, appear an equal number of times in each grade level. The problems appear the same number of times in the ordinal positions, designated by T_1, T_2, and T_3 in the diagram. In this respect the design is balanced.

The Latin square defines three unique sequences of problems, but this does not exhaust the possible sequences. For example, the sequence $P_3P_2P_1$ does not appear. The specific Latin square used in a design is randomly determined.

The counterbalanced design is appropriate only if it can be assumed that there are no interactions of the variables involved. For example, the effect of problems in the diagram could instead be an interaction effect between the grade levels and the ordinal positions. The design is strengthened if replications of Ss are assigned to different Latin squares. In the diagramed design a replication of the same square is indicated.

This replication enables the researcher to separate out certain variance components, which would not be possible if different Latin squares were used. Whether such separation is necessary depends upon the hypotheses and variables of the experiment.

		T_1	T_2	T_3
	S_1	P_1	P_2	P_3
	S_2	P_3	P_1	P_2
8th grade	S_3	P_2	P_3	P_1
	S_4	P_1	P_2	P_3
	S_5	P_3	P_1	P_2
	S_6	P_2	P_3	P_1
	S_7	P_1	P_2	P_3
10th grade	$\vdots$	$\vdots$	$\vdots$	$\vdots$
	S_{12}	P_2	P_3	P_1
	S_{13}	P_1	P_2	P_3
12th grade	$\vdots$	$\vdots$	$\vdots$	$\vdots$
	S_{18}	P_2	P_3	P_1

FIGURE 4.2.   Diagram for counterbalanced design using a 3 × 3 Latin square and a total of 18 Ss

A modification of this design may be made in which an entire group would follow the same sequence but no two groups would follow the same sequence, instead of each S following a sequence and all sequences being represented at least once in a group. This would apply to an experiment in which the group participated as a unit. In such a design the assumption of no interactions is likely to be less tenable than for the other design, in which single Ss were randomly assigned. A threat to validity under this condition is that selection factors may be operating in groups already established by some other criterion than random selection.

A measurement is made on the dependent variable following each experimental treatment. In the example of Figure 4.2, each S would be measured three times, once after each problem. Thus that particular design would yield 54 scores on a dependent variable. Counterbalanced designs are preferred if no pretesting is necessary. The designs are not considered control group designs, although it may be possible to build in a control group.

There is a potential threat to external validity in the counterbalanced designs that is not encountered in the other designs discussed. This is *multiple-treatment interference,* which is the effect of prior treatments upon subsequent treatments. For example, in the illustration of Figure 4.2 the solution of the first problem may affect performance on the remaining two problems. The S's performance may be different from what it would have been had there been no previous problem. In educational research it is difficult to erase the effects of prior treatments. Other factors, such as not being able to generalize to the nonexperimental setting, may also be operating in counterbalanced designs, as in the posttest-only designs.

The counterbalanced designs have the potential for high internal validity, especially if random assignment is employed along with sufficient replications with different Latin squares. The problem of an interaction effect being interpreted as the effect of an independent variable may be intuitively checked by inspection. If an experimental treatment is consistently high, say in the treatment means, it is unlikely that this is caused by an interaction, since the interaction is unlikely to imitate the independent variable effect throughout the design. On the other hand, if one experimental treatment mean is significantly different from the others, and the big difference lies in only one group, then the alternative conclusion of an interaction is highly tenable. It should be noted that this intuitive inspection is not a statistical test of a hypothesis.

The structure and analysis of extensive counterbalanced designs involving several independent variables are complex. It may be necessary to introduce computational adjustments due to the multiple observations, since observations taken on the same S are not independent, as are observations taken on different Ss. This text can provide only a general overview of the designs. Theoretical and computational details can be found in advanced design texts.[7]

QUASI-EXPERIMENTAL DESIGNS

The educational researcher, especially one who carries on his experiments in the classroom setting, often finds that he has little control over

7. See, for example, A. L. Edwards, *Experimental Design in Psychological Research,* 4th ed., (New York: Holt, Rinehart & Winston, 1972), pp. 285–325.

the assignment of Ss to groups. Random assignment requires that all members of a population have an equal probability of being included in the sample. In considering classes or other natural social assemblages, it soon becomes apparent that various selection factors are operating and that the group is hardly a random selection of a larger population. However, though full experimental control cannot be attained when such groups are involved, it is possible to design studies of them which have some of the characteristics of experimental design. The risk of misinterpretation exists, but the use of such groups may prove valuable. These are called quasi-experimental designs by Campbell and Stanley.[8] The use of such designs is recommended only when better designs are not applicable or are impossible to administer.

The researcher who employs a design that does not have random assignment or selection of Ss should be aware of the uncontrolled variables that the lack of randomness introduces. It then remains for him to decide what possible effects such variables may have and how the data are to be interpreted. Many of the quasi-experimental designs involve only a single group, and in a single-group design there is no comparison group or control group. In some situations a group becomes in essence its own control group when comparisons are made to its previous performance or scores. These kinds of characteristics tend to make for lack of control in the designs; hence the name "quasi-experimental."

Time designs

The time designs comprise a group of quasi-experimental designs commonly involving only a single group of Ss. The time designs essentially involve periodic measurement on some dependent variable, with the experimental treatment injected between two of the measurements. The real question in this design is whether the experimental treatment has an effect on the performance of the group, as measured by the dependent variable.

Whatever the statistic of the dependent variable is, perhaps the patterns of the means, it will have an almost unlimited number of possible forms. The major problem of internal validity is that of alternative explanations for the pattern, other than the effect of the experimental treatment. Figure 4.3 shows three possible patterns. The M_i's on the horizontal axis represent the measurement occasions, and the vertical axis represents the scale of the dependent variable. Data are collected at each of the M_i points.

For any one particular experiment and dependent variable there

---

8. Campbell and Stanley, "Experimental and Quasi-Experimental Designs," p. 204.

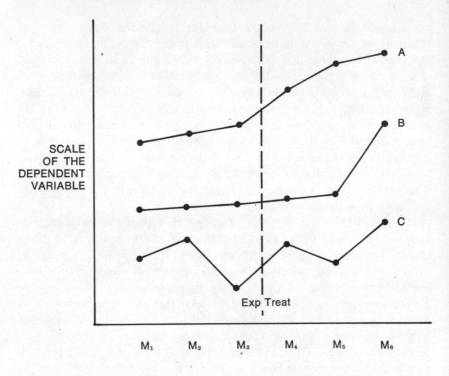

FIGURE 4.3.   Possible outcome patterns of a time design

would be only one pattern. The interpretation of pattern A would be that the experimental treatment is likely to have had an effect. The slope of the line returns to approximately the preexperimental treatment level, especially between the fifth and sixth measurements. On the surface, pattern B appears to include no experimental treatment effect. However, the marked increase between the final two measurements might be the result of a delayed effect. If there is no apparent external event which could have produced this effect, the researcher is in somewhat of a bind to explain it. He should anticipate the time interval between the introduction of the experimental treatment and the appearance of its effect. For certain variables the effect in B is about as definite as it is in A. It should be noted that as the time interval increases, the likelihood of an intervening extraneous event also increases.

The erratic pattern of C almost excludes drawing a conclusion about an experimental treatment effect. Since there is no control group, it is most difficult to infer the pattern without the experimental treatment. The fluctuation between measurements may indicate that other factors are operating which override any experimental treatment effect. It is possible that the experiment requires an increase in control before there can be sensitivity to an experimental treatment effect. The conclusion of no experimental treatment effect cannot be drawn from pattern C, however.

The most serious threat to the internal validity of the time designs is the possibility of external events, which are uncontrolled, giving rise to alternative explanations. The interpretation of the results hangs on the plausibility of ruling out the effects of such external events. The possibility of such events increases as the experimental period is extended in time. The validity of a time design may also be affected by a change in the use of the measuring instruments. Since several measurements occur, a lack of consistency in measurement might produce an effect which in turn would be interpreted as an experimental treatment effect. This could occur, of course, between any two measurements, or it could be a gradual deterioration which would make the final measurement considerably changed from earlier measurements.

The external validity of a time design may or may not be good. With the multiple measurements, the design takes on a sort of sequential pretesting characteristic. Thus the possibility exists of some kind of interaction effect of pretesting which would not be manifest in the unpretested population. However, in conducting research in an actual classroom situation, this is hardly considered a limitation. The measurements can be timed to coincide with the usual testing routine. The possible threats to external validity are not considered serious if the experiment and its measurement are not artificial.

The analysis of the data of quasi-experimental designs is not as straightforward as for the true designs. In the time designs, usually some kind of comparison between pre- and posttest data is made. A pooled pretest and posttest comparison is inadequate because it will not distinguish between certain patterns, and it may not be sensitive to an experimental treatment effect. For example, suppose the group drops back down on subsequent measurements following the measurement immediately after the experimental treatment. The pooling of all these measurements will tend to wash out any experimental treatment effect.

The comparison of the measurements immediately preceding and following the introduction of the experimental treatment is certainly unsatisfactory for a pattern such as B in Figure 4.3. In essentially all cases a single comparison between the two measurements is insufficient. Whatever kind of comparisons are made will be determined in part by the hypothesized pattern. In a pattern such as A, some type of pooled (or other extrapolated) data from the preexperimental treatment measures might be compared with M_4. Some kind of investigation of the slope and intercept of the straight-line fit to the pattern may be involved. Changes in either the slope or intercept may be evidence of an experimental effect. It may be that some pattern other than a straight-line fit would be expected. The researcher should have sufficient knowledge about the variables to have some idea about the possible behavior of the statistics making up the pattern.

A modification of the time designs is one in which there is repeated introduction of the experimental treatment into the sequence. The experimental treatment is inserted randomly into the sequence. Time is controlled by having equal intervals between measurements. The internal validity of a design with repeated introduction of the experimental treatment is strengthened over the single-introduction, time design in that the repeated application of the experimental treatment gives a check on the influence of extraneous events. It is unlikely that an extraneous event would consistently coincide with the experimental treatments.

The repeated measurement of this design is a possible threat to external validity, however. The Ss may be quite sensitive to the experimental arrangements of the change in conditions from experimental treatment to no experimental treatment. For example, suppose that the use of programmed learning materials was the experimental treatment. The Ss would undoubtedly become aware of the experimental nature of the situation. This could be a possible limitation on the generalizability of the results.

A second possible threat to external validity is the multiple-treatment interference discussed in connection with the counterbalanced designs. The experimental treatment–no experimental treatment alternating characteristic of this design makes generalizations to situations in which the experimental treatment is continually present very hazardous. Any one experimental condition (or lack of it) cannot be isolated from the sequence and interpreted as being representative of extended periods under this condition and this condition alone.

In analyzing the data of a time design with repeated applications of the experimental treatment, it is advisable not to make a comparison between single measurements of the experimental treatment and the lack thereof. The effect of an extraneous event could be easily misinterpreted as a significant experimental effect. If means are computed, it may be possible to make some type of comparison between experimental treatment–no experimental treatment means. There should be at least two measurements contained within each. The patterns of the individual Ss might be inspected for consistency with respect to the experimental effect.

The time design can also be constructed to include multiple groups. In this sense it takes on the characteristics of a control group design. The second group, again taken intact as found in some educational setting, would be measured at the same times as the other group but would not have the experimental treatment inserted anywhere in the sequence.

The inclusion of the additional group in the design facilitates interpretation of the experimental treatment effect. The postexperimental
treatment data can now be checked against the preexperimental treatment data of its own group and the data of the control group. Internal
validity is strengthened in that it is possible to check if any selection
factors are operating in the groups prior to the introduction of the experimental treatment. Because of the lack of random assignment, it is
possible that some type of selection–experimental treatment interaction
is operating. A testing and experimental treatment interaction may also
exist. Either of these possible interactions could be a threat to external
validity.

The data analysis of the time design with a control group can be
extended to comparisons between the two groups. Such comparisons are
in addition to the between-measurement, within-groups comparisons.
The difference between the statistics of the two groups can be plotted
over the several measurements. The time design with the control group
is especially well adapted for research in an actual school situation. The
multiple measurements can be built into the routine testing schedule,
and the researcher can often locate another class or even another school
to serve as the control group, but he must be aware that lack of random
sampling may cause a selection bias to operate between the two groups.
The experimenter should be aware of possible factors that make the
two groups nonequivalent.

Any experiment requires some finite amount of time from initiation
to completion. The amount of time required varies greatly from experiment to experiment; for a specific laboratory task, it may be relatively
short. Time designs may appear to be extended because of the multiple
measurements. However, the longitudinal studies in which Ss are measured at various intervals for several years are generally not considered
to be this type of design. While they could be loosely considered to be
based on time designs, usually no controlled experimental treatment is
introduced. Such studies are often strictly of a nonexperimental nature
in which a multitude of factors are operating simultaneously, and experimentation in the formal sense is absent. That is, the researcher is not
deliberately manipulating and controlling variables. The time designs
referred to in this discussion would be used in actual premeditated
experiments.

Nonequivalent control group design

One of the more commonly used designs in educational experimentation
is the nonequivalent control group design.[9] In this design both the group

9. Ibid., pp. 217–20.

which receives the experimental treatment and the control group are pretested and posttested. This design resembles very closely the pretest-posttest control group design but should not be confused with it. The primary difference (and an extremely important experimental difference) is that there is no random assignment of Ss to the groups of the nonequivalent control group design. The groups are taken intact as they exist in some educational setting. Thus the aspect of sampling equivalence prior to the experiment is missing.

The major threats to the internal validity of a nonequivalent control group design are possibilities of interactions between selection factors and other factors which might be mistaken for experimental treatment effects. The external validity of this design may be somewhat questionable. The pretesting gives the possibility of some kind of interaction which would not be present in the nonpretested population. The experiment being carried out in a natural setting lessens the experimental awareness. A selection bias might also be interacting with the experimental treatment. Again, the external validity must be considered in the light of the specific variables and conditions of the experiment.

The real crux of control in the nonequivalent control group design is the similarity between the two groups. The measure of similarity is commonly considered to be the pretest, assuming the pretest has some marked relationship to the dependent variable. It should be noted, however, that the control will not reach the level attained in the pretest-posttest control group design. The occurrence of similar pretest results for the two groups does not rule out the possibility of selection factors interacting with other factors.

The nonequivalent control group design might be strengthened by extending the design to two or more replications of the experimental and control conditions. A disadvantage of this extension is that it quickly runs into large numbers of Ss. Also, because of lack of control, the additional groups may introduce additional uncontrolled factors. For example, suppose several classes were involved in an achievement study. In order to complete the testing the classroom teachers administer the tests. If any ambiguity or extensive flexibility existed in test administration directions, the experiment would be very susceptible to inconsistent measurement procedures, a most undesirable factor.

The replication of the groups might still be worthwhile, for example, in a study involving achievement of average students. Here they would give an added dimension of comparison. Comparisons between the experimental treatment groups can be made to check the consistency or inconsistency of any experimental effect. It is also unlikely that some extraneous event would affect all experimental groups and be misinterpreted as an experimental effect.

The assignment of the experimental treatment to the groups should, if at all possible, be a random assignment. If several groups of both types are included in a relatively homogeneous situation, factors such as the difference in teachers will tend to be equalized over the experimental and control conditions. If a systematic assignment, such as giving all the "innovative teachers" experimental groups, is followed, a bias is definitely introduced. For some experiments in which a new teaching technique is the experimental variable, volunteers are recruited from the teacher ranks. This procedure is somewhat dubious, although sometimes a case is presented for teachers being most effective with techniques toward which they are favorably disposed. By this reasoning, the teachers of the control groups are not less effective, because they are using their preferred method. However, they may be more or less effective for other reasons.

A modification of the nonequivalent control group design may be used if an interaction between pretesting and the experimental treatment is likely. This modification requires a minimum of four comparable groups. Groups that are pretested are not posttested, and vice versa. Thus two experimental and two control groups are required. The decision of which group receives the pretest is based on a random selection. No S is tested twice.

This design, like the usual nonequivalent control group design, can be strengthened by extending the number of groups. As the number of groups is increased the likelihood of a selection interaction with some other factor decreases. The extension of this design involves a marked increase in the number of groups.

The external validity of the nonequivalent control group design with separate groups being pre- and posttested is good. Since no S is tested twice there is no possibility of an interaction between the pretesting and the experimental treatment. With the multiple groups the likelihood of a selection and an experimental treatment interaction is small.

SELECTION OF SUBJECTS

An important aspect of experimental design is the selection of the Ss or the groups to be involved in the experiment. It has certainly been implied in the discussion that it is desirable to have some type of randomization in the assignment. We noted that preexperimental equivalence of groups is attained by a random assignment of Ss to the groups. Sampling for an experiment is a matter that should be taken seriously. A haphazard or "take them as they come" procedure is completely unsatisfactory and essentially invalidates the experiment.

Entire texts have been written on the matter of sampling, which can become very complex, both theoretically and in practice. A few comments are presented here and in Chapter 8 additional attention is given to some of the more common sampling procedures.

The definition of a random sample as given earlier is that all members of the population have an equal chance of inclusion in the sample. Suppose a group of Ss is to participate in an experiment and every S is to be assigned to one of the experimental treatment or control groups. Random assignment means that all Ss, before assignment, have the same probability of being assigned to any one of the groups. A random number table (see the example in Chapter 8) is commonly used to make the assignment. If the experimental design does not exhaust the pool of Ss, those not participating may simply be considered as having been randomly excluded from the experiment.

The procedure of matching Ss in setting up the groups has found some use in educational research. Two Ss are matched on some factor supposedly related to the dependent variable, and then one is randomly assigned to the experimental treatment group and the other to the control group. Matching is an attempt to make the groups equivalent prior to the experiment. It should be noted that matching is not a substitute for randomization in establishing equivalence of groups. In some designs it can serve as a useful technique *with* randomization. As the number of groups increases, matching becomes more difficult. Effective matching precludes the researcher from selecting relevant matching variables. Trying to match Ss on several variables simultaneously generally meets with very limited success. If the variables are highly correlated it may not prove too difficult, but in that case it would be almost as effective to match on only one of the variables.

THREATS TO EXPERIMENTAL VALIDITY

The specific conditions of an experiment determine the extent to which certain factors are an influence on its validity. One of these factors is subject mortality. In a laboratory experiment the conditions may be so structured that all selected Ss participate. It is not serious if an S must be omitted for a reason external to the experiment, especially if the S can be replaced by a comparable substitute. However, if a selective factor is operating among the nonshowers, this omission can be serious.

Experiments carried on with educational classes should involve no more absences and dropouts than normal. If the Ss correctly anticipate the posttest date and a group of low achievers is absent at that time, this would certainly bias the results. Mortality may be encouraged if the experimental treatment group is required to attend special sessions; the elimination of nonshowers is almost certain to shrink this group selectively. Even if dropout rates in the two or more groups are the same, there may be some type of selective dropout operating which would cause differences in the characteristics of the dropouts of the two groups. Any of these difficulties with subject mortality is a threat to experimental validity.[10]

Lack of consistency in the administration of the measuring instruments threatens the reliability of measurement and is therefore a threat to the validity of the experiment. Lack of consistency could appear between groups or between administrations of tests to the same group. This problem is minimized when a fixed measurement device such as a standardized achievement test is used with standardized administration procedures. The grading of essay exams is difficult to standardize; the standards may shift between separate administrations, or a single scorer may shift in his own scoring. Interviews and direct observations are susceptible to change between administrations, and interviewers differ both among interviewers and from time to time themselves. Maximum standardization without destroying the objectives of the interviews or observations is a necessity. Interviewers or observers should be randomly assigned to Ss or groups.

When groups of Ss are included in an experiment on the basis of their extreme scores, a possible threat to internal validity is regression. The extreme scores must be related in some way to the dependent variable. The *regression effect* is an inherent tendency for the extreme scores to regress toward the common mean on subsequent measurements. For example, the highest scorer on an IQ test would not be likely to score highest on a subsequent IQ test. A shift between pretest and posttest scores due to regression could be interpreted as some kind of experimental effect. Experiments involving remedial groups, in which the Ss are included because of their poor scores, are especially susceptible to this type of effect.

The possible effects of external events and pretesting have been discussed in connection with various designs. Undesirable practice effects may appear as a result of pretesting. With groups lacking in preexperimental equivalence, *differential maturation* may take place. Maturation consists of processes operating within the Ss that are functions of time. We usually think of maturation as growing older, but it also includes factors such as fatigue. Differential maturation is a likely threat to

---

10. For a more detailed discussion of ways to analyze mortality, see S. G. Jurs and G. V. Glass, "The Effect of Experimental Mortality on the Internal and External Validity of the Randomized Comparative Experiment," *Journal of Experimental Education* 40 (Fall 1971): 62–66.

validity when classes of different ages make up the experimental treatment and control groups. The random selection or assignment of Ss will do much to enhance experimental validity; any design with random selection tends to be high in this factor. Whenever the condition of randomness is missing, the researcher must be especially cognizant of possible threats to experimental validity.

INADEQUATE EXPERIMENTAL DESIGNS

There are research procedures in education which seemingly take on characteristics of experiments but in fact are inadequate as experimental designs. These are the procedures termed preexperimental designs by Campbell and Stanley[11] and faulty designs by Fred N. Kerlinger.[12] Unfortunately, these designs are still used in educational research, although with the development of adequate experimental designs use of the poorer ones is on the decrease. The basic weakness of these procedures is that they are completely or almost completely lacking in control, and hence for all practical purposes they are entirely void of experimental validity.

A single group, taken intact, pretested and posttested, is an inadequate design. The group receives the experimental treatment between the two testings. No control group is included in the investigation. Thus there is no comparison group, and any number of extraneous factors could have produced the difference between the pre- and posttest scores. These extraneous factors are confounded with the experimental treatment effect.

An attempt may be made to compare the results of the single pre- and posttested experimental treatment group with some ad hoc group which had previously been measured but did not receive the experimental treatment. This extension is entirely inadequate, since there is still a lack of selection control and there is no way of certifying that the groups were equivalent at the respective pretest occasions. Attempts at after-the-fact matching are ineffectual.

A procedure in which a comparison is made between two groups posttested at the same time is the *static-group comparison*.[13] The groups are not pretested and there is essentially no control, except possibly over the measurement, since both groups are measured at the same time. An example involving the use of a static-group comparison would be ascer-

---

11. Campbell and Stanley, "Experimental and Quasi-Experimental Designs," pp. 176–83.
12. Fred N. Kerlinger, *Foundation of Behavioral Research* 2d ed. New York: Holt, Rinehart & Winston, 1973, pp. 317–22.
13. Campbell and Stanley, "Experimental and Quasi-Experimental Designs," pp. 182–83.

taining the effects of a college education by comparing measures on incoming freshmen with those of graduating seniors. The experimental treatment would be a college education. A selective dropout undoubtedly would have occurred in one of the groups, namely the graduating seniors, and there is no certification that the groups were equivalent at their respective times of college entrance. The experimental treatment in such an experiment would span an interval of such time length that a multitude of extraneous factors is likely to be confounded with the experimental effect. At this age level, maturation is likely to have an effect on variables such as social finesse and attitudes.

The posttesting only of a single group or single S which has had the experimental treatment is another inadequate procedure for experimentation. Since there is no pretesting and no control group, inferences made from the data are based on guesses of what the results would have been if the experimental treatment had been omitted. This is a most unsatisfactory procedure for drawing valid conclusions.

Statistical analyses of the data collected in the inadequate procedures serve essentially no experimental purpose. A serious error is to apply statistical techniques and then interpret them as appropriate procedures. A descriptive analysis of the data may be made, and possibly some descriptive statistics of a distribution of scores will be reported. However, this in itself does not comprise an experiment in education. A perceptive educator might be able to make some subjective inferences from the data, but as an experiment, such inadequate procedures do not make the grade.

CONCLUDING REMARKS

This chapter has attempted to provide an overview of experimental design in educational research. The designs presented are general patterns for the pursuit of an experiment. Analysis of the designs has been general, and the details would need to be worked out for a design as it applies to a specific experiment. For example, an important consideration relative to the analysis might be the matter of how many independent variables can be meaningfully and practically included in the same design. In the effort to gain control and efficiency, designs can become very complex. Entire texts are devoted to the intricacies of such designs.

The distinguishing characteristic of experimental research is the manipulation of variables. The experimental design provides the structure for the experiment in which the variables are deliberately manipulated and controlled by the researcher. It might be mistakenly inferred that complexity is a desirable characteristic of an experimental design and that greater complexity is a mark of a more sophisticated experimenter. A truly sophisticated experimenter, however, need only come up with an experimental design that will do the job—meet the objectives of the research and be adequate for testing the hypotheses. An experiment must have definitely stated hypotheses, and the design should test these hypotheses. A meaningful interpretation of the results is another requirement of an adequate design. The statistical analysis of the data is a very intricate part of the design, but it does not necessarily imply that an experiment has been done.

At this point you should have a feeling of the underlying reasoning of experimental design and the logic of the various design structures. Characteristics of a good design were discussed early in the chapter. A well-conceived design will not guarantee valid results, but an inappropriate and inadequate design is certain to lead to uninterpretable results and faulty conclusions, if any can be drawn. The design is conceived prior to the experimentation, and it should be carefully planned and applied. There are no postexperiment manipulations, statistical or otherwise, that can take the place of a well-conceived experimental design.

SUGGESTED STUDY EXERCISES

4.1. Define the concepts of internal and external validity of an experiment. Why do we say that for some experiments an attempt at increasing one type tends to jeopardize the other type?

4.2. A researcher plans to do an experiment in the school setting concerning the effects of class size on achievement in chemistry. He defines class size as an independent variable and has four levels of size, namely, 12, 20, 30, and 38 students. Four high schools are involved in the study, each having eight chemistry classes, two of each class size. The researcher can assign students at random to a class within a school, but he cannot assign students randomly to a school. Two chemistry teachers are used in each school; all teachers teach four classes. The dependent variable is chemistry achievement measured after an instructional period of one semester. Discuss the aspect of control in this situation. Consider possible uncontrolled variables and variables which are or might be controlled. Is there a possibility of confounding of variables in this research situation? State one or more hypotheses for this experiment. Discuss one or more experimental designs which would apply to this situation.

4.3. Discuss two methods by which experimental control over extraneous variables can be increased.

4.4. Discuss in detail an example of an experiment for which the posttest-only control group design is appropriate. Consider such points as why you would not need pretests and the number of groups you would include (you may want to extend the design to more than two groups).

Identify how you are enhancing control in your proposed experiment. Also identify the independent variable(s), dependent variable(s), and constants.

4.5. A researcher is doing an experiment on problem solutions. The experiment is done in a learning laboratory. The Ss for the experiment are college students enrolled in a sophomore-level education course. The problems, although similar, are of two types: geometrical and algebraic. Type of problem is an independent variable. Other independent variables are sex of the student and group size. There are two group sizes: individual and pair. The dependent variable is number of errors to solution, and this is considered to be measured on an interval scale measurement. There are 160 Ss (96 girls and 64 boys) available for the experiment. Each S is to solve only one problem. Present a factorial design that would be appropriate for this experiment. Discuss how you would assign the Ss and how many would be assigned to the various cells. How would you build randomization into the assignment?

4.6. Suppose in the factorial analysis of Exercise 4.5 a significant interaction is found between the independent variables of group size and sex of student. What does it mean that such an interaction exists? Present a possible plot of the means of the four groups involved and interpret your plot.

4.7. Discuss the gains of internal validity when going from the pretest-posttest control group design to the Solomon four-group design.

4.8. To ascertain the effect of Boy Scout training, it is proposed to measure a group of 14-year-old Boy Scouts and a group of 8-year-old boys who have not yet had Boy Scout training. The boys are measured at the same time on proficiency in various skills. This is not a true experimental situation, but what design is being applied? Discuss the weakness related to experimental validity.

4.9. A teacher is interested in the effects of the use of programmed learning materials as supplementary aids in an advanced algebra course. He is interested in the amount of algebra learned during one semester of instruction. There are 83 students enrolled in four advanced algebra classes who are taught by this teacher. These students make up the Ss for the experiment. One group of students has access to the programmed materials and the other has not. Suggest an experimental design that would apply to this situation. Is it necessary that the teacher use a pretest? Consider the matter of control. What procedures would be necessary for adequate internal validity? Comment on the external validity of this experiment.

4.10. Discuss an experimental situation for which a counterbalanced design would be applicable. We say that multiple-treatment interference is a threat to validity when using a counterbalanced design. What does this mean?

4.11. Discuss the differences between "true" experimental designs and quasi-experimental designs. Discuss some of the difficulties introduced when less than a true design is used.

4.12. A researcher desires to do a study of the effects of individual versus massed practice on fifth-grade spelling achievement. He finds three elementary school principals willing to cooperate and then allows the fifth-grade teachers to use the method they prefer. (A single teacher uses only one method.) After an eight-week period the students are given a common spelling test. Discuss the experimental errors in the above procedure. Comment on both internal and external validity for this situation.

4.13. A teacher does a research study on third-grade reading achievement with a class. Two methods of instruction are used, but not simultaneously. The students are tested every four weeks, and a particular method is used for a four-week session. The methods are randomly assigned to the four-week instructional periods, and the procedure continues for the school year. What type of design is being applied in this situation? Discuss its weaknesses and advantages. What might be a special measurement problem that might arise?

4.14. A researcher uses the following experimental design. It involves six groups and is, in essence, a take-off on the Solomon four-group design. The symbols have the meaning indicated in this chapter. Only one experimental treatment, X, is involved.

$$
\begin{array}{llllll}
G_1 & R & O_1 & X & O_2 & \\
G_2 & R & O_3 & - & O_4 & \\
G_3 & R & O_5 & X\!\!-\!\!-\!\!-\!\!-\!\!-\!\!-\!\!-\!\!-\!\!-O_6 \\
G_4 & R & O_7\!\!-\!\!-\!\!-\!\!-\!\!-\!\!-\!\!-\!\!-\!\!-\!\!-O_8 \\
G_5 & R & & X & O_9 & \\
G_6 & R & & \!\!-\!\!-\!\!-\!\!-\!\!-\!\!-O_{10}
\end{array}
$$

a. What is gained (apparently) by including the middle two groups?

b. What comparisons could be made to determine whether or not there is an effect of pretesting?

c. What would you conclude from the following results and comparisons? An equals sign means that the statistics from the indicated observations are about the same, the not-equals sign means they are different. Consider each set of results independently.

(1) $O_2 = O_9$, $O_6 = O_8$, but $O_2, O_9 \neq O_6, O_8$.

(2) $O_2 = O_6 = O_9$, $O_4 = O_8 = O_{10}$, but $O_2, O_6, O_9 \neq O_4, O_8, O_{10}$.

(3) $O_1 = O_2 = O_3$, and $O_3 = O_4$.

(4) $O_2 = O_4 = O_9$, $O_6 \neq O_2$ and $O_6 \neq O_8$.

(Note: Consider only the results given, do not read into the comparison results not specified.)

4.15. Summarize the general characteristics of a well-designed experiment.

4.16. Select one or more research articles which involve experimentation from such publications as the *American Educational Research Journal* or the *Journal of Educational Psychology*. Read the article carefully to determine the design used, the methods and adequacy of control, and the analysis procedures. Comment on the experimental validity of the study.

chapter 5

Nonexperimental research

KEY CONCEPTS

Ex post facto research
Strong inference
Survey studies
Status survey
Survey research
Population surveys and sample surveys
Personal interview
Written questionnaire
Controlled observation
Open-ended question
Structured and unstructured items
Cover letter
Nonresponse
Longitudinal designs: trend study, cohort study, panel study
Cross-sectional designs: parallel-samples design
Coding the data
Historical research
Primary and secondary sources
External and internal criticism

The second large category in classifying educational research according to methodology is nonexperimental research. In defining and discussing its counterpart, experimental research, in Chapter 4, we noted that in order for a research project to be an experiment, at least one independent variable must be manipulated by the researcher, according to some preconceived plan. All research situations in education, however, do not lend themselves to the deliberate manipulation of variables. There are many variables in educational settings whose nature does not allow them to be manipulated by the researcher. Intelligence, aptitude, or socioeconomic background, for example, cannot be randomly assigned to Ss and manipulated in an experiment.

This chapter deals with research methodologies which are not experimental in nature. Generally, nonexperimental research tends to have less control than experimental research, and therefore interpretation of nonexperimental results may be less straightforward and more susceptible to ambiguity. The hypotheses and conditions of the research project determine the appropriate type of methodology. Each type of research has its place in the educational context and makes valuable contributions to the field of education.

EX POST FACTO RESEARCH

Fred Kerlinger's definition of *ex post facto* research, given in Chapter 3, sees it as "systematic, empirical inquiry in which the scientist does not have direct control of independent variables because their manifestations have already occurred or because they are inherently not manipulable." He notes further that "Inferences about relations among variables are made, without direct intervention, from concomitant variation of independent and dependent variables."[1] The term *"ex post facto"* means "from a thing done afterwards"; it implies some type of subsequent action. The researcher studies the variables in retrospect, in search of possible relationships or effects.

The definition above implies a lack of control, at least a lack of direct control in terms of actually manipulating independent variables. The independent variables exist in the situation and are not placed there or manipulated by the researcher. If the researcher draws a sample from a larger population, the sample should be drawn at random. However, there is a difference between drawing *S*s at random and assigning *S*s at random for experimental treatments. Suppose a study were being done on the divergent thinking abilities of high school students in New York and Los Angeles. "City" here takes on the characteristics of the independent variable. It would not be possible to randomly assign high school students to the cities; the students have, in essence, self-selected themselves by living in their respective cities. However, since it is unlikely that it would be feasible to measure all the high school students of both cities, random samples would be drawn. Thus, in *ex post facto* research the researcher does not possess the option to randomize in the experimental sense. Randomization comes in through the sampling process.

The matter of self-selection merits closer attention. Often the groups under study are designated because they differentially possess certain characteristics. Such characteristics may be extraneous to the research problem but may in fact have an effect upon the variables under study. Suppose in a study dealing with mental retardation the *S*s under study were divided into two groups—those mentally retarded and those not. Now the presence or absence of mental retardation becomes the dependent variable, and the *S*s have self-selected themselves into the two

---

1. F. N. Kerlinger, *Foundations of Behavioral Research,* 2d ed. (New York: Holt, Rinehart & Winston, 1973), p. 379.

levels. Suppose that the researcher discovers that the incidence of extremely high fever in connection with childhood diseases was considerably greater for the mentally retarded group. Maybe a statistical test for the difference between the proportions of high fever for the two groups proves significant. The researcher can conclude that there is a relationship between the two variables, but he cannot make the causal connection that high fevers cause mental retardation. There are any number of other variables which singly or in combination could have caused the mental retardation.

The independent variables of an *ex post facto* study are identified, usually, before the data are collected, but because of the lack of control, it is very tenuous to conclude that a causal connection exists between the independent and dependent variables. In most situations there are several uncontrolled independent variables. The control inherent in experimental studies makes it possible for a direct effect to be concluded, but in *ex post facto* investigations this is much more of a gray area. The researcher with this type of study runs a relatively high risk of misinterpreting his results if he begins concluding cause-and-effect relationships. A naive researcher who is oblivious to the variables operating in the situation is very likely to reach unfounded conclusions. The researcher should be sensitive to alternative explanations of the results.

Ex post facto research should be carried on in the framework of defined hypotheses and related theory. Unfortunately, this is not always the case. Sometimes data are collected with apparently no more direction than to see what appears. Then some type of retrospective search begins to determine, if possible, what variables exist that might be the basis for some hypotheses. However, this is usually a less efficient and less desirable approach than using defined hypotheses in conducting the research. While in the definition it is stated that the independent variables have already occurred or do not lend themselves to manipulation, that does not mean the researcher is ignorant or oblivious of them when planning the research. He should be aware of what variables he is considering and conduct the research in the context of existing knowledge.

An example

An example of *ex post facto* research is a cross-national study of characteristics of teacher education students in the United States and British Isles.[2] The two cultures or countries comprised the two levels of at least

---

2. G. E. Dickson *et al., The Characteristics of Teacher Education in the British Isles and the United States,* U.S. Office of Education report CRP 2518, 1965, University of Toledo.

one independent variable. Additional independent variables were identified, such as type of college, either public or private, size of student enrollment, and regional location of the college. (Many more independent variables could have been identified.) In most large-scale *ex post facto* studies, several dependent variables are also included in the same study. The dependent variables of this study included performance on achievement measures and scores on attitude inventories. These were called the "characteristics" of the students.

It is quite apparent that college students cannot be randomly assigned to the country in which they attend college or to the type of college they attend. In this sense they have self-selected themselves. Within a country it would be very likely that some selection factors would be operating in terms of type of college. In looking at the student samples of private and public institutions of higher learning, it would be impossible to make a convincing case for the fact that these two populations are random selections from a common population prior to their entry into college. The *S*s of the study could be classified in terms of the independent variables (assuming unambiguous definitions) but not randomly assigned to the levels of these variables.

The data of a study such as this, assuming adequate sampling, measurement, and data collection, could reveal whether or not the college students of the two countries differ significantly on the dependent variable or variables. However, it should be noted that to say that the college students of the two countries differ does not reveal why they differ. Now the search begins for cause-and-effect relationships between the independent and dependent variables. The differences between countries, which might bring about a difference in college student characteristics, are many. The point of embarkation upon the retrospective search would undoubtedly begin with an analysis of basic differences in the college programs of the two countries. But there are any number of other variables which singly or in combination with others could have brought about, or at least contributed to, the difference. For example, the domestic financial situations may be such that the majority of the students in the two countries come from basically different backgrounds. Also, motivational factors may differ widely between the two countries. Alternate explanations would be plausible and should be entertained as possible explanations of the results.

The identification and definition of independent variables can become somewhat complex. It would be easy enough to classify the students on such variables as country and population of metropolitan location of the college. Classification on variables such as type of college or type of program may not be as straightforward, due to lack of consistency in the meaning. However, operational definitions could be developed for the purpose of classifying the students.

Definite cause-and-effect relationships indicated by the analysis of the data of this *ex post facto* study are not clear, certainly not as clear as in research studies with greater degrees of control. Apparent effects of independent variables may be caused by extraneous, confounded variables. An interaction effect might be the result of one or more unidentified variables. Analyses can be constructed of varying degrees of complexity. But whatever the analysis, the researcher must be aware of what is operating in the situation and the limits or ambiguities that may be attached to the interpretation of results.

Setting and scope

Ex post facto research is not necessarily of a large scale, like the cross-cultural example above. Research studies involving sociological variables, such as social class, socioeconomic status, and social values often are *ex post facto* in nature. Many of these types of studies are limited to a single city or a part of a city, possibly a school district or the area covered by a single school.

Ex post facto studies could be conducted within a classroom setting. For example, we could consider the effects upon student performance of specified variables found in the natural educational setting. In fact, a study could be designed to investigate the possible relationship between student attitude (independent variable) and academic performance (dependent variable). In such a situation, the attitudes of the students would not be manipulated; they would simply be identified. This is in contrast to an experiment, in which the independent variable would be manipulated by the researcher. Attitude of the student is not a variable that lends itself to manipulation in the experimental sense.

Although there is considerable risk of misinterpretation, *ex post facto* investigations can make valuable contributions to educational knowledge and improvement. A large portion of educational research is *ex post facto* in nature. Many nonexperimental empirical studies provide a considerable amount of information, even if cause-and-effect relationships are not definitely established. In the cross-cultural example above, it might be important to know if and how the student characteristics differ even if we do not know precisely why they differ.

Sometimes educational investigations begin on the assumption that a difference exists, without any empirical evidence that this assumption is tenable. It behooves researchers to have evidence about the facts of a situation before they make an attempt to explain it. Otherwise they run an additional risk of trying to explain a situation which does not even exist. Such a procedure goes out of the realm of research and into pure conjecturing or guessing. Conjecturing about the interpretations is tenuous enough without conjecturing about the results.

Guidelines for ex post facto research

Ex post facto investigations can be improved by adhering to some relatively simple guidelines. Hypotheses should be stated and tested whenever possible. The study should also state alternate hypotheses and, if possible, these hypotheses should be tested as well. When alternate hypotheses are tested and refuted, the remaining hypotheses are strengthened as plausible explanations of the results. The procedure of testing multiple hypotheses and zeroing in on the plausible explanations through elimination of refuted hypotheses has been referred to as *strong inference*.[3]

The interpretation of the results of an *ex post facto* study, as with any type of research study, should be supported by a thorough knowledge of the independent variables in the context of the dependent variables. Such knowledge will tend to guard against profuse and improper interpretations. Any conjectures should be recognized as just that. The researcher should recognize the empirical results of the study and should limit the discussion to these results in preference to pursuing conjectures for which there is little or no basis.

One specific analysis technique is not exclusively used in *ex post facto* research. Correlational analyses are often included, since relationships between variables are of interest. A substantial correlation between two variables does not necessarily imply that one variable causes the other, however. In the nonexperimental setting, alternate explanations involving uncontrolled variables cannot be experimentally discounted, and a relationship between two variables may be caused by one or more other variables. The lack of correlation between two variables certainly lessens the credibility of a causal hypothesis. A high correlation, on the other hand, allows the causal hypothesis to survive one possibility of disconfirmation.

We have recognized that *ex post facto* research does have weaknesses, a primary one being the lack of control. However, this should not be interpreted as a reflection on the value of *ex post facto* research. Many educational research problems, especially those involving social and psychological variables, must be researched in an *ex post facto* manner because of their nature. Variables such as aptitude, teacher characteristics, school climate, and hosts of others are primarily *ex post facto* in

---

3. J. R. Platt, "Strong Inference," *Science*, 146, 16 October 1964, 347–53. Platt describes the process of strong inference as the simple, old-fashioned method of inductive inference, applied in a systematic manner. The procedure is, of course, not unique to *ex post facto* research. For example, in an experimental setting it might involve a series of experiments, at each turn discarding those hypotheses not supported by the results.

nature. Many of these variables are certainly important factors in the educational setting, and the importance of *ex post facto* research could be argued solely from that fact.

SURVEY STUDIES

Studies in education conducted to determine the status quo go by such names as school surveys, status surveys, or just surveys. Such studies are concerned with the gathering of facts rather than the manipulation of variables. A school survey may be taken to determine the number of students who eat in the school cafeteria or ride the buses, average student load per teacher, and so on. While such surveys might qualify under a broad definition of research, in many instances they take on more of the characteristics of skilled clerical work concerned with sorting and tabulating. Nevertheless, school surveys do provide information that is not only important but necessary to the educational enterprise.

Status studies are not the only educational research endeavors to come under the survey umbrella. Survey has a broader meaning, and there are different types of survey studies. Since both surveys and *ex post facto* research are nonexperimental, the difference between them is not as distinctive as, say, the difference between experimental and *ex post facto* research. Basically surveys can be distinguished from other types of nonexperimental research by the types of research questions posed. Regardless of the type of survey, they specifically deal with questions about what is rather than why is it so.

Survey research as defined by Kerlinger[4] deals with the incidence, distribution, and interrelations of sociological and psychological variables. These studies deal with how people feel or perceive and how they behave, in addition to things such as role and group status. (Both role and group status could be actual or perceived.) The objectives of a survey research study might be to determine how the psychological and sociological variables are related. Often the relationships among the psychological (or sociological) variables are studied as well. In any event, more is involved in what we call survey research than a tabulation of tangible objects.

Before considering the classification of surveys it should be mentioned that for many surveys, whether status studies or survey research, a sample is used. Undoubtedly, most large-scale studies use sampling rather than measuring the entire population. Although the sampling plans involve random sampling, they are usually more complex than

---

4. Kerlinger, *Foundations of Behavioral Research*, p. 410.

simple random sampling. In some cases, the most sophisticated part of the study is the selection of the sample. Different approaches to sampling are not discussed in this chapter but are considered in detail in Chapter 8.

Classification of survey studies

In educational research, studies are often classified according to some criteria in order to enhance definition and understanding. In classifying experimental designs into various types (see Chapter 4), one criteria used was basically the extent of experimental validity of the design. Different criteria are used for classifying types of survey research. The classification schemes are quite arbitrary, and their value lies in their usefulness, especially as they enhance understanding. We will use three criteria in our classifying system.

One criterion has already been presented in the definition of status surveys and survey research. This might be called the nature of the variables that are under investigation. If a survey study involves the tabulation of tangible variables, it is classified as a *status survey*. A survey dealing with people's perceptions and feelings in connection with sociological and psychological variables would be classified as *survey research*.

A second criterion for the classification of surveys is the group measured, a sample or a population. We shall refer to these as a sample survey and a population survey. *Population surveys* (sometimes called censuses) can be used effectively with small populations, but they are rarely used with large ones. It may be physically or financially impossible to include the entire population. In the case of large populations, the time involved in measuring the entire population might actually reduce the accuracy of measurement. That is, during the extended time required for measurement, the population might change with respect to the dependent variable, and the passing of time would reflect a change in the measurement between Ss measured earlier and those measured later in the survey. Thus, a random sample could actually provide greater accuracy than measuring the entire population because it would not contain this effect of the longer time span.

A *sample survey* involves selecting a random sample and attempting to make inferences about the population from the sample observations. If the entire population is measured there is no inferential aspect concerning the statistics of the study. It would not be proper to use inferential statistics to generalize to the population when the entire population is included, and descriptive statistics would undoubtedly be used. For a sample survey, inferential statistics would be expected to play a major role in the analysis of the data.

A third classification of surveys is by method of data collection. There are several procedures for data collection; for surveys, we will consider three: the personal interview, the written questionnaire, and controlled observation. Questionnaires and interviews are commonly associated with surveys, and their construction and use will be discussed in some detail. Controlled observation is used for several types of surveys, such as those in which the data collected consist of scores on achievement tests, attitude inventories, or some type of physical performance scores. Another type is represented by the trained observer who goes into a classroom or other natural setting to observe the incidence of some phenomena, perhaps something as complex as the interaction of students and teachers. In controlled observation, the measurement or data collection is controlled directly by the researcher, to a larger extent than with questionnaires and interviews.

In the cross-cultural example of teacher education students discussed under *ex post facto* research, if the purpose of the research had been limited to determining the status of achievement and attitude (defined as characteristics) of the Ss, the research would have been a survey. In that case, the use of the standardized achievement tests would have been an example of controlled observation. It should be noted that the control here is on the observation or measurement, and the term "control" is not being used in an experimental sense.

We have proposed three criteria for classifying survey studies, two of them dichotomous and one with three categories. Any survey fits into one of the classifications of each criterion. When the three criteria are superimposed upon one another, a single classification schema with 12 mutually exclusive classes or cells is formed. This schema can be represented by a three-dimensional diagram partitioned into the appropriate number of parts on each of its three dimensions (see Figure 5.1). Each dimension represents one of the three criteria. Note that classifying a survey in any one of the 12 cells identifies it in terms of all three criteria. Other classification schemes are certainly possible, and this particular system may not cover all possible types of surveys, but from a practical standpoint it is adequate for surveys in education.

The three criteria used in this classification scheme comprise the factors determining the survey. The nature of the variables is essentially the basis for doing the survey, and decisions on them provide direction for it. The definition and identification of the variables should be precise enough so that there will be no ambiguity about what is being studied.

The group measured will influence the quantity of data collected as well as subsequent analysis procedures. The analysis for a sample survey will be directed toward inferential statistics, and that of a population survey toward descriptive techniques. In a sample survey, it may be necessary to apply rather complex and sophisticated sampling pro-

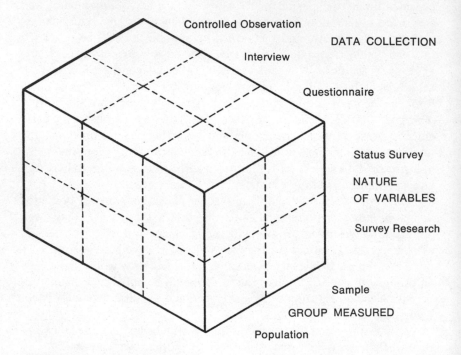

FIGURE 5.1.   Diagram for a 3 × 2 × 2 classification of surveys

cedures. It is not sufficient to open a text and follow some sampling procedure as a recipe. The researcher will have to weigh the advantages and disadvantages of several different procedures and consider available information. Matters such as these must be taken into consideration when designing the survey.

Interview and questionnaire: Definitions

Interviews and questionnaires are data collection instruments or procedures that are closely associated with survey research. The *interview* is a face-to-face confrontation between an interviewer and an S or a group of Ss. It is an oral exchange between individuals. The *questionnaire* is a list of questions or statements to which the S is asked to respond in writing; the response may range from a check mark to an extensive written statement. In an interview, the response may be limited to a single word (for example, yes or no), or it may require a rather lengthy oral discussion.

A questionnaire is sometimes referred to as a written, self-administered interview, and by the same token we could consider an interview as an oral questionnaire. The two types of data collection have a great deal in common relative to item construction and use. Interview and questionnaire have rather broad meanings in educational research, and there are other definitions for these terms. Since there is some ambiguity associated with the terminology, you should check the definitions in any specific discussion.

Use of interviews

The interview has the advantage of being a flexible measurement device. The items of the interview usually are open-ended questions to which the S can offer a fairly free response An *open-ended question* is one for which the S constructs his own response rather than selecting from a group of alternative responses. The interview provides further flexibility in that the interviewer can pursue the response with the S, and can ask for an elaboration or a redefinition of the response if it appears incomplete or ambiguous. The S's response may also reveal factors or feelings the interviewer may choose to pursue and probe.

Flexibility is basically a matter of item structure. Items allow varying degrees of flexibility; they could be considered on a continuum from unstructured to completely structured. An example of an unstructured item would be: "What do you think of the honors program in mathematics?" A partially structured question would be: "What do you think about the effectiveness of the mathematics honors program relative to advanced placement in college?" A structured question would be: "Do you feel that the present honors program in mathematics should be (a) continued without modification, (b) continued but modified, or (c) discontinued?" The term "honors program in mathematics" is assumed to refer here to a specific program with which the respondent is familiar.

The items of a single interview would undoubtedly vary in degree of flexibility. They can follow some type of sequence, in which they become more structured as the interviewer focuses on specific feelings or points. Care should be taken to avoid eliminating flexibility and the opportunity to probe by overstructuring the items.

The interview may be applicable as a data collection procedure when other procedures are not possible. An illiterate or near-illiterate could not respond to a written inventory, for example. A study involving the responses of educationally disadvantaged adults might require an interview, since motivation for responding to a written inventory might be entirely lacking, even if the items were written in a manner that the respondent could understand.

The interview is well suited for probing the feelings and perceptions of the Ss. However, the items of the interview itself will not ensure accurate measurement of these feelings. The S must be able to respond accurately with adequate oral expression, and he must be willing to do so. Difficulties arise if the S does not have the information necessary to answer the question or if he feels uneasy about divulging the information. An S may misunderstand the question or misinterpret the type of response needed. The interviewer must be able to recognize misunderstanding and uneasiness. He must be able to make on-the-spot decisions as to what the S is saying and what additional probing is necessary.

Since the interview is a face-to-face confrontation between individuals, a good rapport is essential between S and interviewer. Perceptive probing is of little value if some hostility has developed so that the S will not respond accurately. Usually the interview begins with gathering factual information about the S, and it is during this period that the rapport of the interview is established. Personal and controversial questions generally appear later in the interview, if they appear at all. The timing and inclusion of such questions must be left to the judgment of the interviewer. The interview should proceed in a businesslike manner in a friendly atmosphere, but excessive informality should be avoided.

The data of the interview are the responses of the S. The accuracy of these data depends on whether the S is telling the truth. Does he really feel the way he says he feels? Truthfulness of the data is always a potential problem when conducting an interview, because responses can be faked. Any of several factors may threaten the accuracy of the data. The S may be inclined to give a response that he thinks is socially or professionally preferable, regardless of the way he really feels. He may have suspicions about the interviewer or the reason for being interviewed that will influence his responses. Personal or controversial information may not be readily forthcoming. If the S is forced (or feels that he is forced) into responding when he does not have adequate background or does not want to reveal the information, he is likely to prefabricate responses.

There is no methodological technique that can ensure the accuracy of the data, but it may be possible to enhance truthful responses and to construct somewhat crude checks. The interviewer must be careful not to imply preferable responses. Controversial questions should be avoided until the proper background and rapport have been established. In the context of the interview, the interviewer may form an opinion of whether or not the S is telling the truth, and it may be possible to construct questions which check on the consistency of responses. Observation of past, present, or future behavior can provide a possible check. For example, if an S responds very favorably toward building new schools and then vigorously campaigns against a school bond issue, his responses might be questioned. The direct observation of behavior in this context is not always possible, and even if possible may be prohibitive in terms of time and effort.

The data recording of the interview should be efficiently structured so that it does not interfere with the process of conducting the interview. Tape recorders can retain the entire oral communication, but before they are used the respondent should agree to this type of data recording. If taping an interview is not practical or feasible, shorthand records of the interview must be developed. Structured questions may require only a check mark indicating one of several alternative responses. The responses to unstructured questions must be recorded briefly but completely, covering all main points. The recording of data should be as unpretentious as possible and should not arouse suspicions in the S; for example, if the S gives a short response, the interviewer should not engage in extensive writing. Materials and equipment for data recording should be arranged prior to the interview so that there is no confusion on this matter.

The interviewer must be well trained in the procedures for all of the activities of conducting an interview. For a particular survey study, he should be well informed about the variables under investigation so that he can make perceptive probes, and he will usually benefit from a training period in interviewing techniques. If there is no training period the early interviews essentially become the training sessions, and they may differ in style and competency from later interviews by the same interviewer. When two or more interviewers are used for a survey, attention must be given to training for interviewer consistency. Each interviewer should conduct a number of practice interviews (depending on the complexity of the interview schedule) until he has mastered the technique to be used. During the training period there should be some provision for more than one interviewer to interview the same S independently, in order to check on inter-interviewer consistency. Possibly a single S's responses could be taped and the responses recorded independently by two or more interviewers. The records of different interviewers could then be compared, the differences discussed, and the process repeated until the consistency is judged adequate. The S's responses should not be a function of the specific interviewer. The requirement of considerable manpower, training, and time is often viewed as a disadvantage of the interview.

The construction of questions for an interview should follow the principles that apply to item construction for questionnaires, which are discussed in the following section. By no means should the questions be a haphazard or off-the-cuff collection.

Use of questionnaires

As in any research study, the initial task of a survey involving a questionnaire is to spell out the objectives of the study. Once this task has been adequately done, the task of constructing the questionnaire follows. The questionnaire must cover the objectives by providing adequate data for the survey. Constructing the individual items so that they will provide these data is a task that requires careful attention to detail. As in the case of the interview, questionnaire items may range from unstructured to structured. Several criteria that can be used in constructing items for questionnaires are discussed below.

Item construction. The burden of communication is upon the questionnaire constructor, who should eliminate ambiguities as much as possible. Once the questionnaire has been sent or administered there is no longer an opportunity to straighten out any items that may not be clear. For one thing, an item should not include several questions to be answered by one response, such as: "Are you in favor of team teaching and the use of teaching machines?" If the S responds no it is not clear whether he does not favor either one, team teaching or the use of teaching machines, or both. The S may also misinterpret the question to mean that if he favors either or both he should respond yes. Items should be phrased and partitioned so that the response can be definite and there is no confusion as to meaning.

The question of whether or not the item can convey to the S a meaning different from the intended meaning should be considered. For example, if the S is asked where he teaches, he may conclude that the type of school—elementary, high school, inner city, suburban—is the required response. Another S may conclude that a geographical region is wanted, and still a third S may give the name and address of a specific school. An S responding hurriedly may simply state that he teaches in a classroom. Such an item would be improved by rephrasing the question as: "List the name and address of the school in which you teach." Or, if the type of school is desired, and to avoid confusion as to what criterion is being used to define type, it would be well to provide a set of alternative responses such as: (a) elementary, (b) junior high, (c) senior high.

The items should not be personally offensive or embarrassing to the S, and he should not be asked questions he cannot possibly answer; they should fit his informational background. An effort should be made to vary the questions, so they are not pedestrian or monotonous. Suspicions should not be raised, and there should be no indication of hidden motives for securing the information. The items should not be suggestive as to a preferred response, and they should be so constructed that responses will not be superficial but will contain adequate depth for the purposes of the study. Checklists or categories for responses should be exhaustive, with the different possible responses mutually exclusive. For many kinds of items it is necessary to provide a middle-of-the-road or neutral response, such as "no definite feeling" or "undecided," to avoid forcing the S to make an undesirable choice. Form of response should be straightforward and uniform.

The items of a questionnaire should·be constructed in a manner that facilitates data tabulation. Many times this is simply a mechanical matter of arranging the space for responses appropriately on the questionnaire. Anticipated coding schemes, such as assigning responses on a five-point ordinal scale to certain numerical codes, should be developed in advance. If a computer is to be used in the analyses, coding schemes must conform to IBM card formats. The space allotted for open-end items should conform to the extent of anticipated response. The S may take a cue from the space as to the expected length of his response, and specified space lessens the likelihood of a rambling response. However, space should be adequate so that the S does not feel restricted in his response.

Before preparing the final form of the questionnaire, the items should be tried out with a small group, as a sort of pilot run. The group need not be a random sample of prospective Ss, but the members of the group should be familiar with the variables under study and should be in a position to make valid judgments about the items. The results of the pilot run should identify misunderstandings, ambiguities, useless items, and inadequate items. Additional items may be implied, and mechanical difficulties in matters such as data tabulation may be identified. Difficulties with the directions for completing the questionnaire may also be uncovered. On the basis of the pilot-run results, necessary revisions should be made for the preparation of the final form.

The questionnaire as a whole should be attractive to the S. Certain physical characteristics can be utilized, such as multicolor printing to draw attention and make the questionnaire more appealing. The length should be such that responding does not become a tedious or burdensome task and unreasonable demands are not made upon the S's time. For many questionnaires, the items follow a logical sequence which can be developed to enhance the interest of the S.

The cover letter.   The cover letter is the vehicle for introducing the S to the questionnaire and getting him to respond to the questions. In a sense the cover letter is the rapport-establishing device. This very important item should be carefully constructed.

The cover letter should be straightforward and explain the purposes and value of the survey. The S should be made to feel that his response is important. There should be nothing in the cover letter to arouse suspicions about the purpose or nature of the survey. The S should be assured that the researcher is interested in the overall responses of the group and that individual responses will not be singled out and associated with him. A procedure may be set up by which replies remain anonymous, but in any event the S should be assured that all responses are confidential.

The matter of who signs the cover letter can be of some importance. Response may be improved if the cover letter carries the signature of someone who is (or appears to be) associated in some way with the Ss. For example, the cover letter of a questionnaire about guidance institutes being sent to guidance counselors might well carry the signature of the institute director on the staff of a university that conducts such institutes. A graduate student who sends out a questionnaire, giving as a reason the data collection for a thesis, can expect a limited and disappointing response.

Figure 5.2 reproduces a cover letter sent with an extensive questionnaire used to evaluate 1970 National Science Foundation summer institutes.[5] Note that the purpose of the survey is given, and the importance of response is emphasized. Directions are given to the respondent on returning the questionnaire, and he is guaranteed complete anonymity. The respondent is not given a deadline for returning the questionnaire but is asked to return it promptly. The cover letter is signed by a division director of the National Science Foundation.

Nonresponse. The problem of nonresponse is often viewed as the primary disadvantage of questionnaire surveys. Unfortunately, a rather common practice is to ignore the problem; without preplanning, this may be the only alternative. While there are procedures for increasing the number of returns, these procedures often meet with limited success. Rate of response depends upon the unique conditions of the survey.

The cover letter signature has already been mentioned as having some influence on the rate of response. The length of the questionnaire also should be considered. Lengthy questionnaires discourage response. If an S can respond in a matter of five minutes, he is more likely to do so than if he must spend an hour or two in order to respond to the items adequately. It may be well to look for items that can be eliminated if a questionnaire seems overly long. Items also can be reconstructed to lessen the necessary time of response.

The S should be encouraged to respond immediately to the question-

---

5. Thomas Gibney, *Evaluation of 1970 Summer Institute for Secondary School Teachers of Sciences and Mathematics Programs,* Final Report, Contract NSF-C677, 1972, University of Toledo.

NATIONAL SCIENCE FOUNDATION
WASHINGTON, D.C. 20550

October 5, 1971

Dear 1970 NSF Summer Institute Participant:

The National Science Foundation is conducting a national survey of the participants of *1970 Summer Institutes.* The purpose of the survey is to evaluate the effects of institute attendance upon the participant and his subsequent professional performance. You have been selected as one of the respondents. Completion of the enclosed questionnaire will take a small amount of your time, but your responses are of great importance to NSF and the Summer Institute Program. Future directions for the Foundation's education programs will be influenced by the results of this evaluation.

We have engaged the University of Toledo, Center for Education Research as the contractor for this evaluation. University of Toledo staff, in cooperation with NSF officials, have designed the questionnaire. Therefore, all completed questionnaires are to be returned to the University of Toledo as indicated on the envelope. Please use the enclosed, stamped envelope for the prompt return of your completed questionnaire.

Please read the instructions carefully, since the format for response differs from section to section. The numbers in parentheses on the left side of each page are for information coding purposes; disregard those numbers as you respond to the items. The questionnaire number will be used only to exclude your name from follow-up mailings. You are guaranteed complete anonymity as an individual respondent.

Your cooperation in responding to the questionnaire and its prompt return are deeply appreciated.

Sincerely yours,

Charles A. Whitmer
Division Director
Pre-College Education in Science

Enclosures

Note: Reproduced with permission from the National Science Foundation.

FIGURE 5.2.   Cover letter used with questionnaire on the evaluation of NSF summer institutes

naire. Deadlines of two weeks or a month hence should not be implied or stated; this will tend to encourage the S to put off responding and, although his intentions may be good, he is likely to forget the entire matter. Of course, a self-addressed, stamped return envelope should be provided. Mechanically, it should be as easy as possible for the S to return the questionnaire.

Follow-up questionnaires are a must for practically any questionnaire survey. The follow-ups should come shortly after the initial mailing and, as in the original cover letter, the S should be encouraged to respond immediately. Follow-ups should be planned in advance and in some cases two or more follow-ups may be desirable. Sometimes an appeal to professional interest is made, or inducements such as money or a report of research findings are offered to encourage returns. The use of telegrams, telephone calls, or special delivery letters may prove effective, though expensive. Promised anonymity may also increase returns, depending on the nature of the questions.

Unless the researcher administers the questionnaires to a captive audience and collects them on the spot, some nonresponse is inevitable and should be anticipated. The researcher should decide in advance what percentage of nonresponse can be tolerated. This will be determined somewhat by the variables and the population under study, but generally 75 percent is considered a minimum rate of return.

The difficulty with a low return rate is that the data may be biased. If this is true the data do not represent the group under study. For example, suppose a survey on need for mathematics teachers is conducted on a statewide basis, and the following response pattern occurs: Practically all the large school systems respond, but for some reason small school systems do not return the questionnaire. The data of the returned questionnaires could indicate an average need for mathematics teachers that is in excess of the total number of mathematics teachers in most schools throughout the state. Nonresponse can result in a data gap that markedly distorts the real situation. It is very tenuous to assume that nonresponse is randomly distributed throughout the group.

The researcher should plan in advance some procedure for dealing with nonresponse. It may be possible to interview a sample of nonrespondents and acquire some information about their characteristics and reasons for not returning the questionnaire. Another alternative is to identify subgroups in the sample (or population) and check if certain subgroups are high in nonresponse. This procedure does not reveal the feelings of the nonrespondents but it does identify the nonresponding groups. If nonresponse is associated with a certain type of feeling toward the questionnaire items, that is, nonrespondents have what they interpret as unfavorable attitudes toward them, the sample of responses will be definitely biased, since response and nonresponse are associated with the variables under study. A check of subgroups may indicate this type of phenomenon, but it will not eliminate or correct it. The researcher will be required to take this into consideration when he reports the results.

One possibility of dealing with nonresponse when discussing results is for the researcher to calculate the effect on the statistics if all nonrespondents had responded in a manner to cause the greatest change in the results. This would be relatively easy to do for items that have only two alternative choices. For example, suppose an item has yes-no alternatives, and 800 out of 1,000 questionnaires sent had been returned. Of the 800, 500 or 62.5 percent responded yes. The extremes would be that the 200 nonresponders would have all responded either yes or no. If all had responded yes, the yes responses would have totaled 700 out of 1,000, or 70 percent. If all had responded no, there still would have been a 500 out of 1,000, or 50 percent, yes response. Therefore, although the actual observed percentage of yes response was 62.5 percent, the range of 50 to 70 percent represents the possible extremes. The researcher would take this into consideration when reporting the pattern of results.

An accurate and complete record should be kept of outgoing and incoming questionnaires. Mailing dates, destinations, dates of return, and by whom returned should be recorded. Incoming questionnaires should be inspected for ambiguous and incomplete responses. Questionnaires returned late after repeated follow-ups may be inadequate or worthless, and the date of return may be a basis for checking bias in the responses. The responses to the various follow-ups should be kept separate and checked against the initial responses for any bias due to persistence. Reluctant respondents, returning their questionnaires late, differ in their responses from earlier respondents. Factors such as these can aid in the interpretation of the data.

SURVEY DESIGNS AND METHODOLOGY

The researcher anticipating a survey has a number of design options available, depending on the objectives and conditions of his study. These designs for the most part would be used with sampling studies rather than with censuses. The designs discussed below by no means exhaust the possible variations in survey designs, but for purposes of surveys in educational research they provide an adequate base.

Longitudinal designs

Longitudinal designs involve the collection of data over time and at specified points in time. Some longitudinal studies are of short duration, others span a long period, possibly several years. One type of longitudinal design is the *trend study*. In a trend study a given general population is studied over time by taking random samples at various points. Different samples are selected at different times, but the samples represent the general population. Trend studies are often used for studying attitudes over an extended period. For example, a community's attitude toward the schools and its subsequent change over time could be researched through a trend study. The general population would be the community as it exists at the specified time. The Gallup Polls conducted over the course of a political campaign are a good example of a trend study.

A variation on the trend study that is also a longitudinal design is the *cohort study*. Random samples are selected at different points in time, but from a specific rather than a general population. The difference between trend and cohort studies can be shown by an example. Suppose a researcher were interested in studying the attitudes toward professional unions of the teachers in Region A. The attitudes are surveyed every three years for a period of 15 years. At any given time, the random sample of teachers surveyed is selected from the teacher population at that time. The population would have changed in membership from the previous time, at least partly, but at that time it is the teacher population (in this case called a general population). Conducting the survey in this manner would be an example of a trend study.

If the researcher were interested in studying the attitudes, again toward professional unions, of the beginning teacher population of 1975 in Region A, this would be the specific population to be studied. Three years hence, the next random sample would be drawn from what remains of this population, which will in 1978 be teachers of three years' experience. Throughout this study, although some of the original beginning teachers will leave teaching along the way, the study focuses on the attitudes of the population of teachers who were beginning teachers in 1975. Conducting the survey in this manner would be an example of a cohort study.

In some populations that turn over very rapidly, the actual members of the population may practically all change over time. For example, if a survey of undergraduate attitudes at a college were conducted every four years, there would be a large percentage of change in the actual members of the undergraduate population. However, the undergraduates at each point in time would still be the general population under study.

Trend and cohort studies enable the researcher to study change and process over time. However, because at each data collection point in time, different random samples are selected, the trends are studied for the group, not individuals. If changes are taking place the researcher cannot determine specifically which individuals are causing the change. A variation on longitudinal designs which involves collecting data on the same sample of individuals over different times is the *panel study*. The sample of *S*s used is called the panel. Of course, it should be randomly selected at the outset of the study.

An advantage of panel studies is that they enable the researcher not only to measure net change but also to identify the source of change, in terms of the specific individuals who are changing. Panel studies can also provide information on the temporal ordering of variables. Such information is important if the researcher is attempting to establish cause and effect, since an effect cannot precede its cause. Suppose we are surveying attitude toward central administration and promotion patterns among college professors. If a full professor has an excellent attitude is it because he was promoted, or did he have an excellent attitude and was he promoted because of it? Without some kind of ordering of what occurred first, there is no way to establish a possible cause and effect. (Note that the ordering does not necessarily establish cause and effect. It only indicates whether or not a cause-and-effect relationship is possible.)

Panel studies have some definite disadvantages, an obvious one being attrition in the panel across the data collection points. Therefore, they tend to be of relatively short duration, compared to other longitudinal studies. Another disadvantage is that the panel study is demanding of the panel members, as well as demanding of the researcher in following up and locating panel members. Another disadvantage may be that the panel members become conditioned to certain variables, so that they are better at recall or exceptionally skilled in responding. Conditioning can also work the other way, causing panel members to become fatigued, bored, or careless. If the population from which the panel was selected is highly mobile and changing, the original panel may no longer be representative of that population at later data collection points. Panel studies are most applicable with quite static populations over short time periods. For example, surveying school board members quarterly over one calendar year might involve a panel study.

Longitudinal designs are used for studying change or status over a period of time. The length of time and the number of data collection points involved in a specific longitudinal design depend upon the objectives of the study. The trend study involves different random samples from a general population, the cohort study different random samples from a specific population, and the panel study a single random sample measured at multiple times.

Cross-sectional designs

In contrast to longitudinal designs, cross-sectional designs involve the collection of data at *one* point in time from a random sample representing some given population at that time. A cross-sectional design in its simple form would not be likely to be used for studying change, although it certainly could be used for studying relationships between variables. By "simple" form, we mean a single population is studied and no antecedent or succeeding populations that are related to the major population in time are included. For some types of surveys, however, it might be possible to use a cross-sectional design and still study change phenomena. Consider the following example.

Suppose a researcher were to survey mathematics achievement of the senior high school students (grades 10–12) in a region. Mathematics achievement is operationally defined as performance on a comprehensive, standardized mathematics test. This is an example of controlled observation. A random sample is selected which includes tenth, eleventh, and twelfth graders, and each individual is identified in terms of grade level. Another way of viewing the sampling is that random samples are selected from each grade level. The sample is tested, and the researcher now has data on all three grades.

Even though the data were all collected at the same point in time, a case could be made that since three different grade levels were represented, the researcher could investigate the patterns of gains in mathematics achievement across the three years. We could view the samples from the three grades as samples from different populations taken at the same time. If a longitudinal design had been used with three data collection points, we would have had the same population, either general or specific, sampled at three points in time. If the researcher had been interested in only the seniors (twelfth grade) we would have had a simple cross-sectional design. The juniors and sophomores represent antecedent populations; that is, they are antecedent to the seniors, since in time the members of these populations will become seniors.

A parallel-samples design can be used as a variation of either a longitudinal or cross-sectional design, but it is more likely to appear with a cross-sectional design, especially if used in educational research. By a *parallel-samples design* we mean that two or more populations are studied simultaneously as related to the same research problem. For example, a study of attitudes toward professional unions might include samples of teachers, school administrators, and school board members. Each of these three samples could respond to similar, if not identical, attitude inventories or questionnaires. The results of the different samples could then be compared.

The cross-sectional designs have some obvious logistical advantages over longitudinal designs. The data collection is not spread over an extended time period, and tedious follow-up of individuals is not necessary, as in a panel study. However, the type of design used depends upon the objectives of the survey. If trends for the same populations are to be studied over time, a longitudinal design is necessary. If single-time description is to be provided or relationships that can be established at a given point in time are to be studied, a cross-sectional design is used.

Methodology of survey research

The methodology of conducting a survey involves a series of detailed steps, each of which should be carefully planned. Lack of planning is certain to result in confusion of data collection, unorganized data, and uninterpretable results. The initial step is to define the objectives of the study and to develop the survey design. The definition of the research problem or objectives should include a good background of the variables to be studied. Variables involved in the survey must be operationally defined, and the investigator should have information about the relationships of the sociological and psychological variables from past studies. This information is valuable in constructing the items for the measuring device.

The next step is the development of the sampling plan, if it has been decided to sample rather than measure the entire population. Various factors must be considered. The population to be sampled must be defined, and the sampling plan, which may be quite complex, must be developed and described in detail. (Chapter 8 describes approaches to sampling applicable for surveys.) Factual information about the population is necessary for planning the sample. The sample selection must be conducted in such a manner that valid inferences can be made to the population and any subpopulations.

Although some activities can be conducted simultaneously, the construction of the interview or questionnaire items is usually the next major step. This is often the most difficult and taxing part of the survey. Since it is so crucial, time and effort should be devoted to this task. Considerable revision of items is commonly involved. The items should be tried out on small groups, and, if interviews are used, the interviewers need to be trained. This in itself is no small task.

Analysis procedures should be considered during construction of the items. It is necessary that the items produce data that can be analyzed to meet the objectives of the survey. The initial questions of both interview and questionnaire often pertain to factual information about the S, such as sex, marital status, and so on. This information is important in that it identifies the S in terms of classifying variables for the analysis. For example, if the responses of men and women are to be analyzed separately or comparatively, it is important to know the sex of the S. The measuring device should reflect the anticipated analysis procedures.

When the measurement instrument is judged to be satisfactory, the data collection begins. It is important to adhere to the sampling plan in collecting the data. If interviews are used, there should be some provision for systematically checking the interviewers. This may be accomplished by having multiple interviews (usually no more than two) of the same S by different interviewers; every 15th interview could be checked by having two interviewers interview the same S, for example. It is important that there be some measure of consistency between interviewers. For certain types of interviews it is also well to get a measure of the consistency of a specific interviewer. This can be accomplished by taping responses and having the interviewer record the responses on two independent occasions.

The data analysis depends upon several factors, but first the responses must be translated into a form which can be analyzed. This involves some kind of quantification, such as assigning numbers to responses. Responses will need categorization, and for open-ended questions, category systems will have to be constructed. Such systems may be based on a content analysis of responses or on an *a priori* basis. The translation of data is known as *coding*. Considerable counting and categorization are usually involved in assembling and coding the data.

The data and corresponding analyses must ultimately take a form that allows the researcher to meet the objectives of the survey. If inferences are to be made to populations, the analyses should provide for this. A number of separate analyses are commonly conducted on the data of a single survey. Not only separate analyses but different types of analyses may be in order. For example, data comprised of frequencies on factual information items would be analyzed differently from the data of an attitude scale. The former might involve proportions, while the latter would most likely involve ordinal scale measurement. Correlation coefficients are often computed between responses from various items. Such coefficients indicate the relationship between responses, but they do not explain the relationship as a cause-and-effect situation. Note that determining the relationship deals with the question of what is, not necessarily why it is so. The results of the various analyses are usually synthesized by the researcher.

The methodology of conducting a survey can be summarized in a flowchart which illustrates the major steps and the sequence of these steps (see Figure 5.3). Although some procedures can be done simultaneously, the various steps do follow a definable sequence. The details for any specific survey, such as developing the survey design to be used, would, of course, be provided at each step. The left part of the figure includes the major steps of the survey, and the activities on the right suggest the major procedures that come under each step. In some cases procedures overlap into two steps. Not all of the procedures would necessarily be applicable for a specific survey; for example, training of interviewers is not necessary for a mail questionnaire study.

The successful completion of a survey is not a simple task. Several

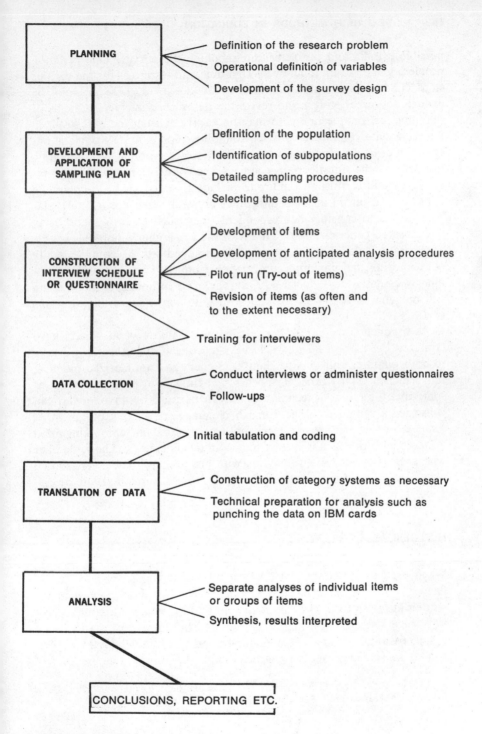

FIGURE 5.3.   Flowchart for the steps of conducting a survey

possible pitfalls and problems can sabotage the survey. One common problem is the failure to allow enough time and resources for the various steps. The sampling procedure can break down, or there may not be enough resources to test and revise the items adequately. The items of the interview or questionnaire may be poorly constructed and result in unusable data. Failure to provide for follow-ups is a very obvious but common difficulty. Inadequate procedures for assembling and tabulating the data as the questionnaires are returned are often a source of inefficiency and confusion. Failure to include the analysis in the planning is liable to result in analysis difficulties or results that are uninterpretable. Failure to consider nonrespondents may bias the results and bring unwarranted generalizations. Finally, if the researcher reports his results as separate, isolated analyses without some synthesis, he is undoubtedly not acquiring the maximum information from his survey. Careful planning is essential for a successful survey, and although such planning will not guarantee success, it will go a long way toward attaining this goal.

As a concluding remark it might be noted that several writers have criticized the lack of adequate surveys in educational research, relative to both quantity and quality. Sam D. Sieber[6] has summarized much of this criticism. Many times it appears that the survey is looked upon as some inferior research technique that can be used by anyone who can construct a sentence in the English language, regardless of how that sentence comes out. This is clearly not true, and anyone embarking upon a survey with this idea is certain to encounter difficulties. The researcher who anticipates doing a survey, as with any research endeavor, should give careful attention to the appropriate research methods to be applied in his survey.

HISTORICAL RESEARCH

When used in the context of educational research, history may be defined as "an integrated narrative or description of past events or facts, written in the spirit of critical inquiry, to find the whole truth and report it."[7] Since historical research involves a description of past events, there is no possibility of control or manipulation of variables in the experimental sense. The aspect of critical inquiry is important. As control

6. Sam D. Sieber, "The Case of the Misconstrued Technique," *Phi Delta Kappan,* 49 (January 1968): 273–76.
7. C. V. Good, *Essentials of Educational Research* (New York: Appleton-Century-Crofts, 1966), p. 145.

and manipulation of variables are essential to the experimental approach, so is critical inquiry essential to historical research.

A review of related literature is necessary for any research endeavor, and in a sense this itself is historical research. To be sure, it may be a relatively modest portion of the overall research project, but, nonetheless, a review of related literature serves an important function. Essentially it provides a context for conducting the research and interpreting the results. On a larger scale, a research study consisting entirely of historical research provides perspective for interpreting a part of the contemporary educational context. Historical research provides information that aids in making educational decisions. In order to meet this function adequately, the information must be accurate and must be viewed in the context of when the events occurred. Historical research requires standards of objectivity that are as demanding as those for other methods of educational research. The nature of historical data—that is, events that cannot be observed firsthand—often makes it more difficult to meet these standards.

Sources of information in historical research

Historical research concerns the critical evaluation and interpretation of a defined segment of the past. Therefore it is necessary to acquire some records of the period under study. The most common source is some type of written record of the past: books, newspapers, periodicals, diaries, letters, minutes of organizational meetings, and so on. However, written documents are not the only sources. Physical remains and objects (relics) of the past are other possible sources. Information may be orally transmitted through media such as folksongs and legends. Pictures, records, and various other audiovisual media can also serve as sources of information about the past.

The sources of historical information are commonly classified as primary and secondary. A *primary source* is an original or first-hand account of the event or experience. A *secondary source* is an account which is at least once removed from the event. The written record of a war correspondent as he viewed a battle would be an example of a primary source of information about the battle. The memoirs of a general who was not present at the battle would be a secondary source, assuming he reconstructed the battle from the description given him by officers and enlisted men of his command. The writings of John Dewey are primary sources of his views, whereas an interpretation of John Dewey's writings by one of his students would be considered a secondary source.

Hypotheses in historical research

The methodology of historical research does not consist of the undirected collection of information. A collection of unrelated or loosely related bits of information would not be viewed as a valuable research contribution. The historical researcher uses his information to explain and interpret conditions, events, and phenomena that existed during the period under study. Like the experimenter, the historical researcher also formulates hypotheses to direct his research activities. These hypotheses are attempts at explaining and interpreting the phenomena of the period under study. After the hypotheses have been formulated, the search begins for information that will confirm or refute them.

Hypotheses in historical research are usually not stated in a statistical sense. The null hypothesis form is not used in the context of testing hypotheses by statistical techniques. Rather, in historical research hypothesis takes on a broader meaning as a tentative statement or conjecture of the situation. As in any research endeavor, more than one hypothesis may be used.

Suppose a researcher were conducting historical research concerning the decline of the humanistic curriculum during the 17th and 18th centuries. Undoubtedly this decline was due to a combination of factors. One hypothesis might be that the elevation of the common man and his vernacular through the Industrial Revolution reduced the importance of the humanities as an avenue to culture. A second hypothesis might be that the advances of science made unwelcome inroads into the curriculum, and this was detrimental to the humanities.

It should be noted that the above hypotheses rest on an assumption of fact, that is, that the humanistic curriculum did decline during this period. If this assumption were not correct, the hypotheses would have no basis. Having established any necessary assumptions (or facts) and stated the hypotheses, the researcher would then set out to assemble the necessary information to confirm or refute his hypotheses. In the above case, when dealing with the initial hypothesis he would look for increased use of the common vernacular in the curriculum materials of the period. The researcher would investigate the different avenues to culture that developed during the period and the relationships between these and the humanities. On the basis of the evidence he would then retain or discard his hypothesis.

Consider a second example. Suppose a researcher is doing historical research on the development of professional education in the United States, specifically as it relates to secondary teachers. Undoubtedly there would be several hypotheses, but one might be that the teachers college developed as an outgrowth of the normal school, due primarily to the inadequate supply of teachers produced by the colleges and universities. The researcher would then collect evidence about the various possible factors that influenced the development of the teachers college. He would need information about the supply and demand of secondary teachers and how this was related to the numbers of teachers produced by colleges and universities. This hypothesis is based on the assumption that the teachers college was an outgrowth of the normal school. The hypothesis considers the inadequate supply not only as a factor but as the primary factor.

The matter of basing hypotheses on accurate assumptions may seem obvious, but failure to do so is not unknown. A false assumption or misconception is likely to persist in leading to a false conclusion. For example, in the late 19th century many liberal arts colleges took the position that it was unwarranted to grant a baccalaureate to graduates of professional schools. This position was based on the assumption that it was not in the tradition of higher education to award bachelors degrees for the profession of education. Careful historical research would have revealed that the arts degree of the medieval university originated almost exclusively for teaching purposes.

Methodology of historical research

The methodology of historical research can be summarized in four essentially overlapping steps. Assuming that a research problem has been adequately identified and initial hypotheses have been formulated, the first step is the collection of source materials. If the researcher has no information upon which to base initial hypotheses, it may also be necessary to collect some source materials prior to formulating hypotheses. The second step consists of subjecting the materials to a critical evaluation as to their trustworthiness and value in the light of the research problem. The third step is a synthesis of the information from the source materials. It is at the third step that the hypotheses may be revised or new ones formulated. Additional inferences may be made relative to the problem, and initial and tentative interpretations are also made at this step. The fourth step, a continuation of the third, is an analysis and synthesis procedure by which the historical researcher rejects or accepts hypotheses, makes final interpretations, and draws conclusions.

Collection and evaluation of source materials

The collection of source material does not consist of simply assembling all available documents which appear to have some relevance to the research problem. A basic rule of historical research is to use primary sources whenever possible, although it is not always possible to locate them. The researcher must decide which are primary and which are secondary sources. The source materials must be subjected to *external criticism,* the tool for establishing the validity of the document. The question to be answered is: Is the document genuine, authentic, and what it seems to be?

Establishing the validity of materials concerns several possible factors, any of which could make the document invalid. With written material, the status of the author in the context of the event is important. Was the author in a position to make a valid record of the event? Was he an on-the-spot observer, if the document appears to be a primary source? Are factors such as time and place consistent with what is known about the event?

Since the practice of using ghost writers is common, a document which appears to be the product of a direct observer may in fact be a secondary source. The ghost writer's unique contributions may inadvertently or deliberately threaten the validity of the document. There are also possibilities of inadvertent mechanical errors. A word may be mistranslated or an error made in typing or transcribing documents. For source materials produced before the advent of printing, copy errors in reproduced documents are very likely. Printing has not eliminated the possibility of such errors, but it has reduced their likelihood.

The possibility of deliberate frauds, distortions, and forgeries may be very real. Modern technology has developed methods of checking the authenticity of objects and documents, including X-ray and radioactivity procedures to establish age of materials. Alterations in the original document can also be detected by technological methods. In subjecting material to external criticism, the historical researcher must make a decision as to whether he finds the material genuine. Since, obviously, the researcher cannot relive the experience of when the material first came into being, his decision must be somewhat arbitrary. If the researcher finds damaging evidence, the acceptance of the material is highly questionable. Lack of such evidence does not guarantee authenticity, but it does have a positive aspect in that the material has survived the initial round of scrutiny.

The second step of critical evaluation is the step of *internal criticism,* which establishes the meaning of the material along with its trustworthiness. There may be some overlap between external and internal criticism, but the shift in emphasis is from the actual material to the content of the material. In a broad sense, external criticism precedes internal criticism in the sequence, since there is little point in dealing with the content of the material if its authenticity is doubtful. However, consider the external criticism directed toward the author of what appears to be a historical document. In establishing his status it may very well be necessary to evaluate some of the content he has written. This essentially becomes internal criticism. The distinction between external and internal criticism is not one of methodology but one of purpose.

The author is an important factor in evaluating the content of a document as well as establishing the authenticity of the document. A pertinent question of internal criticism is whether the author was predisposed, because of his position or otherwise, to present a biased rather than an objective account. Biographies and autobiographies may tend to shift the emphasis from the event to the person. Fictitious details may be included by the author because of some personal factor. An author who was opposed to an existing educational policy will tend to emphasize different factors than one who was favorable toward the same policy at the same time would. For situations such as this, the position or status of the author is very important in ascribing meaning to his statements.

An analysis of the author's style and use of rhetoric is important in evaluating his statements. Does the author have a tendency to color his writings by eloquent but misleading phrases? Is part of the writing figurative rather than a record of the real event? If the question of figurative and real meaning arises, the researcher must be able to distinguish between the two. Does the author borrow heavily from documents already in existence at the time of his writing? If he does, is his document an objective restatement of the facts, or do his own interpretations come into his writings? The latter is more likely the case. The researcher should check the reporting of the author for consistency with the earlier sources. This process should also give indications of the separation of fact and interpretation.

The question of accuracy runs through all of internal criticism (as well as external criticism). There are two parts to the question of the accuracy of a specific author. Was he competent to give an accurate report and, if competent, was he predisposed to do so? A competent reporter may, for some reason, give a distorted account of the event. In checking several authors there may be inconsistencies even about such facts as the date of a specific event. In such a case the researcher must weigh the evidence and decide upon what appears to be the most accurate account.

A single document, even a primary source, can seldom stand on its own. Internal criticism involves considerable cross-referencing of several documents. If certain facts are omitted from an account, this should not be interpreted to mean that the author was unaware of them or that they did not occur. Each document should be evaluated in its chronological position; that is, it should be evaluated in the light of the documents that preceded it, not in the light of documents that appeared later. If several sources contain the same errors, they are likely to have originated from a common erroneous source. If two sources are contradictory, it is certain that at least one is in error, but it is also possible that both are in error. The discounting of one account does not establish the trustworthiness of another. A specific document may prove valuable for certain parts of the overall research problem and essentially useless for other parts.

Synthesis, analysis, and conclusions

Internal criticism carries over into the third step of the methodology, that of synthesis of the information. The researcher now has his materials and, at least to his own satisfaction, has established the authenticity and value of the materials. However, the relative value of the various materials must be considered. As the researcher systematically checks through the evidence on which he will retain or reject his hypotheses, he must weigh the evidence of the various sources. It is a serious error either to overestimate or underestimate a source. The researcher guards against such errors by taking into account the factors used to establish the validity and value of the sources. For example, a primary source may be given more weight than a secondary one.

Synthesis leads to the fourth and final step of the methodology of historical research, although there is no clear-cut separation between the third and fourth steps. The final step is characterized by decision making on the research problem. The entire evidence must be weighed, central ideas or points pulled together, and inconsistencies resolved, at least to the satisfaction of the researcher.

The researcher must be careful at this fourth step not to introduce the error of bias. Bias could enter, for example, if the researcher is partial to a hypothesis and tends to retain it even if the evidence points against it. The problem of avoiding the error of bias involves remaining objective in analyzing the data. Judgments will have to be made, but they should be as objective as possible.

The educational research problems investigated by historical research generally deal with either policy or practices. The nature of history and historical inquiry places this limitation on historical research. In a certain sense the problems investigated by historical research have an ongoing characteristic. Many of the important educational issues are temporarily dealt with by relying on the perspective supplied by the history of the issue. Curriculum change is often viewed in the light of past philosophy, ideas, developments, and curriculums. Historical research is necessary to define the situation of the past and its meaning in the light of the present problem. Interpretations based on historical research thus can aid in defining a course of action dealing with a present educational problem.

The historical researcher may be looking for any one or a combination of things in his research endeavor. He may be searching only for accuracy of the facts. More likely, he will be looking for cause-and-effect situations of the past; he may carefully scrutinize the interactions of two or more relevant factors that were present during the period under study. A valid and adequate interpretation, whether new or old, of some event or idea may be the basic purpose of the research. The specific goals will depend upon the specific research problem. Sometimes problems need redefinition. This could go in both directions— narrowing and broadening the problem. It may be that the initial statement of the research problem is too broad to provide a direction of attack. On the other hand, the available source material may be too limited to provide a satisfactory resolution of the problem. Additional related ideas, points, or topics may be required in order to research the problem adequately. The isolation of the problem may be impossible, and a broadening may be necessary for this reason. That is, the materials cannot be adequately evaluated and interpreted without the addition of factors which broaden the original problem.

A good summary of the methodology of historical research is presented in the definition given by Walter Borg and Meredith Gall: "The systematic and objective location, evaluation, and synthesis of evidence in order to establish facts and draw conclusions concerning past events."[8] A historical research study involves a great deal of attention to detail. In addition to a knowledge of the methodology, the researcher must possess a background knowledge of the problem. Critical appraisal and adequate evaluation are necessary. The researcher who is planning to do historical research should prepare himself in the methodology, just as an experimenter learns about experimental design and a survey researcher masters survey design.

CONCLUDING REMARKS

This chapter has discussed research methodology of a nonexperimental nature. Three broad types of research were discussed: *ex post facto, survey,* and *historical.* Other nonexperimental methods of inquiry might have been included, such as case studies and philosophic research. The

8. W. R. Borg and M. D. Gall, *Educational Research, An Introduction,* 2d ed. (New York: David McKay Co., 1971), p. 260.

fact that they are not discussed in this text should not be interpreted to mean that these methods are not recognized as legitimate research methods. Rather, they have limited application in education as research techniques. Case studies, for example, find greater use for guidance and diagnostic purposes than for research purposes.

The research situation in education, as in any behavioral discipline, is one in which both experimental and nonexperimental research is conducted. Both types of research have their functions, and both have unique situations of application. Since this is the case, the general question of which type is better is not applicable.

Any researcher should keep in mind that nonexperimental research does not have the degree of control found in experimental research. However, it does not follow that educational problems will be solved if we concentrate on rigorous experimentation, to the detriment or elimination of nonexperimental research. Good experimental and nonexperimental research are both needed in education. Research should be conducted in the context of hypotheses, and the research procedures should test the hypotheses. Care should always be taken in treating and interpreting the results, but with nonexperimental research such as an *ex post facto* study the degree of care and caution required is greater.

SUGGESTED STUDY EXERCISES

5.1. A researcher is interested in what effects location of the school, grade level, and sex of the student have upon performance on a critical thinking test. He locates his population, draws a random sample, and measures the sample. Discuss why this is an example of *ex post facto* research rather than an experiment. Identify the "independent" and "dependent" variables. Grades seven through nine are included and two locations of school, rural and urban. Suppose critical thinking is measured on an interval scale. What would it mean if an interaction was found between location of school and sex of the student?

5.2. A researcher hypothesizes that there is a relationship between family instability as evidenced by divorce and poor academic performance of junior high school students. How would one go about determining the existence or lack of such a relationship? Suppose the researcher found evidence of such a relationship. What alternate hypotheses other than the existence of divorce might explain the poor performance?

5.3. The director of institutional research at a college is concerned about the reasons why undergraduates drop out before graduation. Each student who drops out is sent a questionnaire, as soon as it is known that the student is not returning. Construct items that might be used in this questionnaire. Discuss the reasoning that would go into your items. Suggest possible checks on the "truthfulness" of responses. Is nonresponse likely to be a problem, and what information could be obtained about those not responding? Classify this type of survey in the classification scheme presented in this chapter.

5.4. The Department of Guidance and Counseling in a state department of education is planning to survey the secondary guidance counselors of the state, in an attempt to determine their specific professional duties and the time spent weekly on each duty. A random sample of guidance counselors will receive the three-page questionnaire by mail. Prepare a cover letter for this questionnaire. Whose signature (position, not the individual) would you suggest for the cover letter?

5.5. A survey is made of the attitudes of teachers toward the new mathematics. A brief one-page questionnaire of items is sent to a random sample of teachers in a tristate area. Primary, junior high, and senior high teachers are included in the sample. Construct three or four items for the questionnaire that might reflect the relationship between the attitudes and one or more other educational variables. Discuss how you would deal with nonresponse which is likely to occur. What provisions would you make ahead of time for checking the nonrespondents?

5.6. Suppose the study of Exercise 5.5 were changed to a status survey, involving the same sample and a questionnaire, with the purpose of determining the number of teachers and the extent to which teachers use the new mathematics in instruction. Construct a short questionnaire (one page or less) of items whose responses are fixed and easily tabulated. With this change in the purpose of study, do you think your nonresponding group would change? If so, how?

5.7. Discuss the advantages and disadvantages of the use of an interview for survey research. Do the same for the questionnaire, and then compare the circumstances under which each would be the preferable technique.

5.8. In a liberal arts college of approximately 6,000 undergraduate students, a study of student attitudes toward the general education requirement is to be conducted. The researcher is also interested in the change of attitude throughout the college career. One approach would be to design a longitudinal study, beginning with the present freshman class and surveying a sample of this population at four yearly points. Another approach would be to use a cross-sectional design, selecting random samples from the four undergraduate populations and surveying them at one point in time. Discuss the merits and disadvantages of the two types of designs.

5.9. An educational products publishing firm is conducting a five-year longitudinal survey of teacher opinion and use of its products. The survey is conducted in a large city system, and a random sample of teachers is selected to serve as a panel for a panel study. Data will be collected from the panel every six months. What is to be gained by using a panel study as the longitudinal design? Discuss some disadvantages and potential difficulties of this panel study.

5.10. The parents of the students in a single school are to be surveyed about their opinions of a new grading system and report card. Under what conditions would you suggest a longitudinal design over a cross-sectional design, and vice versa? Suppose the school has around 350 students. Would you suggest selecting a random sample or surveying the entire population? Present at least one reason for your answer.

5.11. Select an article from a research (or other) publication which deals with an example of historical research. Read the article carefully to detect the methodology used by the author in collecting information and arriving at conclusions. Consider such things as whether or not primary sources were used and the synthesis of the available information. Identify the author's hypotheses and the evidence used in making decisions about the hypotheses.

5.12. The individual who engages in historical research is limited in the matter of validity in terms of the documents from which he acquires information. Discuss possible procedures that might be used in establishing validity of information. Contrast this with the validity of information when conducting an experiment.

5.13. Consider individually, and possibly discuss in small groups, a list of criteria for deciding when to use experimental or nonexperimental research designs.

5.14. For each of the examples listed below indicate what type of research is most likely called for: experiment, *ex post facto*, survey, or historical.

   a. An indicator of the likelihood of passing a school district's bond proposal.
   b. The effects of drill exercises upon the development of computational skills in arithmetic.
   c. The basis for the age-graded school.
   d. The relationship between psychomotor skills and achievement in academic areas.
   e. Precedents for the establishment of a dress code.
   f. The effect of attitude toward school upon achievement in science.
   g. The attitude toward school of science students.

chapter 6

Concepts of measurement

KEY CONCEPTS

Rules of measurement
Observed score
Error component and true component
Reliability of measurement
Coefficient of reliability
Parallel forms
Coefficient of equivalence
Test-retest procedure
Coefficient of stability
Split-half method
Spearman-Brown step-up formula
Kuder-Richardson techniques
Test norms
Objectivity in test scoring
Validity of measurement
Content validity
Concurrent and predictive validity
Criterion measure
Construct validity
Test score stability
Common factor variance
Coefficient of validity

The educational researcher of any degree of sophistication realizes that if his data are inadequate or incomplete the entire study is destined for failure. No matter how carefully the hypotheses are stated or how precise the analysis, adequate measurement is essential to research, and in any research project careful attention must be given to the measurement through which the data are to be obtained. This chapter will discuss basic concepts of measurement that are relevant to the procedures of a research project.

THE MEANING OF MEASUREMENT

The four general types or levels of measurement scales—nominal, ordinal, interval, and ratio—were defined in Chapter 2. Measurement can be defined as "the assignment of numerals to objects or events according to rules."[1] A numeral is a symbol of the type 1, 2, 3 . . . , devoid of either quantitative or qualitative meaning unless such meaning is assigned by a rule. The *rules of* a particular *measurement* situation are the guides by which the assignment of numerals proceeds in a particular situation. It is with the rules that most difficulties that can result in haphazard and inadequate measurement arise.

Adequate rules are necessary for adequate measurement. If we want to weigh a group of adult males for a research study, determining the weight to the nearest pound may be adequate for the purpose of the particular study. However, for a chemist experimenting with rare compounds, measurement to the nearest pound is entirely unsatisfactory from an experimental point of view. In the case of the chemist, a modified rule is necessary. If he can empirically define his requirements, then measurement is at least theoretically possible.

Educators are involved in a great deal of measurement. Before entering the public schools, a child has several measurements taken, including age and height. Generally, these are variables for which the measurement rules are well defined and present no difficulty. Entire texts have been written about measurement procedures, and many complicated and unresolved measurement problems can arise in specific situations.

The problems of measurement in a research context can essentially be resolved with adequate answers to the two questions of what to measure and how to measure it. While the first of these may seem somewhat superficial, in fact it is not. Naïve researchers have been known to assemble a considerable quantity of data, tabulate the numerals in orderly fashion on sheets of paper, and, upon being asked what the data represent, be at a loss for an adequate answer. The primary question in their minds is what to do with the data, which is putting the cart before the horse. In measurement, it is good policy to know what you want to measure before you attempt the measurement.

The first step in measurement, then, is an attempt to operationally define what is to be measured. Note the emphasis on an operational definition. For example, a researcher might be interested in measuring the ability of his Ss to solve problems using the deductive method. A commonly accepted definition of deduction is reasoning from a premise to a logical conclusion. Thus, to measure performance using the deductive process in problem solving, it would be necessary to provide items posing problems to be solved by reasoning from a premise to a logical

1. F. N. Kerlinger, *Foundations of Behavioral Research,* 2d ed. (New York: Holt, Rinehart & Winston, 1973), p. 426.

conclusion. The researcher must also consider the level of his *S*s, since items must be so constructed that the *S*s can understand them. As a sample, the following item presents a problem in deduction:

From the statements below reason to the logical conclusion
All dogs are animals
Rover is a dog
The logical and correct conclusion would be
Rover is an animal.

Responding to items such as the above provides operational evidence of the *S*'s mastery of the deductive process.

Assuming an operational definition, the researcher can then consider the rules by which to accomplish the measurement. The data analyzed in many research studies consist of the performance scores on one or more tests. A single performance score is a sampling of one *S*'s behavior. In research, we are usually interested in groups of *S*s rather than individual *S*s. The test itself is a procedure for comparing the behavior (or samples of behavior) of two or more *S*s.

The word "test" is used in this discussion to mean a data gathering device for research purposes. A single test may serve several purposes in the educational setting. For example, the same test, in fact the same score or set of scores on the test, may be used for grading, diagnostic, or research purposes.

QUANTITATIVE CONCEPTS OF TEST SCORES

After the researcher has operationally defined what is to be measured and completed the assignment of numerals according to his rules, he is confronted with a distribution of scores, each representing the performance of one *S*. What does any one score represent quantitatively with respect to the *S*? Suppose a certain *S* has attained a score of 82 on an achievement test. Can this score and others in the distribution be partitioned into meaningful segments?

It is generally recognized that few, if any, tests are perfect. Hence, the scores obtained on tests are fallible and not free from error. A single *observed score* contains what we shall call an *error component*. The error component may be due to any of a number of factors, usually unknown, associated with a specific administration of the test to the *S*. The remainder of the observed score may then be considered a nonerror or *true component*.

The true component may be viewed as the *S*'s score if we had a perfect measuring device. Suppose the test had been independently administered a large number of times to a single S and we assume that the error components are randomly distributed around zero. That is, both positive and negative error scores would appear and would tend to cancel each other over a large number of scores. Under these circumstances, the true component can be defined as the mean of this large number of scores. This is a theoretical concept of the true component, since a large number of independent administrations to the same S is usually physically impossible.

Suppose that we let Y_o represent the observed score, Y_t the true component, and Y_e the error component. We can then express the observed score as the sum of the two components. In equation form, this expression would consist of $Y_o = Y_t + Y_e$. This represents a partitioning of the observed score of a single S into the two independent parts.

The researcher has to consider not one score but a *distribution of scores*. If we think of the observed scores in terms of their two components, we have three distributions, two of which are theoretical. We can assume that in a large distribution of scores the error components are uncorrelated with the true components. That is, the size of the true component does not influence the size of the error component. Also, error components are assumed to be both positive and negative, and in a large distribution of scores the mean of the error scores would be zero. If in any one of the three distributions we summed all scores and divided this sum by the number of scores, we would have the *mean of the distribution*. (This is operationally possible only for the observed distribution, however.) Since the true and error components are independent, the relationship between the means may be expressed as $\overline{Y}_o = \overline{Y}_t + \overline{Y}_e$. However, we have assumed that for a large number of scores the mean of the distribution of error components ($\overline{Y}_e$) is zero. Therefore, the observed mean is equal to the mean of the true components.

The variances of the three distributions must also be considered. The concept of variance was introduced in Chapter 2, where is was noted that *variance* is a measure of the dispersion in a distribution. The variance of the observed distribution can be represented by s_o^2. The theoretical components would also have their respective variances, if the distributions were known. Since the true and error components are uncorrelated, the variance of the observed scores may be expressed as the summation of the variances of the component distributions. In keeping with our notation, the s_o^2 may be expressed as $s_o^2 = s_t^2 + s_e^2$. This expression is helpful in developing the concept of reliability, which is discussed in the following section.

RELIABILITY OF MEASUREMENT

An important concept of measurement is reliability. In a word, *reliability* means consistency—consistency of the test in measuring whatever it does measure. Reliability can be conceptualized in terms of the theoretical partitioning of a test score into the true and error components, which were introduced in the preceding section. We have seen that a score can be partitioned into these two parts and, correspondingly, if we have a distribution of observed scores, this variance can also be partitioned into two variances: one that of the true components and the other that of the error components. A theoretical definition of *reliability* is the ratio of the true variance to the variance of the observed scores, that is, reliability is the proportion of the variance in the observed scores that is nonerror. If we let r represent the reliability, the expression $r = s_t^2 / s_o^2$ defines the reliability. We know that $s_o^2 = s_t^2 + s_e^2$. Therefore, an equivalent expression for reliability is $r = 1 - s_e^2 / s_o^2$. The symbol r is called the *coefficient of reliability* or the *reliability coefficient*. From the theoretical expression of reliability it can be seen that r can range from plus one when there is no error in the measurement to zero when the measurement is all error. (If there is no error, s_e^2 is zero, and if measurement is all error, $s_e^2 = s_o^2$.) Empirically, negative reliability coefficients are possible.

Reliability is strictly a statistical concept. Coefficients of reliability cannot be determined by a subjective investigation of the test items. The test must actually be administered to a group of Ss and the reliability coefficient computed from the scores. The greater the value of the coefficient, the higher the reliability of the test. There are several different methods for empirically estimating the reliability of a test. For a specific test only one method is used, depending upon conditions of the test administration. Three methods commonly used are discussed in the following section: parallel forms, test-retest, and split-half methods. Kuder-Richardson single-test techniques are also mentioned.

Empirical procedures for determining reliability

The publishers of standardized tests commonly use two or more equivalent forms of a test in establishing reliability. The forms, called *parallel forms,* have equal means and variances when administered to a defined group of Ss. If more than two parallel forms exist, we would expect the intercorrelations between forms to be approximately equal. The parallel forms are usually administered to a group of Ss, with a short time interval between the administrations. (As the time interval increases, the possibility of extraneous fluctuation of the scores also increases.) The scores of the two administrations are then correlated. If the test is reliable, we would expect a high positive correlation coefficient; Ss who score high on one form should be the high scorers on the other form. The correlation between the two forms is called the *coefficient of equivalence*.

Parallel forms of a test are not always available. Sometimes, even if two forms are available, it is not feasible to administer two separate tests. When only one form of a test exists or the administration of only one form is feasible, it may still be possible to establish reliability through the use of such a technique as the *test-retest procedure*. This involves administering the same test to a group of Ss more than one time, after an intervening time period. The correlation between the scores of the two administrations of the same test is a measure of reliability. Such a correlation is called the *coefficient of stability*.

The test-retest method may be unavailable for several reasons. It may be impossible to administer the test a second time, or the second administration may be delayed for a considerable time. Such a delay is likely to introduce new and possibly relevant factors. In the educational setting, performance on achievement tests is especially susceptible to such factors. A one-form method which requires only one administration is the *split-half method*. The test is split into two halves, each half scored independently of the other with the items of the two halves matched on content and difficulty. The scores of the two halves are then correlated, and this correlation coefficient is the reliability coefficient on the half test. A special formula known as the *Spearman-Brown step-up* is used to estimate the reliability of the whole test. This formula is given by:

$$r_w = \frac{2r}{1 + r},$$

where r_w is the reliability of the whole test and r is the correlation between the two halves.

The split-half technique has the advantage of requiring only one administration of the test. A difficulty with this method is that it requires matched halves of the test, which may be difficult to achieve. If the test items are arranged in order of increasing difficulty, the odd-even method of splitting the test is commonly used. The application of the Spearman-Brown formula also assumes equal variability in the two half-test distributions.

An inspection of the formula for the split-half method reveals that empirically the reliability coefficient could take on negative values if the correlation between the two halves is negative. If negative correlations appeared with parallel forms or test-retest methods, we would also have a negative reliability coefficient, but negative correlations under these conditions would be very unusual and would indicate a complete lack of reliability. In the theoretical formula this would mean that the error variance would exceed the total variance, a theoretical impossibility. However, due to lack of reliability and unique fluctuations of the scores, it is empirically possible to have a negative reliability coefficient.

Formulas also exist for the estimation of reliability without splitting the test. These were devised by George Kuder and M. W. Richardson and go by various KR numbers. Unfortunately, the computational procedures are rather laborious. Books devoted to measurement usually contain detailed discussions of the *Kuder-Richardson techniques*.[2]

A word of caution relative to speeded tests: A *speeded test* is one on which the Ss would perform better if given additional time. The Kuder-Richardson formulas and the split-half technique do not apply to speeded tests because they tend to overestimate the reliability of such tests.

The empirical procedures for estimating reliability are susceptible to factors that can cause the scores to fluctuate. Robert Thorndike and Elizabeth Hagen have identified four such sources as:

1. Variations arising within the measurement procedure itself.
2. Changes in the individual from day to day.
3. Changes in the specific sample of tasks.
4. Changes in the individual's speed of work.[3]

All of the methods for estimating reliability discussed above are susceptible to variations arising within the measurement procedure itself. The test-retest method is susceptible to changes in the individual's speed of work, and if there is an intervening time interval between administrations, this method is also subject to changes in the individual from day to day. If parallel forms with an intervening time interval are used, all sources of variation can be present. Parallel forms administered with a very short time interval between administrations eliminate day-to-day changes in the individual, however. The split-half method and the Kuder-Richardson single-test procedures are susceptible to changes in the specific sample of tasks, but are not affected by

2. As an example the reader is referred to W. A. Mehrens and I. J. Lehmann, *Measurement and Evaluation in Education and Psychology* (New York: Holt, Rinehart & Winston, 1973), p. 113.

3. R. L. Thorndike, and E. Hagen, *Measurement and Evaluation in Psychology and Education,* 2d ed. (New York: John Wiley & Sons, 1961), p. 182.

changes in the individual from day to day or in the individual's speed of work. These factors should be kept in mind when considering reliability coefficients based on the various procedures.

The educational researcher must pay close attention to the measuring devices used in his study. If standardized tests are used, the manuals usually contain discussions of reliability. The manual for a battery of standardized tests commonly has a table of reliability coefficients, as well as *norms* consisting of descriptive statistics about a reference group of *S*s on whom the test was standardized. The researcher should check to be certain that his population corresponds adequately to the normative group, because reliability coefficients for one group will not necessarily hold for another. Norms presented in a test manual must be relevant to the study being conducted.

Objectivity in test scoring is defined as the extent to which equally competent scorers get the same results. Objectivity should not be confused with accuracy of scoring (inadequately trained scorers can exhibit a great deal of inaccuracy). Rather, objectivity is closely associated with reliability. Generally, an objective test has higher reliability than a subjective test. Note that objectivity is not concerned with type of item. Objective tests do not necessarily consist of short-answer or factual type items, although we often associate multiple-choice, short-answer items with objective tests. The objectivity is in the scoring, not in the type of item.

Objective tests are occasionally criticized on the basis that they do not do the job, that is, they do not measure adequately. The criticism arises from the fact that ensuring objectivity may impose undesirable characteristics on the items, such as too much structure or providing the examinee with the alternatives. Overemphasis on objectivity can reduce the range and depth of measurement. However, since increased objectivity tends to increase reliability, it is advisable to retain as much objectivity as possible without sacrificing adequate measurement.

The reliability of a test is influenced by the range on the scale of measurement of the group being tested. As the range increases, the reliability tends to be higher. The reliability coefficient is an indication of how consistently the test places each *S* relative to the others in the group. As the scores become more spread out, that is, as the range of the scores increases, it becomes easier to place the *S*s. For example, if a standardized test of science achievement had a range of measurement spanning 50 points it would be easier to consistently place *S*s in their positions relative to each other than if the range of measurement were only 20 points.

The reliability of a test tends to increase with increased length, assuming that any new items added are homogeneous with the original items. Homogeneous in this context means of equal difficulty and of similar content. In terms of the variances, the component of error variance is associated with individuals and will tend to remain stable as the length increases. The true variance component is associated with the content of the test, and as the length is increased this component tends to increase. Thus, when we increase the length, the true variance component tends to encompass a greater proportion of the total observed variance.

The question of high and low reliability and, more appropriately, the minimum reliability that is acceptable does not have a specific answer which covers all tests and situations. The business of high and low is, of course, a relative thing. The question must be answered in the light of existing information and previous results. An achievement test with a reliability of .65 might be undesirable if existing tests in the academic discipline have reliabilities in the .90's. On the other hand, a reliability of .65 on a theme-writing test may seem very good if previous results indicate reliability coefficients of .50 and less.

VALIDITY OF MEASUREMENT

A second important concept of measurement is validity. The _validity of a test is defined as the extent to which a test measures what it is supposed to measure._ The objective determination of validity is not a simple matter. There are two basic approaches to this problem. One is through a logical analysis which is essentially concerned with the measurement of a trait; this is essentially a judgmental analysis. The other approach, through an empirical analysis, is concerned with criterion measurement. The criterion measure might be the performance on a task or test, or it could be a measure such as job performance. In the empirical approach we are basically interested in correlation between the test performance and the selected criterion.

Content validity

An approach to validity through a logical analysis is the consideration of content validity. _Content validity_ refers to the extent to which the test items reflect the academic discipline or behavior under study. It involves a systematic investigation of the test items to determine whether they make up a representative sample of the behavioral dimensions or traits to be measured. This approach to validity is commonly used in achievement tests.

The basic idea may appear to be simple, but the actual procedure can be quite tedious and involved. Several precautions must be taken. For example, when using an achievement test the researcher must be certain that all the major topics are adequately covered and in the corresponding proportions. A difficulty which may arise is that a specific topic is overrepresented because its content lends itself especially well to the construction of certain kinds of items.

When establishing the content validity of a test the specific objectives of the activity which the test is designed to measure should be well defined. For example, if in an experiment the levels of the independent variable were two or more instructional treatments, the objectives of that instruction should be defined. This definition is necessary so that the objectives will be adequately reflected in the measurement device. For example, an objective of instruction may be the acquisition of factual information, but this may be only one of several instructional objectives. Nevertheless, the test may be so constructed that it reflects only a knowledge of factual information. If all the objectives cannot be adequately measured by items requiring only factual knowledge, the test will be lacking in content validity. For this reason, test content must be broad enough to cover the objectives specified adequately. The test must contain the application of procedures which reflect all the objectives. Test items also should reflect the desired behavior and not only an apparent behavior. Close scrutiny of a test item can fail to reveal the S's behavior in responding to the item; for example, the logical sequence used in solving a concept-attainment problem may not be apparent from the S's correct or incorrect responses alone.

When considering content validity care must be taken not to overgeneralize what the item (or test) is measuring. For example, in an item concerned with the selection of reasons for statements in a geometry proof, the correct association of reasons with given statements should not be interpreted as meaning that the S could construct the entire proof, that is, actually select the statements. Neither does identifying errors in a given proof measure the ability to construct a correct proof from memory.

Factors that are irrelevant to the content tested but not to the S's responses can influence performance on the test. Examples include the mechanics of marking a special answer sheet and confusion between item numbers and their response numbers on the answer sheet.

Content validity may be checked by some empirical analysis. If two parallel forms of a test are available, before and after instruction scores may be compared. From the standpoint of test construction this procedure is entirely acceptable; for research purposes, however, the validity may be confounded with an effect built into the research design. For example, in an experiment using the pretest-posttest control group design, the validity would be confounded with the experimental effect.

The determination of content validity usually involves detailed analyses of content, objectives, and representativeness of a universe of items as well as the test items themselves, and opinions of experts in the area. These procedures are usually adequate for evaluating achievement tests. However, for measurement in the areas of aptitude and personality, content validity is not sufficient. Here some empirical analysis is necessary, usually involving concurrent validity or predictive validity.

Concurrent validity and predictive validity

Concurrent and predictive validity involve the relationship between the test scores and measures of performance on an external criterion. Correlation coefficients are usually computed between the test score and the performance score on the criterion measure. *Concurrent validation* is used if the data on the two measures, test and criterion, are collected at or about the same time. *Predictive validation* involves the collection of the data on the criterion measure after an intervening period, say six months from the time of data collection for the test being validated. This is the basic operational distinction between the two. There is also a distinction in the objectives of validation. Concurrent validity is based on establishing an existing situation, in other words, what *is,* whereas predictive validity deals with what is *likely* to happen. Specifically, the question of concurrent validity is whether or not the test scores estimate a specified present performance; that of predictive validity is whether or not the test scores predict a specified future performance.

The criterion measure of concurrent validity is not necessarily another test score given at the same time as the test being validated. It may consist of concurrent measures such as job success or grade-point average. The criterion measures used with predictive validity are often some types of job performance, certainly subsequent performance. Predictive validity is especially relevant when test results are used for the selection of personnel to fill positions.

Various techniques may be used for concurrent validation. Correlations may be computed between test scores on the new test and scores on a previously constructed test. This technique is often used when attempting to validate a more efficient test from the standpoint of time or administration, for example, a shorter test might be an adequate replacement for a longer one. This might be especially desirable in a research setting if a large sample were to be included in the study and long testing periods for data collection would not be feasible. It would then be well to test a small sample on both the short and long tests and determine the correlation between the measures. This correlation, along with the content of the shorter test, should indicate whether or not it is an adequate replacement for the longer test. The sample tested on both measures should be a random sample from the same population as the samples to be included in the research study.

Selection of a suitable criterion measure. Several possible sources of difficulty may be associated with the selection of the criterion measure. Performance in many areas may be difficult to quantify, if various facets of performance on a task or job do not yield any objective information. Then, too, extraneous factors over which there is essentially no control can affect performance, especially during the measurement period. An *S* may be required to perform under less than desirable conditions, for example with faulty equipment. Another difficulty is that criterion measures may be only partial in that they do not measure the performance under study because of practical limitations. For example, it is impossible to measure everything that makes for success as a college student.

What, then, makes for a good criterion measure? Thorndike and Hagen identify four desirable qualities: (1) relevance, (2) freedom from bias, (3) reliability, and (4) availability.[4]

Relevance is the extent to which the performance on the criterion measure is determined by the same factors that determine performance on the original or predicted measure. The degree of relevance may be based on a professional judgment of the test content in terms of its adequate representation of the measurement objectives. *Freedom from bias* means that all *S*s have equal opportunity of performing on the test or task. Examples of a bias would be a portion of the *S*s performing with faulty equipment or poorly printed tests. *Reliability* was discussed earlier; in this context, it means that the criterion measure remains stable. *Availability* means that the criterion measure is available and applicable for the specific situation.

Construct validity

Construct validity is a type of validity that can be established by both logical and empirical analyses. The term "construct" refers to the theoretical construct or trait being measured, not the technical construction of the test items. A construct is a postulated attribute or structure that explains some phenomenon, such as an *S*'s behavior. Because constructs are abstract, and are not considered to be real objects or

---

4. R. L. Thorndike and E. Hagen, *Measurement and Evaluation in Psychology and Education,* 3rd ed. (New York: John Wiley & Sons, 1969), p. 168.

events, they are sometimes called hypothetical constructs. Theories of learning, for example, involve constructs such as motivation, intelligence, and anxiety.

Quite often we relate one or more constructs to behavior in that we expect individuals to behave (or not behave) in a specified manner. The theory of frustration embraced by the researcher might include specific behavior patterns. For example, frustration increases as the individual unsuccessfully persists in a problem-solving task. The construct may be informally conceptualized with only a limited number of propositions, or it may be part or all of a fully developed theory. When using construct validation we are assuming that the individual's performance on the test reflects the attribute under study.

Construct validity involves a broader concept than the other types of validity, and establishing construct validity is more complex than establishing the other types. Concurrent validity, for example, can be examined by a single statistic, the correlation coefficient between the test scores and the criterion scores. Not so with construct validity, which involves a more long-term procedure including imagination, reasoning, and observation. There is an initial formulation of the construct, various deductions are made and tested through observation, and there is reformulation of the construct. The process is much like that of theory developing and testing. Lee J. Cronbach has suggested three parts to construct validation:

(1) Suggest what constructs might account for test performance. This is an act of imagination based on observation or logical study of the test. (2) Derive testable hypotheses from the theory surrounding the construct. This is a purely logical operation. (3) Carry out an empirical study to test this hypothesis.[5]

The three parts do not necessarily represent such a neatly ordered sequence of procedures in actual practice.

While establishing construct validity does not involve a single clear-cut procedure, we can suggest some general procedures that have proved effective for test validation. Certain informal procedures can be used, such as a close examination of the items and a pilot administration of the test with verbal description by the examinees. The latter may reveal that the meaning of scores is not consistent across individuals, since two individuals attaining similar scores can give quite different verbal descriptions.

Correlation coefficients between scores on the test and other tests related to the same general theory or construct are often cited as

5. L. J. Cronbach, *Essentials of Psychological Testing,* 3rd ed. (New York: Harper & Row, Publishers, 1970), p. 143.

empirical evidence of construct validity.[6] When using such tests, moderately high correlations are usually involved. However, correlations that are too high may be undesirable, since such correlations are indications that the test being validated measures nothing new. It may be desirable to show that the test is relatively free from the influence of other factors. For example, a spatial relations test should have a low correlation with performance on a reading achievement test. That is, we do not want the spatial relations test to be unduly influenced by reading achievement. A high correlation would tend to make the test invalid in that it is heavily influenced by reading achievement, a supposedly irrelevant factor. In a sense this is a negative approach, since the low correlation does not guarantee that the test measures spatial relations; the fact that the test does not measure reading achievement does not mean that it does measure spatial relations. It should be noted that test scores can also be correlated with performance on some practical criteria. It is not required that the measure be another test score.

We may also get some evidence of construct validity by studying the effect of an experimental treatment or some intervening variable on test performance. This involves a test-retest situation. Actually, the retest could be administered with only the normal events of the intervening time period coming between testings. This approach to validation is sometimes referred to as *test score stability*. Whether or not a high degree of stability is desirable depends on the theory underlying the construct. The intervention of certain factors might require a lack of stability in order to be consistent with the theory. The results of the test-retest must be interpreted accordingly.

The formulation of the construct may lead us to expect two groups, for example, men and women, to differ on the test. If the two groups are available for testing, this assumption can be tested. This is a relatively crude procedure for establishing validity, since most constructs in educational research are of such a nature that we would expect considerable overlap. Therefore, too great a differentiation between groups may indicate a lack of validity. For example, physical ability test items may correspond somewhat to age, but if performance on a task correlated around .90 with age, the validity of the task would certainly be questioned.

Construct validity plays an important role in many research efforts. This is due in part to the fact that many research activities involve the formation of constructs that cannot be operationally defined, at least

---

6. Correlation matrices and factor analysis can be used in construct validation. Although factor analysis for construct validity is beyond the scope of this book, the reader is referred to L. J. Cronbach, and P. E. Meehl, "Construct Validity in Psychological Tests," *Psychological Bulletin* 52 (1955): 281–302.

not immediately. Whenever this is the case, construct validity is involved in establishing the measurement of the attribute.

Validity and variance

In the previous discussion on reliability we saw that, theoretically, reliability may be expressed as the proportion of the variance in the observed scores, that is, true variance. For validity, we consider the variances of two distributions, the scores on the test and those on the criterion measure. Then to relate the two we consider the variance that the two measures have in common. Suppose we theoretically quantify the variances in terms of Venn diagrams, as in Figure 6.1. Let S_o^2 be the variance of the observed test scores, s_c^2 the variance of the criterion measure, and s_{co}^2 the *co-variation* or variance that the two have in common. This is also referred to as the *common factor* variance. In the diagram, s_o^2 would still contain error variance (s_e^2) and any variance not error or common with the criterion measure is variance specific to the observed distribution, represented in the diagram by s_{so}^2. The validity of a test is then defined as the proportion of the total observed variance that is common variance with the criterion measure. In symbol form, validity $= s_{co}^2/s_o^2$, or validity $= 1 - (s_{so}^2 + s_e^2)/s_o^2$.

The variance relation between reliability and validity is also relevant here. The true variance or s_t^2 introduced with reliability would be made

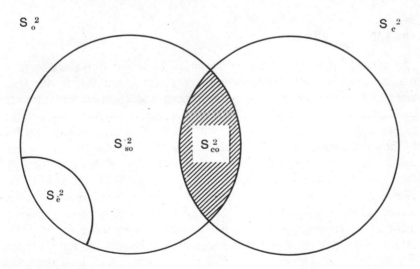

FIGURE 6.1. Theoretical partitioning of the variances of test and criterion measure distributions

up of the s_{so}^2 and s_{co}^2 of Figure 6.1. The total variance of the observed scores is composed of three parts, that is,

$$s_o^2 = s_{so}^2 + s_{co}^2 + s_e^2.$$

If we divide this equation by s_o^2 we get

$$\frac{s_o^2}{s_o^2} = \frac{s_{so}^2}{s_o^2} + \frac{s_{co}^2}{s_o^2} + \frac{s_e^2}{s_o^2}.$$

From this equation we can see that the proportion

$$\frac{s_{so}^2}{s_o^2} + \frac{s_{co}^2}{s_o^2} = \frac{s_{so}^2 + s_{co}^2}{s_o^2} = \frac{s_t^2}{s_o^2}$$

represents the reliability and the proportion s_{co}^2/s_o^2 represents the validity.

The variance equations show us that a test cannot be valid if it is not reliable. The s_{co}^2 is part of s_t^2, and hence if there were no true variance component there could be no covariation component. However, the reverse is not true. The test could be reliable but not valid. The true variance component could be made up entirely of the specific variance, and hence the covariation component would be zero.

A test must be reliable in order to be valid, but a test can be reliable without being valid. This relationship can be logically developed. A test that is consistently measuring the wrong thing is reliable but not valid. A test that is not consistent (reliable), however, can hardly be measuring what it is supposed to measure, and thus it cannot be valid.

The validity coefficient

The determination of validity by empirical techniques involves correlation between variables. The validity coefficients associated with tests are based on the correlations between tests and criterion measures. In some cases, especially when tests are used for prediction, parts of the criterion measure may be weighted differently. Validity is always specific to the particular measurement task. When a test manual or other literature reports that a test is valid (often supported by validity coefficients), the researcher must ask in what instance it is valid. The measuring device must be evaluated in the light of the specific objectives of the research study. A test that is valid for measuring the mathematics achievement of heterogeneous classes may not be valid for measuring the achievement of high-ability students in an experiment involving a modern mathematics curriculum. Validity coefficients must be interpreted in the context of the area of measurement and the specific research endeavor.

CONCLUDING REMARKS: THE NECESSITY
OF RELIABILITY AND VALIDITY

An ultimate objective of the educational researcher is to make a meaningful interpretation of his results. In order to do this, the measuring device or test must be reliable. Reliability is not a sufficient condition for good measurement, but it is certainly a necessary condition. The lack of reliability causes difficult and essentially insurmountable problems. Suppose a researcher is interested in the effect of an experimental treatment upon spelling achievement. Two samples are drawn, and one sample of Ss receives the experimental treatment while the other receives traditional instruction. A spelling test is used to measure spelling achievement, the dependent variable. Now suppose it is revealed that the spelling test used to measure achievement is unreliable. Whatever the results between the two samples, it is now impossible to ascribe the results to the experimental effect, since they could be due to the low reliability of measurement. Suppose the means of the two samples were being compared and the experimental group had a much higher mean score on the spelling test. Is this higher mean due to an experimental effect or unreliable measurement? This question cannot be answered, and no decision can be made on the results. The researcher's investigation has broken down for one apparent reason—the measurement was unreliable.

Validity is, of course, an essential requirement in a measuring device. In the above example, the researcher could hardly check an experimental effect upon spelling achievement if he did not have a test which measures spelling achievement. Inadequate measurement cannot be tolerated in educational research. The measuring devices must be examined logically and empirically for their validity and reliability.

In this chapter two basic concepts of measurement, reliability and validity, have been described. Most educational research projects are not primarily concerned with researching measurement per se, but adequate measurement is nevertheless essential to any empirical research study. Reliability is the consistency of the measuring instrument in measuring whatever it measures. Validity is the extent to which the measuring instrument is measuring what it is supposed to measure. The measurement instruments used in a research project should be both reliable and valid.

SUGGESTED STUDY EXERCISES

6.1 Discuss the distinction between the concepts of validity and reliability. Why do we say that measurement can be reliable without being valid, but that the reverse cannot be true?

6.2 Examine a standardized achievement test and propose a research problem for which it might serve as the measurement device. Identify the Ss for which the test would be appropriate and the population under study. Check on reliability and validity information of the test. The accompanying manual is the most likely source of such information.

6.3 A researcher plans to do a study about the extent of hostility in upper elementary classrooms taught by teachers classified as autocratic or democratic. Discuss the problem of establishing validity in measuring hostility. Assume that hostility can go both ways: from students to teacher and vice versa.

6.4 Define objectivity of a measuring instrument. Why is it an error to conclude that objectivity is limited to short-answer, factual type items? If a test item requires a response of around 200 words, how would objectivity be built into this item?

6.5 Discuss factors that affect the reliability of a test, such as the length of the test. Suppose a researcher plans to do an experiment on the teaching of science in grades three through eight and the dependent variable is to be performance on a science achievement test. What suggestions would you give in order to enhance the reliability of science achievement measurement?

6.6 A distribution of test scores has a variance of 90, and 65 of this variance is variance that the test has in common with the variance of a criterion test. What is the validity coefficient of this test? What sources of variance are contained in the proportion of variance not common with the criterion test?

chapter 7

Measurement and
data collection

KEY CONCEPTS

Objectively scored items
Direct observation
Self-report
Fixed-alternative and open-end responses
Measurement of achievement
Standardized achievement tests
Self-constructed tests
**Measurement of aptitudes: aptitude tests, intelligence tests, or
    mental ability tests**
Measurement of attitudes: Likert-type scale and Thurstone method
Response set
Unidimensionality
Measurement of personality
Trait
Personality inventory
Task measurement
Ethical considerations in conducting research

Since educational research can be broadly defined and it encompasses
a host of types of research, it is to be expected that the kinds of data
in educational research projects are also varied. To obtain this variety
of data, educational research utilizes a large number of different types
of measurement instruments or devices. In some research projects the
measurement requirements can readily be met through the use of
existing tests or instruments. For others, developing adequate measurement procedures may involve a substantial portion of the research effort. In any event, the researcher must know what kinds of data his
measurement is acquiring for him, as well as the reliability and validity
of the measurement.

TYPES OF MEASUREMENT DEVICES

The types of measurement devices considered here are not the measurement scales (nominal, ordinal, interval, and ratio) that were defined

in Chapter 2. Rather, they are types of tests, inventories, or instruments through which the data for a research study are collected.

In many research situations the S responds directly to some type of stimulus and in this way generates the research data. Examples would be a paper and pencil performance test on objectively scored items administered to a group of Ss or a self-report of experiences by the S. Data can also be collected when the researcher or someone not an S in the study records information on an inventory or schedule of some sort. Classroom observation of student-teacher interaction would be an example of this type of data collection. In some special instances data collection requires the use of equipment, such as a device to accurately measure an S's heart rate.

Objectively scored items

A common approach to the measurement of a phenomenon is to assemble a set of objectively scored items which relate to that phenomenon. The S's responses directly reflect the existence, absence, or extent of the phenomenon. Objectivity simply means that there is no question about whether or not a certain response reflects the phenomenon.

This approach to measurement is commonly used when testing achievement in academic and skills areas. The S responds to each item, the items are then scored on the basis of right or wrong, and the S is assigned a numerical value which is his score. Inferences are then made from the score to the S's behavior and to the behavior of his group. Multiple-choice and simple response items grouped together into tests are examples of such measuring devices. However, it should not be inferred that simplicity is a necessary condition for objectivity; an essay test might also be objectively scored. The objectivity is in the scoring, as was noted in the preceding chapter.

It should be noted that objectivity is a matter of degree. All tests contain some element of objectivity, and there is no sharp dichotomy between objective and nonobjective techniques.

Direct observation

Another measurement technique is the direct observation of behavior by a trained observer. This entails watching and noting what actually occurs. The basic problem with this technique is the interpretation of what is seen; different observers see different things in the same situation. The problem of inconsistency in the observation, even multiple meanings for terminology, is not easy to overcome. For example, in classroom observation, what is a dull class or a flexible class? What is a serious discipline infraction? In any research study, these types of terms must be defined as precisely as possible. Such definition is certainly helpful, but observed behavior often is dependent, at least in part, upon observer judgment for interpretation.

The data collected from direct observation are usually categorized as part of the analysis and may even be directly categorized during the observation. The establishment of categories is usually to some extent arbitrary. In order to establish a meaningful and useful set of categories, the researcher must be well informed in the area of study.

Although the establishment of the categories may be quite subjective, the classification of observed behavior (or whatever is being observed) into the categories should be made as objective as possible. For various studies direct observation might be highly objective, for example, if we were simply counting the number of times a student leaves the classroom. However, for most research situations more complex variables are under study.

Direct observation has its limitations, but there are many observational systems presently available for the study of educational phenomena. An example of a direct observation scheme for classifying the interaction in a classroom is the *Flanders interaction model*.[1] This model for classifying classroom behavior has had considerable use, especially in educational research. If observers are adequately trained, relatively high interobserver reliability (coefficients in the neighborhood of .90) has been established with the use of such models. The Flanders model involves a category system in which classroom interaction as interpreted by a trained observer is recorded (through a coding system) every three seconds. The coded information of the model presents a systematic account of the classroom proceedings. When direct observation is used in this manner, considerable effort and time must be reserved for the development of the system and mastery of its use. This is essential for usable data and interpretable results.

Direct observation does have some advantages. Assuming careful planning of the observational procedures and adequately trained observers, it provides a record of actual behavior which should be relatively free from observer bias. Direct observation can be effectively used in situations where other data-gathering procedures are not applicable, for example, with young children for whom written com-

---

1. N. A. Flanders, *Interaction Analysis in the Classroom* (Minneapolis: University of Minnesota Press, 1960). Also, for a more general discussion, see D. M. Medley and H. E. Mitzel, "Measuring Classroom Behavior by Systematic Observation," in N. L. Gage (ed.), *Handbook of Research on Teaching* (Chicago: Rand McNally & Co., 1963).

munication is impossible and verbal communication difficult. Direct observation is usually used in a natural situation, eliminating some of the artificial factors that can arise in a structured testing situation.

Self-report

Information also can be acquired by having an S tell what happened or relate an experience. An experience might be something like solving a problem, and the S could be asked to describe the logic by which the solution (right or wrong) was obtained. However, data obtained through self-report can become quite tenuous, because an interpretation by the S is included in addition to the interpretation of his remarks by the researcher. This procedure may also be quite laborious and time-consuming, since in almost any group certain Ss become highly verbal when asked to respond. Other factors associated with the Ss may also become extraneous factors which have an effect on the data.

With all its limitations, self-report can provide useful information, depending, of course, upon the conditions of the research situation. Suppose an educational psychologist is doing research on "learning to learn" and has his Ss perform a unique learning task. The Ss are learning how to do the task. After successfully completing one or more trials, the S is asked how he learned to do the task. If the researcher expects a relatively unsophisticated description of mental procedures, this may be forthcoming; if, however, he expects a technical psychological description, he is likely to be disappointed. The adequacy of the self-report also depends upon the sophistication of the Ss. Under certain conditions the S may simply not know how to respond, and such situations should be avoided with self-report. When studying selected sociological and cultural variables in the natural situation, self-report may be not only effective but, in essence, the only applicable procedure for securing the necessary information.

Interview and questionnaire items

Interviews and questionnaires are techniques used principally in survey research, as discussed in Chapter 5. The type of items commonly found in questionnaires and interviews is a matter related to data collection. Many of the comments on types of items are equally applicable for interviews and questionnaires. There is, however, a major difference in the delivery of the data collection, since the interview is a face-to-face confrontation, while the questionnaire is usually a written inventory, delivered and collected through the mail.

There is a great deal of variety in types of interviews and questionnaires, ranging from highly structured to almost completely unstructured. Structure refers primarily to the types of questions and anticipated responses; for example, must the respondent select one and only one of several options, or can he say as much and what he wants as a response? The purposes of the research and the situation in which the response is elicited influence the degree of structure.

The items or questions of an interview or questionnaire may take several forms, the two most common ones being the fixed-alternative response and the open-end response. The *fixed-alternative items* are exactly what the name implies: The respondent is asked to select one of two or more given alternatives. This type of item has the advantage of increasing consistency of measurement and hence reliability. The forced choice of one of the fixed alternatives is sometimes cited as a disadvantage; since the S is *required* to select one of the given alternatives, his choice may only approximate his true feeling. Also, this type of item in itself allows for no probing by the interviewer or any elaboration of response on the questionnaire. In an interview, probing might be pursued with additional items leading out of the S's response.

The *open-end question* imposes no restrictions on the respondent except that he stay within the framework of the specific question. The open-end question has obvious advantages and disadvantages. Such questions are more flexible and allow for probing, if this is desirable. They enable the interviewer to detect things such as ambiguity and respondents' feelings, and if a misunderstanding develops the interviewer may detect it and get it cleared up. With both the interview and questionnaire, open-end questions may elicit unanticipated responses which shed a new light on the research problem. Also, the respondent may be more cooperative when he is less restricted in his answer.

The open-end question may introduce additional variables associated with the Ss. Because the data may be quite diverse, the lack of uniformity may make the analysis difficult. The responses therefore are usually categorized by the investigator to impose some degree of uniformity on the data. Category systems are to a large extent arbitrarily constructed by the researcher. This in itself is no problem, but it is important that the category system be used consistently as the data are tabulated.

The construction of questions for an interview or questionnaire is a task which should be approached carefully and critically. The questions should, of course, reflect the objectives of the research, and the anticipated information should relate to the hypotheses. The statement of the question must be clear and unambiguous to the respondent; the fact that it is clear to the instrument constructor does not guarantee that it will be clear to the respondent. Questions should not be personally offensive to the respondent, nor should they suggest that one response is more desirable than another. Responses which are obviously socially or professionally preferable tend to invalidate the results, because the respondent may choose these even though this is not the way he feels. Above all, the respondent must be able to answer the questions; if he lacks information on the question, invalid data will tend to be produced.

THE MEASUREMENT OF ACHIEVEMENT

Because academic achievement (or lack of it) is one of the principal outcomes of the educational experience, considerable research is done on this topic. Multitudes of achievement tests, commonly known as *standardized achievement tests,* are commercially available. The measurement requirement of a research study in achievement is not met by simply taking the first standardized test available in the area of investigation and testing the Ss, however. To be sure, many standardized tests are excellent for research purposes, but the researcher must be careful in his selection. The test must be adequate for the objectives of the study and should not be inherently biased toward one or more of the groups. It would hardly be adequate to use a standardized American social studies test to ascertain whether United States or British students have greater knowledge in social studies, for example.

Standardized tests are usually broad and based on general content of the achievement area. This may be an advantage or disadvantage, depending upon the objectives of the research. The same is true about the information in the manual concerning reliability, validity, and norms. If norms are available for groups comparable to those being researched, this is a definite advantage. A misconception can result if the norms are not relevant and they are interpreted to be relevant. For many research studies, however, it is not necessary to have norms, since the emphasis is on comparison between the groups in the study and not with external groups.

The construction of a standardized test usually involves considerable effort on the part of experts. The researcher may not have comparable resources to devote to the construction of his measuring instrument. Standardized tests also can often be quickly and efficiently scored by the publisher. This is a definite advantage, especially for research studies which involve large quantities of data.

Thus the use of a standardized test greatly reduces the effort connected with the measurement of the data. However, it is not always possible to find a published test which will meet the objectives of the research. For example, in a study by Donald Dessart,[2] various types of programmed learning materials and traditional teaching were used to ascertain the effects upon learning the concept of limit. The study was conducted with elementary algebra students at the junior high school level and involved an instructional period of ten days. The unit or topic to be learned was very specific, and it is unlikely that a standardized test could be found which deals specifically with that topic. There may be items in standardized mathematics tests which relate to the limit concept, but it would not be efficient to use the entire test for a limited number of items. In such cases, it is necessary to construct an achievement test for the specific situation. The validity of such *self-constructed tests* can usually be established by a logical analysis of test content, and if at all possible reliability measures should be made on them. Such tests should be subject to investigations of validity and reliability prior to their use in a research project.

When self-constructed tests are used for research in achievement it is usually because they can meet the objectives of the measurement better than standardized tests can. They may also be preferred because of greater efficiency, since a standardized test may be much longer than is actually needed. Whether a standardized or self-constructed test is more efficient depends on the research situation. Flexibility can be built into a self-constructed test which is not possible in a standardized test.

Achievement tests are usually made up of objectively scored items, which can adequately measure the acquisition of factual knowledge. Other outcomes of learning, such as the application of concepts, can also be measured using such items. Achievement tests need not be limited to short items; free-response items of varying types and lengths can also be used. For example, in geometry achievement the *S* might be required to produce an entire proof of a theorem. Such an item could be objectively scored, although scoring time would be increased. Less objective items can also be used in achievement tests, although the use of such items might raise some difficulties relative to validity and reliability.

THE MEASUREMENT OF APTITUDES

Actual achievement and the potential ability for achievement are not the same thing, although operationally they may not be easy to separate.

2. D. J. Dessart, "A Study in Programmed Learning," *School Science and Mathematics* 62 (October 1962): 513–20.

The potential for achievement is called *aptitude*. Intelligence tests are the most commonly known measures for achievement in academic and skills areas, but other terms, such as "general scholastic ability" and "general mental ability" are being increasingly used to replace the term "intelligence." The difficulty with the term "intelligence" comes with the long-standing belief that intelligence tests somehow measure an inborn capacity, regardless of the individual's background, experiences, and the like. Many intelligence tests, however, are validated against tests of academic achievement. Lee J. Cronbach alludes to this problem as follows:

Much misuse or misinterpretation of mental tests arises simply from the labels "intelligence" and "capacity," as they suggest that inborn potentiality is being measured. Performance on the tests is influenced by many things not included in this concept of "intelligence." Each test calls for knowledge, skills, and attitudes developed in Western culture, and better developed in some Western environments than in others. A mental test gives only indirect evidence on "potentialities," as we can observe potentiality only when it has flowered in performance.[3]

The importance of Cronbach's remarks to the educational researcher is caution in assigning to the aptitude test a task that it clearly cannot do. This task is the identification of potential, independent of factors such as already existing achievement (or the lack thereof). When diverse groups, possibly those from subcultures within the larger culture, are being measured by aptitude tests, it should not be assumed that the tests are equally valid for all groups.

Aptitude tests, intelligence tests, and mental ability tests (whatever terminology is used) come in a variety of forms, commonly designated as individual or group tests. Individual tests tend to be more elaborate and may involve manipulation of objects, while group tests are usually limited to items on paper. The *Wechsler Adult Intelligence Scale* is an example of an individual test, and the *California Test of Mental Maturity* is an example of a group test.

The tests mentioned above are largely designed to measure global intelligence or ability. There are also aptitude tests that focus more on specific abilities. For example, the *Scholastic Aptitude Test* is highly oriented to the types of abilities learned in formal schooling, with the items emphasizing verbal and mathematical abilities. There are numerous batteries of aptitude tests that measure multiple aptitudes through a series of subtests or subscores, such as the *Differential Aptitude Test*. Such tests contain subtests of abilities such as mechanical reasoning, numerical ability, and space relations, to mention just a few.

---

3. L. J. Cronbach, *Essentials of Psychological Testing,* 3rd ed. (New York: Harper & Row, Publishers, 1970), p. 205.

An educational researcher using aptitude tests must carefully define their purpose in the research project. Specific tests anticipated for use must be considered in light of the Ss or groups of Ss to be included in the project. Aptitude measures find some use in educational research as control variables. For example, scores on an aptitude test may be used to classify Ss into the levels of an independent variable to be built into the design. Aptitude test scores may also be used as statistical controls.

The development or construction of an aptitude test is a difficult matter which requires a good deal of information, effort, and resources. For this reason aptitude tests are seldom self-constructed for a research project. Excellent sources of information about aptitude tests are found in testing books and books about tests.[4] The educational researcher must carefully select the test best suited to meet the needs of his project.

THE MEASUREMENT OF ATTITUDES

Tests of achievement or ability are concerned with the maximum or "best" performance of the S and are designed to measure maximum performance. Tests or measures of attitude and personality are concerned with *typical* performance. Maximum or best performance is a meaningless concept for most attitude and personality inventories.

Attitudes deal with existing feelings of an S toward such things as ideas, procedures, and social institutions. Note that the attitude is *toward* something. Usually we think of attitudes in such terms as acceptance-rejection or favorable-unfavorable. The intensity of feeling is not dichotomous but is usually considered to be measured by some kind of continuum between the extremes. It is placing the Ss on this continuum that is the job of the attitude inventory.

The items of an attitude inventory are commonly measured on a scale consisting of a number of points on the theoretical continuum to which the S can respond to indicate the intensity of his feeling. The minimum number of points would be two, although there are usually at least three, giving the S a neutral choice such as "undecided."

The Likert-type scale

A common type of attitude scale is the *Likert-type scale*, which consists of items assumed to have equal value. The various possible responses

---

4. See, for example, O. K. Buros (ed.), *The Seventh Mental Measurements Yearbook* (Highland Park, N.J.: Gryphon Press, 1972).

are assigned numerical values, and these values are summed over all items to give the S an attitude score. The sum or average, computed by dividing the sum by the number of items, may be designated as the score. However, this average is not a mean in the sense of interval scale measurement, it is a score indicating position on an ordinal scale. This score places the S on the agree-disagree continuum of the attitude under investigation.

As an example in which a Likert-type scale could be used, consider a researcher interested in the attitudes of high school seniors toward the school administration. Items are constructed consisting of statements to which the seniors respond. The possible choices for each item are: strongly disagree, disagree, undecided, agree, and strongly agree. The numerical values range from 1 to 5, respectively. (This assignment of numbers and the direction of agreement or disagreement are arbitrary. For example, zero to 4 could have been used, or the "agree" end of the scale could have been assigned the low numbers.)

The responses of each senior are assigned the values and summed (or averaged), and this becomes his score. In this case a high score would indicate agreement with the items and presumably a favorable attitude toward the administration. It is important that the items be so constructed that they are consistent in direction and scoring. That is, an "agree" response should not reflect an unfavorable attitude and be scored 5. Items which reverse direction may be retained if a corresponding adjustment is made in the scoring procedure. Usually the items are constructed so that the scoring is not complicated by reversing directions.

The construction of a Likert-type attitude scale is not simply a matter of writing a set of statements. This is only the initial step. The scale should be used in a trial run, which may reveal items that are ambiguous or inconsistent with the rest of the items. A further step is to correlate the scores of each item with the scores of the total test; this also may eliminate inconsistent items. If desirable the scale can be constructed with subscales, and scores can be acquired for the various subscales. If it is difficult to place an item in a subscale, or if it seems to fit in more than one scale, the scores on this item can be correlated with the subscale scores. The item is then placed in the subscale with which it has the greatest correlation. If appropriate, an item can be used for more than one scale.

The number of possible responses in the scale is arbitrary. Five or seven responses are common. The advantage of additional responses is that the greater variance in scores seems to make the scale more sensitive to differences in attitudes. If the variance is truly due to the differences in attitudes, this is fine, but confounded factors may contribute to the variance. Ss have a tendency to develop a *response set,* a tendency to respond in a certain manner due to a reaction to the construction of the scale, independent of the attitude being measured. For example, the middle-of-the-roader will respond near the center of the scale no matter how strongly he feels. Sometimes reversing the direction of certain items is used as a deterrent against response set, but as was mentioned above, reversing directions complicates the scoring.

The Likert-type attitude inventory yields numerical scores which appear to be measured on an interval scale. Although the scores can certainly be ordered, it may be difficult to make a case for equal units. In the scoring, the difference between "undecided" and "agree" is one point, as is the difference between "agree" and "strongly agree." It would be difficult to say that the two one-point differences represent the same difference in feeling. This lack of an equal unit is, of course, reflected in the total score.

The Thurstone method

Louis Thurstone grappled with this problem and developed what is called the *Thurstone method,* or equal-appearing interval scales. This is an attempt to place the Ss on a continuous scale having equal-appearing units, so that, for example, the difference in scores of 60 and 65 would be comparable to the difference in scores of 68 and 73. In the Thurstone method, each item is given a scale value ranging from zero to 11, from the unfavorable to favorable direction. Note that the items are scaled. The S then simply checks the items with which he agrees or a specified number of items with which he agrees most strongly. The score is an average of the numerical values of the items checked by the S.

A difficulty may arise in assigning the values to the items. The usual procedure is to have a panel of experts scale the items independently. If there is marked disagreement on the scaling of an item, the item is discarded. An item which is retained is given the median value assigned by the members of the panel. The initial choice of items to be used is the responsibility of the researcher. The choice is arbitrary, but the items should be carefully chosen in the light of existing knowledge and research about the attitudes.

The items retained by the panel should be tested in a trial run. Preferably the attitude inventory should be tested with Ss whose attitudes are known. This procedure may reveal items which are incorrectly scaled or are measuring different attitudes than the other items are measuring. Items that are ambiguous or poorly constructed should be exposed by the trial run.

Unidimensionality

Both the Thurstone-type and the Likert-type scales assume *unidimensionality;* that is, they deal with a single trait or dimension of the trait. A difference between the two types of scales is the methods by which the unidimensionality is attained. The Likert-type empirically establishes the unidimensionality of the scale through correlation, which consists of correlating the scores of each item with the total test score. Items correlating low with the total score are not measuring the same thing as the total score. Such items measure, if anything, a different trait. Items with low correlations are omitted, and the remaining items all measure one thing. Thus unidimensionality of scale is arrived at.

The unidimensionality of the Thurstone-type scale is arrived at through a judgmental process. The judges independently rate or scale the items, as was discussed before, and each judge places the items in position. If the items are unidimensional they will be ranked in relatively the same positions by all judges. If judges fail to rank an item in about the same position, apparently the item is not unidimensional but multidimensional. Such an item is then discarded, and by this process of elimination only the unidimensional items are retained.

Reliability, validity, and construction

A Thurstone-type scale is more laborious to construct than a Likert-type scale. Both scales are susceptible to invalid self-report by the S. However, the Thurstone type is not affected by response sets. The Likert type may yield more information in that the S is required to respond to all items. In studies that used comparable scales of both types, the correlations between the scores was found to be quite high, some as high as the low .90's. On this basis the scales may be considered interchangeable.

Validity is a primary concern of attitude measurement. Any self-report device has the possibility of being faked, that is, in attitude measurement the S may report attitudes which are quite different from his true feelings. It is usually difficult to find an external criterion with which to compare the reported attitude. The actual behavior of Ss may provide such a criterion, but this may be difficult to observe or measure.

Reliability coefficients on attitude inventories can be computed by the usual techniques. The range on reliability coefficients is typically greater than for achievement tests in a specific area. While some coefficients go up into the .90's, more modest coefficients are the usual result.

The construction of an attitude inventory requires a careful selection of items, with a reworking of original statements. A trial run of some sort is essential, and the elimination of ambiguity is a requirement that is necessary but not sufficient. The items must consistently measure the attitude under study.

Published attitude inventories are not as extensively available as achievement tests, but there are some available which cover broad areas. The *Minnesota Teacher Attitude Inventory* is one that is used in teacher education. In research projects the purposes and topics of investigation are often so specific that the researcher has little alternative but to construct his own attitude inventory. The construction of this inventory can comprise a major part of the research effort.

The Thurstone and Likert types of scales are the most commonly used methods for measuring attitudes. Other techniques have been developed, but they will not be discussed in this text. The entire topic is treated in detail in texts on psychological measurement.

THE MEASUREMENT OF PERSONALITY

When we consider characteristics such as motivation, attitudes, and emotional adjustments, we are dealing with the individual's personality. Anne Anastasi[5] describes personality tests as being designed to measure the affective or nonintellectual aspects of behavior. Some psychologists use the term "personality" in a broader sense to include the sum total of an individual's mental and emotional characteristics. Intellectual characteristics such as achievement would also be included in such a concept of personality. However, most personality testing deals with emotional and affective, rather than intellectual, characteristics.

Trait measurement

The measurement of personality has certain inherent difficulties. One of these concerns what to measure. Although there is some ambiguity associated with the term, the consensus is that personality measurement deals with the measurement of traits. The term "trait" has been used previously; here it is more formally defined for use in the context of personality. In this sense, a *trait* is a tendency for the individual to respond in a certain way to situations. For example, a pessimistic individual will tend to respond by emphasizing the unfavorable aspects of almost any situation. A person will tend to respond in a certain manner in any situation that tests his honesty.

5. Anne Anastasi, *Psychological Testing,* 3rd ed. (New York: Macmillan Co., 1968), p. 17.

A trait, however, is not usually so "pure" that the response is consistent for all situations. An individual might be pessimistic about money matters but optimistic about other matters. Honesty for one individual might be reflected in business matters but lacking in a golf score, whereas another sportsman would not consider adjusting his score. Thus honesty may differ, and yet two individuals might be viewed as possessing the same amount of this trait.

It would be inefficient to classify every habit or specific response as a trait. The attempt, rather, is to identify general traits which encompass a large number of situations. The trait should adequately describe significant differences of behavior. Traits should be different in more than name only. Two supposedly different traits, upon careful analysis, may be comprised of the same factors and essentially represent only one trait.

Methods

The methods of personality measurement may seem crude and inadequate when compared with analytical measurement in a chemistry laboratory, for example. In a certain sense personality measurement is in its infancy. Though the techniques used may not be precise, they still are of value. The researcher should be aware of the measurement limitations and consider them in his interpretation of results.

The most straightforward approach to personality measurement would be by observing the S's responses, that is, his behavior. This procedure may prove satisfactory when a competent observer is working with a single S or a very limited number of Ss at one time, but it is inefficient for large numbers of Ss. If the S is aware of the fact that he is being observed, his responses may be based on what he perceives to be acceptable rather than his usual response. This also applies to a group of Ss.

Personality measurement can also take place through the opinions of associates of the individual. A formal rating scale of several items may be used in an attempt to instill some uniformity into such a measurement. This method has a number of potential pitfalls, including the raters' own personalities and their ability to do the rating.

The obvious approach to personality measurement is to consult the individual himself. For large numbers of Ss a personal interview technique would hardly be efficient, so the S is asked to respond to a paper and pencil *personality inventory* which consists of one or more kinds of items. He may be asked about his preferences, asked to rate things or activities, or asked to respond to a situation presented in the item. With a large number of items the S is commonly given the possible response choices for each item, rather than being permitted a free response.

Inventory construction

The *a priori* approach to constructing a personality inventory is simply an attempt to construct items that reflect the trait under study. For example, to measure honesty, items are presented which involve situations in which a choice related to honesty is made. This approach to constructing a personality inventory may seem straightforward, and inherently it is, but special care must be taken in constructing the items. Specific items may not measure what they are supposed to measure, and the problem of ambiguity is usually present in the early stages. The validity of an inventory so constructed would likely involve both content and construct validity.

Empirical evidence can be used in constructing a personality inventory. The items may be tried out on a group whose personality characteristics are known; for example, with the honesty trait, the items would be given to a group whose honesty characteristics have been conclusively established. The responses of a group considered to be 100 percent honest would reflect a 100 percent honesty trait. The individual items would be separately analyzed, and those for which responses were not consistent would be deleted from the personality inventory. To strengthen this analysis, the items should also be tried out on a group of *S*s known to be low in honesty. This is necessary to see how their responses differ from those of the honest group. Without the contrasting group it would be necessary to assume that the responses of the two groups would be different, an assumption which may not be tenable.

The items may be an indirect approach to the trait. If we want to distinguish between authoritarian and democratic teachers, it might be undesirable, because of certain terminology, to use direct items. If the reading habits of these two types of teachers differ, this would be a possible source for measuring the trait. Two groups of teachers who have been identified as democratic and authoritarian are administered the items on reading habits. The difference in responses of the two groups, if such a difference exists, is then attributed to a difference in the trait. There is no causative relationship implied here. The point is to find something that differentiates the two groups, not to explain why the groups differ in reading habits. This procedure usually requires a great deal of searching for relevant items.

There are other measurement techniques for personality traits, such as the projective technique, which is essentially built around an unstructured task and allows for an almost unlimited number of possible responses. These techniques are not commonly used in educational research; their primary use is in clinical and diagnostic procedures. The discussion of this text only touches upon the business of personality measurement, and then only in the context of educational research. For comprehensive discussions of personality measurement, you should consult texts devoted to testing and measurement.[6]

The foremost problem of measuring personality is validity; the question of whether we are measuring what we claim to measure is often difficult to answer. The actual construction procedure using known groups does make an attempt at validation. The *a priori* approach is essentially a content-validity technique. The matter of estimating reliability is not as troublesome, since it can be technically handled with the reliability procedures.

Many personality inventories are commercially available, and the educational researcher will save a lot of time and effort if he can find a published inventory that is adequate for his purposes. The construction of a satisfactory personality inventory requires someone well-trained in psychological testing. In the educational research setting, which deals with relatively large numbers of "normal" *S*s, traits are broadly defined, such as personal adjustment or social adjustment. Published inventories are available for such broad traits, but for a very specific measurement, especially with an atypical group of *S*s, the researcher may be required to construct his own measurement instrument. In such a case, a considerable amount of the research effort should be allotted to the construction of the instrument.

The educational researcher does not always find ready-made tests available for the purposes of his study. Suppose a study is conducted in which creativity is to be measured. It is difficult to define creativity, and even more difficult to measure what has been decided upon as a satisfactory definition. It may be possible to use modifications of existing tests, however. In a study by Herbert J. Klausmeier and William Wiersma[7] in which divergent thinking tests were used, the measuring instruments included adaptations from tests by Joy Paul Guilford, Norman Kettner, and Paul Christensen.[8] The modifications were made in order to use the tests with fifth- and seventh-grade students.

---

6. As an example of such a text, see J. C. Nunnally, Jr., *Introduction to Psychological Measurement* (New York: McGraw-Hill Book Co., 1970).

7. H. J. Klausmeier and William Wiersma, "Relationship of Sex, Grade Level, and Locale to Performance of High I.Q. Students on Divergent Thinking Tests," *Journal of Educational Psychology* 55 (1964): 114–19.

8. J. P. Guilford, N. W. Kettner, and P. R. Christensen, *A Factor Analytic Study across the Domains of Reasoning, Creativity and Evaluation: II. Administration of Tests and Analysis of Results.* University of Southern California Psychological Laboratory Reports No. 16, 1956. (Modifications in tests made by Frank B. May.)

SPECIFIC TASK MEASUREMENT

The data for a research study do not always consist of scores on some sort of paper and pencil inventory. In a learning task, for example, the measure of learning may be time required to solve a problem, number of errors in a solution, or some measure of redundancy, to mention just three. The definition of the task is often so specific that it exactly reflects the purposes of the research. In these situations, reliability and validity are often not treated in a technical manner.

All specific task measurement may not directly reflect the factors, characteristics, or behavior under study. An example would be a basket-ball skill test that involves putting coins in cups. The validity of such a task should be considered: Does it test basketball skill? Also, with certain specific task measurements dealing with skills such as selected motor or cognitive skills, the researcher may find it necessary to conduct one or more trials in order to secure the necessary reliability in the measurement. Certainly, if two or more examiners are used there should be some measure of interexaminer consistency.

This type of research involves a very specific task. The rationale behind such research and its measurement must be carefully developed. It should reflect a definite, defined area of education or a related matter such as a learning theory. The area may be general, such as learning, or very specific, but the research procedures and the measurement should be carefully developed, and the research should be relevant to the educational context in some manner, theoretical or applied.

ORGANIZING DATA FOR ANALYSIS

Once the data have been collected through the use of the measuring instruments, some type of tabulation and possibly a transformation of the data in preparation for the analysis may be necessary. If answer sheets or tests are to be hand scored, routine precautions should be taken to ensure accuracy of scoring. Such precautions would include supervised practice for scorers and accuracy checks while the actual scoring is being done.

Research projects that include the collection of considerable data using standardized tests should make provision for machine scoring. There are IBM answer sheets with spaces for responses up to 150 items, and the Electronic Scoring Punch 9002 is an IBM machine for test scoring. Test-scoring machines not only provide for obtaining the actual scores, they commonly provide tabulations, summaries, and conversions to various types of standard scores. In some cases the machines are connected to a computer to provide certain kinds of analyses.

Machine scoring of tests is usually less expensive than hand scoring. Other advantages of machine scoring are its accuracy and its preparation of the data for computer analysis if necessary. Not all educational research data are collected in a form that can be machine scored, however, and the organization of data for analysis when a machine is not to be used to transmit data from the answer sheet to the computer is an important part of the research procedure.

With high-speed computers generally available, any research project that generates even a small amount of data or requires anything but very simple statistical analyses would allow for the use of a computer in compiling data. But the computer usually does not take research data directly from the forms used for recording during the data collection, and, the data or scores must be transmitted from the data sheets to data cards, commonly IBM cards, which feed the information to the computer. The standard IBM card has 80 columns. A single number or letter may be punched into each column.

The format for the data card, indicating the information that goes into each column, must be defined by the researcher. Information is commonly of two types—identification and scores or responses. If the number of bits of information on an *S does not exceed the 80 columns, one card per* S is sufficient. The identification information consists of such things as the *S*'s classification on the independent variables and his unique number. It may include other information, such as age or sex. Usually the identification comes in the early columns of the card, but this is not essential. The scores, commonly the scores on the dependent variables, are punched into the card using as many columns as necessary; a two-digit test score, for example, requires two columns. If there are ten different tests, each giving a two-digit score, these data would require 20 columns. If tests with varying numbers of digits in the scores are used, the number of columns used for each score is sometimes held constant, namely the greatest number of digits for any score. This may facilitate setting up the analysis for the computer, but it is not essential that the number of columns be the same for all test scores.

The data should be so organized that minimum effort is required to transmit the data from its original form to the IBM card. Any confusion should be eliminated to minimize the number of copy errors. The person punching the card can work most efficiently if the data for each *S* are presented in a line or row on a sheet in the exact order they are to appear on the card. It is very inefficient for a keypunch operator to have to fish around to assemble the data. The punched cards should be verified, a process of checking for possible errors in the original card-punching operation. The corresponding information for all Ss should appear in corresponding columns on the IBM cards.

If the data are analyzed on a desk calculator, it is important to classify and organize all scores so that there is no confusion as to the identification of a score. The scores should be presented so that errors are minimized in transmitting them from the data sheets to the calculator. The computations on the calculator should be performed in such a manner that several internal checks can be made during the calculations.

ETHICAL CONSIDERATIONS IN CONDUCTING RESEARCH

Any researcher who involves human Ss in his research has certain responsibilities toward them. Since the activities of the Ss are often closely associated with the data collection, it is appropriate to consider ethical considerations here. We will not review ethical principles as defined by agencies or associations, but we will introduce ethical considerations in using human Ss in research and suggest references that discuss such considerations in detail.

The American Psychological Association (APA) has issued a monograph developed by an ad hoc Committee on Ethical Standards in Psychological Research entitled *Ethical Principles in the Conduct of Research with Human Participants* (Washington, D.C.: American Psychological Association, 1973). This is probably the most comprehensive statement on ethics involved in research with human Ss. The content is relevant for educational research, since like psychological research it often involves human Ss. An editorial in the *Educational Researcher,* "Ethical Standards for Research in Education," by Richard Schultz, Vol. 2, No. 2 (February 1973), discusses the content of the APA monograph in relation to education. It also discusses ethical standards for research with children as presented by the Society for Research in Child Development.

The Department of Health, Education, and Welfare (HEW) has a policy governing the protection of human Ss. A discussion of this policy is provided by James Welsh, "Protecting Research Subjects: A New HEW Policy" in *Educational Researcher,* Vol. 1, No. 3 (March 1972). The HEW policy is particularly relevant to any researcher receiving funds from agencies within HEW.

Numerous important points are made in these publications, including the following. The researcher must protect the dignity and welfare of the human Ss. The S's freedom to decline participation must be respected, and the confidentiality of research data must be maintained. The researcher must guard against violation or invasion of privacy. The responsibility for maintaining ethical standards remains with the individual researcher, and the principal investigator is also responsible for the actions of his assistants.

By no means do these points exhaust all the specific details. Any researcher anticipating the use of human Ss should consult an "ethics" statement or policy statement such as those cited above. As a general rule, he must respect the human Ss used in his specific research project.

CONCLUDING REMARKS

Measurement in numerous areas has been discussed in this chapter. The particular measurement and data collection techniques used are specific to the research project. Published tests may be available for the researcher to use for his study, but in some cases special measurement instruments must be constructed. If specific tasks are required of the Ss, the data of the research study consist of performance scores on such tasks.

Measurement and data collection are very important aspects of the research study. The measurement, which should be carefully defined in terms of the objectives of the research, follows the development of the research objectives. It is not acceptable research procedure to collect a mass of data and then begin searching for research objectives to fit those data. Validity and reliability must be considered, and the coefficients should be reported if they are available.

Good measurement does not ensure a good research study, but poor measurement certainly destines the study to failure. Adequate measurement, in sum, is a necessary but not sufficient condition for good educational research.

SUGGESTED STUDY EXERCISES

7.1. Construct a short culture-fair intelligence test. By "culture-fair" is meant a test that does not reflect a specific culture; that is, the performance of an S is not influenced by his culture. Thus, assuming communication, the test should be as valid for a South Pacific native as an American high school student. Consider such things as the types of possible items and the content of the items.

7.2. Suppose a teacher wants to do a study on the attitudes of junior high students toward a compulsory "orientation to the school" program.

Assume that the Ss have completed the program. Construct five items that would fit into such an attitude inventory. Designate the scoring for your items.

7.3. Select an article from a research journal which involves the measurement of attitudes or personality characteristics. Read the article carefully and check to see if the author discusses such things as validity, reliability, and type of measuring device. Are the data quantified in some way? Were standardized tests used for the study?

7.4. In the preceding chapter, exercise 6.3 dealt with a researcher doing a study about the extent of hostility in upper elementary classrooms. Discuss some of the measurement difficulties the researcher is likely to encounter in preparing for the data collection. What is a possible operational definition of hostility? Is it possible to quantify hostility in any way?

7.5. Suppose a researcher is doing research on the science achievement of students in grades five through seven. Another researcher is doing research on personality characteristics of junior high students. Contrast the measurement of these two research studies with respect to:

a. The availability of published measuring instruments.

b. The type of validity of major concern.

c. The data collection procedures.

7.6. A research director for a large city school system conducts an extensive study of achievement in grades three through eight. He measures achievement in several areas with subscores in the areas so that there are 18 different achievement scores for each participating student. Ten of the scores require two digits and the remainder three digits. The sample of students is drawn from 74 city schools. The total sample size is over 1,000, and each student in the sample is to be identified by a number. In addition to the specific school and grade level, the students are classified according to sex and ability level: high, average, and low. The student's age is recorded. The city is divided into eight socioeconomic districts, and this information is also recorded in terms of the location of the school the student attends.

Produce a possible card layout for an IBM card that includes all of the above information. Consider the number of columns you would use for identification and achievement scores. The order is somewhat arbitrary, but construct a possible grouping of scores. Recall that 80 columns are available on an IBM card.

7.7. Discuss some of the more common errors or difficulties that can arise in the mechanics of data collection. By mechanics is meant actually obtaining the necessary data and not constructing the measuring instruments.

chapter 8

Sampling designs

KEY CONCEPTS

Probability sampling
Random selection and random assignment
Sampling fraction
Table of random numbers
Sampling design criteria: goal orientation, measurability,
     practicality, and economy
Stratified random sampling
Proportional and optimum allocation
Cluster sampling
Sampling through an intermediate unit
Systematic sampling
Periodicity
Determination of sample size
Homogeneity of population
Nonresponse or nonparticipation
Oversampling

A major link in the chain of reasoning for inferential statistics (see Chapter 2) is the sample. Samples are selected from populations, and measures computed from the samples (statistics) are used to make inferences about the population measures (parameters). A sample is a subset of the population. If the sample is randomly selected, it will reflect the population within the limits of sampling fluctuation.

Empirical research in education, especially survey research, often involves sampling from large populations, and the selection and acquisition of the sample may be a major activity of the research project. All the various designs for sampling discussed in this chapter embody the characteristic of random selection in one way or another. It is assumed that in order for a sample to be representative of its population it must be selected in a random, unbiased manner. The sampling designs discussed here involve what is called *probability sampling*—every member of the population has a nonzero probability of being selected. The nonzero probability is attained through some process of randomization.

RANDOM SELECTION AND RANDOM ASSIGNMENT

If a finite population is relatively small, readily accessible, and homogeneous, a simple random sample is feasible. To meet the criterion of a simple random sample, each member of the population would have the same probability of inclusion in the sample. If sampling from a finite population without replacement, every possible sample of a given size would have an equal probability of inclusion. The probability equals the *sampling fraction,* which is the ratio of sample size to population size.

A simple random sample can be obtained by using a table of random numbers. (Figure 8.1 is a page from a random number table.) Each member of the finite population can be assigned a number, and then as many numbers as comprise the sample size are selected from the table. Suppose we have a population of 70 members and 20 are to be selected at random. Each of the 70 members is assigned a number from 1 to 70. The first 20 numbers that appear, wherever we begin in the random number table, determine the 20 sample members. Since there are only 70 members in the population, we use two-digit random numbers. If we begin with the first row in Figure 8.1 and go across, taking two-digit numbers in sequence, we get 59, 39, 15, etc., until 20 numbers are selected. (The numbers in this table are grouped by fives for visual ease.) If a number exceeding 70 is selected we simply ignore it. If a number appears that has already been selected it, too, is ignored, since a single member of the population would not be included twice in the sample. Any kind of sequencing in the table is random, and it is not necessary to go across the rows. We could go in columns or take the numbers in blocks.

The random number table can also be used for assigning Ss at random. Suppose a researcher has available a pool of 90 Ss for an experiment and his experimental variable has three levels. To randomly assign 30 Ss to each level, he would assign each of the 90 Ss a number and use the random number table in the manner described above. The first 20 numbers selected would designate the Ss for level 1, the second 20 those for level 2, and the remaining 20 those for level 3. If an S were assigned to level 1 and his number appeared again in the selection of the second 20, the second time it would simply be passed over, since any one S can be assigned to only one level.

	50–54	55–59	60–64	65–69	70–74	75–79	80–84	85–89	90–94	95–99
00	59391	58030	52098	82718	87024	82848	04190	96574	90464	29065
01	99567	76364	77204	04615	27062	96621	43918	01896	83991	51141
02	10363	97518	51400	25670	98342	61891	27101	37855	06235	33316
03	86859	19558	64432	16706	99612	59798	32803	67708	15297	28612
04	11258	24591	36863	55368	31721	94335	34936	02566	80972	08188
05	95068	88628	35911	14530	33020	80428	39936	31855	34334	64865
06	54463	47237	73800	91017	36239	71824	83671	39892	60518	37092
07	16874	62677	57412	13215	31389	62233	80827	73917	82802	84420
08	92494	63157	76593	91316	03505	72389	96363	52887	01087	66091
09	15669	56689	35682	40844	53256	81872	35213	09840	34471	74441
10	99116	75486	84989	23476	52967	67104	39495	39100	17217	74073
11	15696	10703	65178	90637	63110	17622	53988	71087	84148	11670
12	97720	15369	51269	69620	03388	13699	33423	67453	43269	56720
13	11666	13841	71681	98000	35979	39719	81899	07449	47985	46967
14	71628	73130	78783	75691	41632	09847	61547	18707	85489	69944
15	40501	51089	99943	91843	41995	88931	73631	69361	05375	15417
16	22518	55576	98215	82068	10798	86211	36584	67466	69373	40054
17	75112	30485	62173	02132	14878	92879	22281	16783	86352	00077
18	80327	02671	98191	84342	90813	49268	95441	15496	20168	09271
19	60251	45548	02146	05597	48228	81366	34598	72856	66762	17002
20	57430	82270	10421	05540	43648	75888	66049	21511	47676	33444
21	73528	39559	34434	88596	54086	71693	43132	14414	79949	85193
22	25991	65959	70769	64721	86413	33475	42740	06175	82758	66248
23	78388	16638	09134	59880	63806	48472	39318	35434	24057	74739
24	12477	09965	96657	57994	59439	76330	24596	77515	09577	91871
25	83266	32883	42451	15579	38155	29793	40914	65990	16255	17777
26	76970	80876	10237	39515	79152	74798	39357	09054	73579	92359
27	37074	65198	44785	68624	98336	84481	97610	78735	46703	98265
28	83712	06514	30101	78295	54656	85417	43189	60048	72781	72606
29	20287	56862	69727	94443	64936	08366	27227	05158	50326	59566
30	74261	32592	86538	27041	65172	85532	07571	80609	39285	65340
31	64081	49863	08478	96001	18888	14810	70545	89755	59064	07210
32	05617	75818	47750	67814	29575	10526	66192	44464	27058	40467
33	26793	74951	95466	74307	13330	42664	85515	20632	05497	33625
34	65988	72850	48737	54719	52056	01596	03845	35067	03134	70322
35	27366	42271	44300	73399	21105	03280	73457	43093	05192	48657
36	56760	10909	98147	34736	33863	95256	12731	66598	50771	83665
37	72880	43338	93643	58904	59543	23943	11231	83268	65938	81581
38	77888	38100	03062	58103	47961	83841	25878	23746	55903	44115
39	28440	07819	21580	51459	47971	29882	13990	29226	23608	15873
40	63525	94441	77033	12147	51054	49955	58312	76923	96071	05813
41	47606	93410	16359	89033	89696	47231	64498	31776	05383	39902
42	52669	45030	96279	14709	52372	87832	02735	50803	72744	88208
43	16738	60159	07425	62369	07515	82721	37875	71153	21315	00132
44	59348	11695	45751	15865	74739	05572	32688	20271	65128	14551
45	12900	71775	29845	60774	94924	21810	38636	33717	67598	82521
46	75086	23537	49939	33595	13484	97588	28617	17979	70749	35234
47	99495	51434	29181	09993	38190	42553	68922	52125	91077	40197
48	26075	31671	45386	36583	93459	48599	52022	41330	60651	91321
49	13636	93596	23377	51133	95126	61496	42474	45141	46660	42338

FIGURE 8.1. Sample page from a table of random numbers

Reprinted by permission from *Statistical Methods*, 6th edition, by G. W. Snedecor and W. G. Cochran, © 1967 by the Iowa State University Press, Ames, Iowa U.S.A.

CRITERIA FOR A SAMPLING DESIGN

There may be any number of reasons why a researcher would depart from simple random sampling and use a more complex sampling design. Probably the most common reason is that the population from which the sample is to be selected is so large that simple random sampling cannot be conducted. The population may also be quite diffuse and consist of several subpopulations. In populations where the members are grouped or clustered, these groups are more readily sampled than individual members. If the population is very heterogeneous, an alternative to simple random sampling will tend to control some of the sampling variation.

Whatever the reason for using a more complex sampling design, a good sampling design should meet certain requirements. Leslie Kish has identified the four broad criteria for a good sampling design as (1) goal orientation, (2) measurability, (3) practicality, and (4) economy.[1]

The first criterion, *goal orientation,* means that the sampling design should be tailored to the research design and based on the research goals or objectives. Thus the sampling design must meet the sampling requirements of the research objectives. The measurement necessary to obtain the data and the anticipated analyses, as based on the objectives, also have important implications for sampling. Too often, a convenient "sample" of available Ss is used in educational research, regardless of what is required by the goals of the research.

The criterion of *measurability* means that the sampling design provides for the necessary computations. It was noted in Chapter 3 that as variance is reduced, precision in computing statistics is enhanced. Measurability is also related to securing valid estimates of sampling variability, which are necessary in order to test statistical hypotheses. The criterion of measurability is essential for applying the chain of reasoning in inferential statistics.

It is one thing to theoretically sketch a sampling design on paper and another to apply the design in a real situation. The criterion of *practicality* means that the actual activities of applying the sampling design are identified and they are feasible in the real situation. Practicality also means attempting to anticipate problems and devising methods for avoiding or circumventing them. Simplicity of instructions and well-defined procedures tend to reduce errors in the real situation. Prac-

1. Leslie Kish, *Survey Sampling* (New York: John Wiley & Sons, 1965), pp. 23–26.

ticality involves making the theoretical design conformable with actual activities.

The criterion of *economy* is largely self-explanatory. Since expenditures for educational research projects are usually limited, economy requires that the research objectives be met with minimum cost and effort. Obtaining data for a research project can be time-consuming and expensive. A good sampling design is not wasteful of data collection efforts.

Attempting to meet these four criteria when developing a sampling design often becomes a matter of balance. For example, in order to enhance measurability, the researcher might continue to increase sample size to the point where economy is sacrificed. The budget of a research project may be so limited that in the interest of economy the remaining three criteria are jeopardized. Each of the criteria must be considered in the context of applying the sampling design in a specific situation.

STRATIFIED RANDOM SAMPLING

In some cases the population to be sampled is not homogeneous but, in essence, consists of several subpopulations. Rather than select randomly from the entire population, the researcher might divide such a population into two or more subpopulations called strata. This approach to sampling is called stratified random sampling because the population is "stratified" into its subpopulations. *All* strata are represented in the sample, and the sample members are selected from each stratum *at random*. Thus the condition of random selection is included in this sampling procedure.

The decision must be made as to the numbers (that is, allotments) that will be selected from each stratum for the sample. One method is *proportional allocation,* whereby each stratum contributes to the sample a number that is proportional to its size in the population. For example, if stratum A contains one-fourth of the population, then one-fourth of the sample members will be drawn from that stratum. The allocation of strata members in the sample is proportional to the numbers of members in the strata in the population. Suppose there are k strata to be sampled and the respective population sizes of the strata are $N_1, N_2, \ldots, N_k$. Total population size can be indicated by N and total sample size by n. We can let $n_1, n_2, \ldots, n_k$ be the sample sizes for the respective strata. Then:

$$\frac{n}{N} = \frac{n_1}{N_1} = \frac{n_2}{N_2} = \cdots = \frac{n_k}{N_k},$$

and

$$n_1 + n_2 + \cdots + n_k = n.$$

The sampling fraction is n/N, and this fraction (proportionality) is held constant for the allocation of the sample to the k strata.

Stratified sampling guards against wild samples and ensures that no subpopulation will be omitted from the sample. It also avoids overloading in certain subpopulations. Simple random samples have a tendency to distribute themselves according to the population proportions. Stratified random sampling with proportional allocation will build this proportionality into the sample.

Another advantage of proportional allocation is realized if there is considerable variability between strata means relative to the variable being measured. Suppose that we are attempting to estimate the population mean from the sample data. This estimate will have associated with it a variance, also estimated from the sample data. Proportional allocation will make this estimate of the variance more precise, that is, it will be smaller than if simple random sampling had been used. Using simple random sampling, the variance estimate contains a component of variance, due to the variance between strata means. Proportional allocation removes this component of variance, and a more precise variance estimate is obtainable. If there is no difference between strata means there is no gain in precision in going from simple random sampling to proportional allocation.

A second method of allocation is *optimum allocation*. In optimum allocation, the strata contributions to the sample are proportional not only to the sizes of the strata populations but also to the strata variances. (In determining strata sample sizes, they are proportional to the products of strata population sizes and strata standard deviations.) With all other factors held constant, the strata with the larger variances will contribute the greater numbers to the sample. Optimum allocation requires a prior knowledge or at least a good estimate of the variances of the individual strata.

The gain in going from proportional to optimum allocation is again a gain in precision. Consider the estimate of variance discussed above in connection with proportional allocation. When proportional allocation is used, the variance estimate contains a component of variance, due to the difference between strata variances. Optimum allocation removes this component of variance, giving a more precise estimate. If there are no differences in strata variances there is no gain in precision in going from proportional to optimum allocation.

Proportional allocation requires information about the relative sizes of the strata in the population. Preferably, the exact population numbers or good estimates of these numbers should be available. In addition to this size information, optimum allocation requires good estimates or exact values of the variances of the strata in the population. The use of poor or inaccurate estimates may result in a sample providing decreased rather than increased precision for variance estimates.

As an example of stratified random sampling with proportional allocation, a researcher might be doing a survey of science achievement of elementary students, grades three through six, in a school district. For simplicity's sake, assume that stratification will be on grade level only. (It could also be on sex of the student, school, etc.) Suppose that the population sizes for these four strata are 350, 300, 470, and 430, respectively, for grades three through six. If the sampling fraction has been set at one in ten, sample size for the total population of 1,550 will be 155. With proportional allocation the sample sizes for the respective strata would be 35, 30, 47, and 43. Members of the sample would be randomly selected from their strata and measured on science achievement.

Since the dependent variable in this study is science achievement, a common test, possibly a standardized test, would be used to measure all 155 sample members. Performance on a science achievement test is generally influenced by grade level. Thus, since considerable variance could be expected between strata means, proportional allocation would result in a gain in precision. If a standardized test were used, information on strata variances might be available in the test manual, and optimum allocation might be possible.

The choice of sample size is, more often than not, an arbitrary one dictated by available resources. A rationale for sample size might be provided by the idea of precision as reflected in proportional or optimum allocation. If the researcher has some basis for designating a desired precision and the variance information is available, a necessary sample size could be computed. This sample size is the size necessary to attain the desired precision. If the variance information is not available, a sample may be drawn and the sample variance used as an estimate. Additional members are then selected for the sample if necessary.

When stratified random sampling is used, all strata are represented in the sample, whether the allocation is proportional or optimum. The sample members are randomly selected from each stratum, according to the allocation. The sample allocations for strata are computed from the population information of strata sizes and, in the case of optimum allocation, information about the strata variances.

CLUSTER SAMPLING

When the selection of individual members of the population is impractical or too expensive, it may be possible to select groups or *clusters* of members for the sample. Cluster sampling is a procedure of selection in which the unit of selection, called the cluster, contains two or more population members. Each member of the population must be uniquely identified with one, and only one, cluster. Cluster sampling is useful in situations where the populations members are naturally grouped in units that can be conveniently used as clusters. For example, pollsters doing surveys sometimes use city blocks as the cluster unit for selecting the sample.

In cluster sampling the clusters for the sample are *randomly* selected from the larger population of clusters. Once a cluster is selected for the sample, *all* the population members in that cluster are included in the sample. Before selecting the sample, not only must all population members be identified in their clusters, but all the clusters must be identified. It is not necessary that all clusters have the same number of population members.

An example of a research situation for which cluster sampling would be appropriate is a survey of fourth-grade achievement in mathematics, using a standardized achievement test, by the research director of a large city system (in excess of 60 elementary schools). It is too expensive to administer the test to all fourth graders in the system, and the logistics of selecting a simple random sample would be quite extensive. Stratified random sampling might be feasible, but it has one disadvantage: the fourth graders are in classes, and it is inconvenient to test some members of the class and not others. Since the fourth graders are "naturally" assembled in classes, cluster sampling could be used, using class as the sampling unit. Then all students in a selected class would be tested.

The tendency is for cluster sampling to be used with large populations. Whatever the sampling unit, it is usually something which groups the population members naturally. In large-scale educational surveys, the school might serve as the sampling unit for cluster sampling. As the size of the cluster increases, however, the sample size also becomes large, since all members of a selected cluster are in the sample. The sampling unit should be carefully selected and well defined, so there is no confusion as to what comprises a cluster in the real situation.

SAMPLING THROUGH AN INTERMEDIATE UNIT

There is a sampling design that applies to relatively large-scale projects in which the members of the population to be sampled are found in large groups and it is undesirable to include all members of a selected group, as in the case of cluster sampling. This design is called sampling through an intermediate unit, the large groups or units in which the population members are found. The members of the population in these units are called primary units. When sampling through an intermediate unit, the intermediate units are *randomly* selected first, and then the primary units are randomly selected from those intermediate units. Thus the probability of a primary unit being selected becomes the product of two probabilities: (1) the probability that its intermediate unit will be selected, and (2) the probability that it will be selected if its intermediate unit has been selected.[2]

The cross-national study of characteristics of teacher education students discussed as an example of *ex post facto* research in Chapter 5 illustrates sampling through an intermediate unit. The individual college students were the primary units of the study, and the colleges in which the students were enrolled were the intermediate units. Practical limitations restricted the number of colleges that could be included, so it was not feasible to select a simple random sample, for example. Cluster sampling would have been a possibility using the college as the sampling unit, but some colleges are very large and their inclusion would have tended to increase the number of primary units so drastically that the study would no longer have been economically feasible. Stratified random sampling without regard to college would have greatly complicated the logistics of data collection.

In this design, the selection of the sample requires information about the number of primary units in each of the intermediate units of the population. One selection procedure is to list all the intermediate units and select the sample of intermediate units, with probability proportional to size. By algebraic manipulation it can be shown that this selection procedure requires the selection of an equal number of primary units from each of the intermediate units selected.

The order of listing the intermediate units prior to their selection requires some aspect of randomization. If there are stratifying variables which subdivide the intermediate unit population, it may be well to order the intermediate units by strata. The order within strata should be random. The stratifying technique will ensure that no strata are inadvertently missed and also that the strata will have proportional representation.

The procedure of selecting intermediate units with probability pro-

---

2. This is somewhat analogous to the situation in which we determine the probability of getting two consecutive 6's on two rolls of a single unbiased die. This probability is 1/6 times 1/6, or 1/36. If we do not get a 6 on the first roll we have no chance of getting the two 6's. By the same token, if a primary unit's intermediate unit is not selected, the primary unit can no longer get into the sample. If we have a 6 on the first roll we still need a 6 on the second roll to meet the criterion of two 6's. If an intermediate unit is selected the primary unit must still be selected in order to get into the sample.

portional to size and then selecting the primary units can be summarized by the following steps:

1. Determine the number of intermediate units (k) to be included in the sample. This is often an arbitrary decision based on available resources.

2. Let N equal the number of primary units in the population and N_i the corresponding value for the ith intermediate unit; determine N/k, which we will call a sampling interval, and let $N/k = I$.

3. List all the intermediate units of the population in random order or some predetermined grouping if stratification is used with random order within strata. Determine the cumulative frequencies of the N_i's. Each intermediate unit thus has a number (cumulative sum) associated with it consisting of the sum of its N_i and all preceding N_i's.

4. Select a number (j) at random from numbers 1 through I, inclusive. The first intermediate unit selected is the one in whose cumulative sum j falls. Subsequent units are selected by determining the numbers $j + I, j + 2I, \ldots$, etc., and the units that these numbers "hit." When the process has been applied to the entire list, the k intermediate units have been selected.

5. Randomly select n/k (n is total sample size) primary units from each of the k selected intermediate units.

Special problems may arise, such as what to do if a small intermediate unit is selected and it does not have sufficient primary units. Another problem might be a very large intermediate unit that is selected twice. The resolution of these problems should be considered prior to selecting the sample. There are alternative procedures which can be used. For example, if a large intermediate unit is selected twice, a double sample of primary units could be selected within the intermediate unit, or a single sample, or a sample proportional to its size. Unique characteristics of the research study may influence the type of procedure that is most appropriate.

The intermediate units in a large-scale study are often of such a nature that all those selected will not choose to participate. This is especially true for educational research when the intermediate units are individual colleges, school districts, or schools. In these cases a selection procedure for alternates is necessary. Again, this procedure should be developed prior to selecting the initial sample. If the intermediate units have been ordered by strata and then randomly listed within strata, and an intermediate unit chooses not to participate, it can be replaced by the unit immediately following it on the list. This retains the unit within the original stratum. If the intermediate unit being replaced happens to be the final unit of the stratum, the immediately preceding unit can be used as a replacement if the researcher wants to make the selection within the same stratum.

SYSTEMATIC SAMPLING

The use of systematic sampling is quite common in educational research where large populations are studied and alphabetical or possibly other lists of the population members are available. Directors of institutional research often use this technique in selecting a sample. The primary advantage of systematic sampling in educational research is convenience.

Systematic sampling is a procedure by which the selection of the first sample member determines the entire sample. The population members (that is, their names or type of identification) are in some type of order; for example, the names of the population members may be placed in random order on a list. The sample size is chosen and the sampling fraction determined. If the sampling fraction is designated as $1/k$, then the first member of the sample is *randomly* selected from the first k members of the population as they appear in order. Following this first selection, ever k^{th} member of the population is selected for the sample.

Although the first member of a systematic sample is randomly selected, it is possible that this sampling design will yield a biased sample. The most serious and really the only threat to systematic sampling is the existence of some type of periodicity in the ordering of the population members. *Periodicity* means that every k^{th} member of the population has some characteristics, unique to only those members, which are related to, or have an effect upon, the dependent variable. In that case, the sample becomes biased. If the researcher suspects the existence of periodicity and it requires too much effort to rearrange the list of population members in random order, it would be best to shift to another sampling design.

Periodicity may inadvertently enter into the order of the list. Suppose a sample of fifth graders is being selected from a large school system population. The sample is to be measured on an ability test in order to estimate the ability level of the fifth-grade population of the school system. The researcher in charge of the study decides to take a 1-in-30 sample and notes that he can conveniently use class lists, since the fifth-grade classes all contain 30 or very close to 30 students. The researcher calls for class lists but the fifth-grade teachers, instead of sending alphabetical lists, send lists on which the student names in each class are arranged from high to low according to performance on a recent achievement test. The researcher puts the lists together, one class following another, and selects his systematic sample. Since achievement and performance on an ability test are quite conclusively related, marked periodicity has entered into the sampling list. If the first random selection gives the third name on the list, it would mean the 3rd, 33rd, 63rd, etc., students on the list would comprise the sample. This sample would differ from other samples, especially, for example, one beginning with name 26th on the list. Whatever sample is selected would have the effect of periodicity in it.

Systematic sampling is convenient, for example, for an institutional researcher in a college who might want to survey the student body with a brief questionnaire that could be returned by mail. Suppose a one-in-ten sample is selected. Alphabetical lists of the students, usually listed by class (freshman, sophomore, junior, and senior), could be used. The assumption is that the alphabetical listing is not related to whatever variables are to be researched by the questionnaire.

Systematic sampling provides the condition of sampling throughout the population, due to its spacing of selections over the entire list. A definite advantage of systematic sampling over, say, simple random sampling is that it requires less work. However, any list used for systematic sampling should be checked carefully to determine how it is ordered. The researcher should also check the ordering characteristic with the variables under study for the possibility of periodicity.

CONSIDERATIONS IN DETERMINING SAMPLE SIZE

There are several factors that can influence the size of the sample used in an educational research project. Unfortunately, with the exception of cost, information about such factors is usually sufficiently vague that it is difficult to set an exact sample size. Nevertheless, in most educational research projects requiring a sample, the exact determination of the sample size is not that crucial, and usually enough information exists so that sample sizes are adequate. It should not be inferred that it is always desirable to increase the sample size to its maximum. This may be unduly costly and wasteful of effort and information. Also, for some surveys the time required for the data collection of a large sample may be so long that the timeliness of the results is ruined.

Cost refers not only to the expenditure of money but also the time and effort required to obtain the sample data. In any survey, the actual cost of obtaining the data per unit in the sample should be estimated as accurately as possible. If standardized tests are used, what is the cost per test? How much does it cost to score the tests and summarize the data? What, if any, costs will be encountered in locating the sample for testing? What is the cost of test administration? These are all examples of questions that can be raised. A researcher who is securing funds for his project from a funding agency is usually required to produce quite accurate cost estimates. Researchers who are university professors and graduate students have available to them facilities and resources at no personal cost. Nevertheless, they should estimate the costs of a proposed project; at least time and manpower estimates should be made.

A second factor that should be considered in determining sample size is the statistical precision desired. If all other factors are held constant, statistical precision is increased as sample size is increased. Precision deals with the variance in the distribution of the variable studied. It may be possible to obtain some idea of the amount of this variance from a review of the literature, since other research studies may have used variables and Ss similar to those the researcher anticipates using. In rare instances, it might be possible and worth the effort to select and measure a small sample prior to the major sampling in order to estimate variance. This might be done if the cost of data collection per unit is relatively expensive and it is important not to oversample or undersample. Undersampling might result in inability to interpret the results due to a lack of statistical precision.

Related to statistical precision is the factor of homogeneity of the population. The more homogeneous the population is on the variable under study, the more precision is enhanced. Intuitively, it can be stated that in a more homogeneous population, smaller sample size is necessary to represent the population adequately. If a shipment of 500 laboratory mice all born the same day were sampled for the purpose of estimating the average weight per mouse, it would not be necessary to weigh many mice. To estimate the mean performance score on an IQ test for a high school of 500 students from a sample of these students, however, would require a substantial sample size.

With some types of research studies there is the possibility that data will not be obtained from all sample members. Questionnaires mailed in survey research are susceptible to nonresponse, and studies conducted in a laboratory may lose sample members because of inability to perform. It has been noted that uncooperative intermediate units can be replaced. However, if the likelihood of nonresponse or nonparticipation by selected sample members is great, a certain percentage of oversampling may be included. This, of course, has direct implications for sample size. The percentage of oversampling to be used in a specific project will need to be estimated by the researcher, possibly on the basis of previous experience or information from the research literature. It should be noted that oversampling does not solve the problem of possible bias caused by nonresponse. Oversampling only tends to keep the amount of data at an originally desired level.

CONCLUDING REMARKS

The matter of sampling is an important aspect of any research study which is designed to generalize from a sample to a population. The idea of random sampling is relatively simple, but the procedures necessary to achieve random sampling may not be at all simple.

The foregoing discussion is essentially a brief description of some of the more common sampling designs used in educational research. Sampling theory and procedures, especially in large-scale survey research, are extensive topics, and there are entire texts devoted to them.[3]

SUGGESTED STUDY EXERCISES

8.1. Suppose a researcher has a population of 839 members and he wants to select a simple random sample of size 50. Discuss how you would use a random number table for selecting the sample. Use Figure 8.1 in this chapter to select the first ten members of the sample.

8.2. Discuss stratified random sampling, considering the techniques of proportional and optimum allocation. Give an example of a situation for which you would use each technique.

8.3. A study is proposed to determine the mathematics achievement of high school seniors of a statewide area. A sample of seniors is to be measured. Discuss some of the sampling difficulties that would be likely with such a large population. Discuss the possibilities of using stratified or cluster sampling. What would be possible stratifying variables if a stratified random sample were selected?

8.4. Discuss how the condition of random selection differs between stratified random sampling and cluster sampling, in terms of including strata, clusters, and the members of the strata or clusters.

8.5. A population is divided into four strata. The population sizes of the four strata are 830, 660, 480, and 1,030, respectively, for stratum 1 through stratum 4. A sample of size 450 is to be selected, using stratified random sampling with proportional allocation. What is the sampling fraction? Distribute the sample among the four strata using proportional allocation.

8.6. A school board is interested in surveying the attitudes of the district's voters toward a school bond issue. The district comprises a city of approximately 300,000 population. A random sample of voters is to be selected. If stratified random sampling were used, what would be possible stratifying variables? Discuss the advantages and disadvantages of selecting a systematic sample. What kinds of lists would be used if a systematic sample were to be selected?

---

3. Examples of such texts are William Cochran, *Sampling Techniques,* 2nd ed. (New York: John Wiley & Sons, 1963), and Kish, *Survey Sampling.*

8.7. An educational psychologist has a population of 690 undergraduates available for participation in a concept-attainment experiment to be conducted in the learning lab. He requires 120 Ss for the experiment, including 60 men and 60 women. The population contains 381 women and 309 men. Describe how the Ss would be randomly selected for participation in the experiment. Suppose that the independent variable has four levels, and equal numbers of men and women are to be assigned to each level. Describe how the Ss would be randomly assigned to the levels.

PART TWO

TECHNIQUES FOR
HYPOTHESIS TESTING

chapter 9

Testing hypotheses by parametric techniques

KEY CONCEPTS

Significance level, probability level, or alpha level
Parametric assumptions
Student's *t* distribution
Degrees of freedom
Hypothesis for estimation of a mean
Confidence interval and level of confidence
***t* test for difference between two means**
Null hypothesis
Alternate hypothesis
One-tailed and two-tailed statistical tests
One-way and two-way analysis of variance
Error variance, or expected variance
Sums of squares
Pooled variance
***F* distribution**
Mean square
Fixed-effects model
Row-and-column array
First-order and second-order interaction
Analysis of covariance
Covariate
Type I (alpha) and Type II (beta) errors

The discussion thus far has dealt with relatively broad ideas about designing and conducting educational research studies. With this chapter we will turn to the underlying reasoning of specific procedures for testing hypotheses. The discussion of this and the following two chapters centers around the methodology of testing hypotheses by statistical techniques. Examples of research problems and situations are given in order to illustrate the reasoning and procedures involved. Statistical computations appear sparingly and are used only to help illustrate a point. Such computations are made at a minimal level and should not discourage the nonstatistically oriented reader.

BASIC IDEAS OF HYPOTHESIS TESTING

The basic concepts of descriptive statistics and the underlying reasoning of inferential statistics were introduced in Chapter 2. It is important that you be familiar with the definitions of terms given there, to avoid ambiguity and confusion. A distribution consists of scores on a variable, which, as a set of data, have certain characteristics. These characteristics are either statistics or parameters, depending upon whether we are concerned with a distribution of a sample or a population. Generally the distribution under consideration is a sample distribution, and we want to generalize about a population. In using statistical tests we infer from the statistics, which are measures of samples, to the parameters, which are measures of populations. However, we must make the inference in light of both the underlying distribution of the statistic and probability. In the examples of Chapter 2, the normal distribution was the underlying distribution. Additional underlying distributions will be introduced in this chapter.

In the context of this chapter, a hypothesis will be defined as a statement about a parameter. This is a more restricted definition than was used previously. We do not hypothesize about statistics, because the statistics exist in fact and we can inspect them to determine their values. The parameters will never be known for certain, and therefore we do not set out to prove or disprove a hypothesis absolutely; we either reject or fail to reject the hypothesis. Failing to reject means that in the light of the observed data for a specific statistical test, there is not enough evidence to reject the hypothesis. To fail to reject does not necessarily mean we will accept the hypothesis, although in most practical situations this is the case.

The decisions about hypotheses, and hence the parameters, are made on the basis of the statistics. Since the parameters are never known for certain, however, there is always the possibility of making an error in the decision. Possible errors in hypothesis testing are discussed in a later section in this chapter.

THE MEANING OF SIGNIFICANCE LEVEL

Consider an oversimplified, hypothetical example of testing a hypothesis using inferential statistics. The research director of a large school system is requested by the superintendent to determine the mean reading achievement of the fourth-graders in the system. In order to economize and reduce effort, the researcher selects a random sample of, say, 110 fourth-graders from the population of fourth-graders. He tests the sample, using an appropriate reading achievement test. The range of possible scores on the test is from zero to 200. The researcher computes the mean and standard deviation of the sample, the mean being 85 and the standard deviation 16. These statistics represent the corresponding parameters, and random sampling fluctuation. The researcher reports this to the superintendent.

The superintendent receives the news of the sample mean being 85 with much reluctance. He says he suspects the accuracy of this mean because he hypothesizes that the mean reading achievement of the fourth-grade population is 160. Note that the superintendent is hypothesizing about a parameter, a measure of the population that will not be determined empirically but that is to be inferred from the sample results. The researcher is very reluctant to entertain the superintendent's hypothesis, and rightly so, because the probability that a sample mean of 85 would have appeared if the population mean is 160 is very small. The underlying distribution of the mean is such that if it were located with a mean at 160, there is an extremely small probability that the researcher would have selected a random sample with a mean of 85. It is not likely that this large a departure from the population mean would have occurred due to random sampling fluctuation.

Had the superintendent hypothesized a population mean of 86, this hypothesis would be much more tenable. A sample mean of 85 when the population mean is 86 could have easily occurred, due to random sampling fluctuation. Indeed, there is a substantial probability that a sample mean of 85 *would* appear if in fact the population mean is 86.

When the researcher rejected the superintendent's hypothesis of a population mean of 160, he did so on the basis of probability. However, we cannot keep referring to probability as "small" or "substantial" and make decisions on the basis of such vague designations. We must decide on a specific probability level, so that if the probability of a statistic appearing, given a hypothesis, is below this level, we reject the hypothesis. This probability level is called the *significance level*.

The reasoning in hypothesis testing associates the probability with the statistic. This may initially seem like a contradiction, since the statistic is known. However, the parameter has a value (although the researcher will never know its value for certain) and has no probability associated with it. The probability is associated with the value of the statistic appearing by chance if, in fact, the value of the parameter is as stated in the hypothesis. If this probability of the statistic appearing, given the hypothesis, becomes less than a predetermined level (significance level)—usually .05 or .01—we reject the hypothesis. We cannot reject the statistic, since it is a fact. When the probability falls below the significance level and the hypothesis is no longer considered tenable, we say the test of the hypothesis is "statistically significant."

The term *alpha level* is also used to mean significance level, and the alpha symbol, α, often appears in tables to designate the probability level. Alpha level is the level of probability at which we reject the hypothesis being tested.

The significance level is a probability related to the area of the underlying distribution of the statistic. It is the dividing line between rejecting and accepting the hypothesis. Suppose we have the underlying distribution of a statistic and we designate the area as 1. If we can locate this distribution by the hypothesis and we know its shape and dispersion, we can determine where our observed statistic would be in the distribution.

Consider an example involving a mean. A large sample, say 200 or greater, is drawn from a normally distributed population. With such a large sample size the underlying distribution of the statistic is the normal distribution, and the standard error (that is, standard deviation) of this distribution could be estimated from the sample data. Suppose we hypothesize that the population mean is a specified value, and the significance level is set at .05. This example of the underlying distribution in terms of area is illustrated in Figure 9.1. Note that the 5 percent of the area designated by the significance level is divided equally between the two tails of the distribution. This is because extreme values of the sample mean on either side of the hypothesized mean would result in rejecting the hypothesis.

The probability that the sample mean, when computed, would appear by chance in the 2.5 percent of the area in the right tail is less

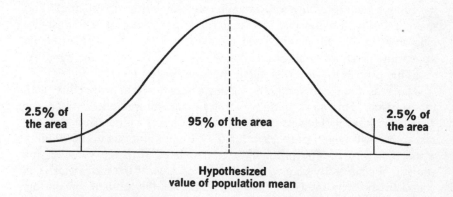

FIGURE 9.1.   Area of the underlying distribution of a statistic with a significance level of .05

than .05 if the hypothesis of the population mean is true. The occurrence of a random sample with a mean located in the extreme right (or left) tail is a rare event, one that has a probability of occurrence that is less than the significance level. We do not entertain the rare event as a tenable explanation of the situation. We cannot reject the statistic, since that has been computed and is therefore a result that has appeared. We must therefore reject the hypothesis and essentially conclude that our underlying distribution is not correctly located and should be shifted to the right. The mean is, of course, a locator of the distribution. The hypothesis concerns the mean of the underlying distribution, and rejecting the hypothesis is rejecting the hypothesized location of the underlying distribution. Note that the probability rests on the statistic but the conclusion rests on the hypothesis. In this example the statistical test is said to be "significant," since the statistic fell in the rejection region as determined by the significance level.

The significance level enables us to make a decision about our hypothesis. We are comparing a statistic with a hypothesized value of a parameter. Usually there is a difference between these two values, and the task is to decide whether or not the difference is so large that we should reject the hypothesis. In order to make the decision we consider the probability that this large a difference would have occurred due to chance, that is, random sampling fluctuation. If this probability is less than the significance level we are not willing to entertain random fluctuation as an explanation, and hence we reject the hypothesis. A difference that is considered too large to be attributed to random sampling fluctuation is said to be a statistically significant difference.

SELECTION OF THE SIGNIFICANCE LEVEL

The choice of the significance level is, to a certain extent, an arbitrary choice of the researcher, but this is not completely the case. The levels commonly used are .05 and .01, which correspond closely to two and two and one-half standard deviations from the mean in a normal distribution. The .05 level is widely used in educational research, most likely because it is considered an adequately good risk. The risk is 5 chances in 100 that such an extreme statistic would occur by chance if the hypothesis is true. The .01 level may be used by a researcher if he wants to be practically certain (99 chances out of 100) he will not reject the hypothesis if it is true. Occasionally the level is set at .10, but this generally is considered quite a high probability of chance occurrence. Decreasing the significance level, that is, going from .05 to .01, is going in what is called a conservative direction. Doing this will require values of the statistic that are more extreme (from the hypothesized values) to reach significance. The .001 level, which appears occasionally in the research literature, is very conservative.

The selection of a significance level depends upon what risk the researcher is willing to take in terms of making an error when making a decision about his hypothesis. This risk is related to the consequences of rejecting a true hypothesis or failing to reject a false hypothesis. If he wants to be very certain that he is right if he rejects the hypothesis, he will set the significance level very small, at possibly .01 or .001. For example, suppose a decision must be made on whether or not a new sixth-grade mathematics text should be adopted because it will result in greater mathematics achievement. However, the old texts are still adequate, and a new adoption will result in a large expenditure. If we hypothesize that the mathematics achievement will be the same using both texts, we want to be certain about rejecting this hypothesis and authorizing the expenditure.

A relatively large significance level (.10 or greater) would be selected if rejecting a true hypothesis is of little importance. Suppose a teacher is trying to decide which of two sets of toys is most appealing to kindergarten children. The two sets are of equal cost. The teacher hypothesizes that the two sets are equally appealing. A large significance level provides a good chance of detecting a preference, if there is one. If no preference exists nothing is lost, regardless of which set of toys is purchased.

We have discussed the significance level as a predetermined probability. Predetermined means that the significance level is set prior to performing the statistical test. An alternate way is to report the significance levels as they occur in the light of the completed statistical test. If we reach the .08 level in the test, this is reported, and the same for the .14 or .013 or any level that might occur as a result of the statistical test. It might be difficult to determine the precise level, since the tables of the values of underlying distributions do not usually report these intermediate values. The actual procedures are not affected by this thinking, only the manner in which a conclusion is reported. For the discussion in this text we will consider the significance level as predetermined. However, actual significance levels, observed after the statistical test, could be reported if adequate tables are available.

PARAMETRIC ASSUMPTIONS

The procedures discussed in this chapter come under the general name of parametric techniques. Underlying the use of these techniques are what are called the parametric assumptions, basically conditions put on the data and the population distributions from which the sample of data is selected. The assumptions come from mathematical derivations of the procedures and formulas that are used in the parametric techniques. The application of parametric techniques when the assumptions are not met will cause difficulty in the interpretation of the results.

One of the parametric assumptions is that the observations are *independent,* that is, the observation or score of any one S on the dependent variable does not in any way influence the observation of any other S. Suppose in an animal laboratory we are taking observations on 30 rats running a maze. If the 30 scores, one for each rat, are independent, then the score of any rat, as indicated by his performance, in no way influences the score of any other rat.

A second parametric assumption is *normality.* This assumption which requires that the observations be drawn from normally distributed populations, is not crucial when sample size increases above 30. It can be shown mathematically that as sample size increases above 30 and the samples are drawn from a population not normally distributed, the statistics which would be computed from repeated random samples would tend to have a normal distribution. It is really the statistic and its underlying distribution that we are testing in a statistical test.

A third parametric assumption is that when two or more populations are being studied, they have *homogeneous variance.* If the populations have equal standard deviations, the population variances must also be equal. What this assumption means, then, is that the populations under investigation have about the same dispersion in their distributions. The populations are not actually measured, but we can estimate their variances through the samples. The sample variances need not be exactly equal; in fact, there can be quite a marked departure from equality before this assumption is no longer tenable. The homogeneity-of-variance assumption can be checked by statistical procedures if the researcher has any reason to believe that it is not being met.

A fourth parametric assumption is that the observations to be analyzed (the scores on the dependent variable) are *measured on at least an interval scale* and these observations are continuous in their measurement. The definition of an interval scale requires that an equal unit be established in the measurement. There is some discussion among writers as to the operational meaning of this assumption.[1] Educational variables which may not possess an equal unit in their measurement are sometimes treated as if the measurement were on an interval scale. An ex-

---

1. See, for example, George Ferguson, *Statistical Analysis in Psychology and Education,* 3rd ed. (New York: McGraw-Hill Book Co., 1971), pp. 15–16, and Edward Minium, *Statistical Reasoning in Psychology and Education* (New York: John Wiley & Sons, 1970), pp. 18–19.

ample might be when a series of item responses which are clearly ordinal are assigned numerical values, and these values are summed for a total score. When the ordinal data are assigned numerical values, to some extent information is inserted into the data that was not obtained through the measurement. The pertinent question is whether or not parametric analyses applied to such data make any sense and can be interpreted in a meaningful way. Often meaningful interpretations are possible. The researcher should understand the nature of the data and know clearly what he is doing so that a decision can be made about the appropriateness of the procedures. Data measured on a ratio scale would, of course, meet this assumption, since a ratio scale does include equal units.

The four assumptions above might be summarized as:

1. Independence of the observations.
2. Observations selected from normally distributed populations.
3. Homogeneity of variance in the population distributions.
4. Interval-scale measurement of the variable to be analyzed.

It should be noted that assumptions 2 and 3, dealing with distributions, are assumptions about the population distributions, not the distributions of sample observations. More complex parametric procedures may require additional assumptions, as in analysis of covariance, a technique discussed later in the chapter.

STUDENT'S t DISTRIBUTION

The concept of underlying distribution was introduced in Chapter 2, and all the examples involving underlying distributions thus far have involved the normal distribution as the underlying distribution. We have seen that the underlying distribution of the mean is the normal distribution with a standard deviation of $\sigma/\sqrt{n}$. But in actual practice the parameter σ is seldom known; it is estimated by the standard deviation of the sample. In order to get an unbiased estimate of the population variance (the square of the standard deviation), we compute the variance of the sample by:

$$s^2 = \frac{\sum_{i=1}^{n_1} (X_i - \bar{X})^2}{n - 1},$$

where n = sample size. Note that this formula has $n - 1$ in the denominator. The positive square root, s, is used as an estimate of σ.

The next logical question concerns what would happen to the expression $\frac{\bar{X} - \mu}{\sigma/\sqrt{n}}$ if σ is replaced by an estimate, s. Is the underlying distribution in fact the normal distribution? The answer is that the underlying distribution for the expression $\frac{\bar{X} - \mu}{s/\sqrt{n}}$ is not normally distributed, at least not for a small sample size. In fact, there is not a single underlying distribution but rather an entire family of distributions, the specific distribution depending upon the size of n. This family of distributions was developed by a statistician who wrote under the name of Student, and the distributions are called the Student's t distributions, or, more commonly, simply the t distributions.

The t distributions are symmetric and upon casual inspection closely resemble the normal distribution. There is a t distribution for each value of the number of *degrees of freedom* (df), or number of ways the data are free to vary. Suppose that we know that the sum of two numbers must be 75. As soon as one number is given (arbitrarily assigned), the second number is fixed. Thus there is only one degree of freedom — the assignment of the first number. If the mean is computed for n values having a fixed sum, the first $n - 1$ values can be arbitrarily assigned, but once they have been assigned, the nth value is uniquely determined. Suppose we have four numbers whose sum is 23, for example, 8, 6, 7, and 2. How many of these numbers could be simultaneously altered and still the sum would equal 23? It can be seen that if three are arbitrarily changed the fourth is fixed. Suppose the first three numbers are changed to 9, 5, and 3. Then the fourth is fixed at 6 in order to meet the condition that the sum be 23. Thus only three of the scores are, in a sense, free to vary.

Degrees of freedom can be defined as the number of observations minus the number of parameters estimated. Suppose we were estimating a mean from a set of sample scores. One requirement of a mean is that the sum of the deviations of the scores from the mean equals zero. Therefore, if we have n scores there would be n deviations, but if $n - 1$ of these deviations were altered the nth would be fixed in order to meet the condition that the sum of the deviations be zero. We had n observations, estimated one parameter, and have $n - 1$ degrees of freedom. In our example of the standard error of the mean $(\sigma/\sqrt{n})$, σ is estimated by s and the correct degrees of freedom would be $n - 1$.

The table of t distributions is found in Table B of Appendix 2. This table differs in certain ways from the normal distribution table. Each row of the t-distributions table represents a different distribution, since the values of each row are associated with a unique degrees-of-freedom value. The proportions of area[2] are given across the top of the table as .10, .05, down to .0005. These proportions indicate the amount of area remaining in the tails of the distributions corresponding to the points in the columns. It would require a vast number of pages to give all possible values for the entire family of distributions, so only the values at certain points in the distributions are given. Six points appear for each distribution. However, the distributions are symmetric and table values are given in standard form, that is, with a mean of zero and a standard deviation of 1. Therefore, actually 12 points are known for each distribution, since each positive point has a corresponding negative point on the other side of the mean. The area underneath the curve of any one distribution is again defined as 1. The t distributions extend from $-\infty$ to $+\infty$.

To illustrate the area in a specific t distribution, consider the distribution with nine degrees of freedom presented in Figure 9.2. Two points,

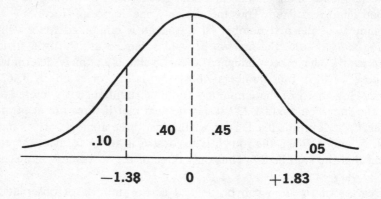

FIGURE 9.2.   Area in the Student's t distribution with nine degrees of freedom

one on each side of the mean, were selected and determined from the table values. Note that the proportion of area indicated is that remaining in the tail of the distribution beyond the designated point.

As an illustration involving the t distribution, suppose we have 20 degrees of freedom and we are selecting a single score from a distribution which we know has a mean of zero and a standard deviation of 1. We also know that the distribution is distributed as the appropriate

2. Table B gives the proportions in terms of significance levels for one- and two-tailed statistical tests. Such tests are discussed in greater detail later in the chapter. For the purposes of this discussion consider the proportions in the top row, that is, those under one-tailed tests.

t distribution. What is the probability that a random selection of one score would result in a score of 1.50 or greater? The first thing to do is to be certain that we are in the correct t distribution. We go down the degrees-of-freedom (df) column until we come to 20. Moving horizontally, we find that the probability of a score of 1.50 or greater appearing by chance is between .1 and .05. We cannot determine it exactly, as with the normal distribution. However, the value we have chosen is closer to the .1 value than to .05, and we can estimate the probability as .08. In terms of area, the scores of 1.50 and greater occupy .08 of the area of the standard t distribution with 20 degrees of freedom. The basic idea of using the t distribution is the same as for the standard normal distribution. When dealing with a specific observed distribution of scores, we must convert to standard form, as when using the standard normal. Then when we compare a computed value with a tabled value, we must select the appropriate t distribution for our degrees of freedom.

Additional underlying distributions will be introduced as they are needed. The concept remains the same, that of determining the underlying distribution of a statistic and considering its area in terms of probability. Underlying distributions are essential in constructing the chain of reasoning from statistics to parameters. Just as a set of scores on an algebra test, for example, has a distribution, so a statistic which is computed from a sample also has a distribution. For the most part, these are theoretical distributions, and the values are provided for us in tables. Once we have determined the underlying distribution of the statistic under study we make our inferences from the statistic to the parameter and then make decisions about hypotheses.

ESTIMATION OF A MEAN

The estimation of a mean, like the other tests of hypotheses, can best be discussed with the help of an example. Consider an imaginary study in which it is desirable to estimate the mean in geometry achievement of a large population of high school sophomores. We will assume that geometry achievement can be measured on a satisfactory equal-interval scale and that such achievement is normally distributed in our population. A random sample is drawn, and members of the sample take the geometry test. The mean computed for the geometry achievement of the sample is 82. (It is not necessary that total possible points be 100, although this may be the case.) If one individual hypothesizes that the mean of the population is 84 and another estimates it to be 81, we could intuitively say that these seem to be reasonable hypotheses. Our reaction to a third hypothesis that the population mean is 50 would be that this hypothesis is untenable. We entertain the hypotheses of 84 and 81 and not of 50 because, intuitively, the mean of 50 seems too distant from the sample mean.

It is hardly satisfactory to make judgments on an intuitive basis alone. This may seem reasonable for the three means of 84, 81, and 50, but where are the points of departure between entertaining and rejecting a hypothesis? The problem is to find two points, one on either side of 82, which represent these points of division. All the values between these two points can be considered as possible values of the population mean. This will provide an interval estimate of the population mean.

If we are testing hypotheses related to the mean in the geometry example and the significance level is set at .05, we will reject the hypothesis if the probability of our mean of 82 appearing, provided the hypothesis is true, is less than .05. Because we are dealing with a mean, we must consider the underlying distribution of the mean to determine the values on either side of it, which includes the middle 95 percent of the area. We leave 2.5 percent of the area in each tail. Since the significance level is .05, 5 percent of the area is left for the rejection region. And since we entertain hypotheses on both sides of the sample mean, the 5 percent is distributed evenly for each tail.

The confidence interval

For the interval estimate of the population mean, we set the condition that the interval we construct will have a .95 probability of spanning the population mean. The interval is constructed symmetrically about the sample mean. In order to decide how far out from this mean we will go, it is necessary to have a standard deviation of the distribution of means. Since it is unlikely that the population standard deviation would be known, we estimate the standard deviation of the distribution of means from the sample standard deviation. The underlying distribution would be the appropriate Student's t distribution, or, if sample size is large enough (for example, exceeding 100), the normal distribution would suffice. We now know where to locate the interval in its appropriate underlying distribution and how to determine its width. Hence we have the necessary ingredients for the construction of the interval.

An interval so constructed is a *confidence interval*. The term "confidence" comes from the fact that we are 95 percent confident that the interval spans the population mean. Note that the probability here is on the interval, based on the statistics of the sample, and not on the parameter. It is incorrect reasoning to infer that the probability is .95 that the population mean falls in the interval. The population mean is something that is not going to change, and it has no probability associated with it. The correct probability statement is that the probability of the interval spanning the population mean is .95. The .95, in this example, is called the *level of confidence*.

Confidence intervals can be constructed without specifically testing hypotheses, but they are quite often considered in this connection. When the level of significance and level of confidence are considered together, they sum to 1.00. The confidence interval in the geometry achievement example above is 95 percent, since the significance level was set at .05. Had the significance level been set at .01 the corresponding confidence interval would be 99 percent. For the same data, a 99 percent confidence interval would be wider than the 95 percent confidence interval. The 99 percent interval leaves only 0.5 percent of the area in each tail of the underlying distribution. Thus, going in a conservative direction (.05 to .01 significance level) tends to widen the confidence interval.

The initial purpose in the geometry achievement example was to estimate the population mean. If one and only one value was demanded in this example, the best estimate would be the sample mean of 82. This would be a point estimate. Although this is the best single-point estimate, it would be rather risky to argue that the population mean is exactly 82. Thus, the estimate provided by the confidence interval gives an interval of estimates which have a 95 percent probability of including the population mean.

Suppose that in the example we computed a 95 percent confidence interval and found this interval to lie between 78.5 and 85.5. This interval is symmetrically located around the sample mean of 82, with 3.5 units on each side. The probability is .95 that this interval spans the population mean. We are 95 percent confident that the population mean is a value between 78.5 and 85.5. Note that we do not put the probability on the population mean. The probability is on the interval which was determined from the sample information, that is, from statistics.

The confidence interval is a test of an infinite number of hypotheses. Any hypothesized value included in the interval will be considered tenable; those that fall outside the interval will be rejected. The confidence interval is a most useful device in estimating a parameter. It gives a basis for deciding on possible values for a parameter, based on probability and statistical reasoning.

THE DIFFERENCE BETWEEN TWO MEANS

The test for a hypothesis regarding the difference of two means can be illustrated by an imaginary situation. A large group of first-grade students is about to embark on reading instruction, and there are two acceptable but quite distinct ways of teaching reading. We can call these method 1 and method 2, designated by M_1 and M_2, respectively. A pertinent question would be: Is there any difference in the effectiveness of the two methods? There might be some discussion as to what constitutes effectiveness, but for the purpose of the example we will define achievement on some acceptable reading test as the measure of effectiveness.

The first step would be to randomly pick two samples from the population of first-grade students being studied. (The two sample sizes need not be the same.) Then we would use M_1 with one sample and M_2 with the other sample, attempting to hold all other relevant factors constant. Upon the completion of the period of instruction, both samples would be tested by the same reading achievement tests and the mean achievement for both samples could be determined. We can designate these means by $\overline{X}_1$ and $\overline{X}_2$, and the difference between the means can be computed by subtracting the smaller from the larger. What about this difference, and what kind of a decision can we make concerning the effectiveness of the methods?

The hypothesis under consideration goes back to the populations. Here we have two populations, although the samples were randomly chosen from a single population. At the time of measuring reading achievement, the samples have been instructed by their respective methods, and thus the samples represent two populations. The one sample represents the population of first-graders taught by M_1 and the other sample the population taught by M_2. We assume that this is the only respect in which the populations differ.

We know that the hypothesis must deal with one or more parameters and that the parameters under consideration in this example are population means. To formulate the statement of the hypothesis, we can use a null hypothesis (see Chapter 1), which hypothesizes no difference or no relationship. In this example, to hypothesize no difference would be to state the hypothesis as: "There is no difference in the population reading achievement means of first-graders taught by M_1 and M_2." The null hypothesis may be represented in symbol form by $\mu_1 = \mu_2$ or $\mu_1 - \mu_2 = 0$. This is the hypothesis to be tested by the statistical procedure.

Each hypothesis has a corresponding alternate hypothesis. The alternate hypothesis of the example would be that the reading achievement means of first-grade populations taught by M_1 and M_2 are not equal. Here we are hypothesizing that there is a difference between these two populations means. Note that in this case the alternate hypothesis does not indicate which of the population means is the greater. In the null hypothesis we are essentially conjecturing that the two methods do not have different effects upon the reading achievement mean. The conjecture in the alternate hypothesis is that there does exist a difference in the effectiveness of the two methods with respect to the mean.

Assuming that the reading achievement test has a substantial number of items and is adequately sensitive to reading achievement, we compute the difference between the sample means, and it turns out to be 1.75 points in favor of M_2. Since this does not seem like much of a difference, our intuitive reaction would be to accept the null hypothesis and conclude that there is no difference between the population means. If the difference in sample means had been 18.9 points in favor of M_2, this result would reflect a marked difference, and we would be inclined to reject the null hypothesis. To determine what magnitude of difference in sample means we will tolerate and still entertain the null hypothesis, we turn to statistics and probability.

The statistic we are dealing with is a difference of two means. If we had the underlying distribution of this statistic we could investigate it to see where our observed difference would fall in light of the hypothesis. In order to determine the standard error (that is, the standard deviation of the underlying distribution) of this statistic we need to work through the standard deviations of the populations. Since it is unlikely that we would know the standard deviations of the populations, we must use an estimate of them, namely the standard deviations of the samples. With the standard deviations of the samples we could compute an estimate of the standard deviation of the underlying distribution. The underlying distribution of the difference of two means is distributed as Student's t distribution, with underlying degrees of freedom, $n_1 + n_2 - 2$ where n_1 and n_2 are the respective sample sizes. The total number of observations is $n_1 + n_2$, and we estimate two parameters, namely the standard deviations of the samples; hence the $n_1 + n_2 - 2$ degrees of freedom.

Since we now have the observed statistic, its underlying distribution, and the standard error of that distribution, we can test our hypothesis. The procedure is known as the *t test for the difference between two means*. We determine the probability of our observed difference appearing, if, in fact, the null hypothesis of no difference is true. If this probability is less than our significance level (say .05), we reject the null hypothesis. Note that the statistic has the probability associated with it, but it has been observed and cannot be rejected. The parameters of the hypothesis have no probability connected with them. If the statistical test is significant the conclusion is that we hypothesized incorrectly. In this example we would then conclude that there is a difference in population means of reading achievement of first-graders taught by M_1 and M_2. If the statistical test is not significant, we conclude that on the basis of this information we cannot reject the hypothesis of no difference.

In light of the hypothesis, we need not determine the exact probability of the statistic. Our only concern is on which side of our significance level the probability falls. If the probability is less than this level, then we say that the difference between means is statistically significant.

An additional comment about the reasoning is in order. Recall that the samples were randomly selected from a common population and that we were attempting to hold constant all relevant factors except the teaching method. If this holds true, the only things operating on the difference in mean achievement are differences due to random sampling error and teaching method. We can check on the probability of the observed difference being due to random sampling. If this probability is less than our significance level, we reject it as the source of difference, leaving the teaching method as the only remaining source. To decide upon the more effective teaching method we inspect the sample means.

A more specific example of a null hypothesis concerning the difference between two means might be as follows. Two samples of size 32 and 30 are randomly selected from a population of first-graders. The samples receive reading instruction by M_1 and M_2, respectively. After the instructional period (probably several weeks in duration), all 62 are given a common reading achievement test. The results are $\bar{X}_1 = 90.00$, $\bar{X}_2 = 81.75$, and the standard error of the difference is 3.5. The null hypothesis is $\mu_1 - \mu_2 = 0$, that is, the means of the populations from which the samples were drawn are equal, and the significance level is set at .05.

The computation of the t value actually is the ratio of the difference between the observed statistic and the hypothesized value of the corresponding parameter to the standard error of the statistic. In symbols this is given by:

$$\frac{(\bar{X}_1 - \bar{X}_2) - (\mu_1 - \mu_2)}{S_{\bar{X}_1 - \bar{X}_2}}.$$

Substituting in the sample values gives:

$$\bar{X}_1 - \bar{X}_2 = 90.00 - 81.75 = 8.25.$$

$\mu_1 - \mu_2 = 0$, from the hypothesis), and $S_{\bar{X}_1} - x_2 = 3.5$. Thus the t value becomes $(8.25 - 0)/3.5 = 2.36$, with $32 + 30 - 2 = 60$ as the associated degrees of freedom. With the null hypothesis of $\mu_1 = \mu_2$, we hypothesized no direction and the rejection region appears in both tails of the underlying distribution.[3] We consult Table B of Appendix 2 and find that for 60 degrees of freedom a value of 2.00 is required for significance at the .05 level. Thus the statistical test is significant. The probability that the observed difference between sample means of 8.25

---

3. This is the condition for a two-tailed test, as explained in the section to follow.

would appear by chance, if, in fact, the population means are equal is less than .05. Therefore we reject the null hypothesis and conclude that the population means are not equal. By inspection we can see that the difference in sample means favored M_1.

ONE- AND TWO-TAILED STATISTICAL TESTS

The hypothesis of the preceding example did not hypothesize a direction. The difference between the reading achievement means of first-grade populations taught by M_1 and M_2, or $\mu_1 - \mu_2$, could, in fact, be on either side of zero. Another way of saying this is that μ_1 may be greater than μ_2 or, vice versa, μ_2 greater than μ_1. Hence we had what is called a *two-tailed test,* designating one-half of the rejection area for each tail of the distribution. The name "two-tailed" comes from the condition that the rejection region is contained in both ends or tails of the distribution. In the preceding example, when we consulted the table to determine the value necessary for significance, we came down the column for two-tailed tests at the .05 level of significance and found the value 2.00 corresponding to 60 degrees of freedom. The right part of Figure 9.3 illustrates the location of the rejection region for a two-tailed test.

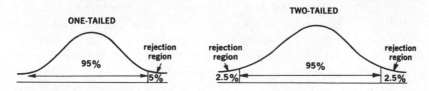

FIGURE 9.3.   Rejection regions for one- and two-tailed tests with $\alpha = .05$

Consider a slightly different situation. Suppose the two teaching methods are of such a nature that M_2 utilizes the existing textbooks and materials and M_1 involves a major change in materials. In order to justify this changeover, the evidence would have to significantly favor M_1. In this case we would hypothesize a direction, namely $\mu_1 > \mu_2$. The alternate hypothesis is that μ_1 is not greater than μ_2.

In determining the rejection region in such a case, we must consider the underlying distribution and its location. Recall that in the two-tailed test the underlying distribution was located by the null hypothesis. However, a directional hypothesis such as $\mu_1 > \mu_2$ does not locate a distribution, since an infinite number of hypothesized values would satisfy $\mu_1 > \mu_2$. With a directional hypothesis, we also use the null hypothesis for locating the underlying distribution. However, instead of having the rejection region located in both tails, as with a two-tailed test, in the circumstances of a directional hypothesis, the rejection region is located in one tail of the underlying distribution. When the rejection region is located entirely in one tail, this is referred to as a *one-tailed test*.

If we consider $\overline{X}_1 - \overline{X}_2$, which goes with the direction of the hypothesis, the rejection region would be in the right tail for this example. The negative values would not concern us because we are not interested in showing M_2 superior to M_1. In this case, the rejection region would be entirely located in the one tail. Suppose the significance level was again set at .05 and we have 60 degrees of freedom. The t value required for significance with a one-tailed test is 1.67, which would not be as great as the corresponding value for a two-tailed test. We do not need to go out as far from the mean in standard deviation units to have 5 percent of the tail remaining as we do for 2.5 percent. Figure 9.3 illustrates the rejection regions in terms of area for one- and two-tailed tests with the significance level set at .05.

In the preceding example, $\overline{X}_1 - \overline{X}_2 = 8.25$ gave a t value of 2.36. This value exceeds the 1.67 required for significance and therefore our statistical test is significant and we reject the hypothesis that μ_1 is not greater than μ_2. Our conclusion is that μ_1 is greater than μ_2 and therefore that M_1 is a superior method of teaching. It should be noted that had $\overline{X}_1 - \overline{X}_2$ been negative, that is, had $\overline{X}_2$ been greater than $\overline{X}_1$, it would not have been necessary to perform any computation, since in this particular example there is no rejection region in the negative tail of the underlying distribution.

A word of caution about the conclusion when using a one-tailed test. Suppose a one-tailed test is computed and found to be significant, that is, the value is in the rejection region. What are we going to reject? The rejection region refers to the hypothesis that μ_1 is not greater than μ_2. Therefore we do not reject our initial hypothesis of μ_1 greater than μ_2. We would conclude that μ_1 is greater than μ_2 and, as noted above, that M_1 is more effective than M_2. The matter of the alternate hypothesis is relative. The rejection region refers to the hypothesis of no difference (two-tailed) or not greater than (one-tailed). It could also be formulated as "not less than" if the situation warranted this direction. Caution should be exercised so as not to become confused in reasoning from the result of the statistical test to the correct conclusion regarding the hypothesis, whether or not this is stated in null form.

It should be remembered that we do not want to make a change from M_2 to M_1 unless we are almost completely certain that M_1 shows a significantly greater mean achievement. If the t test is found to be significant at the .05 level, our conclusion is that the probability is less than .05 (less than 1 in 20) that the observed difference occurred by chance. This probability may still be too great for some skeptics. If this is the case, it might have been preferable to go to a more conservative significance level, say .01. In extreme cases the .001 level might be used, but this is generally not done in educational research. Going in this direction actually lowers the probability of rejecting the hypothesis of no difference.

The preceding examples illustrate a specific use of the t test for comparing the means of two independent samples. The t distribution has many applications in hypothesis testing. The computation is a technical matter and not of importance for the purposes of this text. Whenever a researcher uses computational formulas, they should be checked with a statistics text to be certain of appropriateness and correct application.

ONE-WAY ANALYSIS OF VARIANCE

If we had three teaching methods and consequently three means to test for significant differences, one approach would be to consider the means in combinations of two and apply three separate t tests. But it soon becomes apparent that this procedure would be inefficient. For five means it would require 10 separate t tests; for six means 15 such tests would be necessary. More important than the inefficiency in using multiple t tests in the same analysis is the fact that we would expect some to be statistically significant just by chance. In order to apply multiple t tests appropriately in the same analysis, the significance level would have to be adjusted and a separate level used for each possible number of such t tests to be computed.

A more desirable and more efficient technique is the analysis of variance (ANOVA), which is one of the most powerful and most widely used procedures. The discussion in this text is limited to the ideas relative to application and hypothesis testing. There are many variations of the analysis of variance, and the procedures are extensively involved with the design of experiments. Computational procedures can become quite involved and complex. The basic ideas relative to hypothesis testing remain the same, however, and these are what we are concerned with in this discussion.

The analysis of variance may be summarized as a technique for partitioning the variation in the observed data into parts, each part assignable to different causes or combinations of causes. Analysis of variance is appropriate when it can be assumed that the several groups of observations can be treated as random samples from the populations.

It is further assumed that if the populations differ, they differ only in their means.

To illustrate what is involved in partitioning the variance, consider a situation in which three teaching methods are used, and 30 students are taught by each method. The students are measured on an achievement test, giving 90 observations or scores on the dependent variable. If all 90 scores are exactly the same there would be no variance. This is extremely unlikely, and one possible source of difference is the three different teaching methods. Another possible source is the students. The 30 students within each group were taught by the same methods, presumably had the same teacher, spent the same amount of time in class, and in general have been treated the same. Nevertheless, they do not all have identical scores because there exists what we might term a "natural" variation among the students who receive the same treatment. This variance is more commonly called the *error variance,* or *expected variance.* (This estimate of error variance is also called within variance, as will be noted below. There is also an estimate of variance between groups, which is called between or among group variance). To partition the variance in this example means to consider the variation of all 90 scores and decide what part is attributable to teaching method (between groups) and what part is due to the difference within the three groups. In this example there were only two sources of variation. In more complex analyses there might be several sources, and the variance would be partitioned among all sources.

Consider a research situation in which a mathematics teacher is to have four sections of elementary algebra during the upcoming school year. Prior to the scheduling he arranges with the administration to randomly assign 25 incoming freshmen to each of his four classes. (This is an unlikely freedom in most practical situations.) From the opening of the school year the teacher proceeds to teach each class using different experimental materials. These materials are designated as M_1, M_2, M_3, and M_4. The question under investigation is whether the experimental materials have different effects upon algebra achievement. The independent variable in this study is type of material or, simply, material. It has four levels. The dependent variable is algebra achievement. There are several constants, including school, teacher, and grade level (note that only incoming freshmen are involved in the study).

We are assuming that algebra achievement is continuously distributed and can be measured on an equal-unit scale. Achievement would probably be measured after a considerable instructional period, say one semester. The test might be teacher made but caution would have to be exercised to avoid slanting the questions to any specific type of material. If a standardized test of algebraic achievement is available, it could be used as the measure of achievement, but it would require careful inspection to ensure that it covers the objectives of algebra instruction and adequately applies to the situation.

The actual data collected are the scores of the 100 (or remaining) students who take the algebra test. If a student moves away or for some reason cannot participate to completion this is not serious, because the analysis of variance in this case does not require equal numbers in the four groups. We assume that no systematic dropout is occurring in the groups and any dropouts would be randomly distributed among the four groups. The scores on the tests are the data that go into the analysis of variance.

The null hypothesis of this hypothetical study is that the population means of the four groups taught algebra using M_1, M_2, M_3, and M_4 are equal. Initially it may seem that we do not have four populations, only four samples. However, underlying these samples are four populations to which we hope to generalize our results. The four populations are considered to be alike in all characteristics except the materials used in instruction. The null hypothesis may be written symbolically as: H_0: $\mu_1 = \mu_2 = \mu_3 = \mu_4$. Note that the hypothesis is a statement about parameters, not statistics. No difference between population means is being hypothesized.

Analysis of variance involves a component called "sums of squares." *Sums of squares* means that the difference between an observation and a mean is squared, then these differences squared are summed over the number of observations. For example, in the hypothetical situation of 100 students the total sum of squares would be given by

$$\sum_{i=1}^{100} (X_i - \bar{X})^2,$$

where $\bar{X}$ is the grand mean of all 100 observations. This looks very much like the numerator of the formula for variance. The value of the degrees of freedom corresponds to the denominator of the formula for variance. In the analysis of variance, sums of squares are divided by the appropriate degrees of freedom for an estimate of the variance.

An estimate of the error variance (within or natural variance) is the *pooled variance* within the four groups of the study. To illustrate a pooled variance, suppose the sum of squares is computed individually for each of the four groups. We would subtract each observation from its group mean instead of from the grand mean, square and sum these squares. Within each group the degrees of freedom would be one less than the number in the group. Then we would add the four sums of squares and divide by the sum of the four degrees-of-freedom values for the estimate of error variance. This addition process is called pooling; hence the name "pooled variance." The term "error variance," as noted above, means the estimate of the existing natural or random variance. We assume that the four groups have about equal variance, so we pool these variances. In the actual process, to obtain the estimate, the sums of squares are pooled and this is divided by the pooled degrees of freedom. We will designate this estimate of the error variance by S_W^2. The subscript W denotes the estimate from the difference *within* the group.

Under the assumption that the population means are equal, the variance between the sample means should be a second estimate of the error variance. Even if the population means are equal we would expect some variation in sample means due to sampling fluctuations. When the sum of squares between means is computed and divided by the appropriate degrees of freedom, this estimate would contain only random or error variance. There would be no variance due to differences in population means. This second estimate we will denote by S_B^2. The subscript B denotes the estimate from the difference *between* sample means. Now, under the assumption of equal means, we have two estimates of the same error variance. The only difference between them is the difference due to chance.

In the work with the Student's t test we considered the difference of two means. Here we have two variances, and, since these variances are computed from samples, they are statistics. We do not consider their difference but their ratio. Under the hypothesis of equal means, these two variances estimate the same error variance, and we would expect their ratio to be 1.00. But what kind of underlying distribution does the ratio of two variances have? The answer is the F distribution, which can be found in Table D of Appendix 2.

The F distribution

The F distribution, like the t distribution, consists of a family of distributions. Unlike the t distributions, the F distributions are not symmetrical. F distributions do not take on negative values, in fact, the tabled values provide only values greater than or equal to 1.0. Under the null hypothesis, in the analysis of variance the numerator of the ratio S_B^2/S_W^2 contains as many sources of variance as the denominator, and therefore we would expect the ratio to be at least 1.0.

The F distributions require two degrees-of-freedom values to identify the appropriate distribution; degrees-of-freedom values appear both across the top and down the side in Table D. The term "mean square" is used in the headings. A *mean square* is an estimate of variance, for example $S_B{}^2$ is a mean square, as is $S_W{}^2$. In order to locate the correct F distribution, the two degrees-of-freedom values used are those associated with $S_B{}^2$, the numerator of the ratio across the top (df for greater mean square), and those associated with $S_W{}^2$, the denominator of the ratio down the side (df for lesser mean square). So the degrees-of-freedom values are determined by the degrees-of-freedom values associated with the variance estimates (mean squares) that make up the ratio.

Under the null hypothesis we would expect the ratio of $S_B{}^2/S_W{}^2$ to be around 1, since $S_B{}^2$ and $S_W{}^2$ estimate the same variance. The F distributions as given in Table D give us the values for the probability of .05 and .01. That is, the values determine the rejection regions for testing the null hypothesis with significance levels of .05 and .01, respectively. If values of the computed ratio (F values) are greater than the indicated table values, the probabilities of their appearing by chance are less than .05 and .01. If we have a specific computed F ratio and its value exceeds the tabled value (for the correct degrees-of-freedom values) at .05, we say the statistical test is significant at the .05 level of significance.

Suppose that the null hypothesis is not true, that is, there are real differences between the group means. That means that $S_B{}^2$ not only contains error variance but also variation due to differences in the means. Thus $S_B{}^2$ will tend to be inflated, and, since it is the numerator of the ratio, the ratio will tend to increase. As the ratio increases its probability of appearing by chance decreases. When we reach the significance level of .05 or .01, whichever we have selected, we will no longer entertain the idea that the value of this ratio occurred by chance.

Let us inspect the reasoning carefully. Suppose for the algebra study the analysis of variance produced a significant F ratio. Here, "significant" means that its probability of occurrence by chance is less than the probability (significance) level, say .05. There are now two possible explanations for this F ratio:

1. There are no real differences between the population means from which the sample was drawn, and the F ratio occurred only by chance (random sampling errors); that is, we contend that a rare event has occurred, since its probability of occurrence is less than .05.
2. We reject the null hypothesis and conclude that the F ratio did not occur by chance but due to real differences in the population means of the group.

It is the second of these explanations that we will entertain. Since our significance level is .05, we are running the risk of being wrong about 1 in 20 times.

A word about the degrees-of-freedom values of the F ratio. Earlier it was pointed out that we lose a degree of freedom for each restriction we place on the data. The S_B^2 is determined by squaring the deviations of the group means from the grand mean. In the algebra instruction example, there are four group means, but since the grand mean is known, if three of the group means are known the fourth is also determined. Therefore, the degrees of freedom associated with S_B^2 are $4 - 1 = 3$. In general, if we let k be the number of group means, the degrees of freedom associated with S_B^2 are $k - 1$.

The S_W^2 is a pooled estimate of variance. The deviation of each observation within a group from the group mean is squared. Since a mean is necessary for each group, one degree of freedom is lost in each group. In the example, since each group contains 25 observations we would have 24 degrees of freedom within each group. But, because we pool the degrees of freedom, the degrees of freedom associated with S_W^2 are 96. In general, we know that the sum of the observations across all groups is the total sample size, say n. We lose a degree of freedom for each group mean, and if we have k groups, the degrees of freedom associated with S_W^2 are $n - k$. This value for our example is $100 - 4$ or, again, 96.

The correct degrees of freedom for the F ratio of our example are 3 and 96. By inspection of Table D we see that approximately 2.70 is needed for significance at the .05 level. (In using the table we take the degrees of freedom of S_B^2 across the top of the table. In arriving at approximately 2.70, we go down the column marked 3. We come to the row which has 100 degrees of freedom which is as close as we can come to 96. The tabled value for 100 degrees of freedom is 2.70, for 80 degrees of freedom 2.72. But 96 is much closer to 100 than 80, therefore the 2.70 is used.)

If the F ratio had not been significant we would conclude that on the basis of these results no one of the materials will produce higher mean achievement than any of the others. That is, we fail to reject the null hypothesis of equal population means. The associated probability statement after the statistical test would be: The probability that the sample means, $\bar{X}_1$, $\bar{X}_2$, $\bar{X}_3$, $\bar{X}_4$, would have appeared by chance if, in fact, $\mu_1 = \mu_2 = \mu_3 = \mu_4$ is greater than .05. Note the "greater than," since the test was not significant. Suppose the F ratio *is* significant. Then the associated probability statement would be: The probability that the sample means, $\bar{X}_1$, $\bar{X}_2$, $\bar{X}_3$, and $\bar{X}_4$, would have occurred by chance if, in fact, $\mu_1 = \mu_2 = \mu_3 = \mu_4$ is less than .05. However, we still do not know where the significance lies, that is, what the pattern of significant differences between the sample means is. The first thing we would do is inspect the means and arrange them in descending or ascending order, but it has been pointed out that inspection is not an adequate technique in deciding about the differences in means.

At this point some post-mortem test is necessary to locate the source of the significance. Student's t tests could be computed for the difference of the means in combinations of two, but this is an inefficient procedure because several such tests would be required. The number of t tests would rapidly increase with the number of groups. For example, four groups would require 6 tests; five groups 10 tests; and six groups 15 such tests. Also, if a large number of means are involved a certain number of these tests would be expected to turn up significant by chance. There are other more efficient procedures. Although the computation procedures are beyond the scope of this text, discussions relevant to this topic are treated in more advanced statistics and research design texts.[4]

Assume that in the algebra instruction example the mean of the group taught by M_3 was significantly higher than the remaining three means. We would then conclude that students taught by M_3 attain a higher mean achievement in algebra, and on this basis M_3 is superior to the other three experimental materials. Note that the conclusion here refers to populations of students taught by the use of the four types of materials.

The algebra example involved a one-way analysis of variance. One-way means that only one independent variable was under investigation. The total variance was partitioned into two parts: one part due to differences between group means and a second part due to differences within groups.

TWO-WAY ANALYSIS OF VARIANCE

An important characteristic of the analysis of variance is the possibility of testing more than two group means in a single analysis. It also has other important advantages over less sophisticated techniques. One of these is that two or more independent variables can be investigated simultaneously in the same analysis. When two independent variables are included in the same analysis of variance it is called a *two-way analysis of variance*. There may be any number of groups or levels within an independent variable.

Many research situations involve more than one independent variable. It may be of interest to check not only how the various independent

---

4. For an excellent discussion of multiple comparisons of means, see L. Edwards, *Experimental Design in Psychological Research,* 4th ed. (New York: Holt, Rinehart & Winston, 1972), pp. 130–39.

variables affect the dependent variable but also how combinations of their levels affect the dependent variable. Independent variables in combinations can have an effect which neither one would have singly, and they can influence or affect one another. We have already encountered this concept in Chapter 3, where it is referred to as interaction, or the failure of the effect of one independent variable to remain constant over the levels of another. The analysis of variance can be used to test (statistically) for the existence of interaction.

As an example of a two-way analysis of variance involving interaction, suppose a school has three methods of teaching history and the staff decides to teach it at two different times, say morning and afternoon. We now have two independent variables: teaching method and time of day. The teaching methods will be denoted by M_1, M_2, and M_3: the times by T_1 and T_2. To get all of the levels of the independent variables in all possible combinations with each other, we need 3×2 or 6 groups. These are designated as M_1T_1, M_1T_2, M_2T_1, M_2T_2, M_3T_1, and M_3T_2.

Suppose that the dependent variable is achievement in history which can be objectively and adequately measured on an interval scale. Before the instructional period begins we would randomly assign equal numbers of students to each of the six groups. (If this is a sophomore history class we would assign only sophomores.) After an adequate instructional period the dependent variable would be measured. The analysis of variance would be performed on the scores of the dependent variable.

Three questions are posed in this hypothetical example. Generally they can be stated as follows:

1. Does teaching method affect achievement in history?
2. Does the time of day for teaching affect achievement in history?
3. Do teaching method and time have an interaction effect upon history achievement?

We must now consider the corresponding hypotheses. If there is an effect of any of these independent variables (or their combination), we expect it to show up in the mean achievement of the groups. The null hypotheses are statements about population means. The populations are the populations taught by the different methods and at the different times, and we assume our samples to be representative of these populations. The null hypothesis for method is H_0: $\mu_{M_1} = \mu_{M_2} = \mu_{M_3}$. The μ's represent the respective population means of the populations taught by the three teaching methods, M_1, M_2, M_3. The null hypothesis for time is H_0: $\mu_{T_1} = \mu_{T_2}$.

Recall that the numbers in each of the six groups were equal and assume that they remained equal through the completion of the data collection. Note that the independent variables are balanced with respect to each other. T_1 contains equal numbers of students taught by M_1, M_2, and M_3. The same is true for T_2, and T_2 contains the same number of each as T_1. The methods are balanced in the same manner relative to the two times.

We shall set our significance level at .05. The workings of the analysis of variance are the same in the two-way as the one-way except that the computations are more extensive and there are additional sources of variance. In the one-way analysis of variance we partition the total variance into two parts, one due to differences between groups and the other due to differences within groups. In the two-way analysis of variance we partition the total variance into four parts; that is, instead of having only two sources of variance we have four sources, one part for each of the independent variables. In the example these would correspond to differences between the methods and differences between the times. There is also one component of variance for interaction and one component for differences within the groups.

The purpose in the two-way analysis of variance, as in the one-way analysis, is to get ratios of error variance under the null hypothesis. In the one-way analysis of variance there was only one ratio, the ratio of the between component to the within component. In the two-way analysis of variance there are three such ratios: one for each of the independent variables and one for their interaction. We want to get ratios that are distributed as the F distributions, with the corresponding degrees of freedom.

With the one-way analysis of variance there is no question about how to set up an F ratio because there is only one such ratio—the between estimate of variance over the within. In the two-way analysis of variance there are other possible ways of setting up the F ratios, since there are four estimates of variance. For the purposes of this discussion and in the context of the history-teaching example we will assume that we have a fixed-effects model.[5] A *fixed-effects model* is one for which the levels of the independent variables have been "fixed" by the researcher and have not been randomly selected from a larger population of possible

---

5. The nature of the independent variables in terms of how their levels have been selected and put into the analysis determines the components of variance that are in the respective estimates of variance. This will, of course, influence how we set up our F ratios. In general, we want the numerator of the F ratio to contain one and only one more component of variance than the denominator, that being the component of the effect being tested. Under the null hypothesis this component is no more than error variance. A detailed discussion of different models is beyond the scope of this book. Edwards, *Experimental Design in Psychological Research,* has an excellent treatment of this topic, and the reader who anticipates computing analyses of variance with multiple independent variables would do well to consult the Edwards reference.

levels. In the example, the fact that method is a fixed effect means that the researcher designated and defined the three different methods, and he is attempting to generalize only to these three methods. He did not select the three methods from a larger population of methods. When the independent variables in a two-way analysis of variance are fixed, the denominator of each F ratio for testing the effects of the independent variables and their interaction would be the within estimate of variance. In the example this estimate would be the pooled within variance of the six groups.[6]

The probability statement associated with the method means is: What is the probability of the observed means occurring by chance if, in fact, there is no difference in populations means? Since analysis of variance involves the F ratio, an equivalent way of considering our probability statement is: What is the probability of the observed F ratio occurring by chance if there are no differences in the population means? The second statement is more specific as to what is tested in the analysis of variance. The first may seem more specific to the null hypothesis.

It is not necessary that we determine the exact probability; we are interested only in whether it is less or greater than .05, our significance level. Knowing this will enable us to make a decision about the null hypothesis. Since the table of F ratios is used for making this decision, before a decision can be made we must have an F ratio. In the two-way analysis of variance a different F ratio is computed for each of the two main effects[7] and their interaction effect. The basic procedure is the same as that for a one-way analysis of variance. For example, to determine the F ratio associated with the effect of teaching method we would obtain an estimate of the variance between the three method means and an estimate of error variance. The ratio of these two estimates would make up the F ratio which would test the null hypothesis for teaching method. An analogous procedure would be used to test the null hypothesis for time of instruction and to test for an interaction effect.

If a significant F ratio appears when testing method, we say there is a significant method effect. The same would be true for the time variable. The third effect in this analysis is the interaction between the two independent variables. Interaction has been described above as an effect of combinations of the independent variables. To have a significant interaction effect, the effect of one independent variable does not re-

---

6. In the case of no replication (only one observation) within the cells, a within estimate can be used as the denominator of the F ratios for testing the effects of the independent variables *if* the assumption can be made that there is no interaction effect and hence this component contains only error variance. With no replication there is no way to statistically test for an interaction effect in a two-way analysis of variance.

7. The effect of an independent variable singly is called a *main effect*.

main constant over the levels of the other independent variable. That is, the effect varies with different combinations of levels of the two independent variables. Significant interaction effects may take on several different patterns of means; one such possible pattern was discussed in Chapter 3.

In the context of the history-teaching example, a significant interaction would indicate that one (or more) method shows a greater increase in effectiveness in going from one time to the other than one (or more) of the other methods. For a specific analysis it is well to plot the dependent variable means for all combinations of the independent variables on a graph. The units on the vertical axis represent the dependent variable scale of measurement, while those arbitrarily spaced on the horizontal axis represent the levels of one of the independent variables. These means are sometimes referred to as *cell means*. In our example there would be six such means, one for each of the combinations (or cells), M_1T_1, M_1T_2, M_2T_1, M_2T_2, M_3T_1, and M_3T_2. Figure 9.4 shows a possible pattern of means which would indicate no

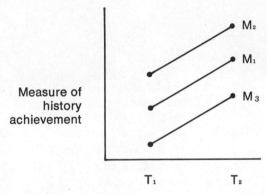

FIGURE 9.4.   Possible plot of means indicating no significant interaction between time and method

interaction. Figure 9.5 shows four possible patterns which might yield a significant interaction effect. The points on the graphs represent the six cell means. To be certain of such an effect the mathematical computations and tests of the interaction F ratio would be necessary.

There could be many more possible plots of the six means, but if an actual analysis were done only one specific pattern would exist. A significant interaction may appear in the absence of significant main effects. An example of such a situation would be the lower left plot of Figure 9.5

The degrees of freedom associated with the interaction are the product of the degrees of freedom associated with the independent variables, in

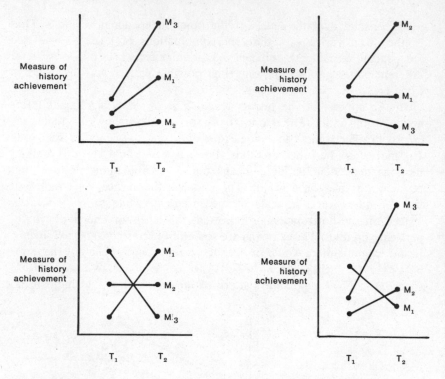

FIGURE 9.5.   Four possible plots of means indicating significant interaction between time and method

the interaction. Suppose we let k and j represent the number of levels of the independent variables. Then the degrees of freedom associated with the interaction are the product of $(k - 1)(j - 1)$. In our example the degrees of freedom would be $(3 - 1)(2 - 1) = 2$. The degrees of freedom for the main effects are determined in the same manner as for the one-way analysis of variance. In this case, method would have two degrees of freedom and time would have one. The number of degrees of freedom associated with the within estimate of variance would be total sample size minus six.

The data for a two-way analysis of variance are sometimes arranged in a *row-and-column array*. This is done only for the purpose of structural convenience. In such an array one variable is placed on the rows and another on the columns. The product of the numbers of rows and columns is then the number of cells in the analysis. In the column-and-row array for the time and method example shown in Figure 9.6, method is indicated by the columns and time by the rows. The row and column means are usually indicated but they are not considered a part of the $k \times j$ (in this case 3×2) array. It can be seen that each row and

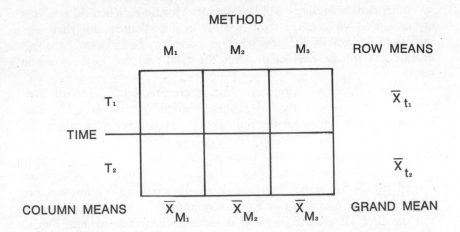

FIGURE 9.6.   Row and column array for a two-way analysis of variance involving time and method

column sum has one restriction, since the dependent variable means of the levels of the independent variables are computed. Inspection of the array indicates that there are $(3-1)(2-1) = 2$ cells free to vary. In general there are $(k-1)(j-1)$ cells free to vary, and this product is the number of degrees of freedom associated with the interaction term.

Advantage of increased precision

The two-way analysis of variance provides for the possibilities of checking on more than one independent variable simultaneously and checking whether there exists an interaction effect, two advantages which were mentioned earlier. Another advantage that can be realized from a two-way analysis of variance is increased statistical precision, because it accounts for additional sources of variance and thus reduces the estimate of within or error variance. Building relevant extraneous variables into a design as independent variables so that the variance they produce can be controlled or accounted for increases statistical precision as well as aids in explaining the results.

Suppose that in the history-teaching example discussed above instead of a two-way analysis of variance the researcher had used a one-way analysis of variance, with method (three levels) as the independent variable. The same number of students are used, and it is assumed that one-half of them participate in the morning and one-half in the afternoon. However, since time is not considered an independent variable, no component of variance will be computed for time. When the students are measured we have the same number of observations, and these observations are exactly the same whether a one-way or a two-way analysis of variance will be computed. Thus the total variance is the same in either case.

In the two-way analysis of variance there are four sources of variance, one being due to the independent variable "time." If the F value for the null hypothesis for the time effect is statistically significant, the variance due to the difference between the means for the two times is more than random or error variance.

When only a one-way analysis of variance is computed, the variance caused by the difference in times is in the error or within variance component, the $S_W{}^2$. But this is the denominator of the F ratio used to test the effect of method. Since it is inflated (contains variance due to time as well as within variance) the F ratio $S_B{}^2/S_W{}^2$ will be less sensitive to a method effect. That is, it will take a bigger difference in the means for method to produce a $S_B{}^2$ such that the F ratio will be statistically significant. It could be that a two-way analysis of variance would produce a significant method effect, while a one-way analysis would not, even though the same data were analyzed. In the one-way, the $S_W{}^2$ would be inflated and the F ratio would not reach statistical significance. In this case, the two-way analysis of variance would have increased precision over the one-way. Similarly, if the interaction effect would be significant, and if it is not computed, it too would inflate the $S_W{}^2$.

The above relationship among the estimates of variance (mean squares) can be shown with formulas. Let $S_M{}^2$ be the mean square for method. It would be the same whether a one-way or two-way analysis of variance were computed. Let the following mean squares come from the two-way analysis of variance: $S_T{}^2$ for time, $S_{MXT}{}^2$ for method by time interaction, and $S_W{}^2$ for within. Consider the F ratios for testing the effect of method, F_1 being the F ratio from the one-way and F_2 being the F ratio from the two-way analysis of variance:

$$F_1 = \frac{S_M{}^2}{S_W{}^2 + S_T{}^2 + S_{MXT}{}^2}$$
$$F_2 = \frac{S_M{}^2}{S_W{}^2}$$

If the $S_T{}^2$ and the $S_{MXT}{}^2$ contain any variance except random variance, the F_2 ratio will be *greater* than the F_1 ratio and therefore it will be more likely to be statistically significant. The two-way analysis of variance is more sensitive to the difference in the means of the levels of method (from which $S_M{}^2$ is computed) and therefore has increased statistical precision over the one-way analysis of variance.

It might be inferred that by identifying more and more sources of variance we could keep on increasing statistical precision indefinitely. Certainly more complex analyses of variance can be structured, but with increasing complexity certain difficulties may be encountered.

MORE COMPLEX ANALYSES OF VARIANCE

The data from two experimental designs discussed in Chapter 4, factorial designs and Latin square designs, are usually analyzed by an analysis of variance. The history-teaching example involving method and time discussed in the preceding section can be considered a factorial design with two independent variables. It is also possible to construct analyses of variance that include more than two independent variables. A detailed discussion of such analyses is beyond the scope of this book, but some general characteristics will be mentioned.

As the number of independent variables is increased, the number of possible interactions between independent variables is also increased, and different types (also called *orders*) of interactions become possible. In the two-way analysis of variance discussed in the preceding section we had one interaction which involved the two independent variables. An interaction involving two independent variables is called a *first-order interaction*. These kinds of interactions are relatively easy to interpret.

In an analysis of variance with three independent variables, we can have three first-order interactions, the independent variables in combinations of two. But, we can also have a *second-order interaction,* one involving all three independent variables. In this type of analysis of variance we have the possibility of eight sources of variance; the three main effects, the three first-order interaction effects, the second-order interaction effect, and the within variance. With additional independent variables included in an analysis of variance, more sources of variance and more complex interactions are possible. Higher order interactions may be impossible, or at least difficult, to interpret. Of course, if they are not statistically significant they cause no problems. In some analyses they are included with the within variance.

The matter of computing a complex analysis of variance is seldom a problem. The basic questions involve research design. What number of independent variables can be simultaneously included in a meaningful way? What assumptions can be made about higher order interactions? Can they be assumed to have no effect? Are there limits on the number of Ss available? (Complex analyses can require large numbers of Ss if within-cell replication is high.) These kinds of questions must be considered in the context of the specific variables and conditions of the research. Complex analyses can be very useful and efficient, but they must be fitted carefully to the specific project.

The Latin square design example discussed in Chapter 4 (see Figure 4.2) is what is called a *repeated measures design*. Repeated measures means that two or more observations are taken on the same *S;* in the example, each *S* was measured three times. Because repeated measures violate the assumption of independence necessary for a parametric technique, when the analysis of variance is set up certain conditions must be considered. One condition is whether the lack of independence has somehow reduced the estimate of within variance. For some analyses there are multiple within terms, and not all *F* ratios computed in the analysis have the same denominator. Thus the identification of the appropriate within or error terms for testing the various effects in the analysis of variance can be somewhat complicated.

A word about the assumptions underlying the analysis of variance is in order. These, of course, are the parametric assumptions. The analysis of variance is a robust technique, that is, for large sample sizes the underlying distributions can depart quite markedly from normality without seriously affecting the application of the technique. This should not, however, be interpreted as an indication that the assumptions may be disregarded. An equal-unit scale is assumed for the measurement of the dependent variable. There is also an assumption called the assumption of *homogeneity of variance,* which assumes that the samples or groups come from populations with equal variance. If there is a reason to believe that this assumption has been violated there are ways it can be checked statistically. A common computational procedure is the Bartlett test for homogeneity of variance, which is discussed in detail in selected research design and statistics texts.[8]

ANALYSIS OF COVARIANCE

A statistical technique for testing hypotheses that is closely related to the analysis of variance is the analysis of covariance, a method of statistical control which adjusts dependent variable scores for initial differences on some variable. It is especially useful for situations in which experimental control over an extraneous or mediating variable is impossible or undesirable. A researcher, especially one who works in a school setting, often must take intact groups such as classes for his research studies. For practical reasons, he cannot equate the groups

8. See, for example, Quinn McNemar, *Psychological Statistics,* 4th ed. (New York: John Wiley & Sons, 1969), pp. 285–86.

through random assignment. The analysis of covariance can often be used effectively in such situations. Many investigations in educational research are or could be strengthened by the use of this technique.

Consider a research situation in which the researcher is interested in determining the effects of team teaching as compared to self-contained classroom instruction upon sixth-grade achievement in mathematics. The research situation is set up in a single school. It is unlikely that the administrative procedures of the school would allow for random assignment of students to the two techniques; the classes would likely have to be taken as they have been set up. Assume that somehow the teachers for the two groups can be equated and that teachers are favorable toward the method they teach. The materials used, instructional time, and other conditions are held constant for both groups.

The question being investigated may be stated as: Do sixth-grade students show higher mathematics achievement when taught in a self-contained classroom or a team-teaching situation? We will define the more effective method as that which indicates the higher mean achievement for the group. Since we want to generalize this to some population of sixth-graders, we will consider the means on our two groups as statistics and test for a statistically significant difference. Thus the null hypothesis is that there is no difference in the mean achievement in mathematics of sixth-graders, as defined by our population, taught in a self-contained or team-teaching situation.

Near the end of the academic year the students are objectively tested by some appropriate test of mathematical achievement. The data are assembled, and for analysis the researcher can use a Student's *t* test or an analysis of variance. If he has decided to control one or more additional variables as independent variables, he would use the analysis of variance. Examples of such variables might be the time of day for the arithmetic instruction and the sex of the students. Suppose the statistical test is computed and the difference between the observed means statistically significant. For illustration purposes, assume that the mean of the group taught by team teaching is the greater of the two. We would reject the null hypothesis and conclude that team teaching is the more effective method.

On the surface, the procedure and conclusion may seem appropriate. But there is no guarantee that the two groups are equal in learning ability. How do we know that the team-taught group which attained a significantly higher mean was not a more able group? Maybe the greater achievement was due not to the teaching method but to more able students. There was no random sampling of students for the two groups, so there is no basis for the argument that learning ability was randomly distributed between them.

A better procedure would be to use the analysis of covariance, for which a measure of learning ability would be needed. For the purposes of this example, assume that a recent IQ score is an adequate measure of learning ability. Preferably the students' IQs would be measured prior to the instructional period. The IQ score would then become the *covariate*. The arithmetic achievement score at the end of the year is still the dependent variable. In the analysis of covariance the dependent variable scores are analyzed for significant differences, but the scores are adjusted for initial covariate differences between the groups.

The suggestion was made that the IQ scores (covariate) should be obtained prior to the instructional period. This would not be absolutely necessary, although it would guard against the possibility of the instruction affecting the IQ score. For some situations, such as a pretest-posttest design, it is necessary to obtain the covariate data prior to conducting the research. The fact that we do not know the team-taught group was not more competent in arithmetic before they started sixth grade suggests that the groups should be pretested on arithmetic achievement prior to conducting the research. Under these conditions, the pretest arithmetic achievement score would become the covariate. An analysis of covariance is not limited to a single covariate. In the example both IQ and pretest arithmetic achievement could be included as covariates. The posttest arithmetic achievement scores would then be adjusted on the basis of a composite of the two covariates.

The analysis of covariance is a parametric technique. As such, the parametric assumptions are to be met. The covariate also requires interval scale measurement. An additional assumption for the analysis of covariance is that the covariate and dependent variable are *linearly related;* that is, if their scores are plotted in a scattergram, they will tend to position around a straight line. In order for the analysis of covariance to be effective, there should be a nonzero correlation, (either positive or negative) between the covariate and the dependent variable.

Like the analysis of variance, the analysis of covariance involves the F ratio. In this case, the F ratio does not test for difference in observed means but rather for differences in adjusted means, the means being adjusted on the basis of the covariate. The hypotheses being tested relate to the adjusted means.

The analysis of covariance enhances statistical precision if there is a nonzero correlation between the covariate and dependent variable. In the F ratio computed, the denominator contains an *adjusted* estimate of within variance. This estimate is called adjusted because a component of variance has been removed from it, due to the correlation between the covariate and dependent variable. If the correlation is nonzero, the component of variance is nonzero, and, therefore, the adjusted estimate of within variance will be less than an estimate obtained without using the covariate. Since the adjusted estimate of within or error variance is used in the denominator of the F ratio, statistical precision is increased.

The analysis of covariance is a technique by which we can gain statistical control over an extraneous but relevant variable that would otherwise be confounded with the independent variable(s). However, the purpose of doing an analysis of covariance is to serve research ends, not statistical ends. We want to be able to make a decision about the effects of our independent variable. In the arithmetic achievement example we want to make a decision about the relative effectiveness of the two instructional situations.

As in the example, intelligence measures are quite commonly used as covariates in educational research, especially that concerned with academic achievement. Pretest achievement in the same academic area can also be used effectively as a covariate. Actually, any variable measured on at least an equal-unit scale could serve as a covariate, although we would generally choose a variable related to the dependent variable.

The actual computation of an analysis of covariance is quite involved, but that is of little concern since computers are almost always used. There are computer programs for including multiple independent variables as well as two or more covariates in a single analysis.

Even though computers have greatly reduced human effort in this technique, the interpretation of the computer output still remains the responsibility of the researcher. Caution should be taken to avoid confusion between observed and adjusted means. The analysis of covariance statistically tests for differences between adjusted means, and the researcher must be careful not to interpret this as a test for differences between observed means. More complex designs, those involving more than one independent variable, may be analyzed by the analysis of covariance, and interaction effects may also be determined. In any case, the hypotheses tested relate to adjusted means. The comments relative to interpretation of interaction made in the discussion of analysis of variance apply in the analysis of covariance.

A research study of the magnitude of the team-teaching versus self-contained classroom study suggested in the example would require considerable effort and time to set up and carry out. The researcher would undoubtedly be interested in all areas of sixth-grade achievement, and the research methodology could also be applied to other areas as long as necessary assumptions are met. The number of dependent variables would be increased and each would be analyzed separately.

When preparing for an analysis of covariance, the assembling of the data is a bit more tedious than for, say, an analysis of variance. Not only are there more data, but the covariate and dependent variable scores of each S must be matched.

Results based on analysis of variance and analysis of covariance frequently appear in the educational research literature. F ratios often are included in tables. The F ratios in the table will be followed by asterisks and the matching reference below the table will indicate the probability level, for example, $*p < .05$. This means that the probability of the observed F ratio appearing by chance is less than .05. Hence the conclusion is that the corresponding independent variable (or interaction) has a significant effect upon the dependent variable.

ERRORS IN HYPOTHESIS TESTING

In hypothesis testing we hypothesize about parameters and through the statistical test reach a conclusion about the hypothesis. This hypothesis about the parameters is either true or false, but we will never be certain about it unless we measure the entire population. Thus, in the testing of hypotheses there exists the possibility that a decision error has been made. The possibility of having made an error is ever present in hypothesis testing.

The test of a specific hypothesis will conclude in one of four possible results, based on the actual situation in the population and the decision of the researcher. This may be diagrammed in a 2×2 table, as in Figure 9.7. The columns in this figure represent the situation in the population, which will never be known for certain. The rows indicate the researcher's decision relative to the hypothesis. The statements in the box indicate whether the researcher's decision is correct or in error.

		True	False
RESEARCHER'S .DECISION	Accept	Correct	Error
	Reject	Error	Correct

FIGURE 9.7. The four possible outcomes in hypothesis testing

If a true hypothesis is accepted or a false hypothesis rejected there is no error. The other two alternatives result in errors, namely, a true hypothesis is rejected or a false hypothesis is accepted. The error of rejecting a true hypothesis is referred to as a *Type I* or alpha (α) *error*. The error of accepting a false hypothesis is a *Type II* or beta (β) *error*. In any one test of a hypothesis the researcher has the possibility of making only one error, since he must either accept or reject the hypothesis. If the researcher rejects he may be making a Type I error; if he accepts he may be making a Type II error.

The problems of reducing and controlling the probabilities of these two types of errors are not simple. For a constant sample size, reducing the risk of a Type I error increases the risk of a Type II error. The probability of making a Type I error is the same as the level of significance. Thus, the significance level could be reduced, to .001 for example, and under this condition there is only a one in a thousand chance of rejecting a true hypothesis. However, since not rejecting is likely to result in accepting the hypothesis, reducing the significance level is inevitably accompanied by an increase in the risk of accepting a false hypothesis. This can be intuitively seen by considering the underlying distribution. As the significance level is reduced, the rejection region decreases in area. Since the total area is constant, this results in an increase of the acceptance region. This means that greater discrepancies between observed and hypothesized values will be tolerated before a hypothesis is rejected. Figure 9.8 illustrates this point. Note that the rejection area is decreased when the significance level goes from .05 to .01. Consider the right tail of each distribution, if we were computing a two-tailed test. The distribution for the .05 level of significance contains 2.5 percent of the area; that for the .01 level only .5 percent of the area. Hence there are values in the rejection area of the .05 distribution which would not fall in the rejection region of the .01 dis-

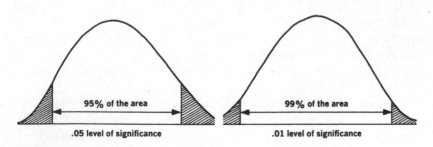

95% of the area

99% of the area

.05 level of significance   .01 level of significance

FIGURE 9.8.   A comparison of rejection regions (shaded areas) for two significance levels, with all other factors held constant

tribution. Therefore, we have decreased the probability of rejecting a true hypothesis.

The probability of making a Type II error is not arrived at in a simple manner. It involves the relation of the actual value of the parameter to the hypothesized value. Since we do not know the true value of the parameter, this involves a second or alternative hypothesis. If, in testing a specific hypothesis, we fail to reject it, we may pose the question: What is the probability of making a Type II error if the parameter is not the hypothesized value but some alternative value? Statistical procedures relative to this problem are commonly discussed in applied statistics texts.[9] For the purposes of this discussion it is sufficient to consider the existence and definition of the two possible types of errors in hypothesis testing.

CONCLUDING REMARKS

In hypothesis testing by parametric techniques, initially we have a statement (the hypothesis) about a parameter. A measure of the corresponding statistic is then obtained from a random sample of observations. A measure of the difference between the observed value and the hypothesized value is studied, and this measure is then considered in terms of what the underlying sampling distribution would be if the hypothesis were true.

At this point the researcher should decide upon the risk he is willing to take, the risk of rejecting a true hypothesis. The risk establishes the significance level, and the significance level determines the regions of acceptance and rejection in the underlying sampling distribution. This is generally accomplished through the use of the appropriate distribution table. On the basis of these regions we either reject or retain the hypothesis.

In rejecting the hypothesis we are in fact saying that the probability of the statistic appearing by chance is too small (less than the significance level), and hence we cannot entertain the hypothesis. Under this condition we say that the statistical test is significant. Thus, statistically significant means that the observed statistic departs from what we would expect by chance. In a nonsignificant test we conclude that this chance expectation is great enough to entertain the hypothesis.

The techniques discussed in this chapter are the most commonly used parametric procedures for hypothesis testing in educational research. The analysis procedure is not dependent upon the type of research. For

---

9. For example see Minium, *Statistical Reasoning in Psychology and Education*, pp. 332–39.

example, analysis of variance would likely be used to analyze the data from a factorial experimental design, but this technique can also be used to analyze data from such nonexperimental forms as *ex post facto* and survey research.

This chapter has dealt specifically with parametric techniques and related examples. The following two chapters also deal with hypothesis testing, by nonparametric and correlational techniques. Although the techniques differ, the basic ideas of hypothesis testing apply.

SUGGESTED STUDY EXERCISES

9.1. One of the parametric assumptions is that the observations are independent. Suppose you selected a sample of 150 American history students from a college population and proposed to measure their knowledge of history by an objective test. What does the assumption of independent observations mean in this context, and how would you assure that this assumption is met?

9.2. We have two teaching methods, each used with a randomly drawn sample of students. (The samples are drawn from a common population.) After a period of instruction we compute the mean achievement for each sample. We want to decide whether or not teaching method affects achievement. We use a Student's *t* test for the difference between two means and get a significant value at the .05 level. What is the null hypothesis tested? Give the associated probability statement.

9.3. Two samples are randomly drawn from a population. The samples are then subjected to different experimental treatments, say T_1 and T_2. The members of the samples are then measured on a dependent variable which has measurement on an interval scale. A difference between the two sample means is then tested to determine if experimental treatment has had an effect. The difference is found to be significant at the .01 level. What would be an appropriate technique to test this difference in means? State the null hypothesis being tested. What is the associated probability statement? What is the conclusion relative to the null hypothesis? What type of error (state in words) in hypothesis testing may be made here? What is the probability of making such an error? Is the difference in means significant at the .05 level?

9.4. Suppose we have a study involving sixth-grade arithmetic achievement. We want to check if there is a difference between the mean achievement of boys and girls. A Student's *t* test is used and found to be significant at the .05 level. State the null hypothesis, the associated probability statement, and your conclusion based on the results of the test. Is the test significant at the .01 level? Why, why not, *or* don't you have enough information to make a decision?

9.5. The mean science achievement on an objective test of a ninth-grade student population is hypothesized to be 85. A sample of 20 students is randomly selected from the population and given the science test. A Student's *t* test is then computed using the sample data, and the *t* value is found to be 3.12. Using the .05 level of significance, find the appropriate t distribution and decide whether or not you would reject the hypothesis. What t value is necessary for rejecting the hypothesis at the .05 level? Was the sample mean larger or smaller than the hypothesized mean?

9.6. A one-way analysis of variance is computed on the scores of a suitable dependent variable. The independent variable has six levels and there are 8 Ss in each level. The F ratio is computed to test for a significant difference between the means. What are the degrees-of-freedom values that designate the correct underlying F distribution? Suppose the computed F ratio is 3.06. Is this value significant at the .05 level? the .01 level? What is your conclusion relative to the null hypothesis? Give the associated probability statement.

9.7. A study of efficiency on a learning task is conducted in a learning laboratory. The Ss are students enrolled in an introductory psychology course at the university. The learning task involves nonsense symbols and meaningful material, both separately arranged on random and ordered displays. Thus, we have two independent variables which we will call stimulus and display. Each independent variable has two levels: stimulus has nonsense symbols and learning materials, and display has random and ordered. The dependent variable is time to solution. Discuss an appropriate parametric technique that would test the effects of the independent variables and their possible interaction. There are really three null hypotheses in this research situation. State these hypotheses. Suppose a total of 80 Ss are equally distributed among the levels of the independent variables. What are the appropriate underlying distributions, and what values are necessary for the test to be significant at the .05 level of significance?

9.8. Discuss the concept of an interaction between two independent variables. From your own experience in education select two variables that are likely to interact. Discuss your choice of variables.

9.9. Discuss under what conditions you would use an analysis of covariance in preference to an analysis of variance; an analysis of variance in preference to an analysis of covariance.

9.10. A researcher is interested in the effect of three sets of instructional materials upon reading achievement in the fourth grade. He selects three random samples of fourth-graders and each is taught by a different teacher using one of the sets. The Ss are pretested and post-tested and an analysis of covariance is done on the data, with pretest as the covariate. What is the null hypothesis? What measures are actually tested by the statistical test? Suppose the statistical test turned out to be significant. What would be your conclusion relative to the instructional materials?

9.11. A researcher is asked to estimate the mean performance score of a large population on a variable we will call X. He decides to build a 95 percent confidence interval and draws a large sample of size 400. He computes the sample mean $\bar{X} = 88$ and constructs the interval to be 85.5 to 90.5. Give the associated probability statement after the interval is constructed. Suppose the standard deviation of the population was estimated by the sample standard deviation. What is the appropriate underlying distribution for constructing the interval?

Would this underlying distribution change if the sample size had been 25? If so, how? Suppose, with the given information, the researcher had constructed a confidence interval of 84.5 to 90.5. Do you think there may have been an error, and if so why? If a 90 percent confidence interval had been constructed, would this interval be shorter or longer than five units?

9.12. Define the two possible types of errors in hypothesis testing. Why do we say that hypotheses are not proved or disproved, only accepted or rejected?

chapter 10

Testing hypotheses by nonparametric techniques

KEY CONCEPTS

Independent and related samples
Chi square distribution
Observed and theoretical frequencies
Goodness-of-fit test
Comparison of two or more independent sample distributions
Contingency table
Test of independence
Sign test
Binomial distribution
Median test for two or more samples
Correction for continuity
Krushal-Wallis one-way analysis of variance by ranks

Parametric techniques, discussed in the preceding chapter, should only be applied when the parametric assumptions can be met. In some research situations there is serious question about the propriety of testing hypotheses by parametric techniques. Sample size may be small, and the necessary assumptions about the population distribution may not hold. Or the data may be measured on an ordinal or nominal scale, so means and variances cannot be computed. The use of nonparametric techniques for testing hypotheses is considered when such conditions exist.

The name "nonparametric" is derived from the fact that these tests do not require the parametric assumptions. It should not be inferred that no assumptions at all are required, however. One assumption is that the individual observations are independent; that is, the score of any one S does not influence the score of any other S. For many of the nonparametric tests the variable under study is assumed to have underlying continuity, even though it cannot be so measured. In generalizing to populations, the chain of reasoning in inferential statistics is kept intact by the use of random samples.

INDEPENDENT AND RELATED SAMPLES

A distinction can be made between related and independent samples. Samples are called related when two measures on a dependent variable are taken on the same sample of S's, as in a before-and-after experimental treatment situation, or when each S of one sample is matched with his counterpart in the other sample. The matching is based on the researcher's judgment of relevant variables. If two samples of distinct S's are drawn and the selection of one sample in no way influences that of the other, the samples are said to be independent samples. In either case random selection is a requirement for generalizing to populations.

The discussion of this chapter occasionally distinguishes between techniques as they apply to related or independent samples. This distinction was not made in the chapter on parametric techniques, in which all samples were considered to be independent samples. There are parametric techniques that apply to related samples, but they are not discussed in this text.

THE CHI SQUARE DISTRIBUTION

In the parametric techniques discussed in the preceding chapter, the Student's t distribution and the F distribution received considerable emphasis as underlying distributions. When dealing with nonparametric techniques another underlying distribution is needed, although the basic reasoning of underlying distributions still applies. The underlying distribution for many of the nonparametric statistical tests is the chi square (χ^2) distribution. Like the Student's t distribution and the F distribution, the χ^2 distribution makes up a family of distributions. The appropriate, specific χ^2 distribution is determined by a single degrees-of-freedom value, in which respect it is similar to the t distribution. A tabulation of χ^2 values appears as Table E of Appendix 2. Selected probabilities are given horizontally; any specific value in the table is the χ^2 value which has the corresponding probability of appearing by chance.

The table of χ^2 values actually gives the critical values for two-tailed or nondirectional tests of significance, but the values of the table are based on one tail only, namely the right tail of the sampling distribution of chi square. Thus only one tail is used, but the critical values given are for two-tailed tests. A one-tailed test is not commonly used in a chi square test of significance. If such a test is required there is a procedure for determining the critical values by relating the normal and chi square distributions.[1]

The chi square distribution should be regarded as another underlying distribution, like the normal or Student's t distributions. In hypothesis testing it is very important, in fact crucial, that the correct underlying distribution be used. The appropriate chi square distribution is the underlying distribution of many of the statistics used with nonparametric techniques.

COMPARISON OF OBSERVED AND THEORETICAL DISTRIBUTIONS

A research situation in which the chi square distribution would be used is one involving a comparison of observed and theoretical frequencies. *Observed frequencies* are those of the sample or group under study. *Theoretical frequencies* are those expected on the basis of some hypothesis, and for this reason they are often referred to in the literature as expected frequencies. The null hypothesis is that there are no differences between the observed and theoretical frequencies. No difference is hypothesized between these two distributions, the observed and the expected, whatever they may be.

Consider a hypothetical example in which the assertion is made that in a certain school the IQ scores of the students are heterogeneous but uniformly distributed within the 80 to 129 range. In the IQ range from 80 to 129, inclusive, there are five 10-point intervals. If the scores are uniformly distributed, we would expect equal numbers of scores in the five intervals. The intervals would be defined as 80–89, 90–99, etc., to make them mutually exclusive; that is, they would have no overlap.

The hypothesis is that the distribution of IQ is a uniform (rectangular) distribution. In the null hypothesis form we could hypothesize no difference between the distribution of scores and the uniform distribution. Assuming that IQ is measured by some generally acceptable intelligence test, we would draw a random sample of students and test them. We can call this sample size n. In the light of our hypothesis we would expect one-fifth of the scores in this sample to fall in each interval. Thus the expected frequencies for all intervals would be the same, namely $n/5$. The observed frequencies are the sample results.

The computation of the χ^2 value for this statistical test is relatively simple. The formula is given by:

---

1. For a discussion of this procedure see George Ferguson, *Statistical Analysis in Psychology and Education,* 3rd ed. (New York: McGraw-Hill Book Co., 1971), pp. 189–190.

$$\chi^2 = \sum_{i=1}^{k} \frac{(fo_i - fe_i)^2}{fe_i},$$

where fo_i is the observed frequency of the ith interval[2] and fe_i is the expected frequency of the ith interval under the hypothesis. The number of intervals is denoted by k. For our example k is five and the fe_i's are all equal to $n/5$, since we hypothesized the uniform distribution. The formula indicates how to determine the difference between the observed and expected frequencies for each interval: Square the difference, divide by the expected frequency, and sum the k quotients.

A decision is necessary relative to the significance level, which we set at .05. Recall that the significance level is a probability. In terms of distributions of our example, we are asking what the probability is that our observed sample distribution would appear by chance, if, in fact, the population distribution is the uniform distribution. However, the χ^2 value is the statistic that we actually compute. Since we have set the significance level at .05, this means that we will reject the hypothesis

TABLE 10.1. Sample distribution of Fifty IQ scores

	Interval				
	80–89	90–99	100–109	110–119	120–129
Observed frequency	8	12	15	9	6
Theoretical frequency	10	10	10	10	10

if the probability of our χ^2 value appearing by chance is less than .05. The χ^2 value is computed, and we make a decision about the hypothesis.

Before this decision can be made, we must determine the specific chi square distribution appropriate for our situation. There are five intervals, but since n is specified, the frequency of the fifth interval is determined when the frequencies of the other four are known. Thus, four degrees of freedom remain in our example. The necessary value for significance at the .05 level with four degrees of freedom, as indicated in Table E, is 9.49. If our computed χ^2 value exceeds 9.49, we have a significant statistical test, and we would reject the hypothesis.

We can illustrate the preceding example with some hypothetical data. Recall that the data being analyzed are frequencies. A sample of 50 IQ scores is distributed according to the distribution in Table 10.1. Since for our example the hypothesized distribution is the uniform distribution, we would expect ten scores in each interval.

---

2. The terms "category," "group," or "cell" are also commonly used. "Interval" is used here primarily because of the context of the example.

The computation of the χ^2 value is presented here solely for the purpose of illustration. The formula given earlier indicates to determine the difference between the observed and theoretical frequencies for each interval, square this difference and divide by the theoretical frequency and then sum these quotients, one for each interval. In the example we have five intervals, and the χ^2 value is given by:

$$\chi^2 = \frac{(-2)^2}{10} + \frac{(+2)^2}{10} + \frac{(+5)^2}{10} + \frac{(-1)^2}{10} + \frac{(-4)^2}{10}.$$

Since we square the difference, it is not necessary to retain the algebraic sign. The signs are included above to enable the reader to identify the difference readily.

The computation of the χ^2 value gives a value of 5.00. This is less than the critical value of 9.49 necessary for a significant test. Thus, the probability of this sample appearing by chance, if, in fact, the population is uniformly distributed, is greater than .05. The conclusion is that we cannot reject the hypothesis that the population is distributed as the uniform distribution.

The probability is relative to the observed distribution appearing, in the light of the hypothesized distribution. In the example the probability question is: What is the probability of our observed sample frequencies appearing by chance, if, in fact, the population distribution is the uniform distribution? We need not determine the exact probability, only the probability in terms of the significance level. If the probability is less than the significance level, we reject the hypothesis.

If the statistical test is nonsignificant, the hypothesized distribution is tenable. If the test is significant, this in itself does not specify the shape of the population distribution. We know that it is quite unlikely that the sample distribution will appear by chance if the population distribution is as hypothesized. Neither does the χ^2 value indicate which intervals had the greatest discrepancies between observed and expected frequencies. There may be one or more intervals with large discrepancies, or the discrepancies may be uniform throughout the intervals. An inspection of the interval frequencies will give an indication of the situation and will reveal which intervals have high and low observed frequencies relative to the expected frequencies.

The above example is somewhat simplified in that all the theoretical frequencies are equal, because the theoretical distribution is the uniform distribution. To be sure, the theoretical frequencies of the intervals are in general not equal but are determined by the shape of the theoretical distribution of a specific research problem. For example, if the normal distribution is the theoretical distribution, the theoretical frequencies of the intervals would not all be the same. However, the underlying reasoning and the procedures would remain the same when comparing observed and theoretical distributions.

GOODNESS-OF-FIT TEST

Closely related to the preceding example is the goodness-of-fit problem. For a random sample drawn from a population, the question might be how well this sample distribution fits a known theoretical distribution. For the purpose of illustration, we will use the normal distribution as the theoretical distribution. The null hypothesis is that there is no difference between the population distribution and the normal distribution, in terms of the variable being investigated. The associated probability statement is: What is the probability of the sample distribution appearing, if, in fact, the population is normally distributed? If this probability drops below our predetermined significance level, we will reject the hypothesis that the population is normally distributed.

The variable under investigation would have a mean and standard deviation and would be measured on an equal-unit or ratio scale. This seems to be data of a parametric nature. However, in the goodness-of-fit test it is not the actual scores that are being analyzed but rather the frequencies of scores in the intervals. Therefore the observed sample distribution is divided into a specified number of intervals. The corresponding normal distribution is determined by computing the expected frequencies in the various intervals if the distribution were normal. In order to do this we need the sample size, say n, and the mean and standard deviation of the scores. It has been noted (see Chapter 2) that the area under the normal curve is 1.00. The points which divide the intervals must be determined in terms of standard deviation units, which will give the proportions of the area expected within the various intervals. The proportions multiplied times n will determine the expected frequencies.

Consider a brief example of how the expected frequency for an interval would be determined if we were computing a goodness-of-fit test using the normal distribution. Suppose we have a sample of 150 observations, and one of the intervals spans 90–95 on the measurement scale. Assume that the end points of this interval correspond to standard scores of $+1.20$ and $+1.47$. The portion of the total area in the normal curve that lies between these two points can be determined by consulting Table A in Appendix 2. Both points lie on the same side of the mean. Recall that the area in the table is given from the mean to the point. To determine the area between the points, subtract the smaller area from the larger as given in the table. The area of the standard score of +1.20, .3849, is subtracted from the area of the standard score of +1.47, .4292, to give .0443 as the portion of the total area in the normal curve that lies between these two points. With 150 scores we would expect 150 times .0443 or 6.645 frequencies in this particular interval. The observed frequency of the interval would be known directly from the sample data. This procedure would be repeated until expected frequencies were determined for all the intervals.

Now we would have a set of observed frequencies from the sample and a set of theoretical frequencies. The total frequency for the theoretical distribution should be n, within rounding errors. The situation is now ready for a chi square test. The number of degrees of freedom associated with the test is the number of intervals minus 3. This is due to the fact that not only do we have a frequency, n, but a mean and standard deviation are also needed for the theoretical normal distribution. These are estimated from the sample mean and standard deviation. Thus, the appropriate chi square distribution is the one with $k - 3$ degrees of freedom, where k is the number of intervals.

The condition of a random sample is essential in the above example. Is this a random sample of a normally distributed population? If the sample were not a random sample but had some sampling bias, no decision could legitimately be made relative to the population. If the χ^2 value were significant we would reject the hypothesis of a normally distributed population and conclude that the population is not normally distributed. But with a sampling bias there would be an alternative conclusion—that the sampling bias has produced the nonnormality in the sample. If the χ^2 value is nonsignificant, the bias may be operating in an opposite direction.

Assuming the sample to be random and the computation to be correct, a significant χ^2 value indicates that the probability of this sample appearing from a normally distributed population is too small to entertain the hypothesis of such a population. Note that the probability is on the sample but the conclusion is relative to the hypothesis, which deals with the population. A nonsignificant χ^2 value, in the context of this example, indicates that there is no evidence on the basis of this statistical test to reject the hypothesis of a normally distributed population.

The researcher should be on the lookout for small expected frequencies, because if the expected frequencies become too small, the chi square distribution is no longer the appropriate underlying distribution. With small frequencies the appropriate underlying distribution may have considerable discontinuity, and the continuous chi square distribution is a poor approximation for the appropriate underlying distribution. In a situation in which there are only two categories, the generally accepted rule is that each expected frequency should be five or greater. In situations in which the number of intervals or categories exceeds two, it is generally required that at least 4/5 of the expected frequencies be five or greater and no expected frequency be less than one. If such intervals or categories appear they should be combined with adjacent categories. At times it may be necessary to combine several categories in the tails of the distribution. Whenever this is done, the combinations should be meaningful and, of course, at least two categories must remain.

The example discussed above deals with a goodness-of-fit test using the normal distribution. The test can involve other distributions, but, of course, the distribution must be known so the comparison between the observed and hypothesized distributions can be made. In any case, the idea is the same, that of testing how well a sample distribution fits a theoretical distribution.

COMPARISON OF TWO INDEPENDENT
SAMPLE DISTRIBUTIONS

The preceding example dealt with a single sample distribution compared with some theoretical distribution. The expected frequencies are based on information about the theoretical distribution, external to the sample information. Suppose we have two independent samples for which the data consist of frequencies in mutually exclusive categories. The variable determining the categories may be of nominal or ordinal measurement. Using the categories, a distribution is determined for each of the samples. These distributions provide the observed frequencies.

The null hypothesis of this situation is that the populations from which the samples are drawn do not differ with respect to the variable, represented by the frequencies in the categories. If, in fact, the populations are the same we would expect the respective category frequencies of the two samples to differ only due to random sampling error. Note that we are not hypothesizing a specific distribution for the populations but only that the population distributions are the same in terms of the frequencies of the categories.

If the populations are the same and the sizes of the two samples are equal, we would expect the same number in each sample for a specific category. This is not to say that we would expect the same frequencies in the different categories, which would be hypothesizing a uniform distribution. Suppose in the samples the total number of frequencies in the kth category is m. Under the null hypothesis, we would expect $m/2$ frequency in this category for each sample. Thus the expected frequencies are determined from the sample information. Under the condition of equal sample sizes, the total frequency for any category would be split equally to determine the expected frequencies for that category.

This procedure does not require equal size for the two samples. In the case of unequal sample size, the expected frequencies in a category are directly proportional to the ratio of the size of the specific sample to the total size for both samples. For example, the expected frequency for sample 1 in the kth category is the product of this ratio times m (m is the total frequency in category k). If the sample sizes are represented by n_1 and n_2, respectively, this expected frequency is given by m times $n_1/(n_1 + n_2)$. A common way of viewing this is by tabulating the observed frequencies in a table, with the two samples in rows and the categories in columns. An example of such an arrangement is presented in Table 10.2. The expected frequency for a specific category is then determined by multiplying row total times column total and dividing this product by n (total for both samples). The specific row and column totals are those in which the specific category appears. The process of determining expected frequencies is the same whether or not sample sizes are equal.

An example of comparison of two independent sample distributions might be a researcher interested in the problem of overweight and underweight among high school freshmen. He can classify freshmen into three categories: overweight, correct weight, and underweight. He wants to make a decision about the populations of girls and boys relative to this variable. In terms of this category classification, do the population distributions of boys and girls differ? The null hypothesis is that these population distributions are not different. It should be noted that the measurement here is at most ordinal. Nowhere is it specified that what is overweight for a girl would also be overweight for a boy. Nor is the shape of the distribution specified. The significance level is designated as .05.

The random samples of size 40 each are drawn from the populations. The observed data appear in Table 10.2. Such a table is commonly called a *contingency table*.

We need the theoretical frequencies under the null hypothesis of no difference between the population distributions of boys and girls in order to complete our statistical test. Since we have equal sample size (40 of each sex), we would expect the same number of boys as girls in a specific category. The theoretical frequency for underweight boys is given by multiplying the row and column totals and dividing by the total of both samples. This turns out to be 10 times 40, divided by 80, or 5. The theoretical frequency for underweight girls is also 5. In like manner we could compute the remaining theoretical frequencies. They

TABLE 10.2. Observed weight distributions for freshmen boys and girls

| | Category | | | |
	Overweight	Correct weight	Underweight	Total
Boys	8	29	3	40
Girls	2	31	7	40
Total	10	60	10	80

would be 30 and 5, respectively, for correct weight and overweight, for both boys and girls.

The χ^2 value can be computed by applying the formula involving observed and theoretical frequencies that was introduced earlier. The computation will not be shown here, but the χ^2 value for these data is 5.27, rounded off to hundredths. We must decide on the degrees of freedom so we can locate the appropriate chi square distribution in Table E. In the computation there is a restriction on the category totals. For example, the overweight category contains ten. When we know that eight are boys, the remainder are girls. A specific sample, such as boys, has one restriction: that when the frequencies of two of the categories are assigned, the frequency of the third is uniquely determined. Therefore, we have two degrees of freedom in our example. An inspection of Table E reveals a χ^2 value of 5.99 is required for significance at the .05 level. Therefore, our value does not reach significance and we do not reject the null hypothesis. The probability is greater than .05 that the sample distributions would have appeared by chance, if, in fact, the population distributions are the same. The conclusion is that the populations of freshmen boys and girls do not differ on this variable. Note that we have not specified the shapes of the population distributions, nor have we said that the distributions would be the same if measurement was on an interval scale. We have only considered classification on the three-category variable.

EXTENSION TO MORE THAN TWO INDEPENDENT SAMPLE DISTRIBUTIONS

The procedure described above can be extended to more than two independent samples. Again, the sample sizes need not be equal. Suppose we have j samples and k possible categories. When this analysis technique is used, the data are usually tabulated in rows and columns, with the possible categories in the columns and the samples in the rows. In this kind of an array there are j times k cells, all of which need an expected frequency. The rows and columns have marginal totals. The totals of the rows are the sample sizes, and the column totals are the total responses to the individual categories. The totals of the row marginal totals and column marginal totals are equal. Call this grand total n_t. The expected value for a specific cell is the product of its marginal totals divided by n_t. This is the same procedure as that for the two-sample case.

The χ^2 value is computed by the usual procedure, summing over all cells. The degrees of freedom associated with this test are $(j - 1)$ times $(k - 1)$ or $(r - 1)$ times $(c - 1)$, if we think of r and c as the numbers of rows and columns in the array. Since the marginal totals exist, this puts one restriction on each row and one restriction on each column. Hence, the correct number of degrees of freedom is as specified.

We can consider an example involving four samples. Suppose at a liberal arts college a researcher is interested in student attitude toward compulsory attendance at college convocations. A student may respond by "agree," "undecided," or "disagree." Thus there are three possible response categories in this very brief measuring instrument.

A random sample is drawn from each of the four undergraduate classes at the college. The sample sizes need not be equal; for some reason, the investigator may choose to draw unequal numbers for the samples. For example, he may determine sample size proportional to the class enrollment of the college population.

The null hypothesis is that the four class populations do not differ relative to the attitude toward compulsory attendance at convocations. This does not hypothesize how many in the class populations agree, disagree, or are undecided. It only hypothesizes that the population distributions do not differ. The associated probability statement is: What is the probability that the four samples would appear, if, in fact, the populations are the same? If this probability is less than the chosen significance level, we reject the hypothesis that the populations are the same.

The responses to the attitude item are tabulated and expected values are computed. In this case there would be 12 cells, and 12 expected values are necessary. The χ^2 value is computed. The degrees of freedom associated with this statistical test are $(4 - 1)$ times $(3 - 1)$, or 6. This determines the appropriate underlying chi square distribution associated with the null hypothesis. According to Table E, the χ^2 value necessary for significance at the .05 level is 12.59. If the significance level had been set at .01, a χ^2 value of 16.81 would be necessary for significance.

Consider some hypothetical data that might result from such a study. We will specify the significance level as .05. The sample sizes drawn from the class populations are 80, 60, 60, and 40, respectively, from freshmen through seniors. The observed sample frequencies on this variable appear in Table 10.3, an example of a 4×3 contingency table.

TABLE   10.3.   Observed sample distributions for response to compulsory attendance at college convocations

| | Category | | | |
Class	Agree	Undecided	Disagree	Total
Freshmen	12	48	20	80
Sophomore	7	20	33	60
Junior	6	19	35	60
Senior	5	3	32	40
Total	30	90	120	240

Since we have 12 observed frequencies, we need 12 theoretical frequencies. We follow the procedure discussed previously for determining the theoretical frequencies. For example, the frequency for "freshmen agree" is 30 times 80 divided by 240, which is equal to 10. In like manner, we compute the remaining theoretical frequencies under the null hypothesis. These frequencies appear in Table 10.4. The observed

TABLE 10.4.   Theoretical distribution for response to compulsory attendance at college convocations*

| | Category | | | |
Class	Agree	Undecided	Disagree	Total
Freshmen	(12) 10	(48) 30	(20) 40	80
Sophomore	(7) 7.5	(20) 22.5	(33) 30	60
Junior	(6) 7.5	(19) 22.5	(35) 30	60
Senior	(5) 5	(3) 15	(32) 20	40
Total	30	90	120	240

*Observed frequencies, from Table 10.3, are in parentheses.

frequencies appear in parentheses to indicate the contrast between observed and theoretical frequencies.

The computation of the χ^2 value by the usual procedure results in a value of 33.588. With six degrees of freedom this is significant at the .05 level (also at the .01 level). Thus the probability that the sample distributions would occur by chance, if, in fact, the population distributions are the same, is less than .05. We cannot entertain the null hypothesis, and we conclude that freshmen, sophomore, junior, and senior populations differ with regard to this variable.

Because the statistical test was significant, we can conclude that the hypothesis of the populations being the same is not tenable. However, this does not tell us the source of difference between the four populations. The cells of one class sample (in this case a row) may differ markedly from the other class samples. As inspection of the differences between observed and expected cell frequencies should give an indication of the situation. A cursory inspection of the sample distributions (see Table 10.4) would reveal that the upper classmen, especially seniors, seem much more decided about compulsory attendance, and they tend to disagree. The freshmen have a high proportion of undecided responses.

The sample distributions may be compared in combinations of two. This would require six chi square tests, each with two degrees of freedom. The hypothesis tested in each case would concern only the two specific populations from which the samples in the test were drawn. In any event, the question of the actual student attitude (agree, disagree, or undecided) has not been tested statistically. If some theoretical distribution of attitude responses is hypothesized, the observed distributions can be tested against the theoretical distribution. The problem would then be reduced to the type discussed in an earlier example involving the comparison of an observed and a theoretical distribution. In an actual research situation, consideration would undoubtedly be given to both questions.

TEST OF INDEPENDENCE

A common use of the chi square test is as a test of independence of two variables. Pairs of observations on two variables are necessary for this situation. The preceding example of attitude toward compulsory attendance at convocations can illustrate this use of the chi square test. Although the actual computation would be the same, the reasoning undergoes a slight modification.

Year in college and attitude toward compulsory attendance are now both considered to be variables. To be sure, they are not variables measured on an equal-unit scale. They may be considered nominal variables or possibly ordinal variables. The question being asked is: Are these variables independent or are they associated? The null hypothesis that the two variables are independent in the population refers to the variables in the college population from which the sample was drawn. Note that now the four classes are considered as one population and the students in the study are considered as a single sample. Year in college is a variable within the population and sample.

The data are set up in a table. The expected cell frequencies are computed from the row and column totals and are the frequencies expected if the two variables are independent. The χ^2 value is computed in the usual way, and the appropriate degrees of freedom are $(r - 1)$ times $(c - 1)$.

Since the expected frequencies are what we would expect in the case of independence, a nonsignificant χ^2 value would indicate that there is no basis to reject the hypothesis of independence of the two variables. If the chi square test is significant we can conclude that the variables are associated. However, the chi square test does not indicate the direction of association. To get measures of magnitude of association and direction of association we would use a correlational technique. Correlation is discussed in the following chapter.

The chi square test of the above example was significant. Therefore, we reject the hypothesis of independence between the two variables in the population and conclude that the variables—year in college and attitude toward compulsory convocation attendance—are associated.

THE SIGN TEST

A nonparametric technique which applies to the situation of two related samples is the sign test. The variable under consideration is measured on an ordinal scale, and it is assumed that this variable has an underlying continuous distribution. The samples are related in the sense that observations are taken on matched Ss or two observations are taken on each S. The latter is usually a before-and-after treatment situation. If matching is used, the pairs are matched on relevant variables.

We define Y_a and Y_b as the two scores for the matched pair or the same S. The Y_a represents the score under one condition or the "before" score and the Y_b represents the score under the other condition or the "after" score. In the sign test we direct our attention to the direction of the difference between each pair of scores and define this direction as plus or minus. If Y_b is greater than Y_a, we assign a plus sign; if Y_a is greater than Y_b, we assign a negative sign. This gives us one dichotomous distribution of plus and minus signs.

The comparison of the Y_a and Y_b scores is open to the possibility of ties. A *tie* occurs when the difference between the two scores for an S is zero, or zero in terms of the measurement. The tied cases are dropped from the analysis, and the total number in the sample is reduced by the number of ties. Thus for the purpose of analysis, we define n as the number of paired scores with a nonzero difference.

Suppose we have a random sample of Ss and two observations are taken for each S, one before and one after an experimental treatment. The distribution of plus and minus signs is determined by the above described procedure. The null hypothesis relates to the population from which the sample was drawn and concerns the effect of the experimental treatment. If there is no effect of experimental treatment we would expect as many plus signs as negative signs in our distribution of signs. Another way of stating this is that the median difference of the Y_a and Y_b scores in the population is zero. Recall that the median is a measure of central tendency (see Chapter 2). A rough median can be computed for ordinal data, whereas it is not possible to compute a mean for ordinal data since in order to compute an arithmetic mean we need an equal unit. The associated probability statement is: What is the probability of our distribution of signs appearing, if, in fact, the distribution in the population has equal numbers of plus and minus signs? To check this probability and test the null hypothesis, we need an underlying sampling distribution.

The theoretical distribution that applies in this case is the *binomial distribution*. This is a distribution based on the expansion of a binomial such as $(p + q)^k$ for example, the p and q could represent the probabilities of obtaining a head or tail on the toss of a coin. Suppose we tossed the coin k times. The expansion would represent the possible outcomes in terms of numbers of heads and tails. Since under the null hypothesis we expect the same number of plus and minus signs, this is analogous to the tossing of an unbiased coin. If we went through repeated sessions of 100 tosses of an unbiased coin, the number of times heads (or tails) would appear would average around 50. The appearance of say 95 heads and 5 tails would be a relatively rare event, and it would be located in the tail of the distribution. Table C in Appendix 2 gives the associated probabilities for the binomial distribution. The vertical axis gives the total number and the horizontal axis the number of one characteristic, such as heads or plus signs. Note that the table is for a one-tailed test and gives probabilities of values as small as observed values. For samples larger than 25 the normal curve is an adequate approximation to the binomial distribution.

In order to use the normal distribution we must convert to a z score. To determine the z score associated with the specific split of our dichotomy we use the formula:

$$z = \frac{(n_1 - .5) - (\tfrac{1}{2}) \cdot n}{(\tfrac{1}{2})\sqrt{n}}$$

where n = total number of nonzero differences in the sample and n_1 = the number with the characteristic such that n_1 is greater than $(1/2)n$. If the z score computed by the above procedure falls in the rejection area determined by our significance level, we reject the null hypothsis.

As with the parametric Student's t test for the difference between two means, the sign test may be two tailed or one tailed. In a two-tailed test it is not hypothesized which sign, plus or minus, will occur with greatest frequency. In a one-tailed test, this is hypothesized, and the rejection region is located entirely in one tail of the distribution.

Now we have a hypothesis to test, a procedure for getting a measure from a random sample, and an underlying sampling distribution. These ingredients, along with a significance level, give us the necessary elements for a statistical test of a hypothesis.

An example involving the use of the sign test might concern a teacher interested in the effect of teaching a certain instructional unit in science on insight in problem solving. Assume that insight in problem solving can be measured on an ordinal scale and that two equivalent forms of an insight measuring instrument are available. The teacher can use a class of 20 students which make up a random sample of, say, an eighth-grade population.

The students are tested before and after the instruction of the unit on insight in problem solving. Results of these tests correspond to the Y_a and Y_b scores. There is a pair of observations for each student. The variable under consideration is insight in problem solving, which we will assume to be continuously distributed. The experimental treatment is the teaching of the instructional unit.

The teacher does not anticipate that the instruction will inhibit insight in problem solving. In fact, he is not interested in retaining the unit unless its instruction shows a significant positive effect. Thus we have the situation for a one-tailed test. The null hypothesis is that in the population there would be as many students who would gain as would regress on the insight measure; that is, the number of plus signs would equal the number of minus signs. By using a one-tailed test we can consider the alternate hypothesis that there will be a greater number of gain frequencies than regress frequencies. A significant statistical test would result in rejecting the null hypothesis and accepting the alternate hypothesis.

When the 20 pairs of scores are compared, the results indicate 13 plus signs, 5 negative signs, and 2 ties. We will set the significance level at .05 and consult Table C for the specific probability. The probability that we are concerned with is the probability of 13 plus and 5 negative signs appearing in a sample of 18, if in the population there are equal numbers of plus and minus signs.

We find the appropriate probability by going down to 18 on the vertical scale and over to 5 on the horizontal scale. The indicated probability is .048. Since this is less than the significance level, we reject the null hypothesis. The conclusion is that the instructional unit in science does have the effect of increasing insight in problem solving. Presumably, the teacher would retain the instruction of the unit.

Another example, this one involving a large sample size, might be an administration of a large university that is concerned with faculty opinion relative to the role of athletics, specifically football. The institutional research director is specifically interested in whether a series of two lectures accompanied by team films will change the opinions of faculty members about the extent of participation in interscholastic football.

A random sample of 150 members is drawn from the university faculty. These members are asked whether more or less participation in football is desirable. Then the members are exposed to the two lectures, after which they are again asked the same question. This is again a situation in which two observations are taken on each S, rather than observations on matched Ss.

The null hypothesis is that the series of lectures would have no effect on the opinions of the university's faculty members. It is the population of faculty members that is under consideration here, and it was not implied that the lectures would tend to make faculty members more or less favorable toward participation. If we say that the lectures and films are merely statements of facts and that opinions could be influenced either way, this hypothesis requires a two-tailed statistical test.

When the distribution of plus and minus signs is determined, the results show 70 plus signs, 60 negative, and 20 ties. The significance level is set at .05. The associated probability statement is: What is the probability that the sample distribution of plus and minus signs would appear, if, in fact, there would be the same number of each sign in the university faculty population?

The normal distribution is used as the underlying distribution, since sample size exceeds 25. The computation of the z score, according to the procedure discussed earlier, gives a z score of 0.79. Since this is a two-tailed test we include .025 of the area in each tail of the distribution as the rejection region. The normal distribution as given in Table A of Appendix 2 indicates that a z score of 1.96 or greater is required for the rejection region. Since our z score is only 0.79, it does not fall in the rejection region. Therefore the probability of the sample distribution appearing under the null hypothesis is greater than the significance level. There is no basis for rejecting the null hypothesis, and the conclusion is that the two lectures have no systematic effect upon faculty opinions toward interscholastic participation in football.

THE MEDIAN TEST FOR TWO SAMPLES

The sign test discussed above applies to two related samples. An analogous test for two independent samples is the median test, which requires that the scores on the dependent variable be measured on at least an ordinal scale and that the samples be randomly selected from the populations under study.

The null hypothesis for the median test is that there is no difference between the medians of the two populations from which the samples are drawn. This hypothesis calls for a two-tailed test. As in the sign test, an alternative hypothesis may be posed, namely that the median of one population is greater than that of the other. Under such an alternate hypothesis, a one-tailed test would be appropriate.

The median test does not require that both samples be of the same size. We can designate n_1 and n_2 as the sample sizes and the sum of n_1 and n_2 as n. The procedure requires that we determine the common median of both samples, that is, the median of all n scores, and then dichotomize the scores for each sample relative to this common median. If some of the scores fall directly on the median, these scores may be removed from the analysis. However, this often is undesirable, since it reduces the total number of scores in the analysis. Therefore, rather than define the dichotomy as above and below median, we can define it as scores that exceed the median and those that do not exceed the median. With this definition, scores on the median are placed in the "do not exceed the median" category of the dichotomy. In this case every score falls into one and only one category, and no scores are deleted. We will define the dichotomy in this manner for this discussion.

Dichotomizing the scores for each sample gives a 2×2 table of the form indicated in Table 10.5. The numbers that appear in this array are frequencies. In order to identify a frequency we must know which sample it came from, 1 or 2, and whether it represents the frequency that exceeds the median or the one that does not. Therefore we use two subscripts on the f. The first indicates sample 1 or 2; the second indicates "exceed median" (a) or "does not exceed median" (b). As an example, f_{1b} indicates the number of scores in sample 1 that do not exceed the median.

Under the null hypothesis that the population medians are the same, we would expect about one-half of the scores within each sample to exceed the median of the combined sample and one-half not to exceed it. That is, we would expect f_{1a} to be approximately equal to f_{1b} (within sampling fluctuation) and f_{2a} to be approximately equal to f_{2b}. These

TABLE 10.5.   Fourfold table for the median test involving two samples.

	Sample 1	Sample 2
Number of scores that exceed the median	f_{1a}	f_{2a}
Number of scores that do not exceed the median	f_{1b}	f_{2b}

in turn would be expected to equal approximately one-half of their respective sample sizes.

We need some combination of the frequencies which will give a statistic for which we can determine a sampling distribution under the null hypothesis. When the total number of the two samples exceeds 20 and no individual sample size is less than 10, the chi square distribution can be used to test the null hypothesis. If the sample size does not meet this requirement, a special sampling distribution which is not discussed in this text is necessary. Therefore the situation in the example is one for which the chi square distribution is applicable.

The determination of the χ^2 value is accomplished by a computational formula involving only observed frequencies from the fourfold table and the total sample size. This formula contains a *correction for continuity*. The correction for continuity is a correction for applying the continuous chi square distribution to our discrete dichotomy. The appropriate distribution in this situation is the distribution with one degree of freedom. To apply the correction for continuity in the case of one degree of freedom, the formula is given by:

$$\chi^2 = \frac{n\left(\left|f_{1a} \cdot f_{2b} - f_{2a} \cdot f_{1b}\right| - \frac{n}{2}\right)^2}{(f_{1a} + f_{2a})(f_{1b} + f_{2b})(f_{1a} + f_{1b})(f_{2a} + f_{2b})}.$$

If this χ^2 value exceeds the critical value given in Table E of Appendix 2, we say the test is statistically significant. In terms of probability we say that a significant χ^2 value indicates that the probability of this large a χ^2 value appearing by chance is less than our significance level. The associated probability statement with the null hypothesis is: What is the probability that the sample frequencies relative to the median would appear, if, in fact, the samples are drawn from populations with the same median? If this probability is less than our significance level we reject the null hypothesis and conclude that the population medians are not equal.

Consider an example in which a researcher is interested in attitudes of board members and teachers toward salary negotiations. An attitude scale is constructed in such a manner that it is possible to identify a direction from unfavorable to favorable toward the salary negotiations concept. Thus the measurement of this attitude variable can be on an ordinal scale.

The researcher defines his populations and randomly selects samples of 30 board members and 40 teachers. Note that he is dealing with two populations and sample sizes of 30 and 40. The null hypothesis of this investigation is that there is no difference between the median scores of the board member and teacher populations. Since no direction is hypothesized, a two-tailed test is appropriate. The significance level is set at .05.

The attitude scale is administered to the 70 Ss, the overall median is determined, and the frequencies are tabulated in a fourfold table. The results of the frequency tabulation of those that do and do not exceed the common median—10 board members and 25 teachers exceed the median; 20 board members and 15 teachers do not—are summarized in Table 10.6.

TABLE 10.6.   Sample frequencies of responses to salary negotiation attitude scale; hypothetical data.

	Sample	
	Teachers	Board members
Frequency for exceed median	25	10
Frequency for do not exceed median	15	20
Total frequency	40	30

The computation of the χ^2 value is done by substituting the frequencies into the formula discussed in the preceding section. This substitution gives:

$$\chi^2 = \frac{70(|(25)(20) - (10)(15)| - 35)^2}{(25 + 10)(15 + 20)(25 + 15)(10 + 20)}.$$

The χ^2 value so computed is 4.725. We consult Table E and note that the critical value for the .05 significance level and one degree of freedom is 3.84. Hence, the probability of the observed χ^2 value appearing by chance is less than .05.

The conclusion relative to the hypothesis is that on the basis of this statistical test, the null hypothesis is rejected. The probability that the sample distributions relative to the common median would appear if, in fact, the population medians are equal is less than .05. Hence, the conclusion is drawn that board members and teachers do differ as to their median scores on attitudes toward salary negotiations. It should be noted that nothing has been said about *how* they differ. If the ordinal scale of the attitude inventory is so set up that exceeding the median indicates a more favorable attitude, it could be noted that teachers have a higher observed than expected frequency in this cell. The opposite situation is true for board members. If a direction had been hypothesized, as may be done in attitude studies, a one-tailed statistical test would apply. However, no direction was hypothesized in this example.

EXTENSION OF THE MEDIAN TEST TO MORE THAN TWO SAMPLES

The median test can be extended to more than two independent samples. The samples need not be of equal size, but the variable being investigated must be measured on at least an ordinal scale. The conditions and the procedure exactly parallel those of the median test for two independent samples.

Let us say that we have j independent samples, with j equal to or greater than three. The procedure for the extension of the median test requires that we determine the common median of all the observations in the j samples. The individual observations of each sample are then assigned plus or minus signs, depending on whether or not they exceed the common median. (The definition of above or below the median may be used instead of exceed or not exceed the median.) This procedure yields two frequencies for each sample. The frequencies may be tabulated in a $2 \times j$ table similar to the one for the two-sample case. The table will contain j columns, one for each sample.

The null hypothesis is that the populations from which the j samples have been selected have the same medians, that is, they have a common median. Under the null hypothesis we would expect one-half of the observations in each sample to be above and one-half to be below the common median in the j samples. Thus we have expected frequencies for each of the cells in our $2 \times j$ table. (If the sample sizes are equal the expected frequencies for all cells would be the same.)

The null hypothesis is tested by the computation of a χ^2 value according to the usual procedure involving observed and expected frequencies. This χ^2 value is distributed as the chi square distribution with $j - 1$ degrees of freedom. The probability statement associated with the null hypothesis is: What is the probability that the observed sample distributions would appear, if, in fact, they come from populations with the same median? Again, this probability need not be determined exactly, only in terms of whether or not it is less than the predetermined significance level. The actual statistical test involves the probability of the χ^2 value appearing under the null hypothesis. On the basis of this probability the decision is made relative to the hypothesis.

Consider an example involving extension of the median test to more than two samples. A researcher at a university is interested in the extent of extracurricular participation of the students enrolled in four of the colleges: Arts and Science, Education, Engineering, and Pharmacy. It is decided that only junior year students will be sampled. Four random samples are drawn from the enrolled juniors of each of the four colleges, using a one in ten sampling ratio. Since the colleges do not have equal numbers enrolled, the sample sizes will be unequal. The records of the students are examined and the number of extracurricular activities is tabulated for each student. An extensive list of possible activities is used in assigning extracurricular scores to the students.

The null hypothesis is that there is no difference in number of extracurricular activities of the junior year student populations of the four colleges in the study. The significance level is set at .05; the null hypothesis will be rejected if the probability of the sample distributions appearing, if, in fact, the population medians are equal, is less than .05.

The four sample sizes appear in Table 10.7. The common median is computed and the plus or minus sign of each student in each sample is determined. To avoid throwing out data, the definition of "exceed" or "not exceed" the median is used for the dichotomy. The frequencies of this dichotomy also appear in Table 10.7.

TABLE 10.7.   Data for median test with four samples

	A & S	Education	Engineering	Pharmacy
Number that exceed median	92	62	41	8
Number that do not exceed median	72	58	57	16
Total in Sample	164	120	98	24

The χ^2 value for these data is 6.52 and the underlying chi square distribution has three degrees of freedom. Consulting Table E of Appendix 2 we find that the probability of this size χ^2 value appearing by chance is between .10 and .05. Hence we have a probability greater than the significance level. On the basis of this statistical test there is no reason to reject the null hypothesis. The researcher now concludes that there is no difference in the median number of extracurricular activities of the juniors in the four colleges of the study.

Note that the generalization is to the populations. Further, it regards only frequency of participation, not anything about the character of the participation. Let us look at the reasoning. The samples are randomly drawn, and the observations are taken and tabulated to acquire the frequencies for the median test. The differences that exist between the observed and hypothesized distributions can be due to two sources: (1) random sampling fluctuations or (2) population distributions that are not as hypothesized (that is, they do not have the same median). The probability of the first source is checked and found to be too great to discard. Hence the conclusion is that the differences may have occurred due to chance, and on this basis the researcher cannot reject the hypothesis that the populations have the same median.

The situation of this example may appear to meet the assumptions for a parametric technique. This may be so. The frequency of extracurricular activities has ratio scale measurement if we consider a zero as no involvement at all. However, simple counting is a rather crude measure of extracurricular activities, and one or more of the parametric assumptions dealing with the shapes and variances of the population distributions may not be tenable.

KRUSKAL-WALLIS ONE-WAY ANALYSIS OF VARIANCE BY RANKS

Nonparametric techniques may be used in doing an analysis of variance of data in ranks. One of these techniques is the Kruskal-Wallis one-way analysis of variance by ranks, a statistical test that is applicable to two or more independent samples. It is used for deciding whether or not the samples are from a common population. The null hypothesis of the test is that the samples are drawn from a common population or from populations with identical averages. Since the data must be in ranks, the dependent variable under study must have measurement on at least an ordinal scale. This variable is also assumed to have an underlying continuous distribution.

Let us say that we have j independent samples, and j is greater than or equal to two. It is not necessary that the sample sizes be equal. Let them be $n_1, \ldots, n_j$, respectively, with n being the total of all samples, that is, the total number of observations.

The computational procedure for the Kruskal-Wallis test requires that the n observations be ranked from 1 to n, inclusive. The smallest score is assigned rank 1, $\ldots$, etc., to the highest score, which is assigned rank n. The data now consist of ranks instead of original scores on the dependent variable.

The statistic of Kruskal-Wallis analysis of variance is denoted by H. The computational form is given below:[3]

$$H = \frac{12}{n(n + 1)} \sum_{i=1}^{j} \frac{R_i^2}{n_i} - 3(n + 1),$$

---

3. Sidney Siegel, *Nonparametric Statistics* (New York: McGraw-Hill Book Co., 1956), p. 185.

where R_i is the sum of the ranks in the ith sample, n_i is the number in the ith sample, and j is the number of samples. It should be noted that the number of observations need not be the same for each sample. If the n_i's are equal, this constant may be moved out in front of the summation sign.

We need an underlying distribution for our statistic H. Under the null hypothesis the statistic H is approximately distributed as the chi square distribution with $j - 1$ degrees of freedom. This approximation is adequate if all the j sample sizes exceed five. If sample size is less than or equal to five, a special table of probabilities associated with H must be consulted. Such a table does not appear in this text but can be found in statistics texts[4] dealing with specialized topics.

At this point we have a hypothesis to test and a statistic which relates to that hypothesis. The underlying distribution of that statistic is known. With the selection of a significance level we have the necessary ingredients for a statistical test of a hypothesis. An example using the Kruskal-Wallis test, taken from an actual research situation, follows.[5]

The purpose of the research was to investigate the frequency of discipline problems between team-teaching and self-contained classroom instructional organizations. The study involved several analyses; only the analysis dealing with a Kruskal-Wallis application is discussed here. Three levels of grades, four, five, and six, were observed by trained observers who recorded the number of relatively minor infractions of discipline. An intermediate team-teaching unit and two self-contained classroom units of the three grade levels were included in the study, the second self-contained unit for reasons of experimental design.

Thus there were three samples, and 12 observations were taken on each sample. An observation consisted of the number of discipline infractions during the first 30 minutes of the class period. The samples were considered to be random samples of the respective populations. Students had been randomly assigned to the instructional units. The null hypothesis was that there existed no differences between the average numbers of minor discipline infractions of the populations from which the three samples were drawn. The significance level was set at .05.

The 36 observations were ranked in the prescribed manner, and the H statistic was computed. The value of the H statistic was 2.64. Under the null hypothesis, this statistic was approximately distributed as the

4. This is the table as given by S. Siegel in *Nonparametric Statistics*, pp. 282–83.

5. The research project is reported in Cooperative Research Project Report No. 1391 of the Office of Education, U.S. Department of Health, Education and Welfare, "Classroom Interaction, Pupil Achievement and Adjustment in Team Teaching as Compared with the Self-Contained Classroom," by Philip Lambert *et al.* The research was conducted at the University of Wisconsin, 1964.

chi-square distribution, with two degrees of freedom. The 2.64 value does not attain the critical value of 5.99 necessary for rejecting the null hypothesis at the .05 level, as specified in Table E. Hence there was no basis to reject the null hypothesis. It was concluded that there was no difference in the average number of minor discipline infractions in the two self-contained populations and the team-teaching population for the grades considered.

Whenever data in ranks are analyzed there is always the possibility of tied ranks. In the use of the Kruskal-Wallis one-way analysis of variance, a correction for ties may be applied in the computation of H. This correction, which is less than 1, is divided into the original value of H. The correction is given by:

$$1 - \sum_{i=1}^{t} \frac{(T_i^3 - T_i)}{n^3 - n},$$

where T_i is the number of tied scores in a tied group and t is the number of tied groups.

The corrected H value will be larger than the initial H value, since the divisor of the fraction is less than 1. As a χ^2 value increases, the probability of it appearing decreases if degrees of freedom are unchanged. In the Kruskal-Wallis test the H value is distributed as a chi-square distribution, and the corrected H will have associated with it a smaller probability than the original H. Thus if the original H value is significant, there is no need to compute the corrected value, since it too will be significant. Actually in most cases the correction is negligible. If the original value is close to significance, the corrected value may attain significance. The degrees-of-freedom value is unchanged when a corrected H value is computed.

We might make some comparisons between the Kruskal-Wallis analysis of variance and its parametric counterpart, the one-way analysis of variance. The Kruskal-Wallis analysis requires at least ordinal measurement, and the parametric technique requires at least interval measurement. Thus the parametric technique is more demanding of the measurement.

The parametric analysis of variance analyzes the actual observed scores on the dependent variable, whereas the Kruskal-Wallis technique analyzes ranks. In the latter case the original scores as observed are changed to ranks, and it is the actual ranks that go into the analysis. Both analyses assume that the variable measured has an underlying continuous distribution. With small sample size the parametric technique would require the assumption of a normally distributed population. The parametric analysis deals specifically with means, and the Kruskal-Wallis technique deals more generally with averages or measures of central tendency. With ranked data the best that can be computed is a rough median. Therefore the parametric analysis tests for difference between means, and the Kruskal-Wallis technique tests for differences between rough medians as indicated by ranks.

As long as we limit the parametric counterpart to a one-way analysis of variance, both techniques involve one independent variable. The parametric analysis can be extended to include two or more independent variables, which opens the door to simultaneously including independent variables and investigating their interactions. There is no comparable extension to the Kruskal-Wallis analysis; the Friedman two-way analysis of variance by ranks, which applies to two or more related samples, does not have the partitioning of variance provided by the parametric technique.

Each type of analysis has its place and application. The correct analysis to be used depends on the hypotheses under study and the tenable assumptions.

The Kruskal-Wallis analysis was discussed as an illustration of a nonparametric analysis of variance by ranks. Other similar nonparametric techniques exist which may be applicable under certain conditions. Like the Friedman two-way analysis of variance, these specialized techniques are not discussed in this text.

CONCLUDING REMARKS: PARAMETRIC AND NONPARAMETRIC TECHNIQUES COMPARED

The testing of hypotheses by parametric and nonparametric techniques involves procedures that are commonly used and find extensive application in educational research. The procedures discussed in Chapters 9 and 10 by no means exhaust the statistical techniques available. When to use parametric or nonparametric procedures is an important consideration.

The type of scale on which the dependent variable is measured should be one of the researcher's primary considerations in deciding which technique to use. If the measurement is on a nominal or ordinal scale, nonparametric techniques are appropriate. Parametric techniques assume the data are measured on at least an interval scale. There are also certain assumptions about the underlying population distributions which are essential for parametric techniques. If these assumptions cannot be met, nonparametric techniques should be applied. If the assumptions are not satisfactorily met and a parametric analysis is nevertheless applied, the validity of the results would be in jeopardy.

It is often stated in research design texts that the parametric techniques are more powerful. The *power* of a statistical test is defined as the probability of rejecting the null hypothesis when in fact it is false. Recall from Chapter 9 that one of the possible errors in hypothesis testing is failing to reject a false hypothesis, a Type II or beta error. The power of a test in mathematical terms is 1 minus the probability of making a beta error. It is generally true that for a fixed sample size the parametric technique is more powerful than a corresponding nonparametric procedure. In general, the power of a statistical test is increased with increased sample size. It may be possible to achieve equivalent power between a parametric and nonparametric technique by increasing the sample size for the nonparametric technique, but this is not always a desirable alternative.

When data measured on an interval scale are converted to ranks, some of the information in the data is lost. However, applying parametric techniques when the data are not measured on an interval scale builds in information which does not exist. This has the end result of manufacturing distortions, which is less desirable than the loss of information if the data are converted to ranks for a nonparametric technique. If the assumptions can be met, parametric techniques are less wasteful of information.

The testing of interactions between independent variables by nonparametric techniques has not been as extensively developed as it has by parametric methods. The parametric analyses are much more sensitive to this type of effect. From a design standpoint the parametric techniques are often more sensitive to differences and to effects of more independent variables and their combinations.

Nonparametric techniques may be used with smaller sample size if the population distribution is not precisely known. The computation of nonparametric methods is generally easier, especially if desk calculators are to be used in the analysis. However, ease of statistical computation is only a technical matter. If computers are readily available, ease and length of computational procedures are of little concern.

The research hypothesis to be tested is, of course, an important factor in the selection of a statistical test. If the hypothesis deals with differences between means, a parametric technique is implied. When it deals with differences in ranks or between rough medians for ordinal data, a nonparametric approach would be feasible. In all cases the statistical test must test the hypothesis. It would be an error to state hypotheses which involve differences between means and then apply, say, the sign test.

The researcher must carefully consider the procedures which apply to the hypothesis, as well as the relevant aspects of assumptions and power. He should have clearly in mind the information he wants from the data and the subsequent analysis. These things should be considered before samples are drawn and data are collected. In the final analysis, only the researcher can make these decisions in the context of his specific investigation.

SUGGESTED STUDY EXERCISES

10.1. Discuss the differences between the parametric and nonparametric assumptions. What assumptions are common to both types of techniques?

10.2. Describe in considerable detail a research situation for which you would use a nonparametric technique. Identify the type of data you would collect. State the hypothesis.

10.3. Suppose that we have a distribution of frequencies within several categories and we test this against some expected distribution, using a chi square test. The test is significant at the .01 level of significance. State the null hypothesis, the associated probability statement, and your conclusion. Can you conclude anything about the .05 level of significance? Why or why not?

10.4. A researcher draws a random sample of 200 Ss and measures them on a performance variable. He wants to test the hypothesis that performance is normally distributed in the population. He divides his sample distribution into 15 categories and runs a goodness-of-fit test. The significance level is set at .05. The computed x^2 value for the statistical test is 23.00. What should the researcher conclude about his population distribution? Give the associated probability statement after the statistical test.

10.5. The median test is computed on two samples of observations. Sample sizes are 15 and 18. The significance level is designated as .05, and the x^2 value is computed as 4.81. Is this value significant? State the null hypothesis and your conclusion relative to the null hypothesis.

10.6. Suppose we have a variable measured on an ordinal scale with five categories. Four independent samples are measured on this variable. The hypothesis is that these four samples were drawn from a common population. A chi square test is computed. What is the necessary x^2 value for significance at the .05 level? Suppose the x^2 value is 23.81; what would you conclude? Give the associated probability statement.

10.7. Contrast the parametric analysis of variance and the Kruskal-Wallis one-way analysis of variance by ranks. What is the null hypothesis for the Kruskal-Wallis technique with five samples?

10.8. The sign test is used with two related samples of size 55. Consider the two samples as the before and after observations on a single group of Ss. The significance level is designated as .01. What is the appropriate underlying distribution, and what value is necessary in this distribution to attain a significant test if this is a two-tailed test? Suppose the value is 3.21; what would you conclude?

10.9. Two samples of entering college freshmen are drawn, one from athletes and one from nonathletes. Two dependent variables are investigated, namely, handedness (right, left, both) and achievement on an entrance mathematics test (interval scale measurement). The question under study is whether or not the populations of athletes and nonathletes differ on these dependent variables. Why would it be undesirable to use the same type of analysis for the two dependent variables? What measures would be tested statistically in the handedness data? In the mathematics test data? What would be an appropriate technique for testing the handedness data? The mathematics test data? Suppose the technique used for the handedness data reached significance at the .05 level. What would be concluded about handedness? After this conclusion, what type of error may have been made?

10.10. A researcher tests the performance of two random samples of Ss on a task. The performance of each S is scored as poor, fair, good, or excellent. A Student's t test is then computed on the sample data. The investigator interprets his results as being significant at the .01 but not at the .05 level. However, he decides to reject the null hypothesis and concludes that the two sample measures are in fact different. He then is concerned about his probability of having made a Type II or beta error. There are several errors in reasoning and procedure in this example. Point out these errors.

chapter 11

Testing hypotheses by correlational techniques

The concept of correlation, introduced in Chapter 2, deals with two variables and their relationship to one another. The measure or index of relationship is the correlation coefficient, which can take on values from -1.00 to $+1.00$, inclusive, depending upon the extent and direction of the relationship. If high scores on one variable tend to go with high scores on the other variable, the relationship is positive; if the opposite is true, the relationship is negative. We can plot the points determined by the scores of the two variables in a two-dimensional grid called a scattergram. Examples of scattergrams appear in Figures 2.10, 2.11, and 2.12 of Chapter 2.

The correlation coefficient is often used as a descriptive statistic; that is, it can be used to describe the relationship between two variables as they appear, without testing hypotheses. The researcher may be interested in describing the relationship within a population rather than in a sample, or he may want to describe the relationship between two distributions without making any further inferences. But the correlation coefficient is also used in an inferential manner. We can consider the correlation as a statistic obtained from a random sample and make inferences about the corresponding parameter. The major emphasis of this chapter will be on the use of correlation coefficients in inferential statistics.

Different types of correlation coefficients are used in educational research. The specific coefficient used in a particular research study depends upon the conditions of the study. Some coefficients are more demanding of the measurement scale of the variables than are others, and necessary assumptions are not the same for all coefficients. In a sense, the situation is analogous to that for parametric and nonparametric techniques. For the use of certain correlation coefficients, more stringent assumptions about the population distributions are necessary. If these cannot be met we turn to other coefficients that are not so demanding in assumptions. In any case the basic idea is the same—the extent of relationship between the variables. When testing hypotheses about correlation coefficients, the basic ideas of inferential statistics apply, as in the case of testing hypotheses with parametric and nonparametric techniques. In this chapter we will consider different types of correlation coefficients and their applications.

PEARSON PRODUCT-MOMENT CORRELATION COEFFICIENT

Probably the most frequently used correlation coefficient in educational research is the *Pearson product-moment coefficient*. This coefficient is the most sensitive measure of correlation for situations in which it applies. However, the Pearson product-moment coefficient requires that both variables be measured on at least an interval scale. An assumption for the Pearson product-moment coefficient is that the distributions of the two variables are continuous and somewhat symmetrical. The distributions need not be normal, but they should be *unimodal,* so that there is only one mode in a distribution. If one of the distributions is skewed, that is, non-symmetrical, it will tend to lower the correlation coefficient, and the researcher should be aware of this fact. Otherwise failure to meet this assumption will not put additional limitations on the procedure.

A linear relationship[1] between the two variables is also assumed. *Linear relationship* means that the plot of the scattergram approximates a straight-line fit when the scale of one variable is plotted on the vertical axis and the scale of the other is plotted on the horizontal axis. A true linear relationship would mean that the graph of the relationship between the two variables would fall exactly on a straight line.

The final assumption for the use of the Pearson product-moment

1. A more precise term would be "rectilinear," which means forming a straight line. However, "linear" refers to a straight line, while a departure from a straight line is referred to as "curvilinear."

coefficient is *homogeneity of variance* or *homoscedasticity*. This means that the dispersions in the rows (vertical axis) and columns (horizontal axis) of the scattergram array are about equal. If we consider the individual values of the variable represented on the vertical scale, for each such value there is a little distribution of values on the other variable. These distributions should have about the same variability in order to meet the homoscedastic assumption. The same is true for the values of the other variable, which would concern the distributions on the horizontal scale, of the scattergram.

Figures 11.1 and 11.2 illustrate the shapes of scattergrams which do not meet certain assumptions. Note that in both figures the Y distributions are much less variable for the X_1 values than for the X_2 values. A straight line would be a poor fit for the data of Figure 11.2. Thus, we say the relationship between the two variables is nonlinear and the assumption of a linear relationship is not tenable.

A possible set of data which would fit the scattergram of Figure 11.1

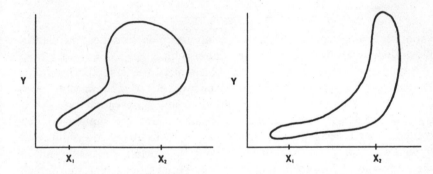

FIGURE 11.1.   Scattergram lacking homogeneity of variance.

FIGURE 11.2.   Scattergram lacking a linear relationship and also lacking homogeneity of variance.

appears in Table 11.1. These strictly hypothetical data include only 18 pairs of scores. The two variables are denoted by X and Y. Note that the Y distribution associated with the X score of 89 is much more variable than the Y distribution associated with the X score of 82. These two X scores correspond to X_1 and X_2 of the scattergram in the figure.

Table 11.2 contains a set of 20 pairs of observations which make a possible fit to the scattergram of Figure 11.2. The scores of 47 and 55 correspond to the X_1 and X_2 values of the figure. The distribution of Y scores for the X value of 55 is much more variable than the Y distribution for the X value of 47. Thus, the assumption of homogeneity of

TABLE 11.1. Hypothetical data on two variables which lack homogeneity of variance.

	Variables	
Subject number	X	Y
1	82	17
2	83	16
3	84	19
4	85	19
5	86	21
6	86	25
7	86	24
8	86	27
9	86	25
10	89	21
11	89	20
12	89	23
13	89	25
14	89	29
15	89	25
16	89	31
17	89	30
18	89	31

variance is not tenable. That the relationship is nonlinear is clearly illustrated by an inspection of the scattergram.

Suppose we have two variables which meet the assumptions for a Pearson product-moment correlation coefficient. A random sample of Ss is drawn from some defined population, and observations are taken on both variables. The correlation coefficient for the sample is then computed and designated as r. In keeping with basic procedures in hypothesis testing, we hypothesize about the correlation coefficient in the population. This coefficient is called rho, symbolized by the Greek letter ρ. A hypothesis which can be statistically tested is the hypothesis that $\rho = 0$. If we are simply concerned whether or not a relationship exists between the variables, this hypothesis takes on the characteristics of a null hypothesis, hypothesizing no relationship between the variables in the population.

The sampling distribution for r under the hypothesis of $\rho = 0$ is known. This distribution is sometimes called the *normal correlation distribution*. It is symmetrical around zero and is dependent upon sample size. When sample size is held constant, as r values become increasingly larger in absolute value, their probability of being selected in random sampling decreases. The associated probability statement is: What is the probability of the observed sample r appearing by chance, if, in fact, the population correlation is zero? If this probability is less than the significance level we will reject the hypothesis that the population correlation is zero. Note that the rejection of the null hypothesis

TABLE 11.2. Hypothetical data on
two variables which lack homogeneity
of variance and a linear relationship.

Subject number	Variables	
	X	Y
1	46	3
2	47	3
3	48	3
4	50	3
5	53	4
6	53	3
7	54	3
8	54	4
9	54	5
10	54	5
11	55	3
12	55	3
13	55	4
14	55	5
15	55	6
16	55	6
17	55	7
18	55	8
19	55	9
20	55	10

does not specify a value for ρ. The rejection simply leads to the conclusion that the population correlation is not zero.

The fact that the sampling distribution of r under the null hypothesis is dependent on sample size implies a family of distributions. It is not necessary for us to compute additional statistics to test the hypothesis of $\rho = 0$, because the critical values for the Pearson product-moment correlation coefficient appear in Table F of Appendix 2.[2] As is the usual case with families of distributions, only specific probabilities appear in the table. The column of degrees of freedom is used to find the proper distribution. The degrees of freedom associated with the proper distribution are given by $n - 2$, where n is the sample size.[3] The correlation values of the table have the indicated probability of appearing by chance if, in fact, the correlation between the two variables in the population is zero.

It should be noted that Table F gives levels of significance for both

2. The statistic underlying this table is $r\sqrt{n-2}/\sqrt{1-r^2}$, which is distributed as the corresponding t distribution with $n - 2$ degrees of freedom. If a table of critical values of the Pearson product-moment correlation coefficient is not available, we can solve for this statistic and use a t-distribution table for testing the null hypothesis.

3. The reason for $n - 2$ degrees of freedom is that when we are computing a statistical test for r we are testing the significance of regression, a concept discussed later in this chapter. A linear regression line involves two constants, and hence two degrees of freedom are lost in fitting the line.

one-tailed and two-tailed tests. The reasoning is the same as for other one-tailed and two-tailed statistical tests. If we would use an alternative hypothesis of $\rho > 0$ or $\rho < 0$, a one-tailed test would be appropriate, since a direction is being hypothesized. In that case, all of the area of the rejection region would be located in one tail of the distribution.

As an example of the use of Table F, suppose for the general situation discussed above we had a sample size of 30 and the computed correlation coefficient for the sample was .42. Recall that the question being posed is whether there is a correlation between the two variables in the population from which the sample was drawn. Since no direction is hypothesized, the null hypothesis is $\rho = 0$ and a two-tailed test is appropriate. The significance level is set at .05. The value for degrees of freedom equals 30 minus 2 or 28. Table F indicates that a correlation coefficient of .361 has a probability of .05 (our significance level) of appearing by chance if the correlation in the population is zero. Since our sample r of .42 is greater than .361, it has a probability of less than .05 of appearing by chance under the null hypothesis. Hence we reject the null hypothesis and conclude that a correlation does exist in the population between the two variables.

CONFIDENCE INTERVAL FOR THE PEARSON PRODUCT-MOMENT CORRELATION COEFFICIENT

The question of whether or not any correlation between two variables exists in a population may be trivial under certain conditions. The researcher may have prior evidence that a relationship exists, and he is really concerned with information about the magnitude of the correlation in the population. The confidence interval for the correlation coefficient can provide an estimate of the correlation in the population. As in the case of the confidence interval for the mean (see Chapter 9), the confidence interval for the correlation coefficient is an interval estimate for a parameter. That is, the researcher is attempting to determine what interval of values he will entertain as tenable values for the correlation coefficient in the population under study.

The procedure is not as straightforward in this situation as it was, say, for constructing a confidence interval for the mean. A special transformation is used in the computation.[4] The sampling distribution for r becomes markedly skewed as we depart from $\rho = 0$. This can be intui-

---

4. This is a logarithmic transformation. For computational details the reader is referred to a statistics text such as G. V. Glass, and J. C. Stanley, *Statistical Methods in Education and Psychology* (Englewood Cliffs, N.J.: Prentice-Hall, 1970), pp. 265–68.

tively seen by considering the restrictions on the possible values the correlation coefficient can take. Consider a situation in which sampling was done from a population with $\rho = .90$. Since the upper bound on the value of r is $+1.00$, the sampling distribution is now very skewed. It will be centered around .90, and the left tail can take on values from .90 to -1.00, while the right tail can only go from .90 to $+1.00$. In addition, there is little exact knowledge about the sampling distribution except when it is centered on zero.

Although the computational procedures are more involved than in the case of the confidence interval for the mean, the principle is the same. Suppose that we are interested in a 95 percent confidence interval. Two values are determined that define the interval. The probability is then .95 that this interval spans the population correlation. Our conclusion is that the values of the correlation coefficient within this interval are tenable values for the correlation in the population.

A situation in which the confidence interval might be a useful procedure would be one in which IQ scores are correlated separately with three different achievement measures. The question under investigation has to do with the tenable values of these correlation coefficients in the population under investigation. Note that in this situation three confidence intervals would be constructed, one for each correlation coefficient of the achievement measure with IQ. There would undoubtedly be prior evidence that a correlation exists between IQ and any one of the achievement measures, and the magnitude of such correlation coefficients would be of primary interest. The confidence interval would provide the interval estimate of the population correlation.

Confidence intervals for correlation coefficients are not common in educational research, but they can be used as an effective technique which provides useful information. A confidence interval can be considered a test of an infinite number of hypotheses in that the values within the interval are all tenable values for the population correlation. Values outside the interval would be rejected as hypothesized values.

DIFFERENCE BETWEEN TWO CORRELATION COEFFICIENTS: INDEPENDENT SAMPLES

In considering the difference between two correlations of independent samples, the problem concerns what magnitude of difference is required so that the hypothesis that the two correlations are equal in the population will no longer be entertained. The null hypothesis is $\rho_1 = \rho_2$, or $\rho_1 - \rho_2 = 0$. Note that it is not implied that either or both of the ρ values are zero. In order to complete the statistical computation to test this null hypothesis, we need the special transformation mentioned earlier. The reasoning underlying the statistical test is analogous to that underlying the situation for the difference between two means. In this case we are trying to decide whether or not the correlations of the two populations are the same. A significant statistical test would result in rejecting the null hypothesis, that is, the hypothesis of no difference between the population correlations.

As an example, suppose someone asks whether the correlation coefficients between IQ and science achievement differ significantly for seventh-grade boys and girls. Random samples of seventh-grade boys and girls are drawn from the populations. The sample of boys is considered to be independent of the sample of girls. The correlation coefficients are computed separately for each sample. The null hypothesis states that there is no difference between the correlation coefficients in the populations of boys and girls. In order to entertain the null hypothesis it must be acceptable for the observed difference to be attributable to chance. If this chance probability is less than the significance level, the explanation of chance is no longer acceptable. The alternative conclusion is that there is a real difference in the population correlations, and hence the null hypothesis is rejected.

Suppose the significance level is designated as .05 and the statistical test for the difference between the two correlation coefficients is significant. Then the probability that the observed difference would occur by chance, if, in fact, there is no difference in the populations, is less than .05. The conclusion is that the correlation between IQ scores and science achievement is not the same for boys and girls. Note that the statistical test does not indicate which correlation coefficient is largest in magnitude. An inspection of the sample coefficients will aid in drawing this conclusion.

DIFFERENCE BETWEEN TWO CORRELATION COEFFICIENTS: RELATED SAMPLES

A hypothesis about the difference between two correlation coefficients of related samples can also be tested statistically. Related samples are sometimes referred to as *correlated samples*. In this situation three observations are taken on the same sample of *S*s. The three correlation coefficients that result may be compared in all combinations of two. Any combination is, of course, a single comparison.

The null hypothesis is again that of no difference between the correlation coefficients in the population. Suppose we have three variables on which the sample is measured, designated by 1, 2, and 3. The subscripts on r denote the two variables being correlated. To compare the difference between r_{12} and r_{13} we compute the statistic:

$$\frac{(r_{12} - r_{13})\sqrt{(n - 3)(1 + r_{23})}}{\sqrt{2(1 - r_{12}{}^2 - r_{13}{}^2 - r_{23}{}^2 + 2r_{12} \cdot r_{13} \cdot r_{23})}},$$

which is distributed as the Student's t distribution with $n - 3$ degrees of freedom.

To consider the question of whether there is a difference between the correlations of IQ and science achievement and IQ and mathematics achievement, a random sample of Ss is drawn from a defined population, and the Ss are measured on the three variables. In addition to the two correlation coefficients mentioned in the question, the correlation between science and mathematics achievement is determined. The three computed correlation coefficients can be designated as follows:

r_{12} = Correlation between IQ and science achievement
r_{13} = Correlation between IQ and mathematics achievement
r_{23} = Correlation between science achievement and mathematics achievement

The null hypothesis is: $\rho_{12} = \rho_{13}$ or $\rho_{12} - \rho_{13} = 0$. That is, we hypothesize no difference between these respective correlation coefficients of the population. A significance level is set, and the computation is carried out as designated by the above formula. If the value of t is significant, the null hypothesis is rejected; if it is not significant, we fail to reject the null hypothesis.

The discussion to this point in the chapter has been concerned primarily with the Pearson product-moment coefficient of correlation. It might be well to summarize the hypotheses that can be tested by this technique. Recall that hypotheses are statements about population characteristics. We can test the hypothesis that the population correlation is zero. Then we can build a confidence interval for a specific correlation coefficient. This is actually an infinite number of tests of hypotheses since it determines which values will be considered tenable and which will be rejected. Finally, the hypotheses of no difference between two population correlations can be tested, for independent or related samples.

SPEARMAN RANK-ORDER CORRELATION COEFFICIENT

The measurement of many variables is not quantitative enough to use an interval scale, yet the relationship between the variables may be of interest. The Pearson product-moment correlation coefficient does not apply in such situations, since the assumption of interval scale measurement is not met. Other correlational procedures must be used in such instances.

Probably the best known correlational procedure for two variables measured on an ordinal scale is the Spearman rank order correlation coefficient. This coefficient is often referred to as the *Spearman rho,* or simply *rho.* This may appear confusing, since we have also designated the population coefficient as rho. For consistency and to avoid confusion we will use r_s and ρ_s to designate the Spearman rank-order coefficients of the sample and the population.

Measurement on an ordinal scale allows us to rank observations. As with any correlation coefficient, measurement on two variables is required. However, the Spearman rank order coefficient does not correlate the actual observations but the ranks representing the observations. If n is the number of Ss in the sample, the Ss are ranked from 1 through $n,$ inclusive, first on one variable and then on the other. Ss with the same score (that is, tied ranks) are assigned the mean rank of the ranks they occupy. The next step is to determine the difference between the two ranks of each S. It is these differences in ranks that actually go into the statistical computation. Because the differences are squared, it is not necessary to retain the algebraic sign but only the absolute values of the difference.

The correlation coefficient of the observations is given by[5]:

$$r_s = 1 - \frac{6\Sigma d_i^2}{n(n^2 - 1)},$$

where the d_i's are the differences in ranks—d_i is the difference for the ith S. The sample size is n. As in all hypothesis testing, we want to make statements about the population correlation and test these statements.

The testing of hypotheses with the Spearman rank order correlation coefficient is somewhat limited for two reasons. If n is small, say less than ten, the standard deviation of the underlying distribution for r_s cannot be estimated, regardless of the hypothesized values of the population coefficient. For any hypothesized value other than $\rho_s = 0$, there is no accepted method for estimating the standard deviation of the underlying sampling distribution for r_s, no matter how large the

---

5. If we use the ranks of the two variables as the scores and apply the Pearson product-moment formula, we get the same result. However, this should not be interpreted to mean that a Spearman ρ computed on interval-scale data converted to ranks will equal the Pearson product moment computed for the same data. The Pearson product moment takes into account the relative distances between scores, as well as their order.

sample size. Note that we are concerned with the standard deviation of the underlying sampling distribution, not that of the sample data. Since the sample data are converted to ranks, we cannot compute a standard deviation for these ordinal data. Hence, we cannot build confidence intervals.

The null hypothesis, $\rho_s = 0$, can be statistically tested with n greater than or equal to ten. If n is less than 25 we can compute the statistic $r_s\sqrt{n-2}/\sqrt{1-r_s^2}$, which is distributed as the Student's t distribution with $n-2$ degrees of freedom. A significant t value would result in the rejection of the null hypothesis. The probability that the observed r_s would appear by chance, if, in fact, $\rho_s = 0$, is less than the significance level. If n is 25 or greater, the normal distribution can be used as the underlying distribution. Under this condition, the standard deviation of the sampling distribution of r_s is given by:

$$\frac{1}{\sqrt{n-1}}.$$

Suppose a researcher is interested in the relationship between attitudes toward school and socioeconomic background. Assume that these two variables are measured on ordinal scales and therefore the Ss could be ranked on the variables. Attitudes toward school and socioeconomic background are variables that may be difficult to measure, but we will assume that satisfactory ordinal measurement is possible. In order to limit the study somewhat, suppose that only the junior high school population of a defined and geographically limited school district is under study. The question may be stated as: Is there a relationship between these two variables in the defined junior high school population?

A random sample of Ss is drawn from the population. The Ss are administered the attitudes-toward-school inventory and scored on socioeconomic background. Each S is then ranked on each variable, and differences between ranks are determined. Using these differences, the r_s is computed. The null hypothesis is that the correlation between attitude toward school and socioeconomic background in the junior high population is zero, i.e., $\rho_s = 0$. Since no direction is hypothesized, the hypothesis implies a two-tailed test. A significance level is specified, say .05.

The appropriate underlying distribution is used to test the null hypothesis. Suppose the statistical test turns out to be significant, which results in the rejection of the null hypothesis. Then the probability that the observed sample correlation coefficient would appear by chance, if, in fact, the population correlation is zero, is less than .05. On this basis we can conclude that there is a relationship between attitude toward school and socioeconomic background. Note that no statement is made as to the exact magnitude of the correlation coefficient.

POINT BISERIAL CORRELATION COEFFICIENT

It is not always possible to acquire measurement of the same type on both variables. One variable may be continuous and measured on an interval scale, while the other variable may be discrete and dichotomous. For example, sex is a two-category variable, and achievement in mathematics is generally considered continuous and measurable on an interval scale. A correlation coefficient which measures the relationship between two such variables is the point biserial correlation coefficient. The dichotomous variable is assumed to be discrete, that is, a genuine dichotomy. The continuous variable essentially requires the assumptions of a somewhat symmetrical, unimodal distribution with interval scale measurement. The point biserial correlations of the sample and population will be designated by r_{pb} and ρ_{pb} respectively.

The point biserial correlation is actually a product-moment type of correlation coefficient. If we artificially assign numerical weights, say zero and one, to the two categories of the dichotomous variable and apply the calculation of a Pearson product-moment coefficient, we would get a point biserial coefficient.

The computation of a point biserial involves the proportions of observations in the two categories of the dichotomous variable. These two proportions we will designate as p and q. Of course, $p + q = 1$. Since the continuous variable is measured on an interval scale, means and standard deviations can be computed for this variable. The computational formula for the point biserial coefficient is given by:

$$r_{pb} = \frac{\bar{Y}_p - \bar{Y}_q}{s_y} \cdot \sqrt{p \cdot q},$$

where $\bar{Y}_p$ and $\bar{Y}_q$ are the means on the continuous variable for those Ss belonging to the respective categories of the dichotomy, and s_y is the standard deviation of all scores on the continuous variable.

The testing of hypotheses when using a point biserial coefficient is somewhat limited. It is possible to test the hypothesis of zero correlation in the population, and this can be done in two ways. From an inspection of the computational formula, it is immediately apparent that the value of r_{pb} is directly dependent upon the difference of two means. Thus, a Student's t test for the difference between two means can be applied. If this statistical test is significant, we reject the hypothesis of zero correlation in the population.

A direct test of the null hypothesis, $\rho_{pb} = 0$, can be made, as in the Spearman rank correlation coefficient. Note that the hypothesis deals with the population correlation. The expression:

$$r_{pb} \cdot \sqrt{\frac{n-2}{1-r_{pb}^2}}$$

is distributed as the Student's t distribution with $n - 2$ degrees of freedom, where n is the total sample size. A significant t value again leads to the rejection of the null hypothesis.

Theoretically, correlation coefficients can take on values between plus and minus one, inclusively. However, with the point biserial coefficient the values of r_{pb} are dependent upon the proportional split of the dichotomous variable, that is, the values of p and q. The maximum and minimum values of r_{pb} do not reach plus one and minus one under any proportional division.

An example for which the point biserial coefficient would apply would be the study of the relationship between type of high school attended, rural or urban, and achievement on a college entrance examination in mathematics. Type of high school attended is a variable that can be dichotomously defined, and the scores on the mathematics examination are assumed to be continuously distributed. A random sample is drawn from entering college freshmen who are then given the mathematics test. Each freshman in the sample is then categorized as to whether he attended a rural or urban high school. The r_{pb} is computed for the sample.

The null hypothesis is that there is no correlation between high school attended and achievement on this entrance mathematics exam. A significance level is designated. Suppose a direct test of the hypothesis is made and the corresponding t value is found not to be significant. Thus we fail to reject the null hypothesis. The probability that the r_{pb} (sample correlation coefficient) would appear by chance, if, in fact, ρ_{pb} is zero, is greater than the significance level. The conclusion is that on the basis of this statistical test we cannot infer that a relationship exists between type of high school attended and achievement on this particular mathematics examination.

BISERIAL CORRELATION COEFFICIENT

A correlation coefficient closely related to the point biserial is the biserial coefficient. It is applicable when the dichotomous variable is an artificial dichotomy and actually has an underlying continuous distribution. A common example of such a variable is the case for which performance on an examination is reduced to pass or fail. The second variable is again continuous and measured on at least an interval scale.

The computational formula for the biserial correlation coefficient is similar to the point biserial coefficient. The biserial correlation of the sample is designated by r_b. The formula is given by:

$$r_b = \frac{\bar{Y}_p - \bar{Y}_q}{s_y} \cdot \frac{p \cdot q}{y^1}.$$

The symbols have the same definitions as in the formula for r_{pb}. The one new symbol is y^1, which is the ordinate of the standard normal distribution at the point of division for the proportions p and q. Since the normal curve is symmetrical, the division may be made on either side of the mean. The value of y^1 can be determined directly from an area table of the standard normal distribution, like Table A in Appendix 2. The area under the standard normal curve is designated as 1.00, or unity. Suppose that $p = .60$ and $q = .40$. This means that for p we have all the area in one-half of the distribution, plus an additional 10 percent located between the mean and the split in the dichotomy. Coming down the area column until we come to .10 we find the corresponding ordinate or y^1 value to be .386.

The hypothesis of zero correlation in the population, i.e., H_0: $\rho_b = 0$, may be statistically tested if the sample size is quite large, say 25 or greater. Under these conditions the standard deviation of the biserial coefficient is given by:

$$s_{r_b} = \frac{\dfrac{\sqrt{p \cdot q}}{y^1}}{\sqrt{n}}.$$

The normal distribution can be used as an adequate approximation for the underlying distribution. The null hypothesis states that there is no correlation between the two variables in the population. The test of the hypothesis gives us the probability of the sample correlation coefficient appearing, if, in fact, the variables are uncorrelated in the population. If this probability is less than the predetermined significance level we reject the null hypothesis and conclude that the two variables are correlated in the population. Note that the statistical test does not specify the direction or the magnitude of the correlation coefficient.

Two variables whose relationship might be studied using the biserial coefficient are pass or fail performance on a physical education task and achievement on a science examination. Suppose that the performance on the physical education task is continuous, but for some reason measurement is such that the researcher chooses to dichotomize the scores on this variable. A random sample is drawn from a defined population, and the r_b is computed. The null hypothesis is H_0: $\rho_b = 0$, i.e., the population correlation between the two variables is zero. A significance level is specified, and the null hypothesis is tested. If the probability of the r_b appearing by chance under the null hypothesis is less than the significance level, the null hypothesis is rejected. If this probability is greater than the significance level, we fail to reject the null hypothesis.

The above example is a case in which the statistical test could be strengthened if it were possible to measure the performance on the physical education task on an interval scale. Under that condition an applicable correlation coefficient would be the Pearson product-moment. An interval scale takes into account differences between Ss in terms of a common or equal unit. Chances are that two Ss, one of whom is slightly above and the other slightly below the pass-fail cut-off, are actually quite close in score, closer than a "just pass" and a high scorer. Going to the dichotomy loses this type of information and makes the statistical test less sensitive to an existing correlation between the variables. However, if measurement is not precise enough for an interval scale, it should not be artificially forced upon the data.

The question may arise in a specific situation whether to use the point biserial correlation coefficient or the biserial coefficient. The crucial point is whether the dichotomous variable is a genuine dichotomy or has an underlying continuous distribution. If there is little doubt about the underlying distribution being continuous, the biserial coefficient should be used. In doubtful situations, the point biserial coefficient should be used. The point biserial will yield a markedly smaller coefficient if applied to a situation in which the use of the biserial is justified. A conversion formula can be applied to convert from one to the other, if afterward it becomes apparent that the other coefficient is more appropriate in a specific situation.

COEFFICIENT OF CONTINGENCY

A situation can arise in which there are two or more categories for one or both of two variables measured on nominal scales. In such a case a measure of the relationship between the two variables can be computed using the coefficient of contingency. This coefficient involves the χ^2 value based on a $k \times j$ table, where k and j are the numbers of categories associated with the two variables under study. The coefficient is generally designated by C and the formula is given by:

$$C = \sqrt{\frac{\chi^2}{n + \chi^2}},$$

where n is sample size and the χ^2 value is as determined from the $k \times j$ table.

The contingency coefficient is restricted in size. Its minimum value is zero, that is, it does not take on negative values. Since the concept of direction requires order, it would be without meaning when applied to strictly nominal variables. In a practical situation a researcher might attach a positive or negative sign to indicate a certain type of association in the data, such as left-handedness going with left-footedness. Since n is an integer, an inspection of the formula reveals that the denominator will always exceed the numerator, and therefore the coefficient cannot attain the maximum value of plus one. The maximum value depends upon the number of categories of the two variables—as the number of categories increases, the maximum possible value of the coefficient also increases.

The null hypothesis of no correlation in the population can be tested. It is possible to estimate the standard error of the contingency coefficient, but this is not necessary because another procedure can be used. A simpler procedure for testing the null hypothesis uses the χ^2 value from which C is computed. Under the null hypothesis this χ^2 value is distributed with $(k - 1)(j - 1)$ degrees of freedom. A significant χ^2 value would result in the rejection of the null hypothesis. The conclusion would be that a relationship does exist in the population between the two variables under study.

THE CHOICE OF CORRELATION COEFFICIENT

The reader of educational research literature may note that correlation coefficients such as the coefficiency of contingency and even the biserials do not appear frequently in correlational studies, although there is a considerable number of correlational studies in the literature. Many times the coefficient used is not specified, but it can be assumed that if possible, the investigator has applied the Pearson product-moment coefficient. It is the preferable technique if the necessary conditions can be met. The Pearson product-moment does not waste information and is more sensitive to an existing relationship under the appropriate conditions.

Five correlation coefficients have been introduced in this chapter, and there are other correlation coefficients that find limited use in educational research. In selecting which coefficient to use, the researcher should carefully consider the conditions of the research situation relative to the assumptions necessary for using a specific coefficient. If a coefficient for which the assumptions are not met is used, it would have the result of inserting information that does not exist into the data. On the other hand, using a coefficient when a more sensitive procedure would be applicable is wasteful of information and is not considered good research methodology.

Certainly consideration of the measurement scales of the variables under study is important in selecting a correlation coefficient. Table 11.3

TABLE 11.3.   Correlation coefficients and minimum required measurement of the variables

Correlation coefficient	Measurement of variables (minimum required)
1. Pearson product-moment	1. Both variables on interval scales.
2. Spearman rank order	2. Both variables on ordinal scales.
3. Point biserial	3. One variable on interval scale; the other a genuine dichotomy on a nominal or ordinal scale.
4. Biserial	4. One variable on interval scale; the other an artificial dichotomy on an ordinal scale. The dichotomy is artificial because there is an underlying continuous distribution.
5. Coefficient of contingency	5. Both variables on nominal scales.

lists the five coefficients discussed in this chapter and the minimum measurement scale required of the variables for each one.

Note that the measurement specified for each coefficient is the *minimum* scale required. Other scales also can be used. For example, the Pearson product-moment coefficient can be used with ratio scale measurement. If we had interval-scale measurement on both variables, as we must have for the product-moment coefficient, we could reduce the scores to ranks and compute a Spearman rho correlation coefficient. However, if the other assumptions were tenable, computing a Spearman rho coefficient rather than a Pearson product-moment coefficient would be wasteful of information. Remember, too, that other assumptions than those dealing with the scales on which the variables are measured may be required for the use of specific coefficients.

CORRELATION AND REGRESSION

A term which invariably appears in a discussion of correlation is regression. Actually the idea of regression preceded the development of the correlational methods. The origin of the idea is credited to Sir Francis Galton, in connection with his studies of the relationship between the heights of parents and offspring. One important observation was that the means of offspring for fixed parent height deviated less from their common mean than the corresponding means of parents differed from their common mean. This indicates a sort of "falling back" or regression in the succeeding generation.

In the case of a perfect positive correlation, the data would fall on a straight line. If the standard deviations of the two distributions are equal, the line would have a slope of plus one, the *slope* of the line being the ratio of the change in the variable on the vertical scale to the change in the variable on the horizontal scale.

When the data of two variables are plotted on a scattergram, the points make up some kind of configuration. If this configuration is such that a straight line is an adequate fit and the line is actually fitted, we say the regression between the two variables is linear. The use of correlation coefficients such as the Pearson product-moment assumes a linear relationship or linear regression between the two variables.

There are many variables in educational research that are not linearly related. If the plot of points in the scattergram does not follow the general pattern of a straight line, the regression is nonlinear. Examples of such variables might be efficiency on a learning task and the passage of time. A marked increase in efficiency would be expected early in time and then a plateau would be reached, resulting in a curved rather than straight line. If the task is continued for a considerable time, efficiency might decrease due to a factor such as fatigue. The relationship between performance on a motor skill and chronological age may be nonlinear if the chronological age range is large. Under such conditions the application of a correlation coefficient that assumes linear regression is clearly inappropriate and will give misleading results.

PREDICTION, REGRESSION, AND CORRELATION

One use of the concept of regression is in connection with prediction studies. Prediction in education has a wide range of procedural meanings, extending from subjective prediction based on casual observation to the development of multiple-term mathematical equations connecting two or more variables. *Prediction* is the estimation of one variable from the information of one or more other variables. The variable from which we are predicting is called the *predictor variable,* and the variable predicted is called the *criterion variable.* Two basic questions must be considered in the execution of a prediction study: (1) What variables are related to the variable to be predicted? (2) What is the connecting expression or equation which will make for the most accurate prediction? The regression between the predictor and criterion variables is involved in this second question.

Note that it is not implied that the involvement of a complex mathematical equation is particularly desirable. The type of data and the conditions of the study dictate the specific procedure to be used. We may predict using nominal variables, for example predicting certain behavior patterns from a knowledge of sex. Attempts may be made to predict success in occupations such as engineer, artist, or teacher from a knowledge of ability or aptitude. The variable being predicted may be measured on a nominal, ordinal, or interval scale. Types of variables between predictors and predicted may be used in various combinations. The computational procedure is determined by the specific combination used in a study.

A common example of prediction in education is predicting achievement from an intelligence measure. If we define Y to be the predicted variable (achievement) and X to be the predictor (intelligence measure), we can develop an equation called the *regression equation*,[6] of the form $Y = a + bX$. An equation in this general form is the equation of a straight line, and this is the regression line for estimating Y from X. It is also called the prediction equation for predicting Y from X. The coefficients a and b are the constants of the regression equation. The equation is uniquely determined with the specification of a and b. After the constants or coefficients of the prediction equation are determined, the value of Y for any one S can be predicted by substituting into the equation the S's score or value on X. Thus, the equation is predicting Y from a knowledge of X.

The advantage in using this fitted line for predicting depends upon the strength or magnitude of the correlation between the predictor and the criterion variables. The greater the correlation, the more precisely the line will fit the points in the scattergram and the greater will be the accuracy of prediction. By accuracy of prediction, we mean that the errors in prediction, the differences between observed and predicted scores of the criterion variable, are small. A common misconception is that accuracy of prediction deals with how many predicted and observed scores actually coincide. This is not what it means at all. We are concerned not with the percentage of scores we can predict "right

---

6. An infinite number of straight lines could be fitted to the points in a scattergram. The line that we fit, which we might call the "best fitting" straight line, is the one determined by the least squares requirement. The *least squares requirement* means that the line is fitted in such a manner that the sum determined by taking all differences between the observed and predicted scores for each S, squaring these differences, and then summing is a minimum. In symbol form this is given by:

$$\sum_{i=1}^{n} (Y_i - \hat{Y}_i)^2$$

is a minimum, where $\hat{Y}_i$ is a predicted score.

on the head" but with getting small differences between observed and predicted scores.

Another way of looking at errors of prediction is to consider the distribution of error scores. The difference between an observed and predicted score is an error of prediction. If a distribution of error scores were generated, some would be positive, others negative, and some might be zero, if the observed and predicted scores coincide. This distribution of error scores would have a standard deviation, called the *standard error of estimate*. We want to have the distribution of error scores closely grouped around zero so we will have a small standard deviation (standard error of estimate). The standard error of estimate is given by the formula:

$$s_{\text{est}} = s_y\sqrt{1 - r^2},$$

where s_y is the standard deviation of the distribution of observed criterion scores and r is the correlation between predictor and criterion variables.

The formula above also shows that the greater the correlation coefficient, the smaller will be the standard deviation of the distribution of error scores. If correlation is perfect, that is, plus or minus one, prediction is exact and the standard error of estimate would be zero. That means that all the error scores would be zero. The standard deviation of such a distribution is zero; all the points of the scattergram would fall on the regression line. On the other hand, if correlation is zero, no predictive value is gained because then the distribution of error scores would be as variable as the original distribution of criterion scores ($s_{\text{est}} = s_y$). So, as the correlation between predictor and criterion scores is increased, the errors of prediction are decreased, and accuracy of prediction is enhanced.

It may be desirable to predict a criterion variable from more than one predictor variable. This involves multiple correlation where two or more predictor variables act as a team of predictors. Again, equations are developed, with a coefficient associated with each predictor variable. The idea is essentially the same, that is, the development of a prediction equation. However, instead of having only one predictor in the equation, two or more are included and each has its own coefficient in the equation.

INTERPRETATIONS OF THE CORRELATION COEFFICIENT

One interpretation of the correlation coefficient is in terms of the variation in one variable associated with the variation in the other variable.

The square of the correlation coefficient gives the proportion of the variance in Y associated with the variation in X, or the proportion of the variance in Y predictable from X. This interpretation assumes an association between the two variables, and if the correlation coefficient is significantly different from zero we conclude that there is an association. If there exists no association or relationship, the correlation is zero and hence none of the variance in Y would be associated with the variation in X. At the other extreme, if correlation is perfect, that is, plus or minus one, prediction is exact and all of the variation in Y would be associated with the variation in X.

In determining what is a good correlation, "good" essentially means a coefficient of such magnitude as to be noteworthy. Questions regarding the size of the correlation coefficient cannot be answered without considering the variables under study and the uses to be made of the coefficient. Deobold Van Dalen provides rough guidelines for the interpretation (with reservations) of the magnitude of the correlation coefficient when conducting prediction studies.[7] These guidelines assign a subjective degree of relationship depending on the size of the correlation coefficient (r), as follows:

$r = \pm .00$ to $\pm .20$, negligible relationship
$r = \pm .20$ to $\pm .40$, low relationship
$r = \pm .40$ to $\pm .70$, marked relationship
$r = \pm .70$ to ± 1.00, high to very high relationship

If one were using correlation coefficients in establishing the reliability or validity of a test, the desired or necessary magnitude of the correlation would depend upon the types of tests and content of the tests.

For a researcher working on a theoretical problem, any correlation coefficient significantly different from zero is likely to be noteworthy. Such a coefficient may be indicative of a generalization being sought. The reasons for the coefficient's small magnitude may be due to uncontrolled factors such as inadequate measurement, rather than an inadequate theory. It may be very difficult to achieve isolation for the two variables being correlated, and the contamination of other factors may be suppressing the relationship. Any number of factors may be operating in a specific situation.

The conclusion from these remarks is that the size of the correlation coefficient must always be interpreted in the light of its use in the specific situation. Size of a correlation coefficient is always relative to the conditions under which it was obtained. The researcher must

---

7. D. B. Van Dalen, *Understanding Educational Research,* 3rd ed. (New York: McGraw-Hill Book Co., 1973), p. 231.

specify his variables, measuring instruments, populations, and the like before he can interpret the size of his correlation coefficient.

COMMENTS ON CONDUCTING CORRELATIONAL STUDIES

The emphasis of this chapter has been upon the use of correlational techniques in inferential statistics. Some writers place correlation with descriptive statistics. When so considered, the primary function of the correlation coefficient is to describe the extent of relationship between two sets of scores. To be sure, many correlational studies are descriptive in nature, and the findings are directed only to the observed data and the variables represented by these data. However, in many situations, the researcher is attempting to make inferences about relationships to a population. When this is done, correlational techniques are being used in an inferential context. In any event, the objectives of the specific study dictate whether descriptive or inferential techniques are appropriate.

The initial problem facing a researcher about to embark on a correlational study is the choice of variables. A review of the literature and an adequate knowledge of the educational area should alleviate much of this problem. The procedure of correlating a large number of variables in order to see what kind of coefficients turn up, sometimes referred to as the shotgun approach, is not recommended. It lacks a rationale for the relationships between variables. This is not to say that any study which correlates a considerable number of variables is a shotgun study; it is the thinking behind the study that makes the difference. The good researcher in an educational area generally does not rely on guesses but rather is sensitive to the variables in the area.

Among the possible factors that can have an effect upon the size of the correlation coefficient are inadequate measurement and lack of isolation of the variables being correlated. The researcher should have some knowledge about his particular variables and how they are operating in the light of the measurement and the other specific circumstances of his study. Suppose a Pearson product-moment coefficient is anticipated. The size of the coefficient depends upon the amount of variance in the distributions of the variables being correlated. If one variable is practically reduced to a constant we can expect a very small correlation coefficient. This relates not only to the variable but also to the methods by which measurement for the variable is conducted.

For example, suppose we have a defined population, heterogeneous in intelligence, and an adequate intelligence test for the measurement. We want to correlate intelligence with performance on a mathematics test, and with such a population we would expect a relatively high correlation coefficient. Now suppose we have another population of high-ability students, those within the 130–150 IQ range, and we correlate their intelligence scores with mathematics performance. We would likely get a relatively small correlation coefficient in this case. What is the conclusion—that for high-ability students intelligence is not related to mathematics performance? Obviously not. What has happened is that the variable of intelligence scores is much more homogeneous in the latter situation than it was when it covered an entire range of ability. This reduction in variability limits the size of the correlation coefficient. The same type of outcome would occur if measurement were inadequate. For example, if a large proportion of the students attained the maximum possible score on the mathematics test, this would limit the variability, and the test would fail to differentiate students with different intelligence scores on mathematics performance. The instrument would not be discriminating between the students, and the size of the correlation coefficient would be relatively small. The range of the scores on one or both variables influences the size of the correlation coefficient, with the limited range giving the smaller coefficient, assuming other factors to be the same.

After the variables are identified the researcher should carefully consider his assumptions and select an appropriate correlational technique. A review of the literature should not only contribute valuable information about the variables but may give indications as to the type of correlation coefficient that is applicable. Generally, the researcher should attempt to use the most sensitive coefficient for which the assumptions are tenable. When the correlation coefficients are computed they must be interpreted in the light of existing knowledge and the circumstances of the situation. The fact that a nonzero correlation coefficient exists does not necessarily mean a causal relationship between the variables. Causal relationships may exist, but they cannot be inferred on the basis of the correlation coefficient alone.

CONCLUDING REMARKS: A REVIEW
OF HYPOTHESIS TESTING

Part Two has been devoted to the testing of hypotheses by parametric, nonparametric, and correlational techniques. For the inexperienced researcher, the formulation of hypotheses is often a difficult task. In fact, because the naïve researcher often fails to state the hypotheses of his study precisely and clearly, the procedure becomes muddled and confused.

In the context of hypothesis testing, the hypothesis is a statement about a parameter or a characteristic of the population under study. A sample is drawn, and observations are taken on the members of the sample. The characteristics of the sample are statistics, and from these we make inferences about the parameters. The particular hypothesis to be tested dictates the statistics and procedures to be used in the statistical test. This calls for caution that the procedure chosen applies to the hypothesis.

The statistic is observed, and the underlying distribution of the statistic is presumably known. Then the probability of the statistic appearing under the null hypothesis is determined, and in the light of this probability the hypothesis is retained or rejected. Note that the probability applies to the statistic.

In the discussion of this text, the hypothesis has generally been stated as the null hypothesis. This is not essential however; hypotheses may be stated in alternate forms that hypothesize a direction of results. However, if the hypothesis is stated in alternate form, the researcher must be careful to reject or accept it in light of the results of the statistical test.

The statement of hypotheses, including hypotheses used with statistical tests, is not unique to a particular type of research, such as experimental or survey research. Analyses of variance, for example, can be computed on experimental data, survey data, and any research data which meet the necessary assumptions. A set of survey data might involve computing a two-way analysis of variance, if the hypothesis requires such a procedure. Some statistical analyses, such as factorial analyses of variance, are often associated more closely with experimental design. When factorial designs were discussed in Chapter 4, on experimental design, the implied analysis techniques would invariably be factorial analyses of variance. Data from a Latin square experimental design are also usually analyzed by an analysis of variance. Probably the reasons some statistical analyses are closely associated with experiments is that they were first used with this type of research, continue to be so used frequently, and were initially easier to structure because of the experimental control. Basically, however, the statistical procedures have broader application across types of research. The important thing in selecting statistical procedures is not the type of research but the hypotheses of the research project and the kind of procedures necessary to test the hypotheses and meet the purposes of the research.

In the specific procedures discussed in Part Two, the emphasis has been on inferential statistics. These three chapters are included to give you some concept of the procedures. But formulating and testing hypotheses alone do not comprise the whole of educational research.

The concepts discussed in Part One—research design, measurement, sampling, and so on—are equally important. Essentially, they set the stage for hypothesis testing procedures. The statistical procedures are supportive of the entire research effort; they are tools by which data are analyzed and which permit decisions to be made in a scientific manner. In any specific research study, the more general concepts of designing the study and the concepts underlying the specific procedures are worthy of consideration.

SUGGESTED STUDY EXERCISES

11.1. Review briefly the meaning of a correlation coefficient and describe how the correlation coefficient can be used as a descriptive statistic, and how it can be used in inferential statistics.

11.2. A Pearson product-moment coefficient is computed between two variables on a sample of size 40. The correlation coefficient is .413. Is this coefficient significantly different from zero at the .05 level? State the null hypothesis and the associated probability statement. What is your conclusion about the population correlation?

11.3. Give an example of two educational variables that are not likely to be linearly related. Sketch a possible scattergram for your example.

11.4. Two random samples are drawn from their respective populations. The Ss of the samples are then measured on variables A and $B,$ and the correlations between the two variables are computed. Both variables have interval scale measurement. A statistical test for the difference between the two correlation coefficients is computed and found to be significant at the .05 level. Give the null hypothesis and the associated probability statement. What is your conclusion? What type of error in hypothesis testing could be made here? Can you conclude anything about the .01 level of significance relative to this hypothesis?

11.5. Contrast the Pearson product-moment and Spearman rank coefficients in terms of required assumptions and type of data correlated. What are the scores that actually go into the computation of a Spearman rank coefficient?

11.6. Give an example of two educational variables whose correlation would be determined by using a Spearman rank coefficient. Using your example, state a hypothesis that you could test statistically. Assume random sampling.

11.7. The performances of a sample of 25 student orations are rated as pass and not pass. The same sample is also tested on an English mastery test which has measurement on an interval scale. The problem under study is whether or not there exists a relationship between oration performance and English mastery. Would you use a point biserial or biserial coefficient? Discuss your choice of coefficient. State the null hypothesis. Suppose that your statistical test is significant at the .05 level. What is your conclusion?

11.8. Select a correlation coefficient for correlating each of the following pairs of variables. Discuss your choice of coefficient.

 a. Color of eyes and mathematics achievement.

 b. Science achievement and history achievement as measured by an objective factual test.

 c. Attitude toward the library and rank on an essay writing task.

 d. "Pass or fail" on a speech test and performance on an IQ test.

11.9. A correlation coefficient of .62 is computed on a sample of 120 Ss. This correlation is between performance on an objective punctuation test and the scores on a reading-for-comprehension test. The sample consisted of four classes of students enrolled in sophomore English at a specific high school. What are some interpretations of this correlation coefficient? Suggest one or more hypotheses that might be involved here. What population might possibly be under study? Suggest some difficulty that might arise in deciding about the population because of the method of sampling.

11.10. A researcher is doing a prediction study and finds that the standard error of estimate is just slightly less than the standard deviation of the distribution of criterion scores. Has he selected a very effective predictor? Why or why not? In a situation like this what would be the (relative) magnitude of the correlation coefficient between predictor and criterion variable? Suppose that the correlation coefficient between a predictor variable and a criterion variable is .80. Approximately, what would be the relative sizes of the standard error of estimate and the standard deviation of the criterion distribution?

11.11. Select an article involving correlation from an educational research journal. Read the article carefully and consider the following questions:

 a. Does the author clearly identify the variables and the type of coefficient used?

 b. Are hypotheses identified and if so, what are they?

 c. What are the conclusions in terms of correlation?

11.12. Briefly review the chain of reasoning in hypothesis testing. Consider such points as the meanings of statistic and parameter, the probability, and the inference to the population.

PART THREE

THE RESEARCH
LITERATURE

chapter 12

Reading the
research literature

A review of the related research literature is an initial step in setting a. context for any research project. As was pointed out in Chapter 1, educational research is not (or at least should not be) carried on in an information vacuum. A background of knowledge on a specific topic or area of interest is available to the researcher in a body of literature comprised of reports, journal articles, and complete texts, if he knows how to locate and interpret it. Thus the researcher looking for research information is faced with two broad tasks: (1) he must find information relevant to his topic and (2) he must be able to read the research in a meaningful matter. That is, he must be able to understand and evaluate, in the context of his own study, the research he is reading.

There is no scarcity of reports of research studies related to education in regularly published books and periodicals. Technical reports and academic theses are also abundantly available. The task of finding information is a matter of searching through appropriate sources, and the library is the major source of research literature. Much research is available there on the printed page, and information retrieval systems have been installed in larger libraries such as those at universities. The first part of this chapter will discuss the various sources that are helpful in locating information on educational research topics, described as to the reference information they contain. Examples will be provided as appropriate. This should not be considered as an exhaustive list of research information sources, however, but as examples of the sources commonly used in educational research.

PERIODICAL LITERATURE

Professional journals and periodicals regularly publish a large volume of research information, although some journals are more oriented to publishing research studies than others. The periodical indexes available in libraries provide concise and efficient guides to published contents. Of course, not all content indexed is research information, but the researcher may be interested in more than research results, such as discussion of a theory. Periodical indexes of particular interest to the educational researcher are discussed below.

Education Index

The *Educational Index* is one of the most widely used periodical indexes. Published since 1929, it is a cumulative author-subject index to educational material in the English language.[1] The entries include literature from periodicals, proceedings, yearbooks, bulletins, monographs, and governmental materials of education and education-related topics. The entries are arranged in alphabetical order as a combined author–key word index. Under many primary key word headings (for example, Health Education) are alphabetically ordered subheadings such as Administration and Criticism. Under these subject headings are given references to the related literature which include title, author, and complete bibliographic information. Author entries list all titles of the author's published works which have appeared since the previous volume of *Education Index*.

Examples of entries from the *Education Index* are given in Figure 12.1. The information contained in the entry, including abbreviations, is identified in the legends at the side.

Current Index to Journals in Education (CIJE)

CIJE is one of the most comprehensive cumulative indexes for the periodical literature in education. It is also one of the most recently established (1969) and is constructed to be compatible with the Educational Resources Information Center (ERIC) information retrieval system. *CIJE* is a monthly guide to the periodical literature in which each entry is followed by a consecutively ordered accession number. An example describing all the information contained in *CIJE* entries is provided in the introduction of every volume. (CIJE entries are illustrated in Figure 12.3.)

Research in Education (RIE)

In addition to *CIJE*, ERIC also publishes *RIE*, a monthly guide to reports of recently completed research studies, descriptions of ongoing programs, and other documents not reported in the periodical literature. As in *CIJE*, the entries of *RIE* are followed by consecutively ordered accession numbers. A sample entry describing all the informa-

---

1. *Education Index*, "Prefatory Note," 45 (September 1973): i.

Author's name ——→ HUGHES, Earl F.
Role playing as a technique for developing a scientific attitude in elementary teacher trainees. bibliog J Res Sci Teach 8 no2: 113–22 '71 ←—————— Bibliography

HUISINGH, Donald. See Grimm, F. M. 3d jt. auth. ←—————— Joint authorship (Grimm is primary author)

HUMAN geography. See Anthropogeography
HUMAN information processing. See Cognition ←—————— Cross reference

Subject heading ——→ HUMAN relations
Human relations experiment in a student orientation program M. H. Witkin. J Col Stud Personnel 12:372 S '71
Integrity group seminars; University of Illinois; O. H. Mowrer. il Sch & Soc 99: 333 O '71
On finding soul. W. Strong. il Media & Methods 8:41–5 O '71 ←—————— Illustrations
See also

Cross reference ——→ Brotherhood of man
Intergroup education
Social adjustment and development
Subheading ——→ Teacher education
Effect of intensive human relations laboratory experiences upon student teacher perception and treatment of behavioral problems of elementary school children. R. Dobson and others. Educ Lead 29:159–64 N '71

Source: *Education Index*, 43 (December 1971): 131 (H. W. Wilson Co., Bronx, N.Y.).

FIGURE 12.1. Sample entries in *Education Index*.

TEACHER EDUCATION   140

UF   Teacher Preparation
     Teacher Training
     Teacher Training Education
     University Training Centers
NT   Inservice Teacher Education
     Preservice Education
     Student Teaching
     Teacher Educator Education
BT   Professional Education
RT   Affiliated Schools
     Clinical Professors
     Cooperating Teachers
     Education Majors
     Institutes (Training Programs)
     Laboratory Schools
     Laboratory Training
     Master Teachers
     Methods Courses
     Methods Teachers
     Microteaching
     Practicums
     Protocol Materials
     Schools Of Education
     Science Institutes
     Summer Institutes
     Teacher Background
     Teacher Certification
     Teacher Educators
     Teachers
     Teachers Colleges

Source: *Thesaurus of ERIC Descriptors*
(New York: CCM Information Corp.,
1972), p. 223.

FIGURE 12.2.   Sample descriptors from the *Thesaurus of ERIC Descriptors*

tion contained in *RIE* entries is provided in the introduction of every volume. (RIE entries are illustrated in Figure 12.3.)

Educational Resources Information Center (ERIC)

ERIC is a decentralized national information system administered by the U.S. Department of Health, Education, and Welfare. The ERIC mandate is to screen, organize, and provide access to educational reports and documents by a continual monitoring of the pertinent literature. There are 18 clearinghouses, each established for a single broad topic, for example, the Clearinghouse for Early Childhood Education at the University of Illinois. These specialized clearinghouses are located on major university campuses and in selected organizations throughout the country.

To illustrate the use of the ERIC system and its related indexes, *CIJE* and *RIE*, consider the following hypothetical research situation (expressed in broad terms) and the accompanying search for relevant studies: The science education professors of a college of education require information relevant to the evaluation of the elementary teacher education science curricula, and the relevance of such evaluation to the development of accountability models.

In order to gain entry to the ERIC system, the professors need to know the subject headings used in *CIJE* and *RIE*. These headings are listed in the *Thesaurus of ERIC Descriptors*,[2] a collection of more than 6,800 vocabulary terms related to topics in education. The *Thesaurus*, which is a separate publication, is the collection of major and minor descriptors used as subject headings in both *RIE* and *CIJE*. In the *Thesaurus*, the main descriptor may be followed by words "used for" (UF) the descriptor, descriptors which are narrower terms (NT) or broader terms (BT) than the main descriptor, and related terms (RT), which may provide access to other avenues of search.[3] Examples of descriptors are given in Figure 12.2. By using the *Thesaurus*, the professors determine that the descriptors to be used are as follows: Evaluation, Science Curriculum, Science Education, and Teacher Education. Using these terms and searching the annual cumulations or monthly issues of *CIJE* and *RIE*, the researchers can complete a bibliography of related literature.

Sample information relevant to this problem is presented in Figure 12.3. At the top of the figure are entries from the subject indexes found in *CIJE* and *RIE*. Note that these entries are found under Science Education and Evaluation, two of the descriptors. Following these entries one abstract is presented from the Main Entry section of *CIJE* and the Document Resumés section of *RIE*. Note that these abstracts are for the fourth entry under Science Education and the first entry under Evaluation. After reviewing an abstract the researcher can obtain a complete copy of the reference found in *RIE* by ordering either a hard copy (HC) or microfiche (MC) from:

ERIC Document Reproduction Service
The National Cash Register Company
Bethesda, Maryland 20014

2. *Thesaurus of ERIC Descriptors* (New York: CCM Information Corp., 1972).

3. Frederick Goodman has written an article, "The Role and Function of the Thesaurus in Education," which appears in the Thesaurus on pp. vii to xx. The researcher would do well to read this article for it not only describes the proper use of the Thesaurus but also provides enough general information to aid in the researching of topics listed in other indexes.

The researcher selects two descriptors, Science Education and Evaluation, and locates their entries in the subject indexes. (Science Education and Evaluation are two of four descriptors to be used.) From the entries he selects the fourth under Science Education and the first under Evaluation.

*CIJE**

Science Education
School Science Education for the 70's, *Science Teacher* v38 n8, pp46–51, Nov. 71 EJ 045 564
Florida's New Elementary Program in Science Education, *Science and Children* v9 n3, pp14–16, Nov 71   EJ 045 568
Application of Science Principles to Teaching, *Clearing House* v46 n3, pp143–6, Nov 71
                                                    EJ 045 656
An Evaluation of the Science Pre-Student Teaching Experience for Students Enrolled in the Elementary Education Curriculum at Indiana State University, *School Science and Mathematics* v71 n8, pp707–721, Nov 71   EJ 045 740

RIE†

Evaluation
Accountability: The State of the Knowledge.
                                                    ED 070 146
Achieving Academic and Social Objectives in Kindergarten through Behavioral Analysis. Research and Development Report, Vol. VI, No. 3.
                                                    ED 072 854
Administrator's Environmental Education Evaluation Manual.
                                                    ED 067 231
An Analysis of Content and Task Dimensions of Social Studies Items Designed to Measure Level of Concept Attainment.
                                                    ED 068 410
An Analysis of Content and Task Dimensions of Mathematics Items Designed to Measure Level of Concept Attainment.
                                                    ED 070 660

After arranging the EJ and ED numbers consecutively he can find abstracts of the reference in the Main Entry section of *CIJE.‡*

EJ 045 740   140   SE 504 259
An Evaluation of the Science Pre-Student Teaching Experience for Students Enrolled in the Elementary Education Curriculum at Indiana State University Uhlhorn, Kenneth W.; And

FIGURE 12.3.   Sample entries from *CIJE* and *RIE* and related abstracts for a hypothetical search using ERIC.

FIGURE 12.3.   (continued)

> Others, *School Science and Mathematics*, v71 n8,
> pp707–721, Nov 71
>> *Elementary Education, *Methods Courses,
>> *Preservice Education, *Program Evaluation,
>> *Science Education, College Science, Evalua-
>> tion, Teacher Education, [Indiana State
>> University]
>
> Preservice teachers' success in a science lesson
> presentation was not significantly influenced by
> the number of science courses taken previously,
> the science topic chosen, or grade level selected
> for the presentation. (CP)

and in the Document Resumés section of *RIE*. §

> **ED 070 146**   80   EA 004 652
> *Hanson, Gordon, Comp.*
> **Accountability: The State of the Knowledge.**
> Wisconsin State Dept. of Education, Madison.
> Spons Agency—Bureau of Elementary and
>> Secondary Education (DHEW/OE), Washing-
>> ton, D.C.
>
> Pub Date 72
> Note—12p.
> **EDRS Price MF-$0.65 HC-$3.29**
> Descriptors—*Bibliographies, *Educational Ac-
>> countability, *Evaluation
>
> Identifiers—*Assessment, Elementary Secondary
>> Education Act Title V, ESEA Title V
>
>> This publication comprises a 144-item bibliog-
>> raphy of articles, documents, and books on the
>> subject of accountability. The 40 cited ERIC
>> documents are listed separately. (JF)

Sources:
   * *CIJE*, Annual Cumulation, 4(January–December 1972):669 (Macmillan Information, New York).
   † *RIE*, Semiannual Index, January–June 1973, p. 140 (National Institute of Education, Washington, D.C.).
   ‡ *CIJE*, Annual Cumulation, 4(January–December, 1972):18 (Macmillan Information, New York).
   § *RIE*, Monthly Index, 8(April 1973):33 (National Institute of Education, Washington, D.C.).

Many major university libraries also maintain a microfiche collection of documents cited in *RIE*. The references given in *CIJE* can be
found in the journal collections of most university libraries.

School Research Information Service (SRIS)

SRIS is a computerized information service provided by Phi Delta
Kappa. There is a fee connected with the search. SRIS uses the ERIC
CIJE and *RIE* magnetic tape collections as its reference base. To gain
access to this system a written request is made to SRIS, accurately
outlining the research topics of interest. In order to facilitate the
search, the use of the *Thesaurus of ERIC Descriptors* is recommended.

The user will receive a computer printout of abstracts from the Document Resumés section of *RIE* and the Main Entry section of *CIJE*. The obvious benefit of this service is in the time saved by the researcher who has neither the resources nor the time for a library search.

Psychological Abstracts (PA) and Psychological Search and Retrieval Service (PASAR)

PA is a bimonthly publication that contains abstracts of articles appearing in over 500 journals. *PA* is, of course, oriented to psychology, but much of education is related to that discipline, and many of the periodicals from which articles are abstracted for *PA* are educational journals. Biannual issues of *PA* giving author and subject indexes are published for the six-month periods January–June and July–December.

As a hypothetical example of a search using *PA,* suppose a researcher wishes to examine information about the relationship between achievement and anxiety in programmed instruction. The general area is programmed instruction, with achievement and anxiety as subtopics.

In order to find related literature in *PA* it is necessary to use one of the three volumes of the *Cumulated Subject Index to Psychological Abstracts* (1927–60, 1961–65 and 1966–68). The researcher would look under the key word heading of Programmed Instruction and find numerous subheadings arranged alphabetically by descriptive terms used in the title of the abstract. Each subheading is followed by the last two digits of the year of publication in *PA,* a colon, and the *PA* record number. (This information is illustrated in Figure 12.4.) For example, the article on motivation and test anxiety indicated in the sixth entry under the heading was published in 1966 and its *PA* record number is 4585. Usually a researcher would list the record numbers, with the years of publication ordered consecutively, and obtain the abstracts of interest. The abstract for the article indicated above is shown in Figure 12.5.

If an investigator is interested in the published works of a particular author or authors, there are the combined *Author Index to Psychological Index* (1894–1935) and *Psychological Abstracts* (1927–58), with supplements for 1959–63, 1964–68 and 1969–71. References in these volumes list the primary author followed by up to four coauthors, a complete title of the work (which may be in parentheses if it is in a foreign language), a complete bibliographic reference, and the *PA* volume number and record number in which the abstract may be found.

Since 1967, *PA* has made available to the researcher a computerized search and retrieval service using the abstracts of journal articles, tech-

Programed Instruction
(See also Computer & Computation, Cybernetics; Data
Processing; Instructional Aids; Teaching Machine)
ability to learn, prediction, 68:1240
achievement, attitude, response mode, teacher role,
sixth grade students, 67:10989
statistics students, 67:3479
automated instruction & programed text, introductory
psychology course, 67:3478
knowledge of results schedule, 66:1935
motivation & test anxiety, 66:4585
negative social reinforcement, 67:6682
reinforcement, aptitude, & autonomy effects, 66:749
achievement gain in disadvantaged Negro pupils, programed
vs. flexible learning instruction, 68:17874
addition, mental retardates, 68:1051
advantages of programed instruction, 68:16159
algebra
vs. Algebra I textbook Instruction, eighth graders,
68:4718
vs. conventional classroom approach in teaching
algebra, attitudes & achievement, high school
students, 68:4594
inductive & deductive methods, 66:8048
text, secondary school students, 68:17871
analysis of learning machines & programing techniques,
audiovisual aids, 68:3004
anthropology, fifth graders, 68:19483
anxiety & intelligence quotient, mathematics, 67:12607

Source: *Cumulated Subject Index to Psychological Abstracts,
Second Supplement: 1966–68,* Vol. II (Boston: G. K. Hall & Co., 1971),
p. 149.

FIGURE 12.4   Sample entry from *Cumulated Subject Index to
Psychological Abstracts*

nical reports, monographs, dissertations, books, and other scientific
articles relevant to psychology published in *PA* from 1967 through
the present. The PASAR Request Form and Search Request Guidelines can be found at the end of most monthly editions of *PA*, or they
may be obtained by writing to the American Psychological Association,
1200 Seventeenth St., N.W. Washington, D.C. 20036. The researcher
is asked to formulate his request in terms that are specifically related
to the search and, in particular, to use index terms or key words that
are common to the *Cumulated Subject Index to Psychological Abstracts.* The search can be limited by request to specific populations
(human or other species), age groups, or publication dates. Search
level, either broad or narrow, can also be specified. The researcher will
receive by mail a computer printout of relevant citations and complete
abstracts. Such a search has a fee attached. A search of the literature
prior to 1967 must, of course, be done manually.

4585. Kight, Howard R., & Sassenrath, Julius M. (State U. New York, Buffalo) Relation of achievement motivation and test anxiety to performance in programed instruction. *Journal of Educational Psychology*, 1966, 57(1), 14–17.—A quasi-projective measure of achievement imagery, a test-anxiety questionnaire, and an achievement pretest were administered to 139 undergraduate pupils and related to their performance on programed instruction. Performance was analyzed using 3 criteria: (1) time needed to complete the material, (2) number of incorrect responses, and (3) a short-term retention test. The high-achievement-motivated students performed better on all 3 criteria and hence learned more efficiently with programed instruction than low-achievement-motivated students. High-test-anxiety students also worked faster and made fewer errors than low-anxiety students, but failed to exhibit higher retention scores.—*Journal abstract*.

Source: *Psychological Abstracts*, Vol. 40 (Washington, D.C.: American Psychological Association, 1966), p. 432.

FIGURE 12.5.   Sample entry from *Psychological Abstracts*

Review of Educational Research (RER)

The *RER*, issued five times per year, publishes critical, integrative reviews of research literature bearing on education. From its inception in 1931 through 1969, each issue contained solicited papers organized around a single educational topic or subdivision, such as Educational and Psychological Testing. Topics were reviewed in three-year cycles; more active topics were reviewed every cycle and less active ones on alternate cycles.

Beginning with Volume 40 (June 1970), *RER* has published unsolicited reviews of research on topics of the reviewer's. own choosing. The papers in both the pre-1970 and the post-1970 issues include excellent bibliographies which contain many references to the educational research literature.

Abstracts and reports in periodicals

There are numerous periodicals that are devoted almost exclusively to abstracts or reviews. Some of these are in the academic disciplines, and others are in professional education. Any university library will have on hand at least some of these periodicals and, in most cases, can provide access to all of them. Examples of such periodicals are:

Sociological Abstracts, published 1952–
Child Development Abstracts and Bibliography, published 1927–
Biological Abstracts, published 1926–
Educational Administration Abstracts, published 1922–

These periodicals include but are not limited to abstracts of articles dealing with research.

There is also a large number of periodicals in education-related disciplines and in professional education that contain research articles, some of them do so more than others. It would be impractical to present a comprehensive listing of such periodicals, but at the end of this chapter is a bibliography of selected periodicals that often contain articles dealing with educational research studies or research studies relevant to education.

THESES AND DISSERTATIONS

Theses and dissertations completed to meet the requirements for a graduate degree usually contain descriptions of completed research. The library at a specific university will invariably contain copies of theses completed at that university and will make them readily available. To obtain information about dissertations completed at other universities, the most widely used comprehensive source is *Dissertation Abstracts* and its related services.

Dissertation Abstracts or Dissertation Abstracts International (DAI)

Dissertation Abstracts was renamed *DAI* beginning with Volume XXX, No. 1 (1969). *DAI* is a reference tool which provides a monthly compilation of abstracts of doctoral dissertations submitted to University Microfilms by more than 300 universities and institutions in North America and Europe.

There are two broad topic areas under which the dissertations are abstracted, Humanities and Sciences. These are presented monthly in separate publications, each with a brief keyword title and author index.

When initiating a search of *DAI,* the researcher can explore the *DAI: Retrospective Index,* which contains bibliographic references in nine subject volumes for *DAI* Volumes I–XXIX. The nine subject volumes are as follows:

Volume I   Mathematics and Physics
Volume II   Chemistry
Volume III   Earth/Life Sciences

Volume IV	Psychology/Sociology/Political Science
Volume V	Social Sciences
Volume VI	Engineering
Volume VII	Education
Volume VIII	Communication/Information/Business Literature/ Fine Arts
Volume IX	Author Index

The *DAI Retrospective Index* would be explored pertaining to a broad area or subject of interest, for example, Education, Volume VII. The table of contents of the volume enables the researcher to narrow the scope of search to specific subheadings, for example, Health, Vol. VII, part 2, page 1391). Under the subheading of Health Education, the principal words in the title are used as key words, arranged in alphabetical order in columns. If the area of research involves evaluation of health attitudes, the key words to search for are Evaluation, Health, and Attitudes.

As an example of the search under the keyword Attitudes, the following dissertation reference would appear:

> Attitudes
> The Evaluation of Attitudes toward Selected Areas of
> School Health Education—Moore, Oscar A.
> BOSU 18/03/920
>
>   *24782*

The dissertation reference under Attitudes contains the complete dissertation title followed by a dash before the author's last name, first name, and middle initial. The abbreviation following the author's name represents the cooperating university or college at which the dissertation was completed (in this case, BOSU for Boston University). This is followed by a reference to the volume, issue, and page number in which the dissertation abstract is found. The number in the far right column represents the publication or order number by which a xerographic or microfiche copy of the complete dissertation can be requested from University Microfilms in Ann Arbor, Michigan.

For those dissertations abstracted in *DAI* from Volume XXX, No. 1 to the present, a similar search of the Keyword Title Index of each volume is required. An example of an abstract from *DAI* with the information identified in the margins appears in Figure 12.6.

Direct Access to Reference Information: A Xerox Service (DATRIX)

DATRIX is a development of University Microfilms, where *Dissertation Abstracts* have been compiled since 1928. DATRIX is a computerized retrieval system for *Dissertation Abstracts,* which number over 126,000 documents.

As with other retrieval systems, the researcher must provide DATRIX with key words derived either from his selected subject and other descriptive information or from an updated Key Word List provided by DATRIX which also includes frequency counts of these words as they appear in the dissertation titles. Each separate key word provided increases the number of references cited, because a search of dissertation titles is made for each word separately. However, each key word added to form a compound request restricts the number of dissertations cited, because the computer will cite only those dissertations whose titles include all the key words of the compound request. This enables the researcher to explore his subject in as broad or narrow terms as he desires.

When the computer search is completed, DATRIX will mail a bibliography of references to the researcher. Each reference will include the complete title of the dissertation, author's name, the university at which it was completed, date of publication, and the page and volume of *Dissertation Abstracts* in which the dissertation is listed. Also, price information is shown so that a microfiche or xerographic copy of the complete dissertation desired can be ordered from University Microfilms.

The *DAI* is not the only source of information on theses and dissertations. *American Doctoral Dissertations* lists all doctoral dissertations accepted by United States and Canadian universities. *Research Studies in Education,* a publication of Phi Delta Kappa, also provides references to doctoral dissertations in education.

SELECTED BOOKS

There is a host of books that deal with research, either educational research or education-related research. Books can be located through various bibliographies, reviews, book indexes, and so on. It would, of course, be impossible to provide a comprehensive listing of books that partially or entirely deal with educational research. However, three publications are briefly described below because they are comprehensive and can be especially useful to the educational researcher as he searches the research literature.

The Encyclopedia of Educational Research (EER)

The publication of the EER is a project of the American Educational Research Association. Four editions of the *EER* have been published, the most recent in 1969. The original edition appeared in 1941, with

Disser-   →A SIMULATED HANDICAPPING EXPERIENCE
tation   AS IT EFFECTS ATTITUDE, AWARENESS AND
title ——   RESPONSES TO COUNSELING PROBLEMS

Author——→Nancy Anna Mary INGWELL, Ph.D.
Institution→University of Missouri—Columbia, 1972

Supervisor→Supervisor: Richard W. Thoreson

Abstract →   The investigation studied the effects of a simulated
handicapping experience on (1) attitudes toward the
handicapped; (2) awareness of problems of the handicapped; and (3) counseling responses to problems presented by handicapped college students. Thirty-nine
subjects were randomly assigned to two experimental
groups and one control group. Experimental Ss wore a
bent knee cast on one leg and used crutches, or wore
bent knee casts on both legs and used a wheel chair for a
24 hour period.

It was hypothesized that a simulated handicapping
experience would produce more adequate responses to
problems presented by handicapped students. It was also
hypothesized that the handicapping experience would
produce more awareness of the problems of the handicapped as measured by the Handicap Problems Inventory, and that experimental subjects would adopt
more favorable attitudes toward the handicapped, as
measured by the Semantic Differential and the Attitude
Toward Disabled Persons Scale.

The counseling problems were obtained using the
critical incident technique and were rated for typicality
by handicapped college students. Subjects' responses to
the handicapped problems were judged by three re-
habilitation counselors and five of their clients.

The results of the study did not support the research
hypotheses. However, a posteriori analysis of the data
indicated that the experimental treatment tended to
crystalize pre-existing notions about the handicapped.
Order No. 73–21, 440, 172 *pages.*

Accession number for copy of
complete dissertation ordered
from University Microfilms

Source: *Dissertation Abstracts International,* 34(September 1973): 1081–A.

FIGURE 12.6.   Example of an abstract from *Dissertation Abstracts
International.*

subsequent editions at approximately ten-year intervals. The content of the *EER* represents a compendium of research covering five major issues in education.

The *EER* has not simply cataloged the research that has been done, but each article presented provides critical evaluation, synthesis, and interpretation of much of the literature in educational research, as well as a relatively extensive bibliography. Each edition has over 150 articles authored by noted educators familiar with the literature and research in their chosen topics. The most recent edition of the EER (the fourth) was edited by R. L. Ebel and published by the Macmillan Company, New York.

Handbook of Research on Teaching

There are two *Handbooks of Research on Teaching,* published by Rand McNally and Company, Chicago. The preparation of the *Handbooks* has been a project of the American Educational Research Association. The original one was edited by N. L. Gage and published in 1963; the second, edited by R. M. W. Travers, was published in 1973. The second *Handbook* is original, not a second edition of the first.

The *Handbooks* contain comprehensive presentations of research on teaching, including higher education and the teaching of subject matter. A variety of topics are given in-depth coverage in both volumes. These are large, comprehensive volumes; the first contains 23 chapters and the second 42 chapters. Not only is the content valuable to educational researchers, but each chapter has an extensive bibliography of references (in some cases over 200 references). The bibliographies themselves represent extensive searches of the research literature and can be very helpful to the educational researcher.

Review of Research in Education

This publication of the American Educational Research Association (AERA) is published in cooperation with F. E. Peacock Publishers, Inc., Itasca, Ill. The purpose of the *Review of Research in Education* is to survey disciplined inquiry in education through critical and synthesizing essays.[4] Each of the essays, written by an author selected for his expertise in that area, represents an attempt to appraise, evaluate, and criticize the more recent important empirical studies in the area.

The areas of research methodology and development will receive special attention in the initial volumes of the *Review* (the first volume

4. F. N. Kerlinger (ed.), *Review of Research in Education, 1* (1973); F. N. Kerlinger and John B. Carroll (eds.), *Review of Research in Education, 2* (1974) (Itasca, Ill.: F. E. Peacock Publishers), v.

was published in 1973). Varied topics from the fields of education will be covered, with the more important areas and topics reviewed more often than others. To a large extent the *Review* replaces the pre-1970 editions of the *Review of Educational Research,* which was described earlier in the chapter. Indeed, *Review of Research in Education* was initiated by AERA to fill the void left by the *Review of Educational Research* when it adopted its new editorial policy of publishing unsolicited manuscripts on a variety of topics.

The *Review* is intended to be a source of information that highlights the strengths and weaknesses in educational research. It also provides direction for future research in the areas discussed. While it is intended only secondarily to serve as a bibliographic reference source, it does contain a wealth of information and detailed reference lists with each article, and it can be very useful to the educational researcher.

MEANINGFUL READING AND CRITICAL ANALYSIS

Locating reports of research studies is of little use unless the reader understands the content of the report. The communication of the information in a written report requires a reader as well as a writer. Meaningful and efficient reading of research reports is to a large extent a learned skill which can be somewhat elusive. It is not too effective to tell you to "read critically" without giving any further direction. Suggested guidelines that can be used in doing critical reading of a research report are stated below in question form, as points to look for. For the purpose of this discussion, research report is very broadly defined to mean a written account of a research study. This could be a thesis, article, or a similar type of report.

Not all research reports are well written, nor does the fact that the research has been published necessarily mean that the research was well done or is of substantive significance. Therefore, the reader of research must read with a critical eye and take an evaluative stance. A sincere effort should be made to understand the problem, procedures, results, and conclusions that the writer is attempting to communicate.

When anticipating an analysis of a report you are reading, it is well to prepare an abstract or outline of it as you read. This helps you acquire the understanding of the content that is necessary for the critical analysis. The abstract should list the main points of the article and give a general overview of the content. Some specifics should be included, such as a statement of the problem or the hypotheses. A brief outline for an abstract might be as follows:

1. Statement of the problem.
2. General methods and procedures.
3. Results.
4. Conclusion.

The amount of information under each of these subheadings should be brief and to the point. For an article of average (six to ten pages) length, three to five sentences under each subheading should suffice.

The evaluation of the content of a research report may be considered from two points of view: (1) the value of the research in the educational context and (2) the methodology of the research per se, that is, whether the research was carefully planned and executed. Both points are important. The most perfectly planned piece of research has little value if it has no place in the educational context. On the other hand, a brilliant research idea pursued haphazardly is essentially worthless.

The worth of a problem and the complexity of the methodology are independent factors. Trivial problems may be camouflaged in complex designs, whereas problems with far-reaching implications may be pursued with relatively simple procedures. The research reader should not infer that because a report involves complex procedures the problem is necessarily of comparable importance.

The critical reading of a research report may be approached by posing specific questions to which satisfactory answers will provide a clear analysis. Most of the questions in the following discussion are directed to methodology, while some are related to the value of the research. The questions are organized according to the usual parts of a research report, as set forth in Chapter 1 and developed in Chapter 3. These are: (1) statement of the problem, (2) data collection, (3) data analysis, and (4) drawing conclusions.

Statement of the problem

The statement of the problem is the first item to look for in a research report. An unambiguous statement demonstrates that the researcher had a clear concept of the problem in mind and gives the reader his first clues of what to look for in the report. The questions commonly associated with the statement of the problem are:

1. Is the problem clearly and concisely stated?
2. Is the problem delimited so that it can be researched? (The problems of educational research must be spelled out and delimited. For example, "the teaching of arithmetic" is not a satisfactory way to propose a problem because it is far too broad.)

3. Are the hypotheses and objectives stated in the context of the research problem?
4. Does the research have a setting in the overall educational context or at least in its own research area? Is there evidence that the researcher is aware of the research in the area? Is there a conceptual framework for pursuing the research?
5. Are the terms well defined? Is there confusion in the definition of terms? Do they have multiple or arbitrary meanings? (An example would be the use of terms such as "nonconforming student.") Are the independent and dependent variables clearly identified?
6. Is there a basic rational on which the study rests? If the rationale is implied through assumptions, are the assumptions tenable and in keeping with existing knowledge?

Research procedures and analysis

A discussion of the procedures used in conducting the research usually follows the statement of the problem. The amount of procedural detail given depends upon the type of research report. A journal article often does not spell out a great deal of detail, whereas a graduate thesis or technical report, may have one or more chapters devoted to procedures. In any case, the writer must convey to his readers that he understands the details of his procedures.

The list of questions dealing with the actual research procedures concerns such matters as sampling and testing. Obviously, if no sample was drawn or no tests were given, these questions need not be considered. Some questions are, of course, unique to the type of study. The questions concerning general procedures and methodology are:

1. Are the procedures appropriate for meeting the objectives and testing the hypothesis? Were the assumptions met for the statistical tests used? If an experiment was involved, was adequate time allowed for the appearance of an experimental effect? In the case of a historical study, were primary or secondary sources used?
2. What variables were controlled in the design, and were there any uncontrolled variables? If there were uncontrolled variables, were they relevant to the study, and how were they likely to have affected the results? (A researcher may be under the impression that it is sufficient to acknowledge the existence of the uncontrolled variables, but this does not account for the effects they may have on the study. The researcher should systematically account for their possible influence. Since there is no way to measure the effects of uncontrolled

variables empirically, a knowledge and background of the variables is invaluable.)

3. Are the variables of the study categorized and quantified adequately? Were tests assumed to be valid and reliable without being checked? Are reliability coefficients reported? If standardized tests were used, is there reference to normative data? If measuring instruments were constructed, were they tried out on a pilot group? Are there adequate descriptions of the measuring instruments? Is there a description of the critical evaluation of historical materials, and, if so, were the evaluation procedures adequate?

4. Were the data accurately and objectively collected and recorded? Did the data collection proceed according to plan? Were checks made to guard against possible errors in collecting and tabulating the data? Was a reasonable time schedule followed for the data collection?

5. Is there an adequate description of the population? (This may be included with the statement of the problem.) Was the sample a random sample? Was there any possibility of the introduction of a sampling bias? Was there any mortality in the sample and if so, is there a discussion of the possible relevancy of the mortality? If replacement procedures were used, were such procedures adequate?

6. If the study deals with an experiment, is the design discussed? Does the design seem applicable and carefully administered? Is the design oversimplified or unnecessarily complicated in the context of the problem? Is it clear how the independent variables were manipulated?

7. Are the analysis procedures clearly and completely identified? If several different analyses were done, is it clear how they are related and what contribution is made by each? Were the analysis procedures appropriate for the research problem and the data? Were there violations of necessary assumptions or tenuous assumptions included without being checked?

Reporting results

After analysis of the data, the results of a research study should be clearly identified in the research report and should not be mixed with the results of other studies discussed in the background of the problem. The questions dealing with results are:

1. Are the results a logical product of the analysis? (This may seem like a trivial question, but occasionally results appear which seem

to have no basis in the procedures and analysis. If this occurs, the research writer either did not adequately discuss the procedures or he has a misconception of what the procedures were supposed to accomplish.)

2. Are the results presented in clear and orderly fashion? If tables were used in reporting results, are the tables well organized and understandable? Are the results complete? Is important information implied that was not actually reported? Was there considerable information in the data which has no corresponding results?

3. If several related variables were investigated, are the results consistent? Do the results seem reasonable in the light of what is known about the data? Are the results consistent within themselves? (An example would be if the range or distribution of scores were reported and the value of the mean of the distribution were found to exceed the greatest score used in computing the range.)

4. Are the results, which are facts, mixed with conjecture? (Results and conjecture should be clearly separated, and conjecture should not appear in this part. If it does, confusion is introduced and the impression develops that the researcher is attempting to pass off conjecture as fact.)

Drawing conclusions

The conclusions section of a research report is usually the climax. The perceptual ability, knowledge, and insight of the researcher come to the fore at this point. Preceding sections of the report are more technical in nature. Questions associated with the conclusions of a research report are:

1. Are the conclusions based upon the results? Are there inconsistencies between the results and conclusions? Are the conjectures based upon the results and the existing knowledge of the problem being researched?

2. Is the discussion of the results related to findings from previous research? Are the conclusions consistent with previous knowledge about the problem? Does the discussion follow the outcomes of the research, or is there considerable wandering from the main point? Are the conclusions incorporated into a larger educational frame of reference?

3. Are alternate hypotheses discussed?

4. Is there a discussion of limitations and weaknesses of the study? Is the researcher aware of additional questions, which are implied by almost all research studies?

5. Is there confusion with the meaning of nonsignificant statistical tests? Are these interpreted to be meaningless or unimportant findings? (Nonsignificant statistical tests have meaning and the fact that a statistical test is significant does not necessarily have great substantive importance.)
6. Does the research generalize to other populations? If so, is there a rationale for making a valid generalization?

The conclusions section should indicate the significance of the research in the educational context. Many of the questions asked above relate to this matter, as well as to the methodology. The basic question on the significance of the research in the educational context considers how the results might be used. (An answer to this question may have been implied in the statement of the problem.) The results need not necessarily be ends in themselves; they could be used for theory building, for example. In considering how he might use the research, the reader should ask himself questions such as: Do I find these results useful? What are other possible approaches to the problem? What would be likely to produce more useful results?

The critical perspective

In order to understand the content of a research report you must be able to read with a critical perspective. This section has posed many questions which can be used in the critical analysis of a research report. As such, they can be considered as a checklist. The questions should not, however, be viewed as an exhaustive list; other questions could be raised in reference to specific research reports. Certainly for any specific report, not all of the questions are appropriate. For example, those questions dealing with the methodology of survey research are not appropriate for analyzing the report of an experiment.

The questions above deal with specific items as the reader progresses through a research report as it is usually organized. It is necessary to deal with specifics in any report, but you should not lose sight of the general overview and meaning of the research. It is a good idea to first skim a report for the general overview, without being too concerned with the specifics. Then, with the general problem in mind, you can reread the report, concentrating on the specifics.

While the checklist can give you some help in evaluating a report, you must also have some familiarity with research procedures. Your analysis of the report will only be valid if you are knowledgeable about the research methods used and the area of research. This is one value of Part Two of this text, which discusses techniques for hypothesis testing. Proficiency in reading research reports improves with experience, and generally the more knowledgeable you are about research methods, the more meaningful and enjoyable will be the task of analyzing research reports.

CONCLUDING REMARKS

The discussion of this chapter has been devoted to two major areas: (1) finding research reports in the research literature and (2) critically analyzing such reports. With the massive volume of reported educational research and education-related research that is available, it is important to know how to launch an organized search. Haphazard searching is not only prohibitively time-consuming, it has a high risk of missing important and relevant reports. Critical analysis will hopefully result in understanding of the reported research.

There are a large number of sources that provide information about research results and research methods. The use of indexes such as the *Education Index* is very helpful, especially in searching the periodicals. The ERIC system can also be used effectively; most such search systems provide quite comprehensive cross-referencing so that the omission of relevant studies is kept to a minimum. Numerous publications in related areas such as psychology are helpful in finding research reports relevant to education. The important thing in searching the research literature is that the reader identify his topic or topics clearly and pursue an organized search.

It does little good to find research reports if they cannot be read with understanding. The procedure for analyzing reports suggested in this chapter consists of preparing an abstract or outline of the report and then posing relevant questions as to the methods used in conducting the research and the substantive importance of the research results. As the reader works through this process he can take notes which, along with the abstract, should provide an effective analysis of the report.

SUGGESTED STUDY EXERCISES

12.1. Select a topic of your own interest and compile a list of possible references for this topic, using the *Education Index* as a source. If this is being done in connection with a real project, follow up on the references.

12.2. Suppose that a researcher is interested in finding information about the content of mathematics programs for students aged 8–10 in Western European countries and the United States. If the researcher were using the ERIC system, what are possible subject headings that might be used? Where would these subject headings be found, and for what publications would they be used?

12.3. Select one or more research articles about an educational topic and write an abstract for each article. Follow the four parts of the outline as suggested in this chapter. Limit yourself to not more than five sentences under each of the four parts of the outline.

12.4. Present a critical review of one or more research articles. You may use the articles suggested in Exercise 12.3. The questions presented in this chapter may serve as a guide for your review, but for your specific articles, all of the questions may not be applicable. If the members of a class or group review a common article, compare and discuss the individual reviews. The sharing of views and ideas from the reviews can be a worthwhile learning experience.

SELECTED PERIODICALS CONTAINING RESEARCH INFORMATION ON EDUCATIONAL TOPICS

The following list of periodicals includes entries that frequently publish reports of research on educational topics or topics related to education. Some journals, such as the *American Educational Research Journal,* contain articles about research methodology as well as reports of results of research studies. The list is by no means intended to be exhaustive, but it identifies some of the more research-oriented periodicals in the field.

American Educational Research Journal
    Washington, D.C.: American Educational Research Association, NEA
British Journal of Educational Psychology
    London, England: British-Psychological Society
British Journal of Educational Studies
    London, England: Faber & Faber, Ltd
California Journal of Educational Research
    Burlingame, Calif.: California Teachers Association
Canadian Education and Research Digest
    Toronto, Ontario: Canadian Education Association
Child Development
    Purdue University, Lafayette, Ind.: The Society for Research in Child Development, Inc.
Educational and Psychological Measurement
    Durham, N.C. Copyright by Frederic Kuder
Educational Technology
    Englewood Cliffs, N.J.: Educational Technology Publications
Florida Journal of Educational Research
    Tallahassee, Fla.: Florida Educational Association
Journal of Educational Measurement
    East Lansing, Mich., National Council on Measurement in Education, Inc.

Journal of Educational Psychology
    Washington, D.C.: American Psychological Association
Journal of Educational Research
    Madison, Wis.: Dembar Publications, Inc.
Journal of Educational Sociology
    New York University, New York: The Payne Educational Sociology
    Foundation
Journal of Experimental Education
    Madison, Wis.: Dembar Publications, Inc.
Journal of Experimental Psychology
    Washington, D.C.: American Psychological Association, Inc.
Journal of Research in Science Teaching
    National Association for Research in Science Teaching and Association
    for the Education of Teachers in Science. New York: John Wiley &
    Sons, Inc.
Measurement and Evaluation in Guidance
    Washington, D.C.: The Association for Measurement and Evaluation in
    Guidance, a division of the American Personnel and Guidance Associa-
    tion
NEA Research Bulletin
    Washington, D.C.: National Education Association
Psychological Bulletin
    Washington, D.C.: American Psychological Association
Psychological Reports
    Missoula, Mont.: Southern Universities Press
Psychological Review
    Washington, D.C.: American Psychological Association
Psychometrika
    Richmond, Va.: The Psychometrika Society
Research in the Teaching of English
    Urbana, Ill.: National Council of Teachers of English
School Science and Mathematics
    Kalamazoo, Mich.: Central Association of Science and Mathematics
    Teachers, Inc.
The Research Quarterly
    Washington, D.C.: American Association for Health, Physical Educa-
    tion, and Recreation, NEA
What Research Says to the Teacher (a series of monographs)
    Washington, D.C.: Department of Classroom Teachers and American
    Educational Research Association, NEA

chapter 13

Writing about research: Proposals and reports

The educational researcher eventually arrives at the point where he wishes to communicate the results of his research. Informal or formal discussion is one method by which research results can be communicated, but such discussions usually have very limited audiences. Even presentations at national meetings which may accommodate hundreds of listeners often are supplemented by written reports. A written report of some type is the most widespread use of communicating educational research results. It may take the form of a thesis, journal article, monograph, or a technical report to a funding agency, to mention just a few.

Not all writing about educational research deals with results of completed research. The research proposal has become quite common in education. Such a proposal commonly deals with research that is intended to be done. In practically all cases, it "makes the case" for doing the research. Research proposals, like research reports, have a variety of formats and vary as to length.

The significance of a research study, both scholastically and practically, is usually judged on the content of the written report of the study. In much the same way, the merits of intended research are judged to a large extent by the adequacy of the research proposal. Precise, complete, and clear reporting and description are of utmost importance in both forms. Writing about research requires organization and attention to detail, along with ordinary writing skills.

Preparation for writing the research report or proposal can be a great help in reducing the confusion and inefficiency that can otherwise mark the writing activity. A common error is not having all of the necessary information and references readily available. Another difficulty is a lack of time. If reasonably sized blocks of time are available, efficiency is increased, since whenever the writer stops and starts, and time and events intervene, some repetition is necessary in order to get reacclimated to the task. Continuity is also enhanced by persistence in the writing task.

Once the mechanics of a research project are completed, the writing of the report should not be delayed. Actually, the research project is not completed until the report is finished. Often a good deal of persistence is required to bring the research to the writing stage, which serves both as the concluding activity and the climax of the project. At this point persistence should be increased rather than diminished. If there is a marked delay with the writing task, the research has a tendency to become cold and unfamiliar, and the report may never be written. When the research report is completed at a later date, reactivating the project involves a great deal of additional effort and relearning. Many research problems also lose their pertinence with the passing of time. Generally, delay results in reduced enthusiasm on the part of the researcher.

PREPARING A RESEARCH PROPOSAL

Preparing a research proposal, as we have noted, involves writing about a proposed rather than a completed research project. In proposal writing we discuss *what* research is contemplated, *why* it is being contemplated, and *how* we intend doing it. Proposal writing has developed into somewhat of a necessary art within recent years. The research proposal for the doctoral dissertation, for example, has been around for a long time. However, within the last decade requirements of the Elementary and Secondary Education Act of 1965, the Office of Research Grants of the National Institute of Education, and numerous fund-grating foundations in educational research and development have motivated extensive proposal writing. Proposal writing is required of public school personnel as well as university personnel.

The comments of this section are general suggestions for proposal preparation. As such, they are quite widely applicable to proposals for educational research. Comments on matters such as where to apply and budgetary procedures are usually not applicable to the dissertation research proposal, however.

The researcher attempting to obtain funding outside of his own institution must make a decision about where to apply. Most funding agencies make available descriptive brochures or some type of statement about the kinds of research they are interested in supporting. Once a decision has been made concerning the foundation or agency from which funding for the project will be sought, the researcher should obtain the specific guidelines for preparing the proposal from that agency. These guidelines provide details as to format, number of copies, deadlines, sections required, necessary subheadings, and the like. They must be followed precisely, and any deviation from them must be thoroughly explained. The funding of proposals is generally competitive, and there are usually more proposals that meet the standards of format than there are funds available. Any proposals not meeting the standards will be automatically rejected.

Decisions on funding proposals are usually made on the basis of reviews by informed readers, often external to the funding agency. The proposal reader will decide whether or not to recommend funding. If funding is recommended, there may be other factors, such as budgetary considerations, that can delay or prevent approval. Because the proposal will be rejected if the reader does not recommend funding, it is extremely important to engage his interest and present an adequate case.

Generally, the proposal will stand or fall on its contents. The writer cannot assume that the reader will read between the lines. Readers are generally informed individuals, but research projects are specific, and the writer should not assume that the reader will possess specific information about his particular research topic. The proposal should be written so that the uninformed reader can understand the ideas and procedures.

MAJOR SECTIONS OF THE RESEARCH PROPOSAL

The names of headings and subheadings within the research proposal may differ somewhat for different agencies. For example, some may require a section entitled Procedures, others a Description of Activities, and still others a Narrative section in which the writer can supply his own subheadings. However, there is a general format for the development of a research proposal. This format develops in a logical sequence from the statement of the problem within an adequate context and continues with specifications of methods and procedures. Concluding parts of a proposal contain the budget, resumés of the researchers, and possibly an evaluation or project management section. Usually there is a section somewhere in the proposal that requires discussion of the significance of the proposed research project. It is in this section that the writer makes his case for the value of the project. In other sections, primary emphasis is directed toward the case that the writer can do the project adequately, and the emphasis is on research methods.

Research problem and background

The statement of the research problem in a proposal should be clearly identified, and the specific problem must be delimited and defined within the educational context and the particular area under study. Regardless of the particular format required, somewhere early in the proposal there should be a statement indicating what the researcher intends to cover. No single project can encompass the entire educational scene nor can any researcher attempt to accomplish everything within a single topic. Proposal writers are more likely to be criticized for stating a problem that is too broad than for not making their topic inclusive enough.

Consider the example of a writer who indicates his problem is the improvement of teacher education. This is far too broad a statement. Although proposal readers may be sympathetic to the idea that teacher education can or should be improved, this type of statement will be viewed unfavorably. There is also an implied conclusion that whatever it is the researcher is intending to do will result in the improvement of teacher education. If this is already conclusive, the suggestion is no longer at the research stage but ready for implementation.

Since the above example is so broad, almost any aspect of teacher education could be included. An example of a delimited research problem in teacher education might be to assess and compare the academic achievement and personality characteristics of secondary education students being trained with three different programs. This statement would be followed by operational definitions of terms such as "compare," "academic achievement," "personality characteristics," and the different programs. This type of study is not an experiment but *ex post facto* in nature. No foredrawn conclusions are implied in the statement of the problem, which would be followed by specific objectives. The significance of the study is implied, although this would be discussed in greater detail later in the proposal. The problem implies a search for facts, and it could certainly be indicated that such facts are necessary and helpful in making decisions about program procedures that might improve secondary teacher education.

After the statement of the problem it is important that the proposal writer provide a background for the research, usually through a review of the literature relating to his area of study. This section should demonstrate that the writer has a comprehensive knowledge of the research area, not only adequate historical knowledge but also familiarity with present activity and developments concerning the problem.

The information available in the literature concerning the specific problem may be quite extensive, but the review of literature in the proposal will be somewhat limited. A suggested length for the entire proposal is usually provided in the guidelines, and the writer must decide as to space allotments for the various sections. Therefore, one of the marks of a knowledgable writer is the ability to select the pertinent facts and tie them together to provide an understandable and accurate background. Continuity between the ideas from the literature and the research problem must be demonstrated. The position of the research problem in the content of the educational area should be established, and there should be an indication as to how the proposed research will contribute to the knowledge of the area. The writer should avoid statements inferring that information on this problem is very limited or that a review of the literature has revealed no information about the problem. The reader will be very suspicious of such statements (and rightly so) and will likely interpret them as a lack of knowledge on the part of the writer rather than as a gap in the literature.

Many research proposals, especially those involving experiments or *ex post facto* studies, include statements of hypotheses. Other types of studies, such as status surveys, may include questions that will presumably be answered through the proposed research. Hypotheses and questions should be specific and to the point. In terms of hypotheses, any acceptable form which enhances the understanding may be used; if statistical tests for differences are anticipated, the null hypothesis may seem most appropriate, for example. If a theoretical construct has been developed, alternate hypotheses may be appropriate. Of course, hypotheses that cannot be tested by the results of the research should be omitted. Also, the writer should not base his hypotheses on only one possible outcome of the results but should be able to make decisions about his hypotheses or questions with any possible outcome.

Some of the possible errors that can be made in the research proposal section dealing with the problem and its background have been identified above. These are errors such as not delimiting the problem or presenting an inadequate review of related literature. Failure to identify the research problem distinctly is quite common. The writer must remember that although he may have the problem clearly in mind, the reader must conceptualize it from his written account.

Gerald Smith[1] identifies two other errors—a trivial problem and a problem peripheral to education. The former is exactly what the name implies, a research problem of little significance to education. A peripheral problem is not central to education, such as a problem dealing with physical activity and its relationship to heart disease. This would undoubtedly be viewed as a significant problem which would touch upon physical education problems, but the central focus would be more applicable in a heart or medical association than an educational agency.

In a tabulation of common deficiencies in research proposals rejected for funding by the National Institute of Health, Ernest Allen

---

1. G. R. Smith, "A Critique of Proposals Submitted to the Cooperative Research Program," in J. A. Culbertson and S. P. Hencley (eds.), *Educational Research: New Perspectives* (Danville, Ill.: Interstate Printers and Publishers, 1963). Although this reference is somewhat dated and the Cooperative Research Program of USOE as such no longer exists, the points made in the critique are still largely relevant.

found that in 58 percent of those rejected deficiencies were connected with the research problem. The most common difficulty was having a problem of insufficient importance or one that was not likely to produce either new or useful information.[2] So it is important that the writer make a case for the merits of his research problem and that he give a favorable impression of it. Otherwise the remainder of the proposal may be looked upon with disfavor or not even considered.

Research methodology and procedures

This section of the research proposal describes in detail what is to be done and how. Although some proposal guidelines may not require subheadings, in this section headings such as Design, Sample, Data Analysis, and any others that might apply to the specific research problem will not only aid the writer in identifying and describing the various activities, but they should help the proposal reader understand the continuity of the activities. One of the most common errors of this section is that the methods and procedures are lacking in detail. The explanation should be complete enough so that the reader has no question about what is anticipated and how it will be accomplished.

The early part of the methodology and procedures section usually contains a discussion of the research design which sets the stage for the specific procedures. The design should reflect the objectives and the specific hypotheses or questions of the research proposal. It should be appropriate for the complexity of the research problem; a common error is to present a simple design for a complex problem, or vice versa. Another common error is to provide a design that does not test all of the hypotheses. Hypotheses dealing with interactions between independent variables are particularly likely to be ignored in the design.

The design should be identified as specifically as possible in acceptable design terminology. In the case of an experiment, it should be apparent how the independent variables will fit into the design; for example, a specific way of indicating a design is a 2×3 factorial design, with the type of materials and ability level as independent variables. The term "factorial" conveys a great deal of meaning in this context. Additional information should be specified, such as the levels of the independent variables and the number of replications in the cells.

The writer should also consider possible weaknesses in the design and describe what will be done to compensate for or eliminate them. A common difficulty is the influence of extraneous variables; their possible effects should be discussed, and how they will be controlled or

2. E. M. Allen, "Why Are Research Grant Applications Disapproved?" *Science*, 132 (1960): pp. 1532–34.

eliminated should be indicated. A similar type of difficulty is the tendency to ignore or dismiss lightly extraneous and confounded variables. Occasionally writers are under the misconception that it is sufficient to identify the difficulty without providing for the solution as in a statement that the effects of variable X are confounded with the experimental treatments, but in the context of the situation the variables cannot be separated and hence we are doing the best we can. The reader is not judging whether or not the researcher is doing the best he can; he is trying to decide whether or not the design is adequate for the proposed research.

The discussion of the procedures usually follows somewhat of a chronological order in terms of conducting the research project. If sampling is to be used, the technique is usually presented early in the procedures section. The instruments used for measuring the variables should also be specified early. If instrument development is involved, detailed discussion will be required.

Consider the matter of sampling. The sampling plan must be viewed in terms of the external and internal validity of the research project. When sampling is used, the researcher is invariably attempting to make inferences to a larger population, so care must be taken in selecting the sample so that it represents the population. If inferential statistics are used, the sample must provide appropriate estimates of random variation.

In a study which would involve a sample of high school seniors from a single state, for example, it is not adequate to say that a random sample of seniors will be selected from the high schools of the state; the sampling plan should be described in detail. Assuming an adequate operational definition of a high school senior, the writer should indicate how he will identify all members of the population. What types of information will be available that will include all seniors fitting the definition? Are there safeguards against omitting segments of the population? Are stratifying variables to be used? If so, what are they, and why are they important? Will it be necessary to sample through an intermediate unit? What will be the replacement procedure if selected units decline to participate?

These types of questions should be carefully answered. For example, if stratified random sampling with proportional allocation is the sampling plan, the stratifying variables should be operationally defined, and it should be clear to the reader that students can be identified in terms of stratifying variables from the population information. It would not be adequate to simply indicate that "size of district" will be a stratifying variable. The definition of the categories for the stratifying variable would have to be given, such as less than 2,000 students, 2,000–5,000 students, and so on. Information should be provided about the source, probably a state document, on which the size of the district will be based, and it would be well to provide a rationale for the specific categories of the stratifying variable. A complete description of this type will provide the reader with evidence as to how and why the researcher will select the sample.

A lack of detail about the sampling plan will leave the reader with the impression that a sample of convenience will be used, another very serious methodology defect. Samples of volunteers should also be avoided. Another possible error is that the sampling procedure will not secure a sample adequate for inferring to the intended population. For example, a sample of seniors from a few large city systems willing to cooperate is not adequate for inferring to the state population of high school seniors.

The anticipated measurement instruments should be identified carefully, since they usually provide the operational definitions of the dependent variables and possibly some independent variables. When applicable, the procedures for dealing with matters such as reliability should be discussed.

The data collection procedures should be presented with some type of flowchart or time schedule, and the data collection must be in accord with the general design for the research project. The writer should guard against the introduction of undesirable factors. For example, if several groups are involved, it may be difficult to maintain consistent measurement. A description of how consistent measurement is to be achieved should be included. Latin square design might be used to balance sequence effects during the data collection. Points such as these should be made to convince the reader that the data collection will be adequate.

The specific procedures of the data analysis should be identified and, of course, such procedures must also be in accordance with the design. If statistical techniques are anticipated it is not adequate to say that statistical procedures will be used; the writer must be specific in identifying the technique; for example, a one-way analysis of variance will be used to test for significant differences between the achievement means of the three experimental groups. The analysis procedures must not only reflect the hypotheses, but the reader must be assured that necessary conditions for the analysis will be met. Certain assumptions about the data may be necessary. A common error is to ignore assumptions that may be tenuous.

The writer should also indicate the availability of necessary equipment or special resources for the analysis. Research projects involving large quantities of data and/or complex analyses invariably require access to a computer or automatic test-scoring machines. The writer should specifically indicate what equipment he expects to use and whether or not it is available at his institution.

Some funding agencies require that there be a specific discussion about how the project will be managed or how progress will be evaluated. A network of major events and activities can be developed which can be used to determine whether or not the research project is on schedule and progressing adequately toward its goals. A system which employs such a network is the Program Evaluation and Review Technique (PERT) management system.[3] PERT, basically a methodology for planning the numerous activities of a project, provides a management system for the actual research project. The inclusion of a management or evaluation system is usually taken as evidence of careful and complete planning for the project. This assumes, of course, that the system suggested is applicable, complete, and well described. Occasionally project evaluation or management requires a separate section in the proposal.

The methodology and procedures section of a proposal should explain clearly and in detail how the research activity will lead to the results. The amount of detail will depend somewhat on the type of project. If a project involves considerable instrument development, this may limit the amount of detail that can be specified in the analysis. Some projects are complete within themselves, others set the stage for continuing research. Whatever the case, this section of the proposal should specify the what and how of the research activity.

Significance of the proposed research

Whether or not a special heading is allocated to the significance of the research in the proposal guidelines, the writer should include a discussion of this topic. The significance may be suggested in the review of literature and statement of the problem or in a section entitled Use to be Made of the Findings.

Research is seldom conducted for the sole purpose of accumulating empirical results. Certainly these results may be important, and the writer can indicate the contribution to the existing knowledge in the area; a scholarly contribution to the field is always significant. However, the writer must project his goals beyond the information purpose to the practical significance of his research. What will the research mean to the practicing educator? Will the results, regardless of outcome, in-

---

3. For a detailed description of PERT, see D. L. Cook, *Program Evaluation and Review Technique* (Washington, D.C.: U.S. Government Printing Office, 1966).

fluence programs or methods? If the research will set the stage for deciding on alternate courses of action for improving education, this can be a significant contribution. What will be improved or changed as the result of the proposed research? How will the results of the study be implemented, and what innovations will come about?

In considering the significance, the writer should not assume that he already knows the outcome, nor should an unreasonable course of action be suggested. For example, he should not imply that the results of his study will require immediate and extensive curriculum reorganization of all senior high schools. Any suggested course of action should be reasonable in the usual context of educational innovation and change.

Funding agencies will usually prefer to fund research projects that have relatively broad significance and whose results are not limited to a local situation. While it is important to note the significance of the proposed project in the specific district or institution, the case for significance should not be limited to local effects. The generalizability of the proposed research and the transferability of any "products" that may result should be stressed. Noteworthy contributions of the proposed research should be explicitly identified.

Other items of the research proposal

Several other items are usually required in a proposal document. The fact that these items are grouped together for this discussion does not mean that they are relatively unimportant. However, most of them are quite straightforward, and the proposal guidelines are very specific as to the information required.

The cover page of a research proposal contains information such as the names of the proposed research project, principal investigator, and institution with which he is associated. This page is often followed by an abstract, or a concise, straightforward summary of the proposed research limited to a certain number of pages or words. Although the abstract precedes the proposal document, it is usually one of the last items completed in the preparation of the proposal. The abstract usually makes the initial impression upon the proposal reader, it is very important that its content be understandable and that it include the major points about the research project. The abstract is the defining statement of the proposed research in terms of its objectives, procedures, and type of research study.

The budget section is required for any research proposal seeking funds. Although budget guidelines are usually very specific, it is well for the writer to discuss the budget with someone familiar with financial procedures in his institution or school district. For the detailed budgets required, there are matters such as partial salaries, fringe benefits, retirement contributions, and overhead that require a knowledge of institutional policy. Overhead rates (such as 25 percent of total budget) can be specified by the funding agency, and they can also vary according to types of research projects. It is the writer's responsibility to be aware of policy that applies to his proposal.

There are basically two types of errors (other than arithmetic errors) that can occur when constructing a budget. The first is to be misinformed on financial policy and apply incorrect formulas in computing budget items. The second error is to omit items. Research projects may require travel allowances and special equipment. The researcher will be required to submit several copies (possibly several hundred) of a final report to the funding agency, which will involve publication costs. The proposal writer should consider all financial requirements from the time the project is approved until the final report is submitted to the funding agency.

The writer should consider each budget item carefully in the light of its contribution to the research project. The budget will be evaluated on the basis of economic efficiency and the needs of the proposed research. That is, the funding agency will consider what it is getting for its money. The budget should reflect the extensiveness of the proposed research. If expensive items or procedures are included that will contribute little to the overall research project, it would be well for the writer to consider ways to eliminate or replace such procedures. Sometimes minor cutbacks in the amount of information to be secured can result in major budgetary reductions. Unusual procedures for developing a budget such as excessive overhead rates should be avoided. The overall budget should appear reasonable in the light of the anticipated contribution of the proposed research.

Another required section of the proposal document discusses the personnel to be associated with the research project. Information should be provided about each individual having major responsibility in the research project, including name, present position, degrees, publications, background related to the project, and percentage of time committed to the project. For many projects research assistants are specified, although they need not be specifically identified. This section of the proposal may also include a description of special facilities or resources that will be necessary and that have been committed to the project if it is funded.

The researcher may want to include some appended items in his proposal document. Such items, of course, appear at the end of the proposal. Appended items consist of any other relevant information that is not contained in another section of the proposal. Examples of information for this section might be letters of support from leading educators who are familiar with the proposed research, names of consultants who were involved in developing the research ideas, and possible support for parts of the research project from another funding agency.

Preparing a research proposal for a funding agency is a major writing task. It requires a great deal of attention to detail, and considerable rewriting is often involved before the proposal is considered satisfactory for submittal. In this discussion several sources of errors have been identified. Generally, the proposal must meet the requirements of technical excellence in order to be recommended for funding.

Various agencies establish their own criteria for evaluating proposals. As an example, the National Institute of Education lists the following criteria to be used in reviewing research proposals and prospectuses for research projects submitted to them for funding:

1. Significance of the proposed research for American education, including:
   a. Importance of the problem area from the standpoint of basic knowledge of problems of American education.
   b. Likely magnitude of the addition that will be made to knowledge if the project is successful, including the generalizability of the results.
2. Quality of the proposed research project, including such considerations as:
   a. Extent to which the application exhibits thorough knowledge of pertinent previous work and relates the proposed research to it.
   b. Likelihood of success of the project.
   c. Adequacy of design, methodology, and instrumentation, where appropriate.
3. Qualifications of the principal investigator and other professional personnel as evidenced by:
   a. Experience and previous research productivity.
   b. Quality of the discussion and analysis in the application.
4. Adequacy of the facilities and arrangements available to the investigator to conduct the proposed study.
5. Reasonableness of the budget for the work to be done and the anticipated results.[4]

Suggestions have been made throughout this discussion that should aid the research proposal writer in meeting these criteria.

---

4. National Institute of Education, *Grants for Research in Education* (Washington, D.C.: Department of Health, Education, and Welfare, 1973), p. 8. Practically identical criteria are listed in the guidelines for research grant proposals.

WRITING THE RESEARCH REPORT

The writing of a research report is usually the concluding task of the research endeavor. Everything is pulled together during the writing of the report. This is the point at which the research must be essentially reproduced in written form. It is a matter of telling what was done, what occurred, and what the results mean in a concise, understandable, accurate, and logical manner.

Since much of what is written in the report is a reproduction of what has gone before, it might intuitively seem that writing should not be a difficult task. Yet many research reports are detained in the writing stage for an exorbitantly long period. Some reports become permanently bogged down at this stage. The anticipated but nonexistent article, the unfinished thesis, and the time-extended technical report are not uncommon. Good research reports are not easily written. Writing, like any skill that must be acquired, demands specific and concentrated attention.

Since the written report is an account of the research project, the organization of the report follows quite closely the organization of the research project. Since a reader reads what someone else has written, the suggestions about what to look for when reading a report which were made in Chapter 12 also apply to writing a report. The questions proposed as a checklist in reading a research report could be considered as requiring satisfactory answers during the writing activity.

Extensiveness of the content depends to some extent upon the type of research report called for. A journal article commonly has a brief lead into the statement of the problem and a brief review of literature with relatively few references, say between three and ten. A technical report to a funding agency or a thesis usually requires a considerable amount of background information. Research procedures and analysis techniques are usually discussed in greater detail for a thesis than for an article.

Although the writing of the report is usually associated with the close of the research project, portions of the writing may be done while the research study is in progress. Certainly, preliminary drafts of the review of the literature can be written and revised and brought up to date later. Research procedures can be recorded as the project is conducted and while they are fresh in the researcher's mind. In any event, precise records should be carefully kept during the progress of the research project. It is difficult to write from memory and avoid serious omissions.

The writer should assemble the available information before beginning the writing task. Mechanical procedures for presenting foot-notes, figures, tables, and the like should be well in mind. The refer-ences on writing procedures listed at the end of this chapter should prove helpful when dealing with the technical aspects in the production of a written report. In the interest of efficiency and continuity, relatively large blocks of time should be reserved for the writing task, and the writer should have the necessary physical resources for efficient pur-suit of the writing task. Preferably he should work with a minimum of interruption.

The research report should contain all the necessary data and at the same time be brief and to the point. First drafts are rarely ade-quate, and there is usually considerable changing and rewriting before the final draft is completed. A general outline of what is to be included in the report is a necessity. For a more extensive report it might be well to outline each chapter.

Statement of the problem and review of the literature

The procedure for writing a research report logically follows the or-ganization of parts of the report—statement of the problem, data collection, data analysis, and conclusions. The statement of the problem includes the review of related literature, for which concrete suggestions were given in Chapter 12.

The statement of the problem should be concise and to the point and should come early in the report. Long, drawn-out introductions pre-ceding the statement are unnecessary; the reader is interested in the research problem, and he should be led directly to it. The purpose of the introduction is only to set the stage for the statement of the problem.

The task of reviewing the literature usually is done quite early in the research project. The review serves multiple purposes, one of which may be aiding in producing a more definitive statement of the problem. When reviewing the literature, complete bibliographical en-tries should be made and some kind of abstracting form set up. File cards, 3 × 5 or 4 × 6, can serve quite effectively, with a separate card (or cards) used for each source. The relevant points of each source should be noted in enough detail so that the researcher has the necessary information to avoid repeated return to the original sources to de-termine what was really said. Since the final research report will require a bibliography, relevant information on the cards must be accurately and carefully recorded. The card procedure facilitates arranging the bibliography in alphabetical order.

The length of the review of literature section or chapter of a research report varies with the type of report. An article commonly has a relatively brief review, which should aid in putting the problem into perspective. Some statement of the rationale for the research problem which leads to the purpose for doing the research and how it ties in with what has already been done in the area is usually included.

The researcher must decide upon some type of organization for presenting the information from the review of literature. In an extensive research study the various sources are usually grouped according to the parts of the study to which they pertain. The information may also be discussed in order of relevance to the problem, the more relevant sources being discussed first. Sometimes the items of the review are discussed in a chronological order, usually beginning with the one most distant in time. This can be especially effective if the research on a topic has been closely related to the passing of time. The progress of the problem can be followed up to its present stage, an effective means for putting it in perspective.

The ideas from the various studies referred to in the review of literature should relate to each other and to the research problem. A common error is to present ideas from individual studies as little packages within themselves, which makes for a disjointed presentation. A related error is to treat each study in a mechanical way, regardless of relative importance.

The writer should avoid the excessive use of quotations. In the context of the research problem, the ideas from several sources can usually be tied together better by the writer's own words than by a series of quotations. The ideas from the review of literature should be integrated into a logical discussion, with the focus upon the research problem.

The researcher is not obligated to discuss information from every source listed in the bibliography. Often in an article three or four main points are brought in from an equal number of sources. Additional references may be listed in the bibliography, complementing the information from the sources discussed. The researcher should indicate in the discussion of the review of literature that he is well acquainted with the problem and the research related to it. An extensive bibliography with almost no discussion is not evidence of an adequate review of literature.

Methods and procedures

The sections of a report dealing with methods and procedures of conducting the research may include several topics. For an extensive report, these topics may be discussed in separate chapters. Such things as measurement, experimental procedures, sampling procedures, design, analysis, and significance levels (if hypotheses are tested) are included under procedures. A good rule to follow in this section is that the description should be detailed enough so that a reader could replicate the study. There should be no areas in which he would be uncertain as to what was done. For example, it is not sufficient to say that the creativity of a sample of third-graders was measured; the procedures and tests used for measuring creativity should be carefully described. The measurement of creativity should, of course, reflect the definition of creativity as given in the statement of the problem.

The procedures section should contain a rationale for the research methodology, especially in a detailed report such as a thesis. Shorter reports often do not state the rationale for applying a specific statistical test, for example. The rationale for the procedure is implied and a statement is given as to what was done. In writing a thesis, however, a graduate student may be required to present quite a detailed rationale for using a statistical test, including a description of the general purpose of the test, because mastery of the research methods may be the primary reason for doing the research. For example, in an article the statement that a student's t test for the difference between two means was computed may appear sufficient. In a thesis there would probably be a discussion of the student's t test and how it can be applied to the difference between two means. This detailed rationale may not always be required, but it facilitates understanding of the research, not only for the writer but also for a reader who is not familiar with the specific techniques. Research reports such as those submitted to a funding agency should contain a rationale for the methods if uncommon or complex procedures have been used. A reader may assume that what was done is accurate, but if he cannot understand the methods, it is unlikely that he will persist in reading the report.

The order of discussing the various items under a procedures section is somewhat arbitrary. One logical order is the sequence in which the procedures were applied in conducting the research project. It is possible that two or more items were worked on simultaneously. Usually the research project progresses through the stages of preparation for data collection, data collection, and data analysis, in that order.

Results

The results of the research procedure are the products of the analysis of the data. In reports which specify a methods and procedures section, the analysis may be discussed near the close of that section. In any case, it should be apparent that the stated results of the project are based upon the analysis.

Probably the most important concern in writing the results section is to present the results in a clear, concise, and well-organized manner. For the sake of brevity, the results and conclusions and recommendations are often included in a single section for a professional journal article. In longer reports, the results usually have a separate section. Whatever the case, it is important that results be clearly distinguishable from conjectures and conclusions. Occasionally writers will attempt to pass off conjectures as actual results, a practice to be avoided. Results of the study should also not be mixed with results reported in the review of literature. Tie-in with the results of research discussed in the review of literature should be done in the conclusions or discussion section.

The organization of results depends upon the specific research project. If several dependent variables are involved, the results may be grouped according to dependent variables; for example, achievement measures might be grouped together, separate from attitude measures. Independent variables may also be used as a basis for organization. An extensive experimental research project may involve several experiments. Assuming the experiments to be somehow sequentially related, the discussion of results would be organized according to order of experiment. The important thing about the organization of the results is that it can be easily followed, to facilitate the reporting of the research.

Tables can be a very helpful device for organizing results. For research reports that involve large amounts of statistical results, they are a necessity. The forms of tables are somewhat flexible. Certain associations, such as the American Psychological Association, are quite specific as to the table requirements for their journals, and directions are usually provided in the publication manuals of these associations.

Some general suggestions can be provided concerning the construction of tables. The title should state specifically what the table contains; if it contains means and standard deviations, for example, this should be stated, and the means and standard deviations should not be referred to simply as results. The title should also include information as to specific means and standard deviations. A table would not be titled simply Means and Standard Deviations, but Means and Standard Deviations of Fifth-Grade Students on Academic Measures.

Immediately below the title should be subheadings indicating the content of the columns. For the table entitled as the example above, the far left column would contain the academic measures. The sources of the means and standard deviations would be identified, such as experimental groups and control group, and means and standard deviations would be differentiated. The title and subheadings of the table for the example would be as shown in Figure 13.1.

TABLE 00.0
Means and Standard Deviation of Fifth-Grade Students on
Academic Measures

Measure	Experimental Group 1		Experimental Group 2		Control Group	
	Mean	Standard Deviation	Mean	Standard Deviation	Mean	Standard Deviation

FIGURE 13.1.   Example of title and column headings for research report table.

More than one type of statistic can be reported in a single table, but running in a large number of different types should be avoided. Means and standard deviations often go together. A correlation matrix may comprise a single table. If means and standard deviations appear with correlation coefficients, this can become cumbersome, because correlation coefficients involve two variables and it may be confusing as to which mean goes with what variable.

The contents of a table should be directed toward a single idea or facet of the research. Spacing is relative and depends upon the type of printing, size of characters, and number of digits in the entries. For the table in the example presented earlier, the spacing is adequate for four- or five-digit entries. If means or standard deviations exceeded five digits, it would be wise to provide additional space. With rare exceptions it is good policy to limit tables to one page in length.

A table should follow as closely as possible the first reference to it in the research report. A table that will not fit into the remaining space on the page should be placed on the page immediately following. A table of one page or less in length should not be split between two pages. Certain periodicals require that all tables appear on separate pages or at the end of the article. This procedure facilitates printing, but it should not be viewed as a general procedure for including tables.

Tables are used for grouping results. However, not all results, including statistical results, appear in tables. If the number of entries is small, say three or four, it is not necessary to construct a table to report the results. For example, if the researcher had three means to report, he might insert a sentence such as: The means of the three experimental groups were 87, 84, and 95, respectively. In the context of the paragraph it should be clear what respectively means.

Diagrams and figures can be used effectively in research reports, especially if equipment is being described or plots of results such as means are being reported. Sometimes diagrams can be used to reduce complex verbal descriptions. A disadvantage of the use of diagrams is that they may complicate or increase the expense of the printed production of the report, and for this reason some professional journals discourage their use. If diagrams or figures are used, accompanying captions should be complete and self-explanatory. Art work, of course, must be accurate and neat, and it may be necessary to have it prepared by an artist or media technician. In this case the author of the research report must provide a sketch for the artist.

The analysis section should contain all of the necessary information for meeting the objectives of the research project. For example, hypotheses should be checked to see if they have been adequately tested and the results of these tests have been reported. Existing patterns should be pointed out. If supplementary analyses are done, these results should appear. (Extensive tables of supplementary results may be placed in an appendix if their inclusion makes this part of the report cumbersome.) Only results should be reported. If a pattern appears, the pattern should be carefully described, but a discussion of why the pattern emerged should be deferred for the conclusions section.

Conclusions, recommendations, and implications

The final section of the research report consists of conclusions, recommendations, and implications. Commonly called the conclusions section, it may also go by names such as Conclusion and Discussion or Conclusions and Recommendations. In any event, the term "conclusions" almost invariably appears in the title of the section.

As the climax of the research report, this section should contain the highlights of the study. In many ways this is the most difficult section to write. The writer's perceptive ability in the area being researched is probably taxed more in writing this section than in any other. The results must be interpreted and the entire study synthesized.

The final section may open with a brief review of the problem and procedures of the research project. This refocuses the reader's attention on the problem and objectives of the study, which may have become somewhat blurred by the attention to details in the analysis. This review should be brief, and the writer should move quickly to the conclusions and the corresponding discussion. The review should not break the continuity with the results section.

The conclusions must follow logically from the results of the investigation. The number of conclusions drawn depends in part upon the complexity of the results. Supposedly at least one substantive conclusion could be drawn, otherwise it would hardly be worthwhile pursuing, much less reporting, the research. A study could also contain a series of conclusions.

A common error in writing the final section is to draw conclusions that are too broad. Educational research, especially research conducted in the classroom and other natural educational settings, involves situations for which there is less than maximum control. Also, there may be inexactness in the data. Therefore caution should be exercised when drawing the conclusions. Qualifying statements such as under specific conditions or subject to such and such conditions are often appropriate, especially when arriving at generalizations. The writer must keep in mind that the conclusions must be backed up by factual information.

The other extreme is for the writer to be too narrow and restrictive in drawing conclusions. This situation, which reflects a lack of information about the research problem, is not as likely to appear in drawing specific conclusions, since they follow from the results, as it is in generalizations.

The final section should contain, in addition to the conclusions, a summary and a discussion. The discussion should be enlightening and creative, characteristics which depend largely on the writer's scholarly understanding of the area under study, past research in the area, and the specific research project being reported.

The discussion should include implications for educational practice and possibly educational theory. At this point in the research endeavor (as at others), the writer should be aware of any weaknesses in his design or procedures. Assumptions should be reviewed, which usually leads to suggestions for additional research in the area. Research in most areas is of a continuing nature; answers or partial answers to research questions invariably raise or imply additional questions. A question may be raised about a variable that was either uncontrolled or not considered in the research at hand. The writer should be aware of the limitations of his research and should have accounted for them; he should not need to apologize for any shortcomings.

The conclusions and summary should be to the point. Conjecture and speculation should be clearly distinguished from direct conclusions. Implications should stay within the mainstream of the research study, and tangential areas should be brought in only when they are relevant to the point under discussion.

Bibliography and appendix

A bibliography or list of references is a necessary part of the research report. Even if no footnote references are made in the body of the report, a bibliography should be included. The writer should adopt a standard procedure for the bibliographical entries. A good policy, one which has been mentioned previously, is to make an accurate and technically correct entry when the source is initially reviewed. This will save considerable time and effort when the final bibliography is being prepared. Entries made on file cards can facilitate putting them in alphabetical order.

While a bibliography should always be given, an appendix is included only if it is necessary, as when there are materials which do not fit well in the main body of the report. Several types of materials can be placed in an appendix: self-constructed measuring instruments such as tests or questionnaires, tables of raw scores, or related data. A bulk of related results tends to make the main report cumbersome and difficult reading, and such results can be placed in the appendix. For example, in discussing hypotheses about testing means, the means are necessary in the results section. However, the standard deviations and other measures of the distributions that may be of interest could be placed in an appendix. Separate appendices should be used for different types of materials. The appendices appear at the end of the report, following the bibliography.

Review and revision of the research report

The writing of the research report is not a task which can be taken lightly or approached haphazardly. Careful preparation is a prerequisite for this task. The writer should not expect to produce a satisfactory final product without some revision. Generally the report is improved with subsequent revisions, additions, and deletions. Research writing is a complex and exacting activity, and revision should be considered a normal part of this task.

Revision may be initiated either by the author himself or by someone's criticism of the report. Self-criticism may be most valuable after the writer has let the report sit for a short time, say ten days to two weeks. This is not to be viewed as a lack of persistence but as an attempt to get a critical perspective of the report. Explanations may not be as obvious as they seemed to be during the initial writing. Omissions and confusing statements may become more apparent, and contradictions may appear which were undetected the first time through. Before releasing the final draft of the manuscript for typing, the writer should make a critical and comprehensive search for omissions, inconsistencies, ambiguous statements, and inaccurate information.

As a matter of course, the writer should subject his report to the criticism of his peers. A graduate student is forced into this due to the channels set up for submitting a thesis and getting it approved. Criticism is offered in a positive and constructive attitude and should be accepted in the same manner. The writer should not interpret criticism as a personal assault. He is not obligated to accept the criticism, but assuming that the critics are competent, their suggestions are likely to improve the report and the manner of presentation.

In conclusion, remember two important points. First: Do not underestimate the task. Prepare for it carefully and attack the problem systematically, with attention to detail. Second: Be persistent. Do not put off the writing when the facts are fresh.

CONCLUDING REMARKS

While in a sense the satisfactory completion of the written research report concludes the specific research project, this should not be the conclusion of an individual's research efforts. A well-done piece of research should be a source of satisfaction and pride. Conducting the research will undoubtedly be a valuable learning experience, regardless of the level of sophistication of the researcher. Completing one research project may stimulate the preparation of a research proposal for another project. The researcher's association with his own research and that of others should stimulate the pursuit of new and related ideas. Educational research should be a continuing activity in which each specific project adds to the store of knowledge.

SELECTED REFERENCES ON WRITING PROCEDURES

The following bibliography presents a list of helpful references on the mechanics and procedures of writing a research report. The references provide suggestions concerning style, presentation of headings and subheadings, typing requirements, and the like. This is in no sense an exhaustive bibliography. Some associations have their own publication manuals; there are many similarities among such manuals, and the content is primarily oriented toward publication in the professional journals. If a writer is preparing an article for a professional journal that has special publication requirements, he should secure the publication manual prior to writing the report.

American Psychological Association. *Publication Manual of the American Psychological Association.* Rev. ed. Washington, D.C., 1967.

Campbell, W. G., and Ballou, S. V. *Form and Style: Theses, Reports, Term Papers.* 4th ed. Boston: Houghton Mifflin Co., 1974.

Dugdale, K. *A Manual of Form for Theses and Term Reports.* 5th ed. Bloomington, Ind.: Indiana University Bookstore, 1972.

Dugdale, K. *A Manual on Writing Research.* 2nd ed. Bloomington, Ind.: Indiana University Bookstore, 1967.

King, L. S., and Roland, C. G. *Scientific Writing*. Chicago: American Medical Association, Division of Scientific Publications, 1968.

Leggett, G.; Mead, C. D.: and Charvat, W. *Prentice-Hall Handbook for Writers*. 5th ed. Englewood Cliffs, N.J.: Prentice-Hall, 1970.

Perrin, P. G., and Ebbitt, W. R. *Writer's Guide and Index to English*. 5th ed. Glenview, Ill.: Scott, Foresman & Co., 1972.

Roland, C. G. *Good Scientific Writing*. Chicago: American Medical Association, Division of Scientific Publications, 1971.

Shannon, J. R. "Tips to Writers from Seventy-Five Editors of Educational Periodicals." *Journal of Educational Research* 1950 (44), 241–68.

Turabian, K. L. *A Manual for Writers of Term Papers, Theses, and Dissertations*. 4th ed. Chicago: The University of Chicago Press, 1973.

Van Hagen, C. E. *Report Writers' Handbook*. Magnolia, Mass.: Peter Smith Publisher, 1969.

Ward, R. R. *Practical Technical Writing*. New York: Alfred A. Knopf, 1968.

Williams, C. B., and Stevenson, A. H. *A Research Manual for College Studies and Papers*. 3rd ed. New York: Harper & Row, 1963.

Woodford, F. P., ed. *Scientific Writing for Graduate Students*. New York: Rockefeller University Press, 1969.

SUGGESTED STUDY EXERCISES

13.1. Select a research topic of limited magnitude and write a hypothetical research report, including the statement of the problem and the anticipated procedures and analysis that would be used. (Since this is a hypothetical study it is not expected that you actually collect data or produce any results and conclusions. Therefore, the sections dealing with results and conclusions would be missing from your report.) Do a brief review of the literature and limit your review and statement of the problem to two or three typewritten pages. Be brief and concise and pay special attention to the continuity of ideas. Use your mastery of the content of previous chapters to present an adequate and correct methodology for doing the research study. Include a bibliography. This suggests a writing task of the magnitude of a short term paper.

13.2. Select a research report, probably an article, which deals with an educational topic in your area or one about which you have some knowledge. Read the report through the results (or data analysis) section but do not read the conclusions. Write a conclusions section of your own. After you have completed your conclusions, subject them to your own critical review and compare them to the conclusions of the report.

Solutions to suggested study exercises

Note: For exercises which (1) have flexible answers, (2) direct the reader to some type of extended activity such as reading a journal article, or (3) indicate considerable discussion, solutions are not provided in this section. The solutions included are brief; for any exercises which require lengthy responses, the solutions given here are overviews only. The purpose of this section is to assist the student in evaluating his own mastery of concepts and to make the solution of exercises a more profitable learning experience.

CHAPTER 1

1.5. The null hypothesis states or implies in its form the characteristic of nondirection. For example, this may take the form of no difference between two parameters. The nondirectional form indicates that we do not hypothesize one parameter to be less than or greater than the other.

CHAPTER 2

2.1. *a.* The *type* of residential dwelling would be nominal scale. If we were interested in number of family units we could go to a ratio scale, but such a quantitative characteristic is not defined when we simply classify according to type.
   b. Calcium deposits could be measured on a ratio scale.
   c. Performance on an essay part of a history test would be measured on an ordinal scale. Considerable objectivity and quantification would have to be defined before such a performance could be measured on an equal-unit or ratio scale.
   d. Rating of student teacher performance would be measured on an ordinal scale.
   e. Ratio scale measurement would be involved.
2.2. The constants are grade level, sex, and school. The independent variables are instructional materials and teacher, although these two

cannot be separated since it is implied that each teacher uses only one type of instructional material. The dependent variable is reading achievement.

TABLE 2.3. Frequency distribution for the 80 scores

Score	f	Score	f	Score	f
20	1	31	2	42	3
21	0	32	4	43	2
22	0	33	5	44	3
23	1	34	3	45	3
24	2	35	6	46	2
25	1	36	4	47	2
26	0	37	5	48	1
27	3	38	4	49	1
28	2	39	3	50	0
29	3	40	3	51	1
30	5	41	4	52	1

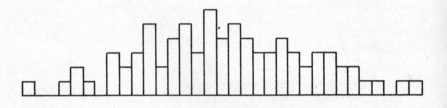

Histogram for the 80 Scores above

2.4. Measures of central tendency are points in a distribution that locate the distribution on a scale. Measures of variability are intervals that indicate the dispersion or spread in the distribution. These two types of measures provide different information that is essential in defining a specific distribution.

2.5. Figure 2.5 indicates that 16 blocks occupy the area for less than 5 or greater than 8. Thus, the probability of getting such a sum is 16/36 or .444. The probability of getting either a 6 or an 8 is 10/36 or .278.

2.6. The 57 is 1.4 standard deviation units above the mean. Table A (Appendix 2) indicates that .0808 of the area lies to the right of a standard score of 1.4. Hence, the probability of getting a score of 57 or greater is .0808. In like manner, between 55 and 65, the probability is .1574; between 40 and 55, the probability is .8185. (It should be noted that for these solutions the actual values were used. The accuracy of measurement was not discussed, but for more precise results this would be necessary. If, for example, measurement was to the nearest integer, then the true boundary for the 57 or greater would be 56.5, since any score exceeding 56.5 would be considered 57 or greater. This would slightly change the standard scores and hence the probabilities.)

2.7. The researcher would select a random sample from which he could compute statistics. The sample would reflect the population within the boundary of sampling fluctuation. Hence, the statistics are used to infer to the parameters, again within the bounds of sampling fluctuations. The statistic involved would be the mean reading level of the sample of first graders measured; the corresponding parameter is the mean reading level of the entire first-grade population. The chain of reasoning follows the inference implied above. The population has certain characteristics called parameters (which will not be known for certain). The random sample which reflects the population has certain characteristics called statistics. The statistics are determined and known, and from these we reason back to the corresponding parameters and draw conclusions about the parameters. In this particular situation the researcher draws conclusions about the population mean from the observed sample mean.

2.8. A statistic is a measure of a sample and a parameter a measure of a population. The underlying distribution is the distribution which provides the theoretical base for how the statistic under study behaves; that is, it identifies the shape, location, and dispersion of the distribution of the statistic of which we have one observation. It is the underlying distribution of the statistic.

2.9. A correlation coefficient is an index of the relationship between two variables. The coefficient can take on values between plus and minus 1, inclusive. The end points of plus and minus 1 indicate perfect relationships. The algebraic sign indicates the direction of the relationship. For a negative correlation, high scores on one variable are associated with low scores on the other variable. For a positive correlation, high scores on one variable are associated with high scores on the other variable.

2.10. (a) Around zero or possibly very low positive. (b) low positive. (c) moderate to high positive (d) moderate positive (e) moderate negative

2.11. *a.* If the researcher were interested only in describing the distributions.
b. If he were inferring the results to a larger population of teacher education students and the 150 students represented a random sample of this population.
c. If he were interested in the relationships between the variables.

CHAPTER 3

3.1. The review of the literature can serve multiple purposes, especially early in (or prior to) the research project. Possible reasons (which reflect the specific information supplied) include to (1) provide a background for the research study, (2) inform the researcher what has been done in the area, (3) provide information about possible procedures or designs, and (4) reveal possible gaps or omissions in the area.

3.3. This would most likely be *ex post facto* research.

3.5. There are undoubtedly characteristics unique to each school that are now confounded with the independent variable "instructional method." The experiment could have been designed so that all five instructional methods are used in each school.

3.7. Two or more variables are said to be confounded when their effects cannot be separated. When variables interact they are affecting each other, and with proper design the effect of interaction can be determined.

CHAPTER 4

4.1. Internal validity concerns the basic minimum control, etc., necessary in order for the results to be interpretable. External validity is the extent to which the results of the experiment are generalizable to existing conditions, populations, and the like. Internal validity is often enhanced by increasing control and thus reducing factors which may be operating in the real situation. This tends to jeopardize external validity. The reverse may also occur when the experiment is essentially a replication of the real situation (has high external validity) but so many factors are operating that it is impossible to interpret cause and effect.

4.2. The fact that the researcher can assign students at random within the school gives a measure of control which would be missing if he had to take existing classes. Existing classes may contain ability biases and any number of relevant factors. The researcher can enhance control by building "school" into the design as an independent variable. Since each teacher teaches four classes, the researcher could assign one class size per teacher. However, "teacher" would be confounded with the independent variable "school," since any one teacher would teach in only one school. The variable "school" might have several uncontrolled but relevant variables associated with it, such as student ability or lab facilities. These variables are essentially confounded with the variable "school." Possible hypotheses: (1) class size has no effect upon the mean chemistry achievement of the population from which these classes were drawn; (2) there is no difference between the chemistry achievement means of the four school populations. The posttest-only control group extended to four groups is a possible design if one class size, say 30, is considered the control group. A factorial design may seem desirable if it is possible to experimentally control additional variables, but the unequality of class size would almost require unequal cell frequencies.

4.3. Possible methods for increasing control over extraneous variables: (1) build them into the design as independent variables, (2) balance their effect over the levels of the other independent variables, (3) the obvious procedure—eliminate the extraneous variable. The various procedures discussed in this chapter for increasing internal validity are essentially procedures for increasing control.

4.5. There are three independent variables with two levels of each, therefore a $2 \times 2 \times 2$ or 2^3 factorial would be an appropriate factorial design. This factorial design has eight cells. However, one-half of the eight cells involve pairs and require two Ss. Therefore, one complete replication requires 12 Ss, six boys and six girls. Since there are only 64 boys and it requires six boys for a replication, the greatest multiple of six we can use is 60. So we would randomly eliminate 36 girls and four boys and proceed with 120 Ss. Sex is a fixed variable but we would *randomly* assign the 60 boys (and girls) to the levels of the independent variables "type of problem" and "class size," assigning 40 to pairs and 20 to individuals, and 30 to each type of problem. Actually we would have the eight cells and the frequencies would be 10 and 20, depending on whether the cell includes an individual or a pair. Thus, randomization is built in by assigning Ss to cells.

4.6. An interaction between the variables sex and class size indicates that effect of class size does *not* remain constant over the two levels of sex. In presenting a plot of means, a change in slope of the two lines would appear. This change may or may not involve a crossover of the two lines.

4.7. The primary gain in validity is that the Solomon four-group design makes it possible to check any effects of pretesting or the interaction of pretesting with the experimental treatment.

4.8. The procedure applied here is a static-group comparison. This procedure is almost entirely lacking in control and hence lacking in experimental validity. There are a multitude of factors in addition to Boy Scout training that could effect performance in the skills. The greater maturity due to age differential, selective dropout, and additional external (to Boy Scout training) experience are examples of factors that would undoubtedly affect the performance and favor the 14-year-old boys. It is impossible to partition out an effect due singly to Boy Scout training.

4.9. Since it is implied that the teacher does not have the option of randomly assigning students, the nonequivalent control group design applies. He could randomly assign two of the classes to the use of programmed materials (experimental treatment), but this does not meet the requirement of a true experimental design. Because the teacher is interested in the amount of algebra learned during the semester, pretesting is necessary, but it would also be necessary as a statistical control. This experiment would most likely be quite high in external validity since testing could occur at natural times and the experiment would be carried on in a natural field setting. The population to which the results are generalized would have to be carefully defined in terms of the students enrolled in advanced algebra classes in this specific type of high school.

4.10. Multiple-treatment interference means that observations taken on the same S immediately following a specific treatment are affected by prior treatments. When an S receives more than one treatment, prior treatments may interfere with the effects of subsequent treatments. This is a threat to validity since it becomes impossible to separate the effects due to specific treatments.

4.11. True experimental designs possess the feature of random assignment of Ss to experimental treatments which is lacking in the quasi-experimental designs. Thus complete experimental control is lacking in the latter designs. The quasi-experimental designs commonly are used when preassembled groups of Ss must be taken intact. The primary difficulty comes with the lack of control, thus making the interpretation of the results tenuous. Also, the matter of inference and applying analysis techniques becomes "muddied" and more difficult.

4.12. There exists no random assignment of Ss to the practice treatments. The use of volunteering schools through the principal may have introduced bias and would certainly limit the generalizability of the results. The teacher variable is very apparent and essentially uncontrolled. The assumption is that teachers are most effective with the techniques they prefer. Even if this is true there is no evidence that different teachers, independent of practice method, are equally effective. With only three schools it would be difficult to make a case for the assumption that the teachers of each method are a random sample of fifth-grade teachers, either in general or as a more specific group. There may be other relevant uncontrolled factors within the schools, and since the method is optional to the teacher, there is no reason to assume a balance between schools on such factors. Thus, internal validity is low because of lack of control. The external validity is also low because of the limits on generalization mentioned above.

4.13. This is an example of a time design. A design such as this is susceptible to multiple-treatment interference. In this case, delayed effects may begin appearing on subsequent observations. The pattern of results may be difficult to interpret. The advantage of using such a design is that it can be applied in a natural setting and can provide information on the reading profile of a specific class. A special measurement problem would be attaining equivalent difficulty levels for the various tests given at four week intervals. Suppose there were a marked drop in performance after one period. This would be interpreted as an effect of the method of instruction, when in fact the drop may be due to a more difficult test.

4.14. *a.* The researcher can determine the possible effect of X extended in time, along with a comparison group extended in time. Also a possible diminishing effect of pretesting could be checked.

b. Compare O_2 and O_9; compare O_4 and O_{10}.

c(1). If an experimental effect exists it is a function of time; there is no pretesting effect nor interaction between X and pretesting appearing in the short-run posttest results of experimental groups.

(2). There is an experimental effect and it is not affected by the different posttest times of the design.

(3). In the short run there is no change due to experimental treatment for pretested groups.

(4). In the short-time there is no experimental effect nor is there an effect of pretesting; there is some kind of experimental effect in the long term with the pretested groups.

4.15. Basically, a well-designed experiment meets the requirements for internal and external validity. This requires the general characteristics of (1) sufficient control to meet the objectives of the research project, (2) bias-free data, (3) necessary information to test the hypotheses; and (4) a design that fits the basic objectives and purposes of the research project.

CHAPTER 5

5.1. This is not an experiment because there is no manipulation of independent variables. This study is *ex post facto* in nature, since the independent variables have already occurred and a retrospective search for cause-and-effect relationships is implied. Grade level, location of school, and sex of the student are independent variables. The dependent variable is critical thinking test performance. If such an interaction were found, it would mean that the effect of location of school is not constant for boys and girls.

5.2. A researcher would need to make some kind of comparison of the academic performance of students from divorced households versus those from intact households. It would be an *ex post facto* type of study, and although it may be possible to do some random selection once the type of household the students come from is identified, it is not possible to randomly assign the characteristic of divorce.

5.7. The interview has the advantages of (1) allowing for deeper probing of the S and possibly pursuing a response, (2) clearing ambiguities, and (3) securing information that would not be forthcoming with a written questionnaire. Also, the problem of nonresponse is many times eliminated and usually not as great as with a questionnaire. The primary disadvantage of the interview is that it requires considerable resources in terms of time, effort, and personnel. The questionnaire has the advantage of not requiring the personnel resources of the interview. The questionnaires can all be sent at the same time so there is no large lapse of time, such as may occur between interviews. This could be a disadvantage of the interview if external events occur which affect the responses. The primary disadvantage of the questionnaire is the usual high percentage of nonresponse. If a great deal of written material is necessary to communicate to the S and elicit his response, the length of the questionnaire may be a disadvantage. Also, if communication breaks down there is no opportunity, at the time, to eliminate ambiguities.

5.9. The panel study allows for the opportunity of collecting data from the same group of teachers at different times. In this way, changes over time within specific teachers could be detected.

5.12. Possible procedures for securing information concerning the validity of documents used for historical research are as follows:

a. Check consistency of the document with related primary and secondary sources; this may involve considerable cross-referencing.

b. Evaluate the writer in terms of his position, possible bias, possibility of deliberate frauds, and so forth.

c. Use of X-ray and radioactivity procedures for establishing age of documents.

It should be noted that the above procedures will not conclusively ensure validity. The advantage that the experimenter has is that of being an eyewitness to the event. The information of the experiment is received firsthand, and assuming that the experimenter knows what he sees, presumably the information is accurate and valid. (Note that having valid information does not necessarily make its interpretation valid.)

5.14. (a) survey (b) experiment (c) historical (d) *ex post facto* (e) historical (f) *ex post facto,* possibly survey (g) survey.

CHAPTER 6

6.1. Validity has to do with whether or not a test measures what it is supposed to measure, while reliability concerns whether or not it is consistent in measuring whatever it does measure. A test can be reliable but not valid by consistently measuring something it was not designed to measure and failing to measure what it was designed to measure. An unreliable test cannot be valid since lack of consistency eliminates the possibility of measuring what it is supposed to measure.

6.4. Objectivity of a measuring device is defined as the extent to which equally competent scorers get the same results. The objectivity is in the scoring and not in the length of response.

6.6. Validity coefficient of .722; the other sources of variance are variance specific to the observed distribution and error variance.

CHAPTER 7

7.4. The primary measurement difficulties deal with classifying teachers as autocratic and democratic and quantifying the variable "hostility." A possible method for quantifying hostility would be the proportion of hostile words used by either the teacher or the students. This would require some kind of definition and list of hostile words, most likely constructed by experts in this area. Hostility would then be defined in terms of the proportion of hostile words. The above procedure would not take into account the context and voice inflection associated with the word. This may be necessary, since certain words may be hostile in one context and neutral in another.

7.5. a. Both researchers have published measuring instruments available, but the one working with achievement would have greater choice, and it would be easier for him to find an instrument specifically suited to his needs.

b. Content validity established on a logical basis would be of concern in the achievement measurement; content validity might also be considered for the personality measures, but construct validity information from the test manual would be of major concern, especially if the researcher is attempting to establish the constructs that underly the junior high personality.

c. Achievement could be measured by a paper and pencil test; personality data might be obtained by some type of written group test or it might require individual testing.

7.6. The following is one possible card layout. Consider first the identification information. There are seven items of information in identification. These items are listed below, with the corresponding number of necessary columns:

a. City school number: two columns; there are 74 schools and each would be assigned a two-digit number.

b. Student identification number: four columns; since there are over 1,000 students and we can assume there are less than 10,000 in the sample.

c. Grade level: one column; numbers 3 through 8.

d. Sex: one column; boys assigned zero and girls one.

e. Ability level: one column; since there are only three classifications, one number assigned to each classification.

f. Age: two columns; record the actual age of the student. If age is measured to the nearest tenth of a year, three columns would be necessary.

g. Socioeconomic classification of the school: one column; assign different one-digit numbers to each of the eight districts.

The achievement variables would require a minimum total of 44 columns, since the ten two-digit variables would require 20 columns and the remaining eight variables 24 columns. Since there is sufficient room on the card, it might be desirable to allow three columns for each variable, thus requiring a total of 54 columns. In that case the two-digit variables would all have their scores preceded by a zero (or blank). That is, a score of, say, 86 would be recorded as 086 on the card. Either 12 or 13 columns would be required for identification but it might be well to reserve the first 15 or 20 columns for identification, in case it would become desirable to add information later. It is not necessary that the identification information appear first or that it be grouped together. Such grouping may facilitate the programming.

CHAPTER 8

8.1. Since there are 839 population members, three-digit random numbers are necessary.

8.2. Stratified random sampling is the technique of dividing the population into nonoverlapping subpopulations and then making random selections from these subpopulations on the basis of some predetermined allocation. Proportional allocation involves sample sizes proportional to the sizes of corresponding strata populations. Optimum allocation involves sample sizes proportional to strata variances as well as strata population sizes.

8.4. In stratified random sampling, all strata are represented in the sample and the random sampling is done within strata according to some allocation. Thus the subpopulations of strata members are randomly selected. In cluster sampling, the clusters are randomly selected from the population of clusters, but if a cluster is selected all its members are included in the sample.

8.5. Sampling fraction is 3/20 or .15. Sample sizes for strata 1 through 4, respectively, are 124.5, 99, 72, and 154. Since partial units can likely not be included, the researcher must arbitrarily decide whether to select 125 from stratum 1 or 155 from stratum 4.

8.7. Sixty men and 60 women would be randomly selected from their respective populations. There would be 15 men and 15 women assigned to each of the four levels of the independent variable. Since selection is random from each population, the first 15 of each sex selected could be assigned to level 1, the second 15 to level 2, etc.

CHAPTER 9

9.1. The dependent variable is the score on the history achievement test. Since each student will produce one score or observation, the assumption of independence requires that no student influence the score of any other student during the testing. To meet this assumption it would be necessary to exclude any group efforts and guard against cheating while the test is being taken. Note that it is not necessary to exclude group study prior to the testing. The thing being measured is knowledge of history at the time of testing, regardless of how the student prepared himself prior to the test.

9.2. The null hypothesis tested is that the population means are equal; that is, there is no difference between the population means. In symbols this is given by $H_0: \mu_1 - \mu_2 = 0$. Since the statistical test was significant, the probability statement is: "The probability that the observed difference in sample means would occur by chance, if, in fact, there is no difference in population means, is less than .05." Note that the difference in sample means is a statistic and the difference in population means a parameter.

9.3. Assuming the parametric assumptions, a Student's t test or an analysis of variance would be appropriate techniques. The null hypothesis is that the two treatment means of the population are equal; that is, $H_0: \mu_{T1} = \mu_{T2}$. The null hypothesis is rejected. The possible error being made here is rejecting a true hypothesis (Type I or alpha error). The probability of making such an error is less than .01. The test is significant at the .05 level, since if the probability is less than .01 it is certainly less than .05.

9.4. The population means of sixth-grade arithmetic achievement for boys and girls are equal; that is, $H_0: \mu_B = \mu_G$ or $H_0: \mu_B - \mu_G = 0$. Since the statistical test was significant at the .05 level, the probability statement is as follows: "The probability that the observed difference between the sample means would occur by chance, if, in fact, the population means are equal, is less than .05." The conclusion is that the population means are different, population means referring to those of boys and girls on sixth-grade arithmetic achievement. There is not enough information to decide whether or not the test is significant at the .01 level. The probability may be less than .05 but greater than .01, that is, it could fall between the .05 and .01 levels.

9.5. We would reject the hypothesis since with 19 degrees of freedom and a two-tailed test (no direction is hypothesized) a t value of 2.09 is required for significance at the .05 level. Since the t value was positive, the sample mean was larger than the hypothesized mean.

9.6. Since there are 6 levels and 8 Ss in each level, there is a total of 48 Ss. Five degrees of freedom are associated with the independent variable and 42 with the within or error term. Thus, the appropriate F distribution has 5 and 42 degrees of freedom. With these degrees of freedom, values of 2.44 and 3.49 are required for significance at the .05 and .01 levels, respectively. Thus, the observed F value is significant at the .05 level but not at the .01 level. In educational research the .05 level is generally considered conservative enough, hence we would probably reject the null hypothesis. The probability statement is: "The probability that the observed sample means would appear if the population means are equal is less than .05." (However, this probability is greater than .01.)

9.7. The analysis of variance would be an appropriate technique. The three null hypotheses deal with (1) the effect of stimulus; (2) the effect of display; and (3) the interaction of display and stimulus. The null hypotheses could be stated as follows: (1) There is no difference in the population means of those students using nonsense symbols and those using learning materials. (2) There is no difference in the population means of those students using random and those using ordered displays. (3) This hypothesis involves four population means which we will denote by $\mu_{NR}, \mu_{NO}, \mu_{MR}, \mu_{MO}$, where the subscripts N and M stand for nonsense symbols or meaningful materials, and R and O denote random or ordered displays. The null hypothesis is that these four population means are equal after the main effects of stimulus and display have been removed. The main effects and the interaction each have one degree of freedom associated with them. If there is a total of 80 Ss, the within or error term has 76 degrees of freedom. Therefore, the appropriate underlying distribution in all three cases is the F distribution, with 1 and 76 degrees of freedom. This distribution requires a value of 3.97 for significance at the .05 level.

9.8. The concept of interaction between two independent variables is sometimes referred to as the effect that one independent variable has upon another. The effect of one of the variables does not remain constant over the levels of the other.

9.9. An analysis of covariance would be used when it is necessary to include a statistical control over a relevant factor. The analysis of covariance may be necessary if it is suspected that the groups differ markedly on a factor relevant to the dependent variable. The hypothesis may be so stated that it becomes necessary for the researcher to adjust for initial differences; for example, if we are interested in the amount learned during a period rather than the absolute amount known at a point in time. The analysis of variance is preferred if no adjustment on dependent variable scores is necessary. Initial differences of S's may be randomly distributed among the groups.

9.10. The null hypothesis is that the adjusted population reading achievement means of students taught using the three sets of instructional materials are equal. Adjusted means of the dependent variable are actually tested. If the statistical test is significant, the conclusion is that the instructional materials have different effects upon fourth-grade achievement.

9.11. The probability that the interval 85.5 to 90.5 spans the population mean is .95. Theoretically the t distribution with 399 degrees of freedom would be the appropriate underlying distribution, but with sample size of 400 the normal distribution can be used as an approximation for the t distribution. If sample size were 25 the underlying distribution would change to the t distribution with 24 degrees of freedom. A confidence interval of 84.5 to 90.5 would indicate a computational error, since this interval would not be symmetrically located around the sample mean of 88. A 90 percent confidence interval would be shorter than 5 units.

9.12. The two possible types of errors in hypothesis testing are (1) Type I, rejecting a true hypothesis, and (2) Type II, accepting a false hypothesis. Hypotheses are neither proved nor disproved because there is always the probability, however small, that an error is being made in the decision on the hypothesis.

CHAPTER 10

10.1. The parametric techniques are more demanding of the measurement scale, assuming the data are measured on at least an interval scale. This is not a necessary assumption for the nonparametric techniques. Nonparametric techniques do not require assumptions about the shape of the population distribution which are crucial with the parametric techniques when sample size is small. Since nonparametric techniques deal with nominal or ordinal data, the parametric assumption of homogeneity of variance does not apply. Both techniques require the assumption of random sampling, since this is a necessary part of any inferential technique. Also, under certain conditions, the assumption of a continuous underlying distribution of the dependent variable (variable measured) is common to both types of techniques.

10.3. The null hypothesis can be stated as: There is no difference between the population distribution (from which the sample was drawn) and the expected distribution. An equivalent statement is that the population distribution is the expected distribution. The probability statement could be: The probability that the observed sample distribution would appear by chance, if the population distribution is the expected distribution, is less than .01. We conclude that the population distribution is not the expected distribution. This statistical test is significant at the .05 level, since probability less than .01 is certainly less than .05.

10.4. With 15 categories the appropriate underlying distribution is the chi square distribution with 12 df. The critical value with a significance level of .05 is 21.03. Since the computed x^2 value exceeds the critical value, the statistical test is significant, and the researcher should conclude that performance is not normally distributed in the population. The probability that the sample distribution would have occurred by chance, if, in fact, performance is normally distributed in the population, is less than .05.

10.5. An inspection of Table E in Appendix 2 reveals that a x^2 value of 3.84 with one degree of freedom is required for significance at the .05 level. Therefore, the value of 4.81 is significant. The null hypothesis tested is that the populations from which the sample were drawn have a common median. The null hypothesis is rejected.

10.6. The appropriate x^2 distribution has 12 degrees of freedom, therefore a value of 21.03 is necessary for significance at the .05 level. A x^2 value of 23.81 is significant, and we would reject the hypothesis that the four samples were drawn from a common population and conclude that the sample distributions came from different population distributions. Probability statement: The probability that the four observed sample distributions would appear by chance, if drawn from the same population, is less than .05.

10.7. The parametric analysis of variance analyzes actual observed scores measured on an interval or ratio scale. The Kruskal-Wallis analysis, in contrast, analyzes ranks which are based on ordinal measurement. The parametric technique deals with the ratio of two variances, while the Kruskal-Wallis technique involves a statistic defined as H. The Kruskal-Wallis technique is a one-way analysis, whereas the parametric technique may include two or more independent variables and their interactions. Null hypothesis: The population distributions from which the five samples were drawn have the same average (or have identical averages). An equivalent statement is to hypothesize that the samples were drawn from a common population with respect to averages.

10.8. Since the sample size exceeds 25, the normal distribution may be used as an adequate approximation to the binomial distribution. Since the significance level is .01, a value of 2.58 is necessary for a significant test. The value 3.21 is significant, and we would reject the null hypothesis. Therefore we conclude that the median difference of the before and after scores in the population is *not* zero.

10.9. It would be undesirable to use the same type of analysis for both dependent variables because the mathematics achievement has interval scale measurement and the handedness data are only nominal scale measurements. Frequencies or proportions would be tested statistically in the handedness data and means in the mathematics achievement data. A chi square test could be used for the handedness data, an analysis of variance or Student's *t* test for the mathematics achievement data. We would conclude that in the population, athletes and nonathletes differ in frequency or proportion of handedness. Assuming that we have been dealing with the null hypothesis that there is no difference in the population proportions of athletes and nonathletes we could be making the error of rejecting a true hypothesis.

10.10. Errors of reasoning or procedure:
   a. A Student's *t* test does not apply to data measured on an ordinal scale.
   b. There is confusion on significance; a test significant at the .01 level is significant at the .05.
   c. Rejecting the null hypothesis would result in concluding that the *population,* not the sample, measures are different.
   d. Since the null hypothesis is rejected, there is no probability of having made a Type II or beta error. The possibility does exist of having made a Type I or alpha error.

CHAPTER 11

11.2. This coefficient is significantly different from zero since Table F indicates that a value of approximately .31 or greater is necessary for a significant test, with 38 degrees of freedom and at the .05 level (two-tailed test). The null hypothesis: The population correlation coefficient between the two variables is zero. Probability statement: The probability that a sample correlation of .413 would occur by chance, if, in fact, the population correlation is zero, is less than .05. We conclude that the population correlation is not zero.

11.4. Null hypothesis: The correlation coefficients of the populations from which the samples were drawn are equal. Probability statement: The probability that the observed difference in sample correlation coefficients would occur by chance, if there is no difference between the population correlation coefficients, is less than .05. We reject the null hypothesis and conclude that there is a difference between the population correlation coefficients. Possible error: Rejection of a true hypothesis (Type I or alpha error). With this amount of information we cannot conclude anything about the .01 level. Probability less than .05 does not indicate whether it is greater or less than .01.

11.5. The Pearson product-moment correlation coefficient requires that both variables possess at least interval scale measurement and that their underlying distributions be continuous, somewhat symmetrical, and homoscedastic. The Spearman rank coefficient does not require interval measurement but only that the scores can be ordered. If the Spearman rank coefficient is used as a substitute for the Pearson product-moment coefficient, the underlying distributions should be continuous and homoscedastic. Both coefficients assume a linear relationship between the two variables being correlated. The scores that actually go into the computation of a Spearman rho are the ranks and not the observed scores.

11.7. The biserial coefficient would most likely apply in this situation. Although dichotomized into pass and not pass, oration performance has underlying continuity. Null hypothesis: The correlation between oration performance and English mastery in the population is zero. An equivalent statement: There is no relationship between oration performance and English mastery in the student population. With a significant statistical test we would reject the null hypothesis and conclude that there is a relationship between these two variables in the population.

11.8. (a) Point biserial, assuming color of eyes to be dichotomy of either blue or brown.
   (b) Pearson-product moment
   (c) Spearman rho
   (d) Biserial

11.9. With sample size of 120 we would interpret the coefficient of .62 as reflecting a relationship (in the population) between reading for comprehension and punctuation skill. Whether this is a low, modest, or high correlation is a relative matter and must be interpreted in the light of other information about the two variables. Possible hypotheses: (1) the population correlation is zero; (2) considering the classes as representing different populations, there exists no difference between pairs of population correlations; (3) since most high school classes contain both boys and girls, there is no difference between the population correlations of boys and girls. The population under study appears to be sophomore English students enrolled in this specific type of high school. A difficulty in sampling arises in that the students of the four classes may not be a random sample of the entire sophomore population of the specific high school. Scheduling of classes or other factors may have introduced a bias.

11.10. The researcher has not selected a very effective predictor because the variance in the distribution of error scores is almost as great as in the criterion distribution. The magnitude of r is small. The s_{est} would be approximately .6 times the standard deviation of the criterion distribution.

11.12. We want to make some decisions about the population characteristics, which are parameters. We draw a sample and compute characteristics of the sample, which are statistics. The statistics reflect the corresponding parameters within the bounds of random sampling fluctuations. We hypothesize about parameters, and the statistics have a certain probability of appearing by chance in light of the hypotheses. It is not necessary to determine the exact probability, only if it is less than or greater than the significance level. We infer from the statistics and the results of hypothesis testing to the parameters and thus make decisions about the population.

CHAPTERS 12 AND 13

The exercises of these two chapters suggest activities such as reading articles, doing a literature search, or in some way working with research reports. Any one exercise may require considerable effort. The reader may want to focus more than one exercise on a single topic.

appendix 2

Tables

TABLE A.   Ordinates and areas of the normal curve (in terms of σ units)

$\frac{x}{\sigma}$	Area	Ordinate	$\frac{x}{\sigma}$	Area	Ordinate	$\frac{x}{\sigma}$	Area	Ordinate
.00	.0000	.3989	.50	.1915	.3521	1.00	.3413	.2420
.01	.0040	.3989	.51	.1950	.3503	1.01	.3438	.2396
.02	.0080	.3989	.52	.1985	.3485	1.02	.3461	.2371
.03	.0120	.3988	.53	.2019	.3467	1.03	.3485	.2347
.04	.0160	.3986	.54	.2054	.3448	1.04	.3508	.2323
.05	.0199	.3984	.55	.2088	.3429	1.05	.3531	.2299
.06	.0239	.3982	.56	.2123	.3410	1.06	.3554	.2275
.07	.0279	.3980	.57	.2157	.3391	1.07	.3577	.2251
.08	.0319	.3977	.58	.2190	.3372	1.08	.3599	.2227
.09	.0359	.3973	.59	.2224	.3352	1.09	.3621	.2203
.10	.0398	.3970	.60	.2257	.3332	1.10	.3643	.2179
.11	.0438	.3965	.61	.2291	.3312	1.11	.3665	.2155
.12	.0478	.3961	.62	.2324	.3292	1.12	.3686	.2131
.13	.0517	.3956	.63	.2357	.3271	1.13	.3708	.2107
.14	.0557	.3951	.64	.2389	.3251	1.14	.3729	.2083
.15	.0596	.3945	.65	.2422	.3230	1.15	.3749	.2059
.16	.0636	.3939	.66	.2454	.3209	1.16	.3770	.2036
.17	.0675	.3932	.67	.2486	.3187	1.17	.3790	.2012
.18	.0714	.3925	.68	.2517	.3166	1.18	.3810	.1989
.19	.0753	.3918	.69	.2549	.3144	1.19	.3830	.1965
.20	.0793	.3910	.70	.2580	.3123	1.20	.3849	.1942
.21	.0832	.3902	.71	.2611	.3101	1.21	.3869	.1919
.22	.0871	.3894	.72	.2642	.3079	1.22	.3888	.1895
.23	.0910	.3885	.73	.2673	.3056	1.23	.3907	.1872
.24	.0948	.3876	.74	.2703	.3034	1.24	.3925	.1849
.25	.0987	.3867	.75	.2734	.3011	1.25	.3944	.1826
.26	.1026	.3857	.76	.2764	.2989	1.26	.3962	.1804
.27	.1064	.3847	.77	.2794	.2966	1.27	.3980	.1781
.28	.1103	.3836	.78	.2823	.2943	1.28	.3997	.1758
.29	.1141	.3825	.79	.2852	.2920	1.29	.4015	.1736
.30	.1179	.3814	.80	.2881	.2897	1.30	.4032	.1714
.31	.1217	.3802	.81	.2910	.2874	1.31	.4049	.1691
.32	.1255	.3790	.82	.2939	.2850	1.32	.4066	.1669
.33	.1293	.3778	.83	.2967	.2827	1.33	.4082	.1647
.34	.1331	.3765	.84	.2995	.2803	1.34	.4099	.1626
.35	.1368	.3752	.85	.3023	.2780	1.35	.4115	.1604
.36	.1406	.3739	.86	.3051	.2756	1.36	.4131	.1582
.37	.1443	.3725	.87	.3078	.2732	1.37	.4147	.1561
.38	.1480	.3712	.88	.3106	.2709	1.38	.4162	.1539
.39	.1517	.3697	.89	.3133	.2685	1.39	.4177	.1518
.40	.1554	.3683	.90	.3159	.2661	1.40	.4192	.1497
.41	.1591	.3668	.91	.3186	.2637	1.41	.4207	.1476
.42	.1628	.3653	.92	.3212	.2613	1.42	.4222	.1456
.43	.1664	.3637	.93	.3238	.2589	1.43	.4236	.1435
.44	.1700	.3621	.94	.3264	.2565	1.44	.4251	.1415
.45	.1736	.3605	.95	.3289	.2541	1.45	.4265	.1394
.46	.1772	.3589	.96	.3315	.2516	1.46	.4279	.1374
.47	.1808	.3572	.97	.3340	.2492	1.47	.4292	.1354
.48	.1844	.3555	.98	.3365	.2468	1.48	.4306	.1334
.49	.1879	.3538	.99	.3389	.2444	1.49	.4319	.1315
.50	.1915	.3521	1.00	.3413	.2420	1.50	.4332	.1295

Source: *Educational Statistics* by J. E. Wert. Copyright 1938 by McGraw-Hill Book Company. Used by permission of McGraw-Hill Book Company.

TABLE A. (continued)

$\frac{x}{\sigma}$	Area	Ordinate	$\frac{x}{\sigma}$	Area	Ordinate	$\frac{x}{\sigma}$	Area	Ordinate
1.50	.4332	.1295	2.00	.4772	.0540	2.50	.4938	.0175
1.51	.4345	.1276	2.01	.4778	.0529	2.51	.4940	.0171
1.52	.4357	.1257	2.02	.4783	.0519	2.52	.4941	.0167
1.53	.4370	.1238	2.03	.4788	.0508	2.53	.4943	.0163
1.54	.4382	.1219	2.04	.4793	.0498	2.54	.4945	.0158
1.55	.4394	.1200	2.05	.4798	.0488	2.55	.4946	.0154
1.56	.4406	.1182	2.06	.4803	.0478	2.56	.4948	.0151
1.57	.4418	.1163	2.07	.4808	.0468	2.57	.4949	.0147
1.58	.4429	.1145	2.08	.4812	.0459	2.58	.4951	.0143
1.59	.4441	.1127	2.09	.4817	.0449	2.59	.4952	.0139
1.60	.4452	.1109	2.10	.4821	.0440	2.60	.4953	.0136
1.61	.4463	.1092	2.11	.4826	.0431	2.61	.4955	.0132
1.62	.4474	.1074	2.12	.4830	.0422	2.62	.4956	.0129
1.63	.4484	.1057	2.13	.4834	.0413	2.63	.4957	.0126
1.64	.4495	.1040	2.14	.4838	.0404	2.64	.4959	.0122
1.65	.4505	.1023	2.15	.4842	.0395	2.65	.4960	.0119
1.66	.4515	.1006	2.16	.4846	.0387	2.66	.4961	.0116
1.67	.4525	.0989	2.17	.4850	.0379	2.67	.4962	.0113
1.68	.4535	.0973	2.18	.4854	.0371	2.68	.4963	.0110
1.69	.4545	.0957	2.19	.4857	.0363	2.69	.4964	.0107
1.70	.4554	.0940	2.20	.4861	.0355	2.70	.4965	.0104
1.71	.4564	.0925	2.21	.4864	.0347	2.71	.4966	.0101
1.72	.4573	.0909	2.22	.4868	.0339	2.72	.4967	.0099
1.73	.4582	.0893	2.23	.4871	.0332	2.73	.4968	.0096
1.74	.4591	.0878	2.24	.4875	.0325	2.74	.4969	.0093
1.75	.4599	.0863	2.25	.4878	.0317	2.75	.4970	.0091
1.76	.4608	.0848	2.26	.4881	.0310	2.76	.4971	.0088
1.77	.4616	.0833	2.27	.4884	.0303	2.77	.4972	.0086
1.78	.4625	.0818	2.28	.4887	.0297	2.78	.4973	.0084
1.79	.4633	.0804	2.29	.4890	.0290	2.79	.4974	.0081
1.80	.4641	.0790	2.30	.4893	.0283	2.80	.4974	.0079
1.81	.4649	.0775	2.31	.4896	.0277	2.81	.4975	.0077
1.82	.4656	.0761	2.32	.4898	.0270	2.82	.4976	.0075
1.83	.4664	.0748	2.33	.4901	.0264	2.83	.4977	.0073
1.84	.4671	.0734	2.34	.4904	.0258	2.84	.4977	.0071
1.85	.4678	.0721	2.35	.4906	.0252	2.85	.4978	.0069
1.86	.4686	.0707	2.36	.4909	.0246	2.86	.4979	.0067
1.87	.4693	.0694	2.37	.4911	.0241	2.87	.4979	.0065
1.88	.4699	.0681	2.38	.4913	.0235	2.88	.4980	.0063
1.89	.4706	.0669	2.39	.4916	.0229	2.89	.4981	.0061
1.90	.4713	.0656	2.40	.4918	.0224	2.90	.4981	.0060
1.91	.4719	.0644	2.41	.4920	.0219	2.91	.4982	.0058
1.92	.4726	.0632	2.42	.4922	.0213	2.92	.4982	.0056
1.93	.4732	.0620	2.43	.4925	.0208	2.93	.4983	.0055
1.94	.4738	.0608	2.44	.4927	.0203	2.94	.4984	.0053
1.95	.4744	.0596	2.45	.4929	.0198	2.95	.4984	.0051
1.96	.4750	.0584	2.46	.4931	.0194	2.96	.4985	.0050
1.97	.4756	.0573	2.47	.4932	.0189	2.97	.4985	.0048
1.98	.4761	.0562	2.48	.4934	.0184	2.98	.4986	.0047
1.99	.4767	.0551	2.49	.4936	.0180	2.99	.4986	.0046
2.00	.4772	.0540	2.50	.4938	.0175	3.00	.4987	.0044

TABLE B.   Critical values of *t*

df	Level of significance for one-tailed test					
	.10	.05	.025	.01	.005	.0005
	Level of significance for two-tailed test					
	.20	.10	.05	.02	.01	.001
1	3.078	6.314	12.706	31.821	63.657	636.619
2	1.886	2.920	4.303	6.965	9.925	31.598
3	1.638	2.353	3.182	4.541	5.841	12.941
4	1.533	2.132	2.776	3.747	4.604	8.610
5	1.476	2.015	2.571	3.365	4.032	6.859
6	1.440	1.943	2.447	3.143	3.707	5.959
7	1.415	1.895	2.365	2.998	3.499	5.405
8	1.397	1.860	2.306	2.896	3.355	5.041
9	1.383	1.833	2.262	2.821	3.250	4.781
10	1.372	1.812	2.228	2.764	3.169	4.587
11	1.363	1.796	2.201	2.718	3.106	4.437
12	1.356	1.782	2.179	2.681	3.055	4.318
13	1.350	1.771	2.160	2.650	3.012	4.221
14	1.345	1.761	2.145	2.624	2.977	4.140
15	1.341	1.753	2.131	2.602	2.947	4.073
16	1.337	1.746	2.120	2.583	2.921	4.015
17	1.333	1.740	2.110	2.567	2.898	3.965
18	1.330	1.734	2.101	2.552	2.878	3.922
19	1.328	1.729	2.093	2.539	2.861	3.883
20	1.325	1.725	2.086	2.528	2.845	3.850
21	1.323	1.721	2.080	2.518	2.831	3.819
22	1.321	1.717	2.074	2.508	2.819	3.792
23	1.319	1.714	2.069	2.500	2.807	3.767
24	1.318	1.711	2.064	2.492	2.797	3.745
25	1.316	1.708	2.060	2.485	2.787	3.725
26	1.315	1.706	2.056	2.479	2.779	3.707
27	1.314	1.703	2.052	2.473	2.771	3.690
28	1.313	1.701	2.048	2.467	2.763	3.674
29	1.311	1.699	2.045	2.462	2.756	3.659
30	1.310	1.697	2.042	2.457	2.750	3.646
40	1.303	1.684	2.021	2.423	2.704	3.551
60	1.296	1.671	2.000	2.390	2.660	3.460
120	1.289	1.658	1.980	2.358	2.617	3.373
∞	1.282	1.645	1.960	2.326	2.576	3.291

Source: Abridged from Table III of R. A. Fisher and F. Yates, *Statistical Tables for Biological, Agricultural, and Medical Research,* 6th edition, published by Longman Group, Ltd., London, 1974 (previously published by Oliver & Boyd, Edinburgh), and by permission of the authors and publishers.

TABLE C.   Table of probabilities associated with values as small as observed values of x in the binomial test

Given in the body of this table are one-tailed probabilities under H_0 for the binomial test when $P = Q = \frac{1}{2}$. To save space, decimal points are omitted in the p's.

N\x	0	1	2	3	4	5	6	7	8	9	10	11	12	13	14	15
5	031	188	500	812	969	†										
6	016	109	344	656	891	984	†									
7	008	062	227	500	773	938	992	†								
8	004	035	145	363	637	855	965	996	†							
9	002	020	090	254	500	746	910	980	998	†						
10	001	011	055	172	377	623	828	945	989	999	†					
11		006	033	113	274	500	726	887	967	994	†	†				
12		003	019	073	194	387	613	806	927	981	997	†	†			
13		002	011	046	133	291	500	709	867	954	989	998	†	†		
14		001	006	029	090	212	395	605	788	910	971	994	999	†	†	†
15			004	018	059	151	304	500	696	849	941	982	996	†	†	†
16			002	011	038	105	227	402	598	773	895	962	989	998	†	†
17			001	006	025	072	166	315	500	685	834	928	975	994	999	†
18			001	004	015	048	119	240	407	593	760	881	952	985	996	999
19				002	010	032	084	180	324	500	676	820	916	968	990	998
20				001	006	021	058	132	252	412	588	748	868	942	979	994
21				001	004	013	039	095	192	332	500	668	808	905	961	987
22					002	008	026	067	143	262	416	584	738	857	933	974
23					001	005	017	047	105	202	339	500	661	798	895	953
24					001	003	011	032	076	154	271	419	581	729	846	924
25						002	007	022	054	115	212	345	500	655	788	885

Source: Adapted from Table IV B of *Statistical Inference* by Helen M. Walker and Joseph Lev. Copyright 1953 by Holt ,Rinehart and Winston, Inc. Adapted and reprinted by permission of Holt, Rinehart and Winston, Inc.
    † 1.0 or approximately 1.0.

TABLE D. Critical values of F

5 percent (lightface type) and 1 percent (boldface type) points for the distribution of F.

Degrees of freedom for lesser mean square	Degrees of freedom for greater mean square																							
	1	2	3	4	5	6	7	8	9	10	11	12	14	16	20	24	30	40	50	75	100	200	500	∞
1	161 **4052**	200 **4999**	216 **5403**	225 **5625**	230 **5764**	234 **5859**	237 **5928**	239 **5981**	241 **6022**	242 **6056**	243 **6082**	244 **6106**	245 **6142**	246 **6169**	248 **6208**	249 **6234**	250 **6258**	251 **6286**	252 **6302**	253 **6323**	253 **6334**	254 **6352**	254 **6361**	254 **6366**
2	18.51 **98.49**	19.00 **99.01**	19.16 **99.17**	19.25 **99.25**	19.30 **99.30**	19.33 **99.33**	19.36 **99.34**	19.37 **99.36**	19.38 **99.38**	19.39 **99.40**	19.40 **99.41**	19.41 **99.42**	19.42 **99.43**	19.43 **99.44**	19.44 **99.45**	19.45 **99.46**	19.46 **99.47**	19.47 **99.48**	19.47 **99.48**	19.48 **99.49**	19.49 **99.49**	19.49 **99.49**	19.50 **99.50**	19.50 **99.50**
3	10.13 **34.12**	9.55 **30.81**	9.28 **29.46**	9.12 **28.71**	9.01 **28.24**	8.94 **27.91**	8.88 **27.67**	8.84 **27.49**	8.81 **27.34**	8.78 **27.23**	8.76 **27.13**	8.74 **27.05**	8.71 **26.92**	8.69 **26.83**	8.66 **26.69**	8.64 **26.60**	8.62 **26.50**	8.60 **26.41**	8.58 **26.35**	8.57 **26.27**	8.56 **26.23**	8.54 **26.18**	8.54 **26.14**	8.53 **26.12**
4	7.71 **21.20**	6.94 **18.00**	6.59 **16.69**	6.39 **15.98**	6.26 **15.52**	6.16 **15.21**	6.09 **14.98**	6.04 **14.80**	6.00 **14.66**	5.96 **14.54**	5.93 **14.45**	5.91 **14.37**	5.87 **14.24**	5.84 **14.15**	5.80 **14.02**	5.77 **13.93**	5.74 **13.83**	5.71 **13.74**	5.70 **13.69**	5.68 **13.61**	5.66 **13.57**	5.65 **13.52**	5.64 **13.48**	5.63 **13.46**
5	6.61 **16.26**	5.79 **13.27**	5.41 **12.06**	5.19 **11.39**	5.05 **10.97**	4.95 **10.67**	4.88 **10.45**	4.82 **10.27**	4.78 **10.15**	4.74 **10.05**	4.70 **9.96**	4.68 **9.89**	4.64 **9.77**	4.60 **9.68**	4.56 **9.55**	4.53 **9.47**	4.50 **9.38**	4.46 **9.29**	4.44 **9.24**	4.42 **9.17**	4.40 **9.13**	4.38 **9.07**	4.37 **9.04**	4.36 **9.02**
6	5.99 **13.74**	5.14 **10.92**	4.76 **9.78**	4.53 **9.15**	4.39 **8.75**	4.28 **8.47**	4.21 **8.26**	4.15 **8.10**	4.10 **7.98**	4.06 **7.87**	4.03 **7.79**	4.00 **7.72**	3.96 **7.60**	3.92 **7.52**	3.87 **7.39**	3.84 **7.31**	3.81 **7.23**	3.77 **7.14**	3.75 **7.09**	3.72 **7.02**	3.71 **6.99**	3.69 **6.94**	3.68 **6.90**	3.67 **6.88**
7	5.59 **12.25**	4.74 **9.55**	4.35 **8.45**	4.12 **7.85**	3.97 **7.46**	3.87 **7.19**	3.79 **7.00**	3.73 **6.84**	3.68 **6.71**	3.63 **6.62**	3.60 **6.54**	3.57 **6.47**	3.52 **6.35**	3.49 **6.27**	3.44 **6.15**	3.41 **6.07**	3.38 **5.98**	3.34 **5.90**	3.32 **5.85**	3.29 **5.78**	3.28 **5.75**	3.25 **5.70**	3.24 **5.67**	3.23 **5.65**
8	5.32 **11.26**	4.46 **8.65**	4.07 **7.59**	3.84 **7.01**	3.69 **6.63**	3.58 **6.37**	3.50 **6.19**	3.44 **6.03**	3.39 **5.91**	3.34 **5.82**	3.31 **5.74**	3.28 **5.67**	3.23 **5.56**	3.20 **5.48**	3.15 **5.36**	3.12 **5.28**	3.08 **5.20**	3.05 **5.11**	3.03 **5.06**	3.00 **5.00**	2.98 **4.96**	2.96 **4.91**	2.94 **4.88**	2.93 **4.86**
9	5.12 **10.56**	4.26 **8.02**	3.86 **6.99**	3.63 **6.42**	3.48 **6.06**	3.37 **5.80**	3.29 **5.62**	3.23 **5.47**	3.18 **5.35**	3.13 **5.26**	3.10 **5.18**	3.07 **5.11**	3.02 **5.00**	2.98 **4.92**	2.93 **4.80**	2.90 **4.73**	2.86 **4.64**	2.82 **4.56**	2.80 **4.51**	2.77 **4.45**	2.76 **4.41**	2.73 **4.36**	2.72 **4.33**	2.71 **4.31**
10	4.96 **10.04**	4.10 **7.56**	3.71 **6.55**	3.48 **5.99**	3.33 **5.64**	3.22 **5.39**	3.14 **5.21**	3.07 **5.06**	3.02 **4.95**	2.97 **4.85**	2.94 **4.78**	2.91 **4.71**	2.86 **4.60**	2.82 **4.52**	2.77 **4.41**	2.74 **4.33**	2.70 **4.25**	2.67 **4.17**	2.64 **4.12**	2.61 **4.05**	2.59 **4.01**	2.56 **3.96**	2.55 **3.93**	2.54 **3.91**
11	4.84 **9.65**	3.98 **7.20**	3.59 **6.22**	3.36 **5.67**	3.20 **5.32**	3.09 **5.07**	3.01 **4.88**	2.95 **4.74**	2.90 **4.63**	2.86 **4.54**	2.82 **4.46**	2.79 **4.40**	2.74 **4.29**	2.70 **4.21**	2.65 **4.10**	2.61 **4.02**	2.57 **3.94**	2.53 **3.86**	2.50 **3.80**	2.47 **3.74**	2.45 **3.70**	2.42 **3.66**	2.41 **3.62**	2.40 **3.60**
12	4.75 **9.33**	3.88 **6.93**	3.49 **5.95**	3.26 **5.41**	3.11 **5.06**	3.00 **4.82**	2.92 **4.65**	2.85 **4.50**	2.80 **4.39**	2.76 **4.30**	2.72 **4.22**	2.69 **4.16**	2.64 **4.05**	2.60 **3.98**	2.54 **3.86**	2.50 **3.78**	2.46 **3.70**	2.42 **3.61**	2.40 **3.56**	2.36 **3.49**	2.35 **3.46**	2.32 **3.41**	2.31 **3.38**	2.30 **3.36**
13	4.67 **9.07**	3.80 **6.70**	3.41 **5.74**	3.18 **5.20**	3.02 **4.86**	2.92 **4.62**	2.84 **4.44**	2.77 **4.30**	2.72 **4.19**	2.67 **4.10**	2.64 **4.02**	2.60 **3.96**	2.55 **3.85**	2.51 **3.78**	2.46 **3.67**	2.42 **3.59**	2.38 **3.51**	2.34 **3.42**	2.32 **3.37**	2.28 **3.30**	2.26 **3.27**	2.24 **3.21**	2.22 **3.18**	2.21 **3.16**

df																								
14	4.60 / **8.86**	3.74 / **6.51**	3.34 / **5.56**	3.11 / **5.03**	2.96 / **4.69**	2.85 / **4.46**	2.77 / **4.28**	2.70 / **4.14**	2.65 / **4.03**	2.60 / **3.94**	2.56 / **3.86**	2.53 / **3.80**	2.48 / **3.70**	2.44 / **3.62**	2.39 / **3.51**	2.35 / **3.43**	2.31 / **3.34**	2.27 / **3.26**	2.24 / **3.21**	2.21 / **3.14**	2.19 / **3.11**	2.16 / **3.06**	2.14 / **3.02**	2.13 / **3.00**
15	4.54 / **8.68**	3.68 / **6.36**	3.29 / **5.42**	3.06 / **4.89**	2.90 / **4.56**	2.79 / **4.32**	2.70 / **4.14**	2.64 / **4.00**	2.59 / **3.89**	2.55 / **3.80**	2.51 / **3.73**	2.48 / **3.67**	2.43 / **3.56**	2.39 / **3.48**	2.33 / **3.36**	2.29 / **3.29**	2.25 / **3.20**	2.21 / **3.12**	2.18 / **3.07**	2.15 / **3.00**	2.12 / **2.97**	2.10 / **2.92**	2.08 / **2.89**	2.07 / **2.87**
16	4.49 / **8.53**	3.63 / **6.23**	3.24 / **5.29**	3.01 / **4.77**	2.85 / **4.44**	2.74 / **4.20**	2.66 / **4.03**	2.59 / **3.89**	2.54 / **3.78**	2.49 / **3.69**	2.45 / **3.61**	2.42 / **3.55**	2.37 / **3.45**	2.33 / **3.37**	2.28 / **3.25**	2.24 / **3.18**	2.20 / **3.10**	2.16 / **3.01**	2.13 / **2.96**	2.09 / **2.89**	2.07 / **2.86**	2.04 / **2.80**	2.02 / **2.77**	2.01 / **2.75**
17	4.45 / **8.40**	3.59 / **6.11**	3.20 / **5.18**	2.96 / **4.67**	2.81 / **4.34**	2.70 / **4.10**	2.62 / **3.93**	2.55 / **3.79**	2.50 / **3.68**	2.45 / **3.59**	2.41 / **3.52**	2.38 / **3.45**	2.33 / **3.35**	2.29 / **3.27**	2.23 / **3.16**	2.19 / **3.08**	2.15 / **3.00**	2.11 / **2.92**	2.08 / **2.86**	2.04 / **2.79**	2.02 / **2.76**	1.99 / **2.70**	1.97 / **2.67**	1.96 / **2.65**
18	4.41 / **8.28**	3.55 / **6.01**	3.16 / **5.09**	2.93 / **4.58**	2.77 / **4.25**	2.66 / **4.01**	2.58 / **3.85**	2.51 / **3.71**	2.46 / **3.60**	2.41 / **3.51**	2.37 / **3.44**	2.34 / **3.37**	2.29 / **3.27**	2.25 / **3.19**	2.19 / **3.07**	2.15 / **3.00**	2.11 / **2.91**	2.07 / **2.83**	2.04 / **2.78**	2.00 / **2.71**	1.98 / **2.68**	1.95 / **2.62**	1.93 / **2.59**	1.92 / **2.57**
19	4.38 / **8.18**	3.52 / **5.93**	3.13 / **5.01**	2.90 / **4.50**	2.74 / **4.17**	2.63 / **3.94**	2.55 / **3.77**	2.48 / **3.63**	2.43 / **3.52**	2.38 / **3.43**	2.34 / **3.36**	2.31 / **3.30**	2.26 / **3.19**	2.21 / **3.12**	2.15 / **3.00**	2.11 / **2.92**	2.07 / **2.84**	2.02 / **2.76**	2.00 / **2.70**	1.96 / **2.63**	1.94 / **2.60**	1.91 / **2.54**	1.90 / **2.51**	1.88 / **2.49**
20	4.35 / **8.10**	3.49 / **5.85**	3.10 / **4.94**	2.87 / **4.43**	2.71 / **4.10**	2.60 / **3.87**	2.52 / **3.71**	2.45 / **3.56**	2.40 / **3.45**	2.35 / **3.37**	2.31 / **3.30**	2.28 / **3.23**	2.23 / **3.13**	2.18 / **3.05**	2.12 / **2.94**	2.08 / **2.86**	2.04 / **2.77**	1.99 / **2.69**	1.96 / **2.63**	1.92 / **2.56**	1.90 / **2.53**	1.87 / **2.47**	1.85 / **2.44**	1.84 / **2.42**
21	4.32 / **8.02**	3.47 / **5.78**	3.07 / **4.87**	2.84 / **4.37**	2.68 / **4.04**	2.57 / **3.81**	2.49 / **3.65**	2.42 / **3.51**	2.37 / **3.40**	2.32 / **3.31**	2.28 / **3.24**	2.25 / **3.17**	2.20 / **3.07**	2.15 / **2.99**	2.09 / **2.88**	2.05 / **2.80**	2.00 / **2.72**	1.96 / **2.63**	1.93 / **2.58**	1.89 / **2.51**	1.87 / **2.47**	1.84 / **2.42**	1.82 / **2.38**	1.81 / **2.36**
22	4.30 / **7.94**	3.44 / **5.72**	3.05 / **4.82**	2.82 / **4.31**	2.66 / **3.99**	2.55 / **3.76**	2.47 / **3.59**	2.40 / **3.45**	2.35 / **3.35**	2.30 / **3.26**	2.26 / **3.18**	2.23 / **3.12**	2.18 / **3.02**	2.13 / **2.94**	2.07 / **2.83**	2.03 / **2.75**	1.98 / **2.67**	1.93 / **2.58**	1.91 / **2.53**	1.87 / **2.46**	1.84 / **2.42**	1.81 / **2.37**	1.80 / **2.33**	1.78 / **2.31**
23	4.28 / **7.88**	3.42 / **5.66**	3.03 / **4.76**	2.80 / **4.26**	2.64 / **3.94**	2.53 / **3.71**	2.45 / **3.54**	2.38 / **3.41**	2.32 / **3.30**	2.28 / **3.21**	2.24 / **3.14**	2.20 / **3.07**	2.14 / **2.97**	2.10 / **2.89**	2.04 / **2.78**	2.00 / **2.70**	1.96 / **2.62**	1.91 / **2.53**	1.88 / **2.48**	1.84 / **2.41**	1.82 / **2.37**	1.79 / **2.32**	1.77 / **2.28**	1.76 / **2.26**
24	4.26 / **7.82**	3.40 / **5.61**	3.01 / **4.72**	2.78 / **4.22**	2.62 / **3.90**	2.51 / **3.67**	2.43 / **3.50**	2.36 / **3.36**	2.30 / **3.25**	2.26 / **3.17**	2.22 / **3.09**	2.18 / **3.03**	2.13 / **2.93**	2.09 / **2.85**	2.02 / **2.74**	1.98 / **2.66**	1.94 / **2.58**	1.89 / **2.49**	1.86 / **2.44**	1.82 / **2.36**	1.80 / **2.33**	1.76 / **2.27**	1.74 / **2.23**	1.73 / **2.21**
25	4.24 / **7.77**	3.38 / **5.57**	2.99 / **4.68**	2.76 / **4.18**	2.60 / **3.86**	2.49 / **3.63**	2.41 / **3.46**	2.34 / **3.32**	2.28 / **3.21**	2.24 / **3.13**	2.20 / **3.05**	2.16 / **2.99**	2.11 / **2.89**	2.06 / **2.81**	2.00 / **2.70**	1.96 / **2.62**	1.92 / **2.54**	1.87 / **2.45**	1.84 / **2.40**	1.80 / **2.32**	1.77 / **2.29**	1.74 / **2.23**	1.72 / **2.19**	1.71 / **2.17**
26	4.22 / **7.72**	3.37 / **5.53**	2.98 / **4.64**	2.74 / **4.14**	2.59 / **3.82**	2.47 / **3.59**	2.39 / **3.42**	2.32 / **3.29**	2.27 / **3.17**	2.22 / **3.09**	2.18 / **3.02**	2.15 / **2.96**	2.10 / **2.86**	2.05 / **2.77**	1.99 / **2.66**	1.95 / **2.58**	1.90 / **2.50**	1.85 / **2.41**	1.82 / **2.36**	1.78 / **2.28**	1.76 / **2.25**	1.72 / **2.19**	1.70 / **2.15**	1.69 / **2.13**
27	4.21 / **7.68**	3.35 / **5.49**	2.96 / **4.60**	2.73 / **4.11**	2.57 / **3.79**	2.46 / **3.56**	2.37 / **3.39**	2.30 / **3.26**	2.25 / **3.14**	2.20 / **3.06**	2.16 / **2.98**	2.13 / **2.93**	2.08 / **2.83**	2.03 / **2.74**	1.97 / **2.63**	1.93 / **2.55**	1.88 / **2.47**	1.84 / **2.38**	1.80 / **2.33**	1.76 / **2.25**	1.74 / **2.21**	1.71 / **2.16**	1.68 / **2.12**	1.67 / **2.10**
28	4.20 / **7.64**	3.34 / **5.45**	2.95 / **4.57**	2.71 / **4.07**	2.56 / **3.76**	2.44 / **3.53**	2.36 / **3.36**	2.29 / **3.23**	2.24 / **3.11**	2.19 / **3.03**	2.15 / **2.95**	2.12 / **2.90**	2.06 / **2.80**	2.02 / **2.71**	1.96 / **2.60**	1.91 / **2.52**	1.87 / **2.44**	1.81 / **2.35**	1.78 / **2.30**	1.75 / **2.22**	1.72 / **2.18**	1.69 / **2.13**	1.67 / **2.09**	1.65 / **2.06**
29	4.18 / **7.60**	3.33 / **5.42**	2.93 / **4.54**	2.70 / **4.04**	2.54 / **3.73**	2.43 / **3.50**	2.35 / **3.33**	2.28 / **3.20**	2.22 / **3.08**	2.18 / **3.00**	2.14 / **2.92**	2.10 / **2.87**	2.05 / **2.77**	2.00 / **2.68**	1.94 / **2.57**	1.90 / **2.49**	1.85 / **2.41**	1.80 / **2.32**	1.77 / **2.27**	1.73 / **2.19**	1.71 / **2.15**	1.68 / **2.10**	1.65 / **2.06**	1.64 / **2.03**

Table D continued next page

Source: Reprinted by permission from *Statistical Methods*, 6th Edition, by George W. Snedecor and W. G. Cochran, © 1967 by the Iowa State University Press, Ames, Iowa U.S.A.

TABLE D (continued)

Degrees of freedom for lesser mean square	Degrees of freedom for greater mean square																							
	1	2	3	4	5	6	7	8	9	10	11	12	14	16	20	24	30	40	50	75	100	200	500	∞
30	4.17 7.56	3.32 5.39	2.92 4.51	2.69 4.02	2.53 3.70	2.42 3.47	2.34 3.30	2.27 3.17	2.21 3.06	2.16 2.98	2.12 2.90	2.09 2.84	2.04 2.74	1.99 2.66	1.93 2.55	1.89 2.47	1.84 2.38	1.79 2.29	1.76 2.24	1.72 2.16	1.69 2.13	1.66 2.07	1.64 2.03	1.62 2.01
32	4.15 7.50	3.30 5.34	2.90 4.46	2.67 3.97	2.51 3.66	2.40 3.42	2.32 3.25	2.25 3.12	2.19 3.01	2.14 2.94	2.10 2.86	2.07 2.80	2.02 2.70	1.97 2.62	1.91 2.51	1.86 2.42	1.82 2.34	1.76 2.25	1.74 2.20	1.69 2.12	1.67 2.08	1.64 2.02	1.61 1.98	1.59 1.96
34	4.13 7.44	3.28 5.29	2.88 4.42	2.65 3.93	2.49 3.61	2.38 3.38	2.30 3.21	2.23 3.08	2.17 2.97	2.12 2.89	2.08 2.82	2.05 2.76	2.00 2.66	1.95 2.58	1.89 2.47	1.84 2.38	1.80 2.30	1.74 2.21	1.71 2.15	1.67 2.04	1.64 2.04	1.61 1.98	1.59 1.94	1.57 1.91
36	4.11 7.39	3.26 5.25	2.86 4.38	2.63 3.89	2.48 3.58	2.36 3.35	2.28 3.18	2.21 3.04	2.15 2.94	2.10 2.86	2.06 2.78	2.03 2.72	1.98 2.62	1.93 2.54	1.87 2.43	1.82 2.35	1.78 2.26	1.72 2.17	1.69 2.12	1.65 2.04	1.62 2.00	1.59 1.94	1.56 1.90	1.55 1.87
38	4.10 7.35	3.25 5.21	2.85 4.34	2.62 3.86	2.46 3.54	2.35 3.32	2.26 3.15	2.19 3.02	2.14 2.91	2.09 2.82	2.05 2.75	2.02 2.69	1.96 2.59	1.92 2.51	1.85 2.40	1.80 2.32	1.76 2.22	1.71 2.14	1.67 2.08	1.63 2.00	1.60 1.97	1.57 1.90	1.54 1.86	1.53 1.84
40	4.08 7.31	3.23 5.18	2.84 4.31	2.61 3.83	2.45 3.51	2.34 3.29	2.25 3.12	2.18 2.99	2.12 2.88	2.07 2.80	2.04 2.73	2.00 2.66	1.95 2.56	1.90 2.49	1.84 2.37	1.79 2.29	1.74 2.20	1.69 2.11	1.66 2.05	1.61 1.97	1.59 1.94	1.55 1.88	1.53 1.84	1.51 1.81
42	4.07 7.27	3.22 5.15	2.83 4.29	2.59 3.80	2.44 3.49	2.32 3.26	2.24 3.10	2.17 2.96	2.11 2.86	2.06 2.77	2.02 2.70	1.99 2.64	1.94 2.54	1.89 2.46	1.82 2.35	1.78 2.26	1.73 2.17	1.68 2.08	1.64 2.02	1.60 1.94	1.57 1.91	1.54 1.85	1.51 1.80	1.49 1.78
44	4.06 7.24	3.21 5.12	2.82 4.26	2.58 3.78	2.43 3.46	2.31 3.24	2.23 3.07	2.16 2.94	2.10 2.84	2.05 2.75	2.01 2.68	1.98 2.62	1.92 2.52	1.88 2.44	1.81 2.32	1.76 2.24	1.72 2.15	1.66 2.06	1.63 2.00	1.58 1.92	1.56 1.88	1.52 1.82	1.50 1.78	1.48 1.75
46	4.05 7.21	3.20 5.10	2.81 4.24	2.57 3.76	2.42 3.44	2.30 3.22	2.22 3.05	2.14 2.92	2.09 2.82	2.04 2.73	2.00 2.66	1.97 2.60	1.91 2.50	1.87 2.42	1.80 2.30	1.75 2.22	1.71 2.13	1.65 2.04	1.62 1.98	1.57 1.90	1.54 1.86	1.51 1.80	1.48 1.76	1.46 1.72
48	4.04 7.19	3.19 5.08	2.80 4.22	2.56 3.74	2.41 3.42	2.30 3.20	2.21 3.04	2.14 2.90	2.08 2.80	2.03 2.71	1.99 2.64	1.96 2.58	1.90 2.48	1.86 2.40	1.79 2.28	1.74 2.20	1.70 2.11	1.64 2.02	1.61 1.96	1.56 1.88	1.53 1.84	1.50 1.78	1.47 1.73	1.45 1.70
50	4.03 7.17	3.18 5.06	2.79 4.20	2.56 3.72	2.40 3.41	2.29 3.18	2.20 3.02	2.13 2.88	2.07 2.78	2.02 2.70	1.98 2.62	1.95 2.56	1.90 2.46	1.85 2.39	1.78 2.26	1.74 2.18	1.69 2.10	1.63 2.00	1.60 1.94	1.55 1.86	1.52 1.82	1.48 1.76	1.46 1.71	1.44 1.68
55	4.02 7.12	3.17 5.01	2.78 4.16	2.54 3.68	2.38 3.37	2.27 3.15	2.18 2.98	2.11 2.85	2.05 2.75	2.00 2.66	1.97 2.59	1.93 2.53	1.88 2.43	1.83 2.35	1.76 2.23	1.72 2.15	1.67 2.06	1.61 1.96	1.58 1.90	1.52 1.82	1.50 1.78	1.46 1.71	1.43 1.66	1.41 1.64
60	4.00 7.08	3.15 4.98	2.76 4.13	2.52 3.65	2.37 3.34	2.25 3.12	2.17 2.95	2.10 2.82	2.04 2.72	1.99 2.63	1.95 2.56	1.92 2.50	1.86 2.40	1.81 2.32	1.75 2.20	1.70 2.12	1.65 2.03	1.59 1.93	1.56 1.87	1.50 1.79	1.48 1.74	1.44 1.68	1.41 1.63	1.39 1.60
65	3.99 7.04	3.14 4.95	2.75 4.10	2.51 3.62	2.36 3.31	2.24 3.09	2.15 2.93	2.08 2.79	2.02 2.70	1.98 2.61	1.94 2.54	1.90 2.47	1.85 2.37	1.80 2.30	1.73 2.18	1.68 2.09	1.63 2.00	1.57 1.90	1.54 1.84	1.49 1.76	1.46 1.71	1.42 1.64	1.39 1.60	1.37 1.56

df																								
70	1.35/1.53	1.37/1.56	1.40/1.62	1.45/1.69	1.47/1.74	1.53/1.82	1.56/1.88	1.62/1.98	1.67/2.07	1.72/2.15	1.79/2.28	1.84/2.35	1.89/2.45	1.93/2.51	1.97/2.59	2.01/2.67	2.07/2.77	2.14/2.91	2.23/3.07	2.35/3.29	2.50/3.60	2.74/4.08	3.13/4.92	3.98/7.01
80	1.32/1.49	1.35/1.52	1.38/1.57	1.42/1.65	1.45/1.70	1.51/1.78	1.54/1.84	1.60/1.94	1.65/2.03	1.70/2.11	1.77/2.24	1.82/2.32	1.88/2.41	1.91/2.48	1.95/2.55	1.99/2.64	2.05/2.74	2.12/2.87	2.21/3.04	2.33/3.25	2.48/3.56	2.72/4.04	3.11/4.88	3.96/6.96
100	1.28/1.43	1.30/1.46	1.34/1.51	1.39/1.59	1.42/1.64	1.48/1.73	1.51/1.79	1.57/1.89	1.63/1.98	1.68/2.06	1.75/2.19	1.79/2.26	1.85/2.36	1.88/2.43	1.92/2.51	1.97/2.59	2.03/2.69	2.10/2.82	2.19/2.99	2.30/3.20	2.46/3.51	2.70/3.98	3.09/4.82	3.94/6.90
125	1.25/1.37	1.27/1.40	1.31/1.46	1.36/1.54	1.39/1.59	1.45/1.68	1.49/1.75	1.55/1.85	1.60/1.94	1.65/2.03	1.72/2.15	1.77/2.23	1.83/2.33	1.86/2.40	1.90/2.47	1.95/2.56	2.01/2.65	2.08/2.79	2.17/2.95	2.29/3.17	2.44/3.47	2.68/3.94	3.07/4.78	3.92/6.84
150	1.22/1.33	1.25/1.37	1.29/1.43	1.34/1.51	1.37/1.56	1.44/1.66	1.47/1.72	1.54/1.83	1.59/1.91	1.64/2.00	1.71/2.12	1.76/2.20	1.82/2.30	1.85/2.37	1.89/2.44	1.94/2.53	2.00/2.62	2.07/2.76	2.16/2.92	2.27/3.14	2.43/3.44	2.67/3.91	3.06/4.75	3.91/6.81
200	1.19/1.28	1.22/1.33	1.26/1.39	1.32/1.48	1.35/1.53	1.42/1.62	1.45/1.69	1.52/1.79	1.57/1.88	1.62/1.97	1.69/2.09	1.74/2.17	1.80/2.28	1.83/2.34	1.87/2.41	1.92/2.50	1.98/2.60	2.05/2.73	2.14/2.90	2.26/3.11	2.41/3.41	2.65/3.88	3.04/4.71	3.89/6.76
400	1.13/1.19	1.16/1.24	1.22/1.32	1.28/1.42	1.32/1.47	1.38/1.57	1.42/1.64	1.49/1.74	1.54/1.84	1.60/1.92	1.67/2.04	1.72/2.12	1.78/2.23	1.81/2.29	1.85/2.37	1.90/2.46	1.96/2.55	2.03/2.69	2.12/2.85	2.23/3.06	2.39/3.36	2.62/3.83	3.02/4.66	3.86/6.70
1000	1.08/1.11	1.13/1.19	1.19/1.28	1.24/1.36	1.28/1.41	1.36/1.54	1.41/1.61	1.47/1.71	1.53/1.81	1.58/1.89	1.65/2.01	1.70/2.09	1.76/2.20	1.80/2.26	1.84/2.34	1.89/2.43	1.95/2.53	2.02/2.66	2.10/2.82	2.22/3.04	2.38/3.34	2.61/3.80	3.00/4.62	3.85/6.66
∞	1.00/1.00	1.11/1.15	1.17/1.25	1.24/1.36	1.28/1.41	1.35/1.52	1.40/1.59	1.46/1.69	1.52/1.79	1.57/1.87	1.64/1.99	1.69/2.07	1.75/2.18	1.79/2.24	1.83/2.32	1.88/2.41	1.94/2.51	2.01/2.64	2.09/2.80	2.21/3.02	2.37/3.32	2.60/3.78	2.99/4.60	3.84/6.64

TABLE E. Critical values of chi square

df						Probability under H_0 that $\chi^2 \geq$ chi square								
	.99	.98	.95	.90	.80	.70	.50	.30	.20	.10	.05	.02	.01	.001
1	.00016	.00063	.0039	.016	.064	.15	.46	1.07	1.64	2.71	3.84	5.41	6.64	10.83
2	.02	.04	.10	.21	.45	.71	1.39	2.41	3.22	4.60	5.99	7.82	9.21	13.82
3	.12	.18	.35	.58	1.00	1.42	2.37	3.66	4.64	6.25	7.82	9.84	11.34	16.27
4	.30	.43	.71	1.06	1.65	2.20	3.36	4.88	5.99	7.78	9.49	11.67	13.28	18.46
5	.55	.75	1.14	1.61	2.34	3.00	4.35	6.06	7.29	9.24	11.07	13.39	15.09	20.52
6	.87	1.13	1.64	2.20	3.07	3.83	5.35	7.23	8.56	10.64	12.59	15.03	16.81	22.46
7	1.24	1.56	2.17	2.83	3.82	4.67	6.35	8.38	9.80	12.02	14.07	16.62	18.48	24.32
8	1.65	2.03	2.73	3.49	4.59	5.53	7.34	9.52	11.03	13.36	15.51	18.17	20.09	26.12
9	2.09	2.53	3.32	4.17	5.38	6.39	8.34	10.66	12.24	14.68	16.92	19.68	21.67	27.88
10	2.56	3.06	3.94	4.86	6.18	7.27	9.34	11.78	13.44	15.99	18.31	21.16	23.21	29.59
11	3.05	3.61	4.58	5.58	6.99	8.15	10.34	12.90	14.63	17.28	19.68	22.62	24.72	31.26
12	3.57	4.18	5.23	6.30	7.81	9.03	11.34	14.01	15.81	18.55	21.03	24.05	26.22	32.91
13	4.11	4.76	5.89	7.04	8.63	9.93	12.34	15.12	16.98	19.81	22.36	25.47	27.69	34.53
14	4.66	5.37	6.57	7.79	9.47	10.82	13.34	15.22	18.15	21.06	23.68	25.87	29.14	36.12
15	5.23	5.98	7.26	8.55	10.31	11.72	14.34	17.32	19.31	22.31	25.00	28.26	30.58	37.70
16	5.81	6.61	7.96	9.31	11.15	12.62	15.34	18.42	20.46	23.54	26.30	29.63	32.00	39.29
17	6.41	7.26	8.67	10.08	12.00	13.53	16.34	19.51	21.62	24.77	27.59	31.00	33.41	40.75
18	7.02	7.91	9.39	10.86	12.86	14.44	17.34	20.60	22.76	25.99	28.87	32.35	34.80	42.31
19	7.63	8.57	10.12	11.65	13.72	15.35	18.34	21.69	23.90	27.20	30.14	33.69	36.19	43.82
20	8.26	9.24	10.85	12.44	14.58	16.27	19.34	22.78	25.04	28.41	31.41	35.02	37.57	45.32
21	8.90	9.92	11.59	13.24	15.44	17.18	20.34	23.86	26.17	29.62	32.67	36.34	38.93	46.80
22	9.54	10.60	12.34	14.04	16.31	18.10	21.24	24.94	27.30	30.81	33.92	37.66	40.29	48.27
23	10.20	11.29	13.09	14.85	17.19	19.02	22.34	26.02	28.43	32.01	35.17	38.97	41.64	49.73
24	10.86	11.99	13.85	15.66	18.06	19.94	23.34	27.10	29.55	33.20	36.42	40.27	42.98	51.18
25	11.52	12.70	14.61	16.47	18.94	20.87	24.34	28.17	30.68	34.38	37.65	41.57	44.31	52.62
26	12.20	13.41	15.38	17.29	19.82	21.79	25.34	29.25	31.80	35.56	38.88	42.86	45.64	54.05
27	12.88	14.12	16.15	18.11	20.70	22.72	26.34	30.32	32.91	36.74	40.11	44.14	46.96	55.48
28	13.56	14.85	16.93	18.94	21.59	23.65	27.34	31.39	34.03	37.92	41.34	45.42	48.28	56.89
29	14.26	15.57	17.71	19.77	22.48	24.58	28.34	32.46	35.14	39.09	42.56	46.69	49.59	58.30
30	14.95	16.31	18.49	20.60	23.36	25.51	29.34	33.53	36.25	40.26	43.77	47.96	50.89	59.70

Source: Abridged from Table IV of R. A. Fisher and F. Yates, *Statistical Tables for Biological, Agricultural, and Medical Research*, 6th edition, published by Longman Group, Ltd., London, 1974, by permission of the authors and publishers.

TABLE F.   Critical values of the Pearson product-moment correlation coefficient

df	Level of significance for one-tailed test			
	.05	.025	.01	.005
	Level of significance for two-tailed test			
	.10	.05	.02	.01
1	.988	.997	.9995	.9999
2	.900	.950	.980	.990
3	.805	.878	.934	.959
4	.729	.811	.882	.917
5	.669	.754	.833	.874
6	.622	.707	.789	.834
7	.582	.666	.750	.798
8	.549	.632	.716	.765
9	.521	.602	.685	.735
10	.497	.576	.658	.708
11	.476	.553	.634	.684
12	.458	.532	.612	.661
13	.441	.514	.592	.641
14	.426	.497	.574	.623
15	.412	.482	.558	.606
16	.400	.468	.542	.590
17	.389	.456	.528	.575
18	.378	.444	.516	.561
19	.369	.433	.503	.549
20	.360	.423	.492	.537
21	.352	.413	.482	.526
22	.344	.404	.472	.515
23	.337	.396	.462	.505
24	.330	.388	.453	.496
25	.323	.381	.445	.487
26	.317	.374	.437	.479
27	.311	.367	.430	.471
28	.306	.361	.423	.463
29	.301	.355	.416	.456
30	.296	.349	.409	.449
35	.275	.325	.381	.418
40	.257	.304	.358	.393
45	.243	.288	.338	.372
50	.231	.273	.322	.354
60	.211	.250	.295	.325
70	.195	.232	.274	.303
80	.183	.217	.256	.283
90	.173	.205	.242	.267
100	.164	.195	.230	.254

Source: Abridged from R. A. Fisher and F. Yates, *Statistical Tables for Biological, Agricultural, and Medical Research*, 6th edition, published by Longman Group, Ltd., London, 1974, by permission of the authors and publishers.

Glossary of research method terms

Analysis of covariance. A method of statistical control through which scores on the dependent variable are adjusted according to scores on a related, often antecedent, variable.

Analysis of variance. A statistical technique by which it is possible to partition the variance in a distribution of scores according to separate sources or factors; although variance is partitioned, the statistical test tests for differences between means.

Aptitude. The potential for achievement.

Attitude. A tendency to possess certain feelings toward a specified class of stimuli.

Central limit theorem. A theorem which states that given any population with a mean and finite variance, as sample size increases, the distribution of the sample means approaches a normal distribution with mean equal to the population mean and variance equal to the population variance divided by sample size.

Cluster sampling. The selection of groups of elements called clusters rather than single elements; all elements of a cluster are included in the sample, and the clusters are usually selected randomly from the larger population of clusters.

Coding. The translation of raw or observed data into categories or classifications in preparation for analysis.

Coefficient of equivalence. A measure of test reliability based on the correlation between parallel forms of a test administered at approximately the same time to a single group of individuals.

Coefficient of internal consistency. A measure of test reliability computed on an internal analysis of the data secured from a single administration of the test.

Coefficient of stability. A measure of test reliability based on the correlation between a specific test and a retest (usually a parallel form) given at a later time to the same group of individuals.

Cohort study. A longitudinal design (in survey research) in which random samples are selected at different points in time from a specific population, rather than a general population.

Common factor variance (in validity of measurement). The covariation or the variance that the observed test scores have in common with the scores of the criterion measure.

Concurrent validity of a test.   The extent to which scores on the test match performance on contemporary criterion measures.

Confidence interval.   An interval estimate of a parameter constructed in such a way that the interval has a predetermined probability of spanning the parameter.

Confounded variables.   Variables operating in a specific situation such that their effects cannot be separated.

Constant.   A characteristic that has the same value for all observed units of a research study.

Construct validity of a test.   The extent to which a test measures one or more dimensions of a theory or trait.

Contamination of data.   The presence of sampling biases, uncontrolled variables, or other factors which tend to make the data unusable for the purposes of the research.

Content validity of a test.   The extent to which the content of the test items reflects the academic discipline, behavior, or whatever is under study.

Contingency table.   The array into which a set of enumeration data may be grouped according to two or more classification variables.

Continuous variable.   A variable that can take on any value within an interval(s) on the scale of measurement.

Control group (in the context of an experiment).   A group of subjects who do not receive any experimental treatment, included for comparison purposes.

Correction for continuity.   A correction applied when certain techniques are used with small samples and the underlying distribution of the statistic is discrete but a continuous distribution from tabled values is used as an approximation for the underlying distribution.

Correlation.   The extent of relationship between two variables; in statistical analysis the relationship must be quantifiable.

Correlation coefficient.   The measure of the extent of relationship between two variables.

Covariate.   The measure used in an analysis of covariance for adjusting the scores of the dependent variable.

Cross-sectional studies.   Studies in which the data are collected at one point in time from a random sample of a general population, which contains two or more subpopulations, with the intention of comparing subsamples from subpopulations or noting trends across such subsamples.

Degrees of freedom.   The number of ways in which the data are free to vary; the number of observations minus the number of restrictions placed on the data.

Dependent variable.   The consequent (assumed) of the independent variable.

Directional hypothesis.   A hypothesis stated in such a manner that a direction, usually indicated by greater than or less than, is hypothesized for the results.

Discrete variable.   A variable that can take on only a limited, finite number of values.

Distribution. The total observations or a set of data on a variable; when observations are tabulated according to frequency for each possible score, we have a frequency distribution.

Experiment (in educational research). A research situation in which one or more factors are systematically varied according to a preconceived plan, in order to determine the effects of this variation.

Experimental mortality. The dropout of subjects in terms of participation in the experiment; the failure of certain subjects to continue in the experiment until its conclusion.

Experimental validity (two types). Internal: basic minimum necessary in terms of control, measurement, analysis, and procedures to make the results of the experiment interpretable. External: the extent and appropriateness of the generalizability of the experimental results.

Ex post facto *research.* Research in which the independent variable or variables have already occurred and in which the researcher begins with the observations on a dependent variable, followed by a retrospective study of possible relationships and effects.

F *Ratio.* A ratio of two variances or estimates of two variances computed to test the homogeneity of two variances; the underlying distribution is the F distribution and when the statistical test is applied it is referred to as an F test.

Fixed-effects model. A term usually associated with analysis of variance; an analysis in which the levels of the independent variables are determined or "fixed" by the researcher rather than being selected randomly from a larger population of possible levels.

Histogram. A graphical representation of the scores in a distribution, consisting of rectangles, the areas of the rectangles being proportional to the frequencies of the scores.

Homogeneity of regression. The situation of equal or approximately equal regression coefficients within two or more groups, i.e., the same regression.

Homoscedasticity. In the context of correlation, the condition that for all values of one variable the distributions of the values of the other variable have approximately the same variability.

Hypothesis. In general, a conjecture about a situation; in the context of inferential statistics, a statement about a parameter.

Independent variable. In experimental research, the variables deliberately manipulated by the researcher; in nonexperimental research, variables that classify or identify the participants.

Interaction (in context of analysis of variance). The effect of one independent variable upon another; the lack of the effect of one independent variable to remain constant over the levels of another.

Interval scale. A measurement scale which, in addition to ordering scores, also establishes an equal unit in the scale so that distances between any two scores is of a known magnitude; also called equal-unit scale.

Kruskal-Wallis one-way analysis of variance. A nonparametric technique which tests the ranks for two or more independent samples; the null hypothesis tested is that the sum of ranks, and hence the averages of the populations from which the samples were selected, are equal.

Kuder-Richardson methods. Procedures for determining the reliability of a test from a single form and administration of the test without splitting the test.

Latin square. An $n \times n$ square array, including n different letters or symbols so arranged that each symbol appears once and once only in each row and column.

Level of confidence. The probability associated with a confidence interval of the interval spanning the corresponding parameter; commonly used confidence levels in educational research are .95 and .99.

Level of significance. A probability associated with the test of a hypothesis by statistical techniques which determines whether or not the hypothesis is rejected; commonly used levels in educational research are .05 and .01: also called the alpha level.

Likert-type scale. A scaling procedure commonly associated with measuring attitudes which requires a graded response to each item or statement. In scoring, the alternate responses to items are assigned numerical values, and the individual's score is the sum of the numerical values corresponding to his response.

Linear relationship. A relationship between two variables such that a straight line can be fitted satisfactorily to the points of the scattergram; the scatter of points will cluster elliptically around a straight line rather than some type of curve.

Longitudinal studies. Studies which involve measuring the same or different S's two or more times during a period of time (usually of considerable length, such as several months or years); e.g., measuring the mathematics performance of the same students at yearly intervals as they progress from the fourth grade through senior high.

Maturation. Psychological and biological processes operating and causing systematic variation within individuals with the passing of time.

Mean. The sum of the scores in a distribution divided by the number of scores in the distribution.

Measurement. The assignment of numerals to objects or events according to specific rules.

Measures of central tendency. Points in a distribution that locate the distribution in terms of the measurement scale; points within the distribution about which the scores tend to group themselves.

Measures of variability. Interval measures of a distribution that indicate the amount of dispersion or spread in the distribution.

Median. The point in a distribution below which 50 percent of the scores lie.

Median test. A nonparametric technique for testing whether or not two or more independent samples have been selected from populations with a common median.

Mode. The point or score of greatest frequency in a distribution.

Multiple-treatment interference. Carry-over or delayed effects of prior experimental treatments that may affect the results of subsequent treatments when individual subjects receive two or more experimental treatments in succession.

Nominal scale.   A measurement scale that simply classifies elements into two or more categories, indicating that elements are different, but not according to order or magnitude.

Normal distribution.   A family of bell-shaped, symmetrical distributions whose curve is described mathematically by a general equation sometimes called the Laplace-Gaussian normal probability function.

Norms.   Descriptive statistics which summarize the test performance of a reference group of individuals.

Null hypothesis (in context of inferential statistics).   A hypothesis stated so that no difference or no relationship is hypothesized; a nondirectional hypothesis.

Objectivity in test scoring.   The extent to which equally competent scorers get the same results when scoring test performance.

One-Tailed statistical test.   A directional test of a statistical hypothesis so constructed that the rejection region for the null hypothesis is located entirely in one tail.

Operational definition.   A definition expressed in terms of the processes or operations that are going to be used to measure the characteristic under study.

Optimum allocation (in stratified random sampling).   Selecting the sample in such a manner that the strata contributions to the sample are proportional to the strata populations and the strata variances.

Ordinal scale.   A measurement scale that classifies and ranks elements or scores.

Panel studies.   Longitudinal designs (in survey research) in which the same random sample is measured at different points in time.

Parallel forms of a test.   Two (or more) forms of a test that are equivalent in terms of factors such as difficulty.

Parameter.   A characteristic or measure of a population; e.g., the population mean.

Periodicity (in systematic sampling).   A periodic characteristic that follows the listing of the elements and the selection interval so that a bias is introduced into the systematic sample.

Personality.   In general, the sum total of an individual's mental and emotional characteristics; in the context of psychological testing, personality inventories usually are designed to measure characteristics such as emotional and social adjustment.

Pilot study.   A study conducted prior to the major research study which in some way is a small-scale model of the major study, conducted for the purpose of gaining additional information by which the major study can be improved; e.g., an exploratory use of the measurement instrument with a small group of subjects for the purpose of refining the instrument.

Population.   The totality of all elements, subjects, or members that possess a specified set of one or more common characteristics which define it; in inferential statistics, the group to which inferences are made.

Post mortem test.   A statistical test conducted to locate the specific sources of significance when differences between three or more sample means are tested and the null hypothesis is rejected.

Prediction.   The estimation of scores on one variable from the information of one or more other variables.

Predictive validity of a test.   The extent to which predictions made from the test are confirmed by subsequent data.

Projective technique.   A situation in which the individual responds to stimuli in such a way that he projects into his responses his feelings, traits, and the like; commonly associated with personality measurement.

Proportional allocation (in stratified random sampling).   Selecting the sample in a manner such that the sample size is divided among the strata proportional to population sizes of the strata.

Random sample.   A sample selected in such a way that the selection of one member of the population in no way affects the probability of selection of any other member.

Range.   One plus the difference between the two extreme scores of a distribution.

Ratio scale.   A measurement scale which in addition to containing an equal unit also establishes an absolute zero in the scale.

Regression (as a threat to experimental validity).   A tendency for groups, especially those selected on the basis of extreme scores, to regress toward a more average score on subsequent measurements, regardless of the experimental treatment.

Regression equation.   The equation of the regression line for a set of bivariate data.

Regression line.   The straight line of best fit (usually according to the least squares criterion) for a set of bivariate data.

Reliability coefficiency.   A measure of the consistency of a test. There are several methods of computing a reliability coefficient, depending upon the test and the test situation.

Reliability of measurement.   The consistency or accuracy of the measurement.

Response set.   The tendency for an individual to respond to items or other stimuli in a consistent manner, regardless of the content or context of the stimuli.

Sample.   A subset of the population under study.

Sampling ratio.   The ratio of sample size to population size; also called the sampling fraction.

Scattergram.   The plot of points determined by the cross tabulation of a set of bivariate data.

Significant statistic.   A statistic whose appearance by chance in the light of the hypothesis is less than the probability as designated by the significance level; e.g., a significant difference: a difference too large to be attributed to chance (random sampling fluctuation) in the light of the hypothesis.

Sign test.   A nonparametric technique for testing differences between two related samples in terms of direction rather than in terms of magnitude of the differences between pairs of observations. It derives its name from the plus and minus signs assigned to the directions of differences.

Simple random sample.   A sample selected in such a way that all members of the population have an equal probability of selection; in the case of sampling without replacement from a finite population, every possible sample of a given size has an equal chance of being selected.

Split-half method.   A procedure for determining the reliability of a test by which a single form of the test is divided into comparable halves, the scores on the halves are correlated, and the reliability coefficient is computed by applying a special formula known as the Spearman-Brown step-up formula.

Standard deviation.   A measure of variability which is the positive square root of the variance.

Standard error of a statistic.   The standard deviation of the underlying distribution of the statistic.

Standard error of estimate.   The standard deviation of the distribution of errors of prediction, in which an error of prediction is the difference between the observed and predicted scores.

Standard error of the mean.   The standard deviation of the underlying distribution of the mean.

Standard normal distribution.   The normal distribution with a mean of zero and a standard deviation of one.

Standard score.   A score given in terms of standard deviation units from the mean of the distribution; a negative score indicates below the mean and a positive score above the mean.

Statistics.   In the context of descriptive statistics, measures taken on a distribution; in the context of inferential statistics, measures or characteristics of a sample; in a more general sense, the theory, procedures, and methods by which we analyze data.

Stratified random sampling.   A sampling procedure through which the population is divided into two or more subpopulations, called strata, and elements for the sample are then randomly selected from the strata.

Subject (in the context of experiments).   The individual participants in an experiment that are measured on the dependent variable; i.e., the observable units of an experiment.

Systematic sampling.   A selection procedure through which all sample elements are determined after the selection of the first element, since each element on a selection list is separated from the first element by a multiple of the selection interval.

Thurstone-type attitude scale.   A procedure that requires the individual to check all statements or items with which he agrees; all items have a scale value as determined by a panel of judges prior to use, and the individual's score is the median scale value of all the statements checked.

Trait.   A tendency to respond in a certain way to situations.

Trend studies.   Longitudinal designs (in survey research) in which a general population is studied over time by taking different random samples at various points in time.

Two-tailed statistical test.   A test so constructed that when testing the null hypothesis, the rejection region of the underlying distribution is contained in both tails of the distribution; a nondirectional test of a hypothesis.

Type I or alpha error.   In inferential statistics, the error of rejecting a true hypothesis.

Type II or beta error.   In inferential statistics, the error of failing to reject a false hypothesis.

Unbiased statistic.   A statistic computed in a manner such that the mean of its underlying distribution is the parameter that the statistic estimates.

Underlying sampling distribution of a statistic.   The distribution (usually theoretical) of all possible values of the statistic from all possible samples of a given size selected from the population.

Validity coefficient.   A coefficient based on the correlation of the scores of the test with scores on a criterion measure.

Validity of measurement.   The extent to which a measurement instrument measures what it is supposed to measure.

Variable.   A characteristic that takes on different values for different observed units of a research study.

Variance.   A measure of variability which is the average value of the squares of the deviations from the mean of the scores in a distribution.

Bibliography

Anastasi, A. *Psychological Testing*. 3rd ed. New York: Macmillan Co., 1968.

Ary, D.; Jacobs, L. C.; and Razavieh, A. *Introduction to Research in Education*. New York: Holt, Rinehart & Winston, 1972.

Babbie, E. R. *Survey Research Methods*. Belmont, Calif.: Wadsworth Publishing Co., 1973.

Best, J. W. *Research in Education*. 2d ed. Englewood Cliffs, N.J.: Prentice-Hall, 1970.

Borg, W. R., and Gall, M. D. *Educational Research: An Introduction*. New York: David McKay Co., 1971.

Campbell, D. T., and Stanley, J. C. *Experimental and Quasi-experimental Designs for Research*. In N. L. Gage (ed.), *Handbook of Research on Teaching*. Chicago: Rand McNally & Co., 1963.

Clarke, R. B.; Coladarci, A. P.; and Caffrey, J. *Statistical Reasoning and Procedures*. Columbus, Ohio: Charles E. Merrill Books, 1965.

Cochran, W. G., *Sampling Techniques*. 2d ed. New York: John Wiley & Sons, 1963.

Cornell, F. G. *The Essentials of Educational Statistics*. New York: John Wiley & Sons, 1956.

Cronbach, L. J. *Essentials of Psychological Testing*. 3rd ed. New York: Harper & Row, 1970.

Edwards, A. L. *Experimental Design in Psychological Research*. 4th ed. New York: Holt, Rinehart & Winston, 1972.

Englehart, M. D. *Methods of Educational Research*. Chicago: Rand McNally & Co., 1972.

Ferguson, G. A. *Statistical Analysis in Psychology and Education*. 3rd ed. New York: McGraw-Hill Book Co., 1971.

Fox, D. J., *The Research Process in Education*. New York: Holt, Rinehart & Winston, 1969.

Freund, J. E. *Modern Elementary Statistics*. 4th ed. Englewood Cliffs, N.J.: Prentice-Hall, 1973.

Galfo, A. J., and Miller, E. *Interpreting Educational Research*. Dubuque, Iowa: William C. Brown Co., 1965.

Glass, G. V., and Stanley, J. C. *Statistical Methods in Education and Psychology*. Englewood Cliffs, N.J.: Prentice-Hall, 1970.

Gronlund, N. E. *Measurement and Evaluation in Teaching*. 2d ed. New York: Macmillan Co., 1971.

Guilford, J. P. *Psychometric Methods*. 2d ed. New York: McGraw-Hill Book Co., 1954.

Guilford, J. P., and Fruchter, B. *Fundamental Statistics in Psychology and Education*. 5th ed. New York: McGraw-Hill Book Co., 1973.

Harris, C. W. (ed.). *Problems in Measuring Change*. Madison: University of Wisconsin Press, 1963.

Hays, W. L. *Quantification in Psychology*. Belmont, Calif.: Brooks/Cole Publishing Co., 1967.

Helmstadter, G. C. *Research Concepts in Human Behavior*. New York: Appleton-Century-Crofts, 1970.

Kaimann, R. A., and Marker, R. W. *Educational Data Processing, New Dimensions and Prospects*. New York: Houghton Mifflin Co., 1967.

Keppel, G. *Design and Analysis: A Researcher's Handbook*. Englewood Cliffs, N.J.: Prentice-Hall, 1973.

Kerlinger, F. N. *Foundations of Behavioral Research: Educational and Psychological Inquiry*. 2d ed. New York: Holt, Rinehart & Winston, 1973.

Kish, L. *Survey Sampling*. New York: John Wiley & Sons, 1965.

Lindquist, E. F. *Design and Analysis of Experiments in Psychology and Education*. Boston: Houghton Mifflin Co., 1953.

McNemar, Q. *Psychological Statistics*. 4th ed. New York: John Wiley & Sons, 1969.

Mehrens, W. A., and Lehmann, I. J. *Measurement and Evaluation in Education and Psychology*. New York: Holt, Rinehart & Winston, 1973.

Minium, E. W. *Statistical Reasoning in Psychology and Education*. New York: John Wiley & Sons, 1970.

Mouly, G. J. *The Science of Educational Research*. 2d ed. New York: Van Nostrand Reinhold Co., 1970.

Neale, J. M., and Liebert, R. M. *Science and Behavior: An Introduction to Methods of Research*. Englewood Cliffs, N.J.: Prentice-Hall, 1973.

Nunnally, J. C. *Educational Measurement and Evaluation*. 2d ed. New York: McGraw-Hill Book Co., 1972.

Sax, G. *Empirical Foundations of Educational Research*. Englewood Cliffs, N.J.: Prentice-Hall, 1968.

Senter, R. J., *Analysis of Data*. Glenview, Ill.: Scott, Foresman & Company, 1969.

Siegel, S. *Nonparametric Statistics for the Behavioral Sciences*. New York: McGraw-Hill Book Co., 1956.

Slakter, M. J., *Statistical Inference for Educational Researchers*. Reading, Mass.: Addison-Wesley Publishing Co., 1972.

Stanley, J. C. *Improving Experimental Design and Statistical Analysis: Proceedings of the Seventh Annual Phi Delta Kappa Symposium of Educational Research*. Chicago: Rand McNally & Co., 1967.

Taylor, P. A. *An Introduction to Statistical Methods*. Itasca, Ill.: F. E. Peacock Publishers, 1972.

Thorndike, R. L., and Hagen, E. *Measurement and Evaluation in Psychology and Education*. 3rd ed. New York: John Wiley & Sons, 1969.

Travers, R. M. W. *An Introduction to Educational Research*. 3rd ed. New York: Macmillan Co., 1969.

Tuckman, B. W. *Conducting Educational Research*. New York: Harcourt Brace Jovanovich, 1972.

Turney, B., and Robb, G. *Research in Education: An Introduction*. Hinsdale, Ill.: Dryden Press, 1971.

Van Dalen, D. B. *Understanding Educational Research: An Introduction*. 3rd ed. New York: McGraw-Hill Book Co., 1973.

Author Index

Subject Index

American Doctoral Dissertations, 331
American Educational Research Association, 331, 333, 334
American Psychological Association, 327, 328, 359, 364
  Committee on Ethical Standards in Psychological Research, 199
Analysis of covariance, 86, 226, 252-256
Analysis of variance, 88, 314
  complex, 251-252
  fixed-effects model, 245
  Friedman two-way by ranks, 287
  Kruskal-Wallis, one-way by ranks, 284-287
  one-way, 237-243, 245, 286, 287, 350
  two-way, 243-251, 314
Appendix, of a research report, 362-363
Aptitude, 188
Author Index to Psychological Index, 326
Averages, 38

Biased estimate, 55
Bibliography, of a research report, 362-363
Biological Abstracts, 329

California Test of Mental Maturity, 188
Cartesian plane, 58
Central limit theorem, 48
Child Development Abstracts and Bibliography, 329
Clearinghouse for Early Childhood Education, 322
Cohort study, 146, 147
Collate, 77

Confidence interval,
  for correlation coefficient, 296-297, 299, 301
  for the mean, 230-231, 296, 297
Confounding (of variables), 83, 99, 109, 123, 349
Constant, 32, 33, 68
  identification of, 71-72
Contingency
  coefficient of, 305-306, 307
  table, 270, 273
Control
  definition of, 84
  experimental, 84, 95-96
  group (definition of), 96-97
Controlled observation (in connection with survey research), 135, 148
Cooperative Research Program (of USOE), 347
Correction for continuity, 280
Correlation, 57, 291
  coefficient of, 57, 61, 291
    biserial, 303-305, 307
    difference between, 297-299
      correlated samples, 298-299
      independent samples, 297-298
    interpretations of, 310-312
    Pearson-Product Moment, 292-299, 300, 305, 306, 307, 312
    Point biserial, 302-303, 305, 307
    Spearman rank, 299-302, 307
  multiple, 310
Covariate, 254
Covary, 57
Cover letter, 141-142
  example of, 143
Cross-sectional designs, 147-148
Cumulated Subject Index of Psychological Abstracts, 326, 327
  sample entry, 327

THE BOOK MANUFACTURE

Research Methods in Education was typeset, printed and bound by Kingsport Press. Internal design was by the F. E. Peacock Publishers art department. Cover design was by Charles Kling & Associates. The type is Times Roman with Venus Medium Extended display.